Wealth, War, and Wisdom

Barton Biggs

WILEY
John Wiley & Sons, Inc.

Published by John Wiley & Sons, Inc., Hoboken, New Jersey.
Published simultaneously in Canada.

For general information on our other products and services or for technical support, please contact our Customer Care Department within the United States at (800) 762-2974, outside the United States at (317) 572-3993 or fax (317) 572-4002.

Wiley also publishes its books in a variety of electronic formats. Some content that appears in print may not be available in electronic formats. For more information about Wiley products, visit our Web site at www.wiley.com.

Library of Congress Cataloging-in-Publication Data:

Biggs, Barton M., 1932-
    Wealth, war, and wisdom / Barton M. Biggs.
      p. cm.
    Includes bibliographical references and index.
    ISBN 978-0-470-22307-9 (cloth)
      1. Stock exchanges—History—20th century. 2. Investments—History—20th century.
    3. World war, 1939–1945—Economic aspects. 4. Wealth. I. Title
  HG4551.B4623   2008
  332. 609'04—dc22
                                        2007034477

Printed in the United States of America

10 9 8 7 6 5 4 3 2 1

Contents

Foreword

For 30 years Barton Biggs wrote the financial world's most elegant and insightful prose in his regular submissions to the pages of Morgan Stanley's "Investment Perspectives." Barton Biggs knows writing, in part because of his training in English at Yale in the 1950s. Barton Biggs knows markets, in part because of his investing with Fairfield Partners in the late 1960s and early 1970s, in part because of his work with Morgan Stanley in the 1970s, 1980s, and 1990s, and in part because of his investing with Traxis Partners in the 2000s. Readers who care about markets and love the English language will thank Biggs for taking time from his current hedge fund responsibilities at Traxis Partners to write *Wealth, War, and Wisdom*.

Barton Biggs allows facts to drive conclusions. Relentlessly rational, Biggs builds his analysis on the foundation of strong fundamental research. Readers familiar with Biggs' Morgan Stanley research pieces or his book, *Hedgehogging,* already know that the topic on any given page is as likely to be a mountain climbing expedition as it is to be a price-to-earnings or a price-to-book ratio. Yet, Biggs' marvelous stories never fail to enlighten as well as entertain. The unusual combination of depth of research and breadth of experience create a powerful platform for *Wealth, War, and Wisdom*.

In his book, Barton Biggs stretches our conception of market efficiency. In my undergraduate finance seminar at Yale, I teach Burton Malkiel's time-tested tripartite description of market efficiency, which includes the weak, semistrong, and strong forms. The weak form of market efficiency simply states that past stock prices contain no predictive information about future stock prices. In other words, momentum strategies do not work. The semistrong form states that investors cannot benefit from the use of public information to beat the market. In other words, security analysis does not work. The strong form states that investors benefit from neither public nor private information. In other words, even insider trading does not work. Note that all of these definitions focus on market efficiency at the security-specific level. Most of the academic debate on market efficiency concerns the semistrong form of the efficient markets hypothesis, to wit whether investors might benefit from astute security analysis.

Financial economists spend less time studying the predictive power of the stock market as a whole. Daunted by the staggering breadth of variables that influence stock indexes, finance professors generally cite Paul Samuelson's maxim about the stock market having predicted nine of the past five recessions, thereby cleverly dismissing the question of the stock market's prescience.* Barton Biggs, ferocious competitor that he is, positively embraces the question of the market's ability to defeat what John Maynard Keynes characterized as the "dark forces of time and ignorance which envelop our future."

In *Wealth, War, and Wisdom,* Biggs intertwines a gripping narrative of significant personalities and important battles of World War II with a synopsis of stock market moves in the major countries of both the Allied and Axis powers. In his work, Biggs identifies a striking number of instances in which markets reacted to what turned out to represent important

---

*A quick Google search showed a strong preponderance of citations in which Samuelson suggested that the stock market predicted nine of the last five recessions. Also mentioned were 12 of the last nine and nine of the last four. With this numerical diversity, Paul Samuelson joins Woody Allen, whose well-known quote is variously cited as "Seventy/Eighty/Ninety percent of success in life is showing up."

turning points in the course of the war. The stunning conclusion that Biggs reaches is that in many cases the market foresees dramatic shifts in the prospects for the warring parties that completely escape contemporary observers. Barton Biggs challenges us to consider the possibility that the wisdom of crowds, as reflected in the level of stock prices, surpasses the wisdom of even the most astute observers of the current scene.

While Biggs cites an impressive number of associations between stock market moves and significant turning points in the war, he admits that his evidence sometimes falls short. In contrast to particularly impressive records of foresight in the U.S. and U.K. equity markets, Biggs notes that equity investors in France deserve mixed grades, at best.

Biggs adds to our store of knowledge about long-term returns of security markets. In my work at Yale, in my classroom, in my books, and in my speeches, I cite historical market returns to support the argument that stocks deserve an important role in the portfolios of long-term investors. Roger Ibbotson's more than eight decades of data, which he presents in his *Stocks, Bonds, Bills and Inflation,* focus predominantly on the U.S. stock market, which enjoyed more or less continuous operation from its very inception. Jeremy Siegel's more than two centuries of data, which he presents in *Stocks for the Long Run,* pay somewhat more attention to non-U.S. markets, but the centerpiece of his book remains the United States Generally speaking, the most widely used compilations of market returns say little about the more difficult histories of markets that suffered extreme dislocation.

Biggs reminds us that many markets did not enjoy the relatively uninterrupted trading that characterized the U.S. markets. His careful examination of stock, bond, and cash returns in markets that experienced disruptions adds valuable context to the often too broad-brush examination of time series of market returns. Biggs' conclusions about twentieth-century returns for what he calls the "stable lucky ones" that were spared catastrophe (the United States, the U.K., Australia, Canada, et al.) surprise no serious student of markets. Inflation-adjusted returns for stocks trump those for bonds and bills, with all of the asset classes besting inflation. In contrast, some of Biggs' conclusions about the "losers" (Germany, Japan, Italy, France, et al.) give the reader pause. Unsurprisingly, the averages of the twentieth-century asset class returns for the winners exceed those for the losers in all categories. Surprisingly, the asset class returns in the loser countries show the familiar pattern of stocks beating bonds and bonds beating bills. Even more notably, only stocks in the loser countries managed to beat inflation, as both bonds and bills on average produced negative real returns. According to Biggs' analysis, even in those countries in which the most extreme forms of risk were manifest, the risky asset class of stocks produced superior returns and the safe asset classes of bonds and bills underperformed. Biggs reaches the now conventional asset allocation conclusion that stocks deserve a prominent place in investor portfolios, but he arrives at that conclusion via an unconventional route.*

As to market timing and security selection, which along with asset allocation represent the three tools in every investor's toolkit, Biggs articulates some unexpected advice. Even though his entire career—first at Fairfield Partners, then at Morgan Stanley, finally at Traxis Partners— revolved around active management of investment portfolios, Biggs recommends that investors avoid market timing and shun security selection. The justification for his advice comes from the recognition that investors benefit from the long-run returns in the stock market only if investors own stocks. Maintaining exposure to the stock market requires the courage to hold (or even add to) positions in the face of extreme adversity. If a market timing decision, however well considered, causes an investor to underweight stocks and retreat into fixed income at an inopportune time, the investor's portfolio may never recover. Moreover, getting the market return requires holding the market basket of securities. If a series of security bets, however well considered, wreak havoc on a portfolio, the investor's portfolio may never recover. Sticking with a stable, equity-oriented, index-based portfolio represents a good strategy for the overwhelming numbers of investors.

Barton Biggs' *Wealth, War, and Wisdom* entertains us with a creative juxtaposition of a war narrative and a security markets history. He challenges us with a notion that stock markets exhibit incredible prescience. He teaches us that equity-oriented, stable allocations of passively managed assets provide superior investment results. As has been the case

---

*To protect against disaster, Biggs recommends extreme forms of portfolio diversification, including buying a farm or a ranch and burying some gold in the backyard.

throughout his remarkable career, Barton Biggs adds to our store of knowledge with his elegant, wonderfully crafted prose.

—David F. Swensen
Chief Investment Officer
Yale University
November 2007

Introduction

And I looked and behold a pale horse: and his name that sat on him was Death, and Hell followed with him. And power was given unto them over the fourth part of the earth, to kill with sword and with hunger, and with death . . .

—REVELATION 6:8

Two subjects have long obsessed me. First, stock markets on a short-term basis are random, irrational, and undecipherable, but at major inflexion points and in the long-term ebb and flow of events are they truly intuitive and wise in their judgments, or do stock prices mostly just reflect the foolish consensus of crowds?

Second, at least once in every century there has been an episode of great wealth destruction when the Four Horsemen of the Apocalypse—Pestilence, War, Famine, and Death—have ridden rough-shod. World War II was the last time that the pale horse with Death on his back and Hell following him terrorized the world.

How do you preserve wealth in times when the Four Horsemen are on the loose? We know from history that equities are *wealth enhancers* in good times, but do stocks work as true *wealth preservers* when their country, their "home" society, is facing defeat and occupation from a foreign power? If they don't, what should a person with wealth do? How well in *real*–inflation adjusted, purchasing power terms, do public equities perform?

To be the ultimate repository of family or institutional capital, an asset class, an investment vehicle, must be able to preserve as well as enhance wealth over the long run—in bad times as well as good. The value of accumulating wealth is terribly diminished if it cannot be preserved. As you become richer, protecting your fortune against the "slings and arrows of outrageous fortune" becomes at least as important as enhancing it.

The preservation of wealth across time is not an academic matter. The world is and always has been prone to disasters that destroy great globs of wealth. In earlier centuries there were wars, natural disasters, famines, and plagues. Then in the eighteenth and nineteenth centuries came revolutions that confiscated wealth and heads. The last century, the twentieth, was perhaps the most ruinous of all time with World War I, hyperinflations, the Great Depression, and then the inter-connected climax, the worst ravager of them all, World War II. It was truly a world war, and in retrospect, it was a close call whether Western civilization as we know it was going to survive.

The Second World War has long been a fascination of mine. It offers so many lessons about life, politics, financial markets, wealth, and above all, survival. I have read and studied it for years, but as an amateur, not as a professional. World War II was unquestionably the war of the century and probably the war of the millennium because it gripped, ravaged, and tortured almost the entire world. Its effect on the conquered and then occupied countries, and later on the losers of the war was so extreme that it was the ultimate test in modern times of whether public equities or any asset could preserve the purchasing power of wealth in the face of a prolonged and total national disaster. It also was an epic struggle with first the Axis Powers and then the Allies appearing to be prevailing.

The 1930s and 1940s were an incredibly dark time for the world. Until you become really engrossed with the actual diary of events, you don't realize how grim things were and how close the world came to a new Dark Age. Thus, I spend a lot of time in this book on the ebb and flow of the war and on the character and management styles of the leaders on both sides. I think I have found and included some unusual insights on Hitler, Churchill, Mussolini, and others. *Wealth, War, and Wisdom* focuses primarily on the events that occurred between 1938 and 1943 and not the Allies' later victories because it was the *turning points* in the struggle that mattered. Korea is included because of its significance for the Japanese market.

Investors (and for that matter, people in general) have to deal with adversity and hard times. This book relates how dire were the defeats and agonies of the late 1930s and of the early 1940s, and how the leaders—Churchill, Hitler, Stalin, MacArthur, and Yamamoto in particular—managed them, and how they dealt with people. All of us professionals have to practice and endure crisis control, and this is another reason why investors read history and biographies.

Looking back with the perfect vision and the perspective of today, we can identify the victories that were the great turning points. However, at the time, in the fog of war, it was far from clear that the tide had turned. Did equity markets with the unique wisdom of the crowd "through a glass darkly" sense these moments? I think the evidence is that they did, while the press and the so-called expert commentators and strategists mostly did not, and that we should be very respectful of the collective wisdom of stock markets. This means listening to what the market is saying by its action. (Chapter 1 provides more insight on the wisdom of markets.)

I first became fascinated with the subject of the wisdom of markets when, by chance, I discovered that the British stock market bottomed for all time in the summer of 1940 just before the Battle of Britain; that the U.S. market turned forever in late May 1942 around the epic Battle of Midway; and that the German market peaked at the high-water mark of the German attack on Russia just before the advance German patrols actually saw the spires of Moscow in early December of 1941. Those were the three great momentum changes of World War II—although at the time, no one except the stock markets recognized them as such. This, to me, confirmed the extraordinary (and unrecognized) wisdom of market crowds.

This leads to another important point. Today, almost every investor is a contrarian. Everyone knows about the dangers of groupthink and the madness of crowds. But is there a special, intuitive wisdom in the uncoordinated ebb and flow of the investor crowd? I have come to think there is. Mr. Market is a smart, canny old soul, and during World War II he often, not always but often, sensed important tipping points that at the time few of the elite grasped. The ebbs and flows of the stock market reflect the collective opinion of the investor crowd, and in this book, I maintain that markets have great wisdom. The investor ignores their message at his extreme peril.

Another major theme of the book is what happened to wealth before and during the war, and what insurance steps should a wealthy individual take to protect his or her fortune from the Black Swan-like appearance of the apocalypse. I also have studied whether stocks and bonds preserved and enhanced wealth not only in the years of extreme duress from 1930 to 1945 but also over the course of the century. I could not have come to the conclusions that I have without the massive studies of Elroy Dimson, Paul Marsh, and Mike Staunton of the London Business School. I found that equities generally did preserve wealth— over the full course of the century and particularly if you owned the right stocks in the right country (Chapters 9 and 15 especially address this topic). However, stocks (and bonds for that matter) had substantially higher returns if their country of residence was on the winning side. If your homeland lost the war and was occupied, public equities did not work during the years of war and occupation and bonds were even worse. Moreover, for the first 50 years of the twentieth century, equities in both France and Germany adjusted for inflation were a wealth-losing proposition. Government bonds were a disaster.

Asset diversification helped. Real assets such as land, property, gold, or a business were somewhat better than stocks but far from perfect. A working farm protected both your wealth and your life. The other solution was having money outside the country in a safe haven, but of course, that didn't help you keep body and soul together at the time.

As far as I know much of the market data has never been compiled in this form or published before. *Wealth, War, and Wisdom* also relates what happened to other forms of wealth such as bonds, land, gold, jewelry, and property during those years (again, primarily in Chapters 9 and 15).

Anyone with wealth has to care about all this. There is no use working yourself to death to accumulate wealth if it can't be preserved and enhanced. There are definite messages in the book as to what a person of means should do to pass on wealth to future generations in an uncertain world although I concede the next apocalypse may be different from the previous one.

I also find the history of this epic war populated as it was with such extravagant figures to be an endlessly intriguing, incredibly dramatic, and gripping event. Some may quarrel with my judgments about the inflexion points and disagree with my interpretations of the leaders, of their actions, and the moods of the times.

Investors, as opposed to traders and speculators, have to make long-term, slowly evolving judgments about the course of events in economies and the world. The more history they know and understand, the better these perspective decisions will be. An investor simply must know some history as well as be a statistician, psychologist, and a gifted intuitionist.

However I am definitely not a *real* historian. This is in no way a true history book—either of stock markets or of World War II. I have done no original research on World War II, but I have read a number of books that are listed in the bibliography. I have shamelessly borrowed from the ideas, insights, and reminiscences of the true historians and warriors who wrote the tomes listed in the bibliography. In spite of my extensive reading, however, I found no source that deals with what really happened to financial markets and wealth during the war years. There are market statistics, but very little background information. To find the social information I present in this book, I have read old newspapers and interviewed people who lived through that time. Numerous market charts with event references are included in the book. I have written an impressionistic, interpretive account of those times that I hope reverberates today.

Barton M. Biggs
October 2007

Chapter 1

Listen to the Market Crowd

The only one who is wiser than anyone is everyone.
—NAPOLEON BONAPARTE

This book is about what happened to wealth in the throes of probably the most excruciating, destructive global disaster in all history, World War II. The focus is on equities and whether they preserved and enhanced the purchasing power of money. It also looks at what amount of diversification and other assets people with wealth should have to protect the purchasing power of their fortunes.

In exploring these subjects, it became startlingly evident that the equity markets in the principal contenders—the United States, Britain, Germany, and Japan—identified the monumental, epic turning points in the war with uncanny perception. The conventional opinion today is that crowds in general and the stock market crowd in particular are manic beasts. However, as you study the history and read the sociology, you begin to come to the conclusion that there is great wisdom in crowds, that the equity market itself is the epitome of a wise crowd, and that we should pay close attention to its messages, particularly when it reverses its trend.

Much has been disparagingly written about the "madness of crowds." In fact, it has become the deeply entrenched, conventional wisdom. However, as James Surowiecki has pointed out in his original and insightful book, *The Wisdom of Crowds,* it's the collective ***judgment*** of crowds and their intuitions that we should be respectful of.

The great classic is Charles Mackay's *Extraordinary Popular Delusions and the Madness of Crowds,* which is religiously stacked in every professional investor's bookcase. Its most famous lines undoubtedly are: "Men, it has been well said, think in herds. It will be seen that they go mad in herds, while they only recover their senses slowly, and one by one." Friedrich Nietzsche wrote: "Madness is the exception in individuals but the rule in groups."

Another classic on crowd behavior is Gustave Le Bon's *The Crowd: A Study of the Popular Mind* published in 1896. Le Bon, an aristocratic autocrat if there ever was one, believed crowds invariably make bad decisions and act foolishly. "Crowds can never accomplish acts demanding a high degree of intelligence," writes Le Bon, "and they are always inferior to the isolated individual." Le Bon's definition of a crowd was broad in that it included any kind of group that could make decisions.

This disdain for crowds is deeply embedded. There is the old saying, source unknown, "None of us is as dumb as all of us." Then we have that self-proclaimed investment genius Bernard Baruch quoting German poet and philosopher Friedrich von Schiller, "Anyone taken as an individual is tolerably sensible and reasonable—as a member of a crowd, he at once becomes a blockhead." And Scottish historian Thomas Carlyle proclaimed: "I do not believe in the collective wisdom of individual ignorance."

A crowd morphs into a *mob* when it becomes disorderly, violent, and vulgar. The etymology of mob is from the Latin: *mobile vulgus.* The inference is that a crowd, and particularly a mob, can be easily manipulated and turned to dangerous and evil pursuits. The bad reputation of groups or crowds is not undeserved, but what is not appreciated is that when asked or required to make judgments ***independently*** and in a ***rational*** way, the record of crowds is impressive. In other words, the disparagement and mockery of Le Bon and the others are mostly incorrect.

In the investment world today, even a mention of "the crowd" has an intensely pejorative connotation. Everyone knows you don't want to be part of *the crowd* because *the crowd* is always wrong. Avoid "*crowded trades at all cost*" has become a hedge fund maxim. Distrust of the wisdom of crowds has become deeply imbedded in the psyche of professional investors, strategists, economists, and sometimes, the media.

Conversely, it has become very fashionable to be contrarian—in other words, to do the opposite of what the crowd is doing because the crowd is so stupid and is almost always wrong. If everyone is bullish on the equity market, then the contrarian will be bearish and vice versa. Investors assiduously track sentiment indicators in order to do the opposite. Strategists and economists often in the preamble to their reports boast that their view is contrary to the consensus as though that supposition alone is more important than all their analysis. In reaction to the popularity of contrarianism, one of the best investors in the world, George Soros, once described himself as a "contra-contrarian."

It is a truism that human beings are reactive imitators and are subject to emotional extremes of euphoria and despair. Investors and speculators run the gamut from greed to fear as they passionately, blindly stampede after markets and prices. From time to time this leads to excesses and eventually to bubbles. However, as will be discussed, this does not invalidate this book's assertion that collectively the investor crowd often has superb intuitions about long-term events and that these judgments should be respected and followed.

Ignore the Opinion of Experts: They're Not Reliable Forecasters

On the other hand, there is increasing evidence that relying on expert opinion for advice is a loser's game. Philip Tetlock in his new book *Expert Political Judgment: How Good Is It? How Can We Know?* concludes that expert opinion on politics, economics, and business should be ignored as random blather because experts are even less accurate than nonspecialists in guessing what is going to happen. Tetlock tracked

284 experts who made 82,361 forecasts over a period of years. What a tedious labor of sifting and evaluating masses of horse manure! Anyway he found, among other humiliating things, that the alleged experts were right less than half the time, and that they were worse than dart-throwing monkeys in forecasting outcomes when multiple probabilities were involved. As the Danish physicist Niels Bohr said, "Prediction is very difficult—particularly about the future."

After reviewing this accumulation of data, Tetlock concluded that although you need to be reasonably informed on a subject to make credible predictions of events or the economy, knowing a lot, being regarded as a real expert, a wise man, a guru, actually makes someone less reliable as a forecaster. The more facts, information, and history an expert knows, the more likely he is to have pet theories and to have developed complex chains of causation in making a prediction. Tetlock believes this is why experts fail to outpredict nonexperts. The odds tend to be with the simple and the obvious outcome. Tetlock reports that the better known, more quoted, more self-confident, and better credentialed an expert (or should we say *pontificator?*) is, the more likely he is to be wrong.

Another reason that pundits who appear regularly on television are particularly unreliable is because they become obsessed with showmanship. In other words, they strive above all to be original and different, often just for the sake of being original and different. The clever, ingenious, outrageous forecast gets the most attention. Their tenure on the talk shows or CNBC and CNN (and in many cases their compensation) doesn't hinge on their accuracy (because there are so many forecasts being made no one can keep track of them), but on their entertainment shock value. Although they may not even acknowledge this, it complicates their thinking and screws up their expert heads.

After his study of the record of experts, Tetlock came to some other interesting conclusions. First, when experts are wrong, they seldom admit it. Second, experts tend to dismiss new information that doesn't fit with their previous beliefs or actions. This is called *cognitive dissonance,* and it has proved to be an ailment of the George W. Bush administration. Third, and even more disappointing but not surprising, they are much tougher in assessing the validity of new information that undercuts their theories than they are in evaluating information that is supportive.

Finally, Tetlock divided the experts into two groups using the Isaiah Berlin analogy of hedgehogs and foxes. Hedgehogs are experts who know a great deal about one big thing and tend to analyze complex problems from that framework. Within their small circle of competence they are regarded as brilliant. Foxes, Tetlock says, are "thinkers who know many small things, . . . are skeptical of grand schemes, see explanation and prediction . . . as flexible exercises that require stitching together diverse sources of information and are rather diffident about their own forecasting prowess." Tetlock found that the foxes were significantly better predictors than the hedgehogs. The foxes' cognitive diversity gives them a broad structure from which to analyze complex problems.

For example, in the investing world there are highly educated, very intelligent quantitative hedgehogs armed with PhDs and powerful computers. For a while their inventive models produce superior investment performance. Then their success spawns imitating competitors. Before long there are so many of them, that the exploitable valuation anomalies that the brilliant pioneers identified and used to create a portfolio management system, are almost immediately discovered by other quantitative hedgehogs and quickly no longer work. It is the investment world's latest version of "creative destruction."

It's hard to argue with Tetlock's data. However, the skeptic would reply that while Tetlock may be right about all experts as a class, there are some, particularly in specialist areas such as technology and the sciences, that are worth paying attention to. As for political or stock market forecasters, there are few that should be listened to. The problem is that just because someone **has** been right **recently** doesn't mean that individual is going to **continue** to be right. In fact, with professional investors, it's often just the opposite. Nevertheless, it can be amusing and sometimes stimulating to listen to an articulate and erudite forecaster. You just shouldn't be under any illusions about the class's long-term record. All this bashing of prognosticators and strategists is written with a pinch of chagrin since the author once sheltered under that sobriquet.

Global Markets Understood What Was Happening during WWII

Intuition, gut hunches, and common sense count for a lot in making forecasts. But as we will see, it's not the guru's forecast you should be respectful of, it's the wisdom of markets, the collective judgment of many individuals filed individually and then collated that you should pay close attention to. The London stock market deduced in the early summer of 1940, even before the Battle of Britain at a time when the world and even many English despaired, that Britain would not be conquered. Stocks made a bottom for the ages in early June although it wasn't evident until October that there would be no German invasion in 1940 and until Pearl Harbor 18 months later, that Britain would prevail.

Similarly, the German stock market, even though imprisoned in the grip of a police state, somehow understood in October of 1941 that the crest of German conquest had been reached. It was an incredible insight. At the time, the German army appeared invincible. It had never lost a battle; it had never been forced to withdraw. There was no sign as yet that the triumphant offensive into the Soviet Union was failing. In fact, in early December a German patrol actually had a fleeting glimpse of the spires of Moscow, and at the time Germany had domain over more of Europe than the Holy Roman Empire. No one else understood this was the tipping point.

The New York stock market recognized that the victories at the battles of the Coral Sea and Midway in May and June of 1942 were the turn of the tide in the Pacific, and from the lows of that spring never looked back, but I can find no such thoughts in the newspapers or from the military experts of the time. A barrage of defeats and surrenders had engendered intense criticism of the management of the war and the commanders in the field. The wise men of the media were so busy wringing their hands that they didn't grasp the significance of the battles of the Coral Sea and Midway as the high-water mark of Japan's grand design for empire and of its attack on the United States.

In fact, the American media had been wrong on the war from the beginning. Fed by the U.S. War Department, the *New York Times* in the first weeks after Pearl Harbor was exaggerating any small successes of the allies and under-reporting the damage to the Pacific fleet. For example, five days after Pearl Harbor, on December 12, 1941, the banner headlines were **JAPANESE CHECKED IN ALL LAND FIGHTING; 3 OF THEIR SHIPS SUNK, 2ND BATTLESHIP HIT.** The story reported that one of the three ships sunk was also a battleship. It was pure fiction. Only one relatively insignificant Japanese destroyer had been sunk.

Markets Outperform Experts—
Human or Computer

But to get back to crowd theory, in 1945, economist and political philosopher F.A. Hayek wrote a powerful essay to refute the then-popular socialist doctrine of central planning. In it he argued that central planning could never be as economically efficient as the price mechanism. It was impossible, he said, for the central planner, be he human or computer, to accumulate all the bits and pieces of diverse information scattered widely throughout the vast population needed to make as efficient, "good" economic decisions as are accomplished by the price mechanism. Markets function so efficiently because the totality of all relevant information including subjective preferences are aggregated through the price mechanism into a single market valuation which, while perhaps not perfect, is better than any number concocted by a human entity or even a computer.

Decentralization of sources is also very important because it is crucial for the collection of what Hayek called "tacit knowledge." Tacit knowledge is knowledge that is intuitive to individuals or is derived from a particular place or job or way of life. Since it is so intuitive and instinctive, it can't easily be summarized or communicated and, in fact, the people that have it may not even know they have it. Yet it is very valuable because it reflects the deep life experience of human beings dispersed over the world.

This insight was the basis of efficient market theory, but it has remained an observation, not a conclusion. As Henry Manne, Dean Emeritus of the George Mason School of Law, recently pointed out, it does not explain a theory of how this massive amount of information gets so effectively disseminated into the prices of goods and services. He asks: "How does the weighted averaging get done?" Similarly, "The efficient market hypothesis was based almost entirely on empirical observations and did not offer a theory of how the market came to be so efficient." Manne's answer seems to be: *the wisdom of crowds.*

In his book, *The Wisdom of Crowds,* Surowiecki argues convincingly that groups often are more right in their decision making than brilliant experts. In other words, "the many are smarter than the few." He points out that experts have biases and blind spots, and that there is little correlation between an expert's confidence in his prediction and the accuracy of it. You are more likely (but not guaranteed) to get a better estimate or decision from a group of diverse, independent, motivated people than you are from a single or even a couple of experts. Other psychologists have shown that posing a judgment question, then asking a large number of people what they think the answer is and taking the mean is superior to asking a few experts no matter how highly qualified or deliberative and informed a group.

The group, the crowd, the market must have diversity. The mass of investors takes information from their experience and interaction with multiple environments. Stock markets provide an effective aggregation system. This collective judgment system works best when the individuals have some incentive to be right. The aggregation of investors in a stock market essentially is what the social sciences people call "a complex adaptive system." As the market strategist Michael Mauboussin has pointed out in his excellent essays, one of the key lessons of a complex adaptive system is that you can't understand the whole by adding up the parts. The whole is greater than the sum of the parts.

Many people attempt to understand markets by talking with experts or other supposedly astute investors, but if markets really are a complex adaptive system, individual agents will provide little or no worthwhile help on the workings or the course of the market. This is why I will argue it is so important to **listen to the market.** In other words, at crucial turning points observe what markets do and ignore what the experts and the commentators say about what is going on.

Experiments that Prove the Wisdom of Crowds

As an example of a complex adaptive system at work, Surowiecki relates how at a famous contest at a county fair in England to guess the weight of an ox on display, there were 800 guesses entered, some by knowledgeable farmers but most by those who had no expertise whatsoever. Not only was the average of all the guesses of 1,197 pounds almost exactly correct (the weight was 1,198 pounds), but it was far superior to the estimates of the so-called livestock experts. He also conducted an experiment with a group of 56 students who were shown a jar and asked how many jelly beans were in it. The average of the group was 871 which was closer to the correct number of 850 than that of all but one of the students' estimates.

Surowiecki conducted a number of similar experiments. He tells in his book how he would approach random people in New York's Times Square and ask them how many jelly beans were in the plastic jar he was carrying or to estimate his weight. They must have thought he was nuts. On another occasion when he was in front of an audience he succinctly described his study and asked them to guess how many books were in it. At the time he didn't even know himself. In each case the average of the collective guesses was very close to the mark, and the average was better than the vast majority of the individual guesses. He argues the misjudgments that individual people make effectively cancel themselves out leaving you with the knowledge that the group has. Incidentally, the larger the crowd and (as noted previously) the more decentralized it is, the more reliable its decision will be. Obviously a stock market is a very large, decentralized crowd indeed.

Manne goes on to make the point that the literature of "prediction" or of "virtual" markets proves that the more participants in a contest and the better informed they are, the more likely the weighted average of their guesses is likely to be correct. Suroweicki writes of the remarkably successful results of the Iowa Electronic Markets (IEMs) in which speculators make bets on the outcomes of elections. The resulting "predictions" from these wagers have been much better than those of the political pundits and the polls. The bettors in the IEMs aren't predicting their own behavior but are forecasting what the voters of the country will do. Three quarters of the time the IEM's market price on the day each of the preelection polls was released was more accurate than the results of the polls.

In the last five presidential elections the IEM predicted the vote percentages with an absolute average error that was nearly 30% less than the experts. In the 2004 election for Prime Minister of Australia, just before the election the pundits were saying the race was too close to call while Australia's equivalent of the IEM, Centrebet, showed John Howard comfortably ahead. He won easily. The IEM's and Centrebet's superior results also confirm that predictions are best when the predictors are motivated with real money at stake.

Groupthink vs. Crowdthink

Both Manne and Surowiecki maintain that it is essential the participants be diverse and their judgments be independent of each other. The participants also must "care." There should be an economic incentive. Their estimates can't be casual throwaways. They also can't sit around and exchange ideas about what the right answer should be and then finally reach a consensus. If they did, their collective judgment would become *groupthink* with all its well-known and pernicious sins. Groupthink results in decisions that usually are less wise than the knowledge of the collected individuals. When properly collated, *crowdthink* is just the opposite.

James Monitor has written extensively and well on behavioral finance, and he argues that these findings are true but only under a very strict set of circumstances. Three conditions must be met, says Monitor. First, people must be unaffected by others' decisions. Two, the probability of being correct must be independent of the probability of everyone else being correct. Three, the participants must be unaffected by their own vote possibly being decisive. I would add that good group decisions are more likely to occur when most of the members of the group either don't know or don't pay any attention to what other members of the group think. In other words, crowds do have imbedded in them a collective wisdom that is very prescient but it has to be artfully extracted. The price action of a stock market on a longer term basis is a highly efficient collection mechanism.

In a way, isn't the recognition of this truth the basic tenet of democracy with its popular elections? Democracy is predicated on the belief that the majority makes better decisions than a ruling elite. Stock markets are really voting machines, and I submit that often the wisdom of this kind of collective intuition is seen in the ability of stock markets to understand the ebb and tide of human history and events—particularly at crucial turning points. As Surowiecki writes: "The idea of the wisdom of crowds is not that a group will always give you the right answer but that on average it will consistently come up with a **better** answer than any individual could provide." The Japanese stock market was wise during the Second World War and at the onset of the Korean War, but the French bourse was dead wrong in 1941 when it forecast prosperity from the German occupation.

The stock market should be a good case study of whether crowds have some wisdom. Not wisdom on little things, but insights on the ebb and flow of great events. The stock market encompasses a very large, diverse crowd of people, and even in the Second World War years there were at least several hundred thousand active participants in each of the major equity markets of the world. Because of the diversity of this collection of investors and because it is also decentralized with a lot of tacit knowledge, this crowd brings a variety of different intuitions to the process. In addition, it is a relatively intelligent and well-informed crowd. All investors are not rocket scientists but they are not complete idiots either. Just the fact that they have sufficient money to be investors suggest there is some natural selection process at work. Furthermore, the stock market crowd fulfills the motivation criteria because the judgment this group is making involves its own money. It is a crowd of "foxes," not a crowd of "hedgehogs."

As a result, the stock market is a wise and farseeing old thing. It can get panicky and crazy in the heat of the moment, and as we all know it can get suckered into frauds and blow enormous bubbles. Individual investors and clusters of investors can be irrational or become irrational, but the overall market on a longer term basis is generally rational. As Maubossin puts it: "We must be very careful to avoid extrapolating individual irrationality to market irrationality."

In fact, investors with their extremes of fear and greed make the stock market prone to boom and bust cycles. But every mania stems from some degree of substance in a life-changing development whether it was the railroads in the nineteenth century or technology in the waning moments of the twentieth. In retrospect, even in 2000 there was some rationality in the market as a whole. Tech and Internet growth stocks were selling at ludicrous valuations, but other major value segments of the market that were out of favor were ridiculously underpriced. I am not for one moment arguing that the crowd is a good interpreter of individual sectors or stocks.

However, despite the fog of war and the smoke of statistics, the stock market has a great nose and amazing intuitions. This is what the wise old traders are expressing when, in the face of a gloomy environment or bad news, they say "the market is acting well" or vice versa "the market is acting badly." A classic example of all this can be seen in the major stock markets' reactions to the most serious crisis of the twentieth century, the rise and fall of the Axis powers in the 1940s.

I argue that the stock market, because it is the collective conclusion of multiple, independent, diverse, decentralized, motivated judgments, is a far different creature from the mob or the group. This is not to claim that the stock market is all wise or cannot make mistakes or in the short-term misjudge events. I am saying that in general its judgment is good and worth paying attention to. The ultimate test of that thesis and of equities as wealth preservers is World War II—a time of overwhelming anxiety and fear. In the next chapter, I describe a world darkened by fear and the malaise that depressed stock markets.

Chapter 2

A World Darkened
by Fear

*An Overview of Soviet, German, and Japanese
Aggression from 1929–1945*

To understand the malaise and the mood of stock markets in the late 1930s and early 1940s, one has to comprehend the grim state of the world at that time. As everyone who hasn't been in a coma knows, the Great Crash in 1929 was followed by worldwide deflation and a deep depression. Fiscal and monetary policy errors had compounded the despair, and the democratic-capitalist system seemed incapable of the necessary response. Wealth had been obliterated, and equity valuations everywhere had been relentlessly driven to record lows. However, by 1936 the world economy and financial markets had partially recovered, only to sag again in the late 1930s and early 1940s. Capitalism seemed a failed creed, and many thoughtful people wanted to try either communism or national socialism. But there was another reason why investors were so depressed.

From the spring of 1940 through the spring of 1943, the survival of the European and North American democracies and their western tradition of Judaic-Christian freedom appeared to be in extreme peril from three different but equally authoritarian, nationalistic, and evil sources. The first was from expansionist Communism, the Soviet Union, and its sinister leader, Joseph Stalin. The second was from European National Socialism and Adolph Hitler as embodied in Germany, Italy, and as time went on, fringe Eastern European countries. The third, of course, was a militaristic, resource-ambitious, and aggressive Japan. All three practiced terror and were expert in its application.

Soviet Terror, Torture, and Death Camps

In the decade of the 1930s it is estimated that 10% of the total population of the Soviet Union passed through and was consumed by Stalin's penitential machinery. Stalin wanted to insure that there was not and never would be a threat to his reign. He purged his own officer corps, Eastern European Communist leaders who made the mistake of thinking Russia was a sanctuary, and so-called "domestic conspirators." Certain camps were torture chambers for the purpose of extracting confessions. Victims were not only subjected to mutilations, gouging, and other fiendish ordeals, but if they endured the agony without confessing, they were finally broken by being forced to observe the torture of their lovers or children.

Most of the camps were situated north of the 69th parallel and inside the Arctic Circle. The camps ranged in order of intensity and sophistication. There was a Yale and Harvard for the most gifted and dangerous pupils and state universities for the average malcontent. Alexander Solzhenitsyn later described this sadistic system of terror and torture as did Arthur Koestler in *Darkness at Noon,* published in 1940. Koestler's magnificent novel described how prisoners were not strengthened by the brutal and insidious regimen of torture, but were warped, crushed, and eventually destroyed by it. The message fell on deaf official ears in the West, but left sensitive souls depressed and frightened.

Stalin employed work camps to exterminate dissidents, malcontents, and potential enemies. The entrance sign at these camps proclaimed "Labor is a matter of honor, valor, and heroism," but the objective was to get as much work out of the inmates as possible. The men worked 16 hours a day, were subject to savage beatings, slept in unheated barracks with temperatures below zero, and were given meager rations of food. The theory was that it took 20 to 30 days to work a healthy man to the point of death, whereupon he was machine gunned at the weekly mass execution.

The rapid death rate required a steady stream of raw material, which the Soviet secret police, the NKVD, provided with relish. In March 1940, thousands of returning POWs from the embarrassing war with Finland were greeted in Leningrad with a banner "The Fatherland Hails Its Heroes," and marched straight to the railroad yards where they were loaded into cattle cars and sent to the camps. The archives indicate that between 1936 and 1939 four-and-a-half million men and women died in the work camps, and that the total number of deaths from Stalin's "cleansing" policies was around 10 million.

Germany Overruns Europe

Meanwhile, Spain had fallen to Francisco Franco, China was again being raped by Japan, Czechoslovakia bullied by Germany, and Italian aircraft were using mustard gas against Ethiopian tribal villages in Benito Mussolini's quest for empire. "Ah," murmured the complacent, "but he has made the trains run on time."

By 1940, the most imminent threat came from the Fascist or so-called Axis Powers (Germany, Japan, Italy and assorted vassal nations), which seemed poised to rule the world for at least a generation. In the end, it was a close thing. Financial markets, a sensitive gauge of sentiment, in the early 1940s trembled and plummeted. By 1942, a map of the world showed Germany in control of most of Europe with its fierce hegemony stretching from the North Sea to the very gates of Moscow and Leningrad. At the peak of its expansion across Asia, Japan controlled ten percent of the land mass of the world and much of its most precious natural resources.

Since the actual fighting had begun in 1938, no army had been able to prevail in battle against the *Wehrmacht,* the most highly trained, disciplined, and well-equipped army in the world. By 1940, as John Lucaks points out in *The Duel,* Hitler's armies had conquered all of Western Europe with less cost in men and equipment than the Germany army had expended in World War I for a few miles of trenches and mud. The resistance of the smaller European countries to this onslaught could be measured in days, and France, in spite of her large army and supposedly impregnable *Maginot* Line, had ignominiously been routed by the German *Blitzkrieg.* The British Expeditionary Force had barely escaped total annihilation at Dunkirk, and the Royal Navy had suffered grievous wounds at sea, in North Africa, and Norway. Britain still stood resolute in her island home, but she was slowly being starved to death by the U-boats, and no matter how gallant her armies, they had proved ineffective against German technology, discipline, and daring.

Perhaps even more frightening was the inherent evil embodied in the Nazi credo and its dynamic, psychotic leader, Adolph Hitler. The terrible extermination that was under way of Jews, gypsies, and the Slavic people, and the concept of a master race were both deeply terrifying and profoundly depressing because it seemed so few stood against them. The thought of a "Thousand Year Reich" was enough to dismay even the stoutest heart.

In the early 1940s, Hitler, *Der Führer,* with his violent yet magnetic and charismatic personality, loomed over the world like an evil genius. He had single-handedly, with force, terror, but also ideas, saved Germany from unemployment, starvation, and probably a Communist revolution. Never in the modern history of the world had one man so completely hypnotized so many millions. Hitler was a dynamic, passionate public speaker able to lift a crowd with his fanatical ravings. As an orator he could establish an uncanny emotional communication with his audience that went beyond words. He fully understood the value of pageantry and color, and he, like Winston Churchill, recognized the power of the radio. Corporal Hitler in World War I had been twice wounded, and had won two Iron Crosses of the First Rank for extreme heroism, a decoration that was seldom awarded to common soldiers.

Nietzsche had celebrated in academic terms the concept of "the superman." As a frontline messenger, Hitler seemed to have a charmed life. He had accomplished and returned from missions that no one else survived, but he was not foolhardy, just brave, and he fastidiously prepared himself by studying the terrain he had to cross. Between missions in his trench, he read Carl von Clausewitz (a Prussian solider in the late 1790s and early 1800s who later was an influential military theorist), to whom he uniquely granted the title of intellectual master. Part of his puissance with both men and women derived from this aura of courage, infallibility, and invulnerability. In the eyes of many he had assumed the mantle of the German superman.

Hitler was a man of normal size, perhaps five feet nine, about 150 pounds. He was not particularly handsome, his nose was too thick, and he usually dressed simply but neatly. His hands were well-formed with long, graceful fingers, and he gestured with them, both while delivering a speech and in more casual conversations. However, it was the eyes that dominated the otherwise common face. They stared at you with hypnotic, piercing, penetrating power. They were a light blue but with great depth.

Even as dispassionate and cosmopolitan a reporter as William L. Shirer, who was the foreign correspondent for CBS and Universal News, wrote that he had never seen anything like them. "They reminded me of paintings I had seen of the Medusa," wrote Shirer, "whose stare was said to turn men into stone or reduce them to impotence." Women were fascinated by Hitler's eyes; however, they froze men. People said that with them Hitler could see into the future. When you looked at him you were drawn to these bottomless eyes that had such power and perception.

Hitler, like so many Germans, believed the Fatherland had been stabbed in the back by its leaders in the aftermath of the First World War. He maintained hyperinflation, depression, and political chaos for the German people had been the result of this betrayal. His own life had been distorted by poverty and even hunger, and for years even as he was rising to power, he was afflicted by an overwhelming infatuation for his niece. She may well have been the love of his life, but their blood relationship made it a desperate and eventually hopeless relationship politically. She subsequently committed suicide under mysterious circumstances, and one of Hitler's confidantes later told the correspondent, Shirer, that Hitler was never again seriously sexually interested in women. Apparently Eva Braun, his mistress, was a sideshow.

Hitler's intuitions about military and political events from 1935 until 1943 were original, unconventional, and almost infallible. He correctly calculated the weakness of his adversaries and their reluctance to fight, and his tactical decisions and audacious gambles succeeded time and time again to the amazement of the German General Staff. He possessed an extraordinary understanding of human nature and an instinctive insight into the weakness of his adversaries. As Alan Clark wrote in *Barbarosa,* his epic study of the German campaign in Russia, "The Devil's hand guided Hitler, just as it was later to protect his life. His capacity for mastering detail, his sense of history, his retentive memory, his strategic vision—all these had flaws, but considered in the cold light of objective military history, they were brilliant nonetheless."

At the time, William Butler Yeats' great poem "The Second Coming" was widely quoted because it so eloquently captured the mood of despair that prevailed in the late 1930s as Hitler and Nazism seemed poised to conquer Europe.

> Turning and turning in the widening gyre
> The falcon cannot hear the falconer;
> Things fall apart; the centre cannot hold;
> Mere anarchy is loosed upon the world,
> The blood dimmed tide is loosed, and everywhere
> The ceremony of innocence is drowned;
> The best lack all conviction,
> While the worst are full of passionate intensity.

W.H. Auden expressed the same emotion but differently in his poem "September 1, 1939."

I sit in one of the dives
On Fifty-Second Street
Uncertain and afraid
As the clever hopes expire
Of a low dishonest decade:
Waves of anger and fear
Circulate over the bright
And darkened lands of the earth,
Obsessing our private lives;
The unmentionable odour of death
Offends the September night.

Innocent, helpless people trembled as gross, bulging men in black shirts with damp armpits marched on the cobblestones chanting racist slogans, eager to beat senseless anyone who stood in their way.

Moreover, in much of the West after the insane carnage of the trench warfare of World War I where a thousand men would be sent to die as cattle to gain a hundred yards of mud, which would be lost again the next day, there was a deep weariness with war. Wilfred Owen in a much-quoted poem branded Horace's famous words: *Dulce et decorum est pro patria mori* (It is sweet and right to die for your country) "The Old Lie." Many were unwilling to fight again for "King and Country" under any circumstances. In the nineteenth century war had been marching bands, patriotism, and glory but no longer. Poets railed against it. Louis Simpson wrote:

But at Verdun and at Bastogne
There was a great recoil,
The blood was bitter to the bone
The trigger to the soul.
And death was nothing if not dull,
A hero was a fool.

In the poem, the word *recoil,* literally the kickback of a gun, was used to suggest the idea that the user of a weapon inflicts injury upon himself. But perhaps Stephen Crane said it best in "War Is Kind and Other Lines."

Hoarse, booming drums of the regiment,
Little souls who thirst to fight,
These men were born to drill and die.
The unexplained glory flies above them,
Great is the battle god, great, and his kingdom
A field where a thousand corpses lie.
Do not weep, babe, for war is kind,
Because your father tumbled in the yellow trenches,
Raged at his breast, gulped and died,
Do not weep
War is kind.

Japan Overruns Asia

Meanwhile, on the other side of the world, Japan was in the process of changing the face of Asia with its powerful fleet and army. In early 1937 the Chinese had unwisely provoked Japan, and in the fighting that followed the Chinese had been humiliated, climaxing with the notorious Rape of Nanking during which 300,000 Chinese civilians were slaughtered. The "China-lobby" in the United States was appalled and outraged, and Franklin Roosevelt (FDR) in a speech in Chicago equated Japan with the Nazis.

Well before Pearl Harbor, Japanese aggression had spread south, and by the summer of 1942 Japan controlled the richest countries of Southeast Asia. (Chapter 7 will discuss this in more detail.) Not only was Japan gaining control of Asia's vast store of natural resources, the sinews of war, but by routing and humiliating the colonial powers it was ending forever the old era of Western imperialism, gunboat diplomacy, and dispelling the myth of the white man's supremacy. The Greater Southeast Asia Co-Prosperity Sphere struck a responsive chord, and in many areas the Japanese armies were initially welcomed by the local people as liberators from the colonial powers.

In the longer run, the harsh and unnecessarily cruel Japanese occupations and their exploitative nature dissipated the friendly reaction and eventually engendered hatred, but that was not apparent in 1942. Moreover, in Hong Kong and Singapore and what were to become Indonesia, Malaysia, the Philippines, Thailand, and above all, India, there was a deep restlessness and a strong desire for independence. The age of empire building was well and truly over.

The U.S. had been badly bloodied at Pearl Harbor, and had lost all of its Asian possessions except the key island base at Midway in the center of the Pacific. American military incompetence was the order of the day. By the spring of 1942, the Philippines also had fallen and 65,000 men had been taken prisoner at Corregidor. Crushing naval losses had been suffered by the Allies in the Singapore Straits, in the Indian Ocean, and at the Battle of the Java Sea. Hong Kong had been taken in days, Malaysia was overwhelmed, and the great fortress of Singapore had been out-flanked and had ignominiously surrendered. Australia and New Zealand were in mortal danger, and their prime ministers groused at Churchill.

Europe Ravaged

The early 1940s were a time when most of Europe despaired for the future and was desperately hungry. The German occupiers either sent home massive amounts of food or consumed it on the spot. Across Europe agricultural productivity had collapsed as the population in occupied countries became predominantly female. For example, from France alone, in addition to war casualties, 2,600,000 men had been shipped back to Germany as prisoners to do forced labor. Much of Europe believed the Germans would rule for generations, and therefore, at least tacitly, collaborated. After all, the penalty for resistance was the tender ministrations of the Gestapo or death. By the spring of 1942, the surname "Quisling" had become a common noun (denoting a collaborator and traitor), concentration camps were where people disap-peared to, and the Gestapo was a terrifying presence across Europe.

It was a time when many supposedly wise and worldly men and women were convinced the Allies were beaten both in Europe and Asia. Germany had not only won the war but deserved to win it. They ques-tioned the future and spoke of "the abyss of a new dark age" which Churchill warned might be "made more sinister and perhaps more pro-tracted by the lights of perverted science." Capitalism and democracy had failed, and the German and Japanese brand of national socialism rather than Communism might be the palatable answer. After all, the economies of much of the Western world were still mired in a vicious cycle of depression, deflation, soaring unemployment, and social unrest, that capitalism seemed unable to cure. The pessimists argued that democracy was an inefficient and impotent form of government that lacked the forceful leadership, efficiency, and freshness of national socialism.

The British Empire was unraveling. Her crown jewel, India, was rebellious and restless for *Freedom at Midnight*. Gandhi was threatening to negotiate a safe passage for Japanese troops through India to enable them to coordinate with Hitler in return for India's independence. Churchill worried about a Japanese invasion of India. Even in the United States, in many quarters there was no sympathy for the Empire. In early 1942 in a letter to the British people, *Life* (at that time the dominant American magazine) warned "one thing we are sure not fighting for is to hold the British Empire together."

The armed forces of the western democracies seemed weak, inadequately equipped, and poorly led in contrast to the technology, discipline, training, and boldness of the German and Japanese military juggernauts. In Europe, the German mechanized divisions with their *panzers,* half tracks, and motorized infantry had simply trampled and overwhelmed all opposition. In Poland it had been tanks against cavalry. Both the Germans and Japanese immediately established air superiority over any battlefield, and the Japanese had been the first to understand that ship-to-ship gun battles at sea were mostly a thing of the past, and that aircraft carriers were now the crucial factor. They also realized that carrier-based aircraft could sink the most powerful capital ships. In late 1941, Japanese aircraft sank off Singapore the pride of the Royal Navy, *Repulse* and *Prince of Wales,* with only the loss of a few torpedo planes and dive bombers. The German and Japanese strategists also understood the immense advantage of surprise, armor, and mass, and they seemed modern, brilliant, and daring tacticians while the Allies and the Russians appeared to be led by defensively-minded, elderly defeatists.

There were many pessimists on both sides of the Atlantic. Even Churchill admitted that when evenly matched, it seemed the Germans would always prevail. By the late 1930s, Adolph Hitler had created the most successful economy in Europe. German industrial production was up and unemployment had almost disappeared. It was a false bloom of health fed by deficit spending on arms, but few realized that at the time.

Already Hitler was attracting allies in central Europe such as Hungary, Romania, and later Finland. The Japanese were proving themselves a resourceful, cruel, and relentless enemy with their surprise attacks and surgical conquests. Mussolini seemingly had revitalized the Italian economy. How could the forces of freedom prevail?

America: Oblivious and Self-Indulgent

In the midst of all this anguish, the United States seemed isolationist, oblivious, and self-indulgent, and many people around the world maintained the American people were too parochial, too soft and weak to fight. In 1937, the American economy collapsed again. Unemployment soared from 14% to over 19% in 1938, the United Auto Workers shut General Motors with sit-down strikes, and the police fired on workers armed only with slingshots. On October 1, 1937, a day that was christened Black Tuesday, both the stock and commodity markets panicked. The investment banks were caught with large underwriting positions in Bethlehem Steel bonds and a Pure Oil preferred stock issue and there was talk of closing the stock exchange.

Ironically, exactly 50 years later on October 19, 1987, the New York stock market crashed again.

The great Japanese Admiral Isokoru Yamamoto, who had studied at Harvard and been the Naval attaché to the embassy in Washington, D.C., remarked that the U.S. Navy was "a club for golfers and bridge players." How could they have allowed their battleships to be lined up like sitting ducks helplessly in a row at Pearl Harbor? He doubted that in the open sea their crews could competently fight them. Yamamoto had high regard for the industrial prowess of the United States but questioned the quality of her professional officer corps. The Japanese planners discounted any submarine threat because "Americans were inherently unsuited for the physical and mental strain of submarine warfare."

The American Army garrisoned in Asia was not well regarded either. It was the "old army" of polo ponies, long golf games, cheap domestic help, and petty rivalries and dalliances at the Army Navy Club. James Jones in his epic novel *From Here to Eternity* describes this stagnant milieu. In the invasion of the Philippines, the American army proved no match for the battle-hardened, better-conditioned Japanese. The American commander, General Douglas McArthur, was a handsome, imperious man (you called him Mac at your mortal peril), and he had carefully sculptured an image of himself as The Great American Hero.

Others had different views. Harry Truman, who, as we shall see later, was no fan, said: "There was never anybody around him to keep him in line. He didn't have anybody on his staff that wasn't an ass kisser. He just wouldn't let anybody near him who wouldn't kiss his ass." Dwight Eisenhower commented, "I studied dramatics under him for five years in Washington and four year in the Philippines."

MacArthur could be an able and inspiring leader. He certainly didn't lack for arrogance, asserting that he was "the greatest military mind that ever lived," and he was a daring tactician as he later proved in his relentless, island hop-scotching advance to avenge his defeat in the Philippines and then at Inchon in Korea. However, he was also pompous, vainglorious, and affected—he always carried a riding crop. He had graduated first in his class at West Point despite the embarrassment of having his controlling mother move to a hotel near West Point to meddle in his life. His father was a general and a Civil War hero who had won the Medal of Honor. MacArthur was twice decorated for heroism in World War I, and by the end of that war he was commanding a division. Always politically astute and extremely ambitious, he ascended rapidly in the post-war army.

Sent to the Philippines, he operated virtually as an emperor in Manila. In early 1941, he promised Washington he could defend the Philippines with a massive army of mostly native troops. His boasts were fanciful. The Philippine soldiers went into action with World War I rifles that they had never fired and pitiful equipment. In fact, many didn't have helmets or shoes. "These guys barely know how to salute much less how to shoot," said one disgusted American sergeant.

MacArthur's orders to his troops in the withdrawal across Bataan to Corregidor were unrealistic at best and suicidal at worst. "Dugout Doug," was what the Marines who had to dig his dugouts every time he visited the front lines called him. In the first few days of the war, his domineering and imperious chief of staff blocked access to him, and as a result his air force was not deployed or dispersed even after the attack on

Pearl Harbor. Instead, with a Japanese invasion fleet approaching, the planes were inexcusably parked wing tip to wing tip on the runway and easily destroyed by the Japanese 24 hours after the attack on Pearl Harbor.

In 1941, the Philippine government had offered MacArthur the title of Field Marshall and a solid gold baton, and he had against all regulations accepted. Even more amazing, in 1942 when he fled from Bataan to Australia, he accepted a large sum of money from the Philippine government that was virtually a bribe. After he escaped to Australia, FDR, feeling the United States needed a hero, callously awarded him the Medal of Honor, astounding and enraging the officers and men he left behind in the bloody caves and rocks of Corregidor, who felt he had abandoned them. For a superb character study of this complex man read James Webb's historical novel *The Emperor's General.*

Churchill's Belief in American Involvement

After Pearl Harbor and the other disasters in the Pacific, the American press began printing stories about the ineptness of the military in the Pacific and the stumbling setbacks in organizing war production at home. The epithet "red tape" was coined to symbolize the binding coils of bureaucratic inefficiency. Churchill, however, had always believed the United States would be an overwhelming fighting force when finally aroused. In the early 1940s, he had a much higher opinion of the United States' capabilities than many others did, but as he wrote in *The Hinge of Fate:*

> Silly people—and there were many, not only in enemy countries—might discount the force of the United States. Some said they were soft, others that they would never be united. They would fool around at a distance. They would never come to grips. They would never stand blood-letting. Their democracy and system of recurrent elections would paralyze their war effort. They would just be a vague blur on the horizon to friend of foe. Now we should see the weakness of this numerous but remote, wealthy, and talkative people.

It is interesting to ponder who the Americans were that bent Churchill's ear so severely that he referred to us as a "talkative people." In any case, although throughout his great six-volume history of the Second World War, Churchill maintains a stiff upper lip, he, too, was vulnerable to fits of discouragement. He once described his depressions as like a visit from the "black dog" of depression that all his life periodically had haunted him. This huge, hairy, foul smelling creature suddenly would appear and sit heavily on his chest, pressing him down with his stale, sick dog breath.

John Colville, Churchill's private secretary, in *The Fringes of Power: 10 Downing Street Diaries* recounts occasions in 1940 and 1941 when the Prime Minister was depressed, discouraged, and irritable. In January of 1942 Churchill groused that "to us in the British Isles it seemed that everything was growing worse." He suffered through a vote of confidence in the House of Commons, and although he won, he endured some parliamentary humiliations, which clearly rankled him. In 1942 he spoke of the "remorseless tide of defeat and ruin which dominated our fortunes." He frequently berated his military commanders for incompetence and excessive caution. On January 31, 1942, his commanding general in the desert sent him an incredible message, "I am reluctantly compelled to conclude that to meet the German armored forces with any hope of success our armored forces as presently equipped, organized, and led must have at least two to one superiority." On March 5, 1942, in a plaintive message to FDR he wrote:

> When I reflect how I have longed and prayed for the entry of the United States into the war, I find it difficult to realize how gravely our British affairs have deteriorated by what has happened since December 7. We have suffered the greatest disaster in our history at Singapore, and other misfortunes will come thick and fast upon us.

He then went on to enumerate the perils to Malta, Ceylon, India, and the victories of Rommel in Africa. Even more dangerous was the stranglehold of the German U-boats on shipping. As events transpired, the sinking of U.S. and British ships in the first six months of 1942 was almost equal to the entire year of 1941 and exceeded the whole Allied shipbuilding program by three million tons. The Royal Navy suffered heavy losses in the Indian Ocean from Japanese aircraft, and it became clear that the elderly British surface fleet was no match for the modern Japanese capital ships. On April 1, Churchill, the perennial stoic and optimist, ended a private message to FDR with these lines: "I am personally extremely well, though I have felt the weight of the war rather more since I got back than before." In other words, the Black Dog had been visiting him.

American Isolationism

There were plenty of reasons for the pessimism about the United States. Prior to Pearl Harbor, the dyspeptics about the fate of the world maintained the United States would remain neutral, and that Japan, with its need for raw materials, would take British and Dutch possessions in the Far East and carefully avoid hostilities with the U.S. Meanwhile, Germany's U-boats would gradually strangle England and force her to sue for peace. Then the United States and Canada would have to face the Axis Powers alone. However, even if Britain went down, the United States, protected by a vast ocean, would still be secure and prosperous. In the end these "soft" and "talkative" people would negotiate a *modus vivendi* with Germany and Japan.

In fact, there was a strong isolationist movement in the United States. Admittedly, a British War Relief concert could fill Carnegie Hall, but America First Rallies packed the much larger Madison Square Garden. The voices of isolation were loud and strident. Charles Lindbergh, America's aviator-hero, eloquently argued that the war in Europe was just part of the age-old struggle between the European powers and asked why American boys should die to preserve the British Empire. After a visit to Germany in 1938, he said, "England and France are far too weak in the air to protect themselves.... It is necessary to realize that England is a country composed of a great mass of slow, somewhat stupid and indifferent people, and a small group of geniuses." His wife, the beautiful, poetic, and sensitive Anne Morrow Lindbergh, wrote a best seller in which she described the war as a contest between "Forces of the Past (the Allies)" and "Forces of the Future (Germany)." Russell Leffingwell, a prominent partner of J.P. Morgan, intoned: "The Allies cannot sub-jugate the Germans. There are too many of the devils and they are too competent."

Many in Congress argued for a strict policy of neutrality. As late as the spring of 1941, the bill to enact compulsory military training passed Congress by a single vote. If the bill had failed, the U.S. army would have been virtually disbanded. Half of the two million men called up in the first draft were dismissed as physically or mentally unfit for service. Isolationists made noisy speeches about how Wall Street and Big Business wanted war because of their bloodlust for profits. In this vein, a Wisconsin congress-man, Thomas O'Malley, introduced legislation requiring that members of the richest families be drafted first. "It will be Privates Ford, Rockefeller, and Morgan in the next war," he said.

Moreover, after the shock of Pearl Harbor and the initial defeats in the Philippines, the American public panicked. By the spring of 1942, there were rumors and sometimes newspaper stories of spying, sabotage, and even a Japanese invasion of the West Coast. Fanciful stories abounded of night landings on Long Island, and midget submarines in New York Harbor. No less a commentator than the *New York Times'* respected Walter Lippmann predicted coordinated sabotage on a grand scale. On February 19, 1942, the disgraceful decision to intern the entire Japanese-American population was implemented. The national speed limit was reduced to 35 miles an hour to conserve gasoline, and a law was passed that capped after-tax incomes at $25,000 or $250,000 in today's money. It was a grim, desperate time, and it is no wonder that investors were profoundly depressed.

Chapter 3

Stock Markets Struggle

From the Great Depression to the Start of WWII

When war is declared, truth is the first casualty.
—ARTHUR PONSONBY

B y the late 1930s, economies and stock markets around the world had generally made a modest recovery from the Depression-era lows of the early 1930s. However, the economic recoveries had been fragile and most of the stock market rallies, although sharp, faltered after the initial spurt. In the case of the United States, the Dow Jones

Industrial Average by early 1937 had almost quadrupled from the 1932 low but was still down about 60% from its 1929 high. Investors around the world were still licking their wounds. Equities in the United States and Europe sold at five to eight times depressed earnings, at discounts to book value, and had yields considerably higher than bonds. The one exception was the German economy, which was booming by the standards of the 1930s, and the Berlin stock market, which was exhibiting sustained strength.

But in general, the trauma of the Great Crash and the subsequent depression loomed over investors like a vast, dark cloud. The Warren Buffett of the time was a scholarly Columbia Business School professor, Benjamin Graham, who wrote the seminal textbook *Security Analysis*. Buying a stock or bond, Graham taught, was about using rigorous financial analysis to develop a margin of safety because the great bear market had taught that the risk of loss was high. Graham maintained that balance sheets were at least as important as income statements and that stocks had to have higher yields than bonds because they were riskier. Credit worthiness was all that mattered. Treasury bonds were rated quintuple A (AAAAA). It was the financial analysis mantra of depression, deflation, and a secular bear market.

The London Stock Market and the British Economy

The London stock market was somewhat different. In the late 1920s it had indulged in far fewer speculative excesses than New York, mostly because the British economy and company results had been sluggish throughout the 1920s. Although the Great Crash, according to the *Financial Times,* caused "dismay and alarm in the city," there was some "quiet satisfaction" because British investors for several years had been feeling aggrieved at missing the party. They luxuriated in more than a few "I told you so's" about the dangers of speculation. However, as so often happens, the most aggressive British investors were playing in New York, and got hit hard. Among those suffering wounds was the hedge fund run by the economist John Maynard Keynes and O.T. "Foxy" Falk. They had divided the fund into two separately managed segments to get more focus, and Falk who had turned bearish on New York in 1928 against Keynes' advice went back into U.S. equities in the summer of 1929 and was almost wiped out. His segment was down 63% for the year.

Keynes' segment was only down 15%, and for a number of years he had in his own account been speculating in commodities with spectacular success. By the end of 1928 he was a very rich man. However, in early 1929 he was long rubber, corn, cotton, and tin when prices suddenly collapsed. His commodity losses forced him to sell stocks to meet margin calls so by the end of 1929, he had left only tag ends and a large, illiquid position in Austin Motors, which had collapsed from 21 to 5. His biographer, Robert Skidelski, says by the end of 1929, his net worth had fallen 75% from its 1928 high. Ironically, Keynes had been right about the excesses in New York but still was unable to avoid the deluge, which goes to show how difficult it is to sidestep a truly vicious bear market no matter how early and perceptive you are. The price of everything goes down, and liquidity is the ultimate coward—it runs at the first sign of trouble.

After the crash, London benefited for a while as investors, worried about bank failures in the United States and viewing British gilts as a safe haven, moved capital from New York. However, by the fall of 1930, Britain's economy was in as dire straits as that of the United States with unemployment soaring, industrial activity collapsing, and trade suffering from protectionism. Suddenly there were sullen breadlines in Glasgow and Manchester, and now most of England was impoverished. Austerity ruled. In the early 1930s when the prime minister needed to go somewhere, he walked out of Number 10 Downing Street and hailed a cab.

However, both the British economy and stock market bottomed in 1932, by the mid 1930s both began to recover. By the end of 1936, the Financial Times Index had more than doubled to a new all-time high. Keynes, for one, made big money in this new cyclical bull market and was once again riding high. Then, in 1937, stocks fell again as the economic recovery aborted, and both the United States and Britain slipped back into another recession. In addition, as Germany became increasingly more aggressive, European markets became very tender to international developments. These roller coaster rides were very hard on the nerves of investors, and Keynes, who once again was fully invested and leveraged, suffered a severe net worth setback that caused him to have fits of depression (visits from his own Black Dog) and severe insomnia.

The British prime minister at the time was Neville Chamberlain, a good but naïve man. In one of the great misjudgments of history, he judged Hitler to be a "decent, honest chap," and he believed the *Führer* when he told him that after the Sudetenland, he had no further territorial ambitions. On September 28, 1938, in a moment of high drama, Chamberlain told the House of Commons that Hitler had accepted Mussolini's offer to negotiate the Sudeten German question, which basically was the German annexation of Czechoslovakia. The House and the galleries rose in wild applause and shouts of happiness, and Chamberlain modestly murmured: "I believe it is peace in our time." That day, the British pound rose thirteen cents against the dollar and the London stock market surged. On this occasion the market, like the House of Commons, was temporarily fooled. Churchill, by contrast was not. He thought it was appeasement, and he did not join the applause nor did he congratulate Chamberlain. "The government has chosen between shame and war. They choose shame; they will get war," he said.

At this time editorial writers in London and market commentators generally disparaged Churchill and viewed Hitler with cautious optimism. In those days, investors and the public got their information from newspapers and books, and *Mein Kampf* was widely read. In it Hitler praised the fighting spirit of the English race and lauded its firm, imperial administration of India, which he hoped to emulate with an Eastern European empire. In interviews he spoke of a Nordic racial alliance in which England would maintain its dominance of the seas and its Far Eastern possessions, and Germany as its equal partner would dominate Europe. The clear implication was that the common enemy was Russia and Communism. The diaries of some of the general staff suggest that Hitler sincerely desired such an arrangement.

The U.S. Economy: 1929–1937

The Dow Jones Industrial Average had reached 380 in 1929, and at the abyss of the bust, the index touched 50 three years later, a decline of 89%. The market's first response to the election of Franklin Roosevelt was concern that he was too liberal. Many investors considered FDR a traitor to his class and a lightweight. However, the new president delivered an inspiring inauguration address in which he said, "The only thing we have to fear, is fear itself," and followed up with forceful moves to deal with the banking crisis, which had caused the country's banks to be closed. The banks reopened on March 13, 1933, and on March 15, when the New York Stock Exchange (which also been closed since March 3) reopened, the Dow surged 15% on huge volume, its biggest one day rise in its history. Somehow investors sensed that this new president that they initially had so disliked and disdained, held the touchstones to economic recovery with his bold moves and talk of a "New Deal." The 1932 low was the secular bear market low that was never reached again even in the depths of 1942.

This resurgence became a powerful rally in 1935 as the U.S. economy began a recovery, insipid at first, but a revival nevertheless. After hesitating prior to the 1936 election, the rally resumed as the economic expansion broadened and deflation ebbed. By January 1937 the market value of all stocks listed on the New York Stock Exchange had risen from $19.7 billion at the bottom to $62.5 billion. Think of it! The stock market value of listed America in 1932 was about the same as that of a medium-sized company today.

As Figure 3.1 demonstrates, at its recovery peak, the Dow was still at only about half of its 1929 high. The economy was still struggling. Ninety-eight percent of American families lived on less than $5,000 a year, and very few owned their own homes. Most people paid no income tax to speak of, and the top incomes reported to the IRS in 1937 were Louis B. Mayer of MGM with $1,161,735, Thomas J. Watson of IBM at $419,398, and someone named George Washington Hill with $380,976.

In 1937, the stock market rally ran out of gas, and prices fell sharply as Roosevelt's attempt to pack the Supreme Court disconcerted investors and the economy fell back into recession. Furthermore, the administration's agenda of a balanced budget was seen by the Keynesians as ill-advised for an economy still flirting with depression. The year closed with steep losses in the blue chips, as shown in Figure 3.2. Note also that at year-end apparent dividend yields were astronomical. Chrysler yielded over 20% and General Motors and Bethlehem Steel

Stock and Dividend	Price ($)			
	High	Low	Close	Change for Year
American Telephone $9	187	140	144	−40
Bethlehem Steel $5	106	41	58	−17
Chrysler $10	135	46	47	−68
General Electric $2.20	65	34	41	−14
General Motors $3.75	70	28	30	−34
U.S. Steel $1	126	49	54	−20

Figure 3.1   Losses of Leading Issues, 1937
DATA SOURCE: *New York Times;* Robert Sobel, *The Big Board: A History of the New York Stock Market.*

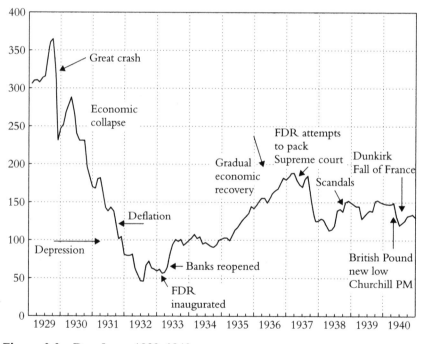

Figure 3.2   Dow Jones: 1929–1940
DATA SOURCE: Dow Jones & Co.; Global Insight.

yielded around 10%. The reason, of course, was that investors suspected that dividends would be drastically cut. They were right! The following year Chrysler paid only $2, General Electric $0.96, and General Motors $1.50.

The U.S. Economy: 1934–1939

The second half of the 1930s was a grim time for stock market investors who were still horribly scarred from the Great Crash and its aftermath. Research on stocks and bonds was superficial, no attention was paid to quarterly earnings, and the emphasis was on a good, solid balance sheet. The pools that manipulated stocks in the 1920s had disappeared. The investment business was rotten and had no appeal for ambitious young men. Wall Street, brokers, investment banking, and money managers were in disrepute.

However, two very different investment religions were rising from the ashes. On the one hand, Ben Graham and David Dodd in 1934 were preaching book value, current yield, and always buying both bonds and stocks with a margin of safety. On the other, T. Rowe Price by 1937 was writing in *Barron's* of the life cycle of companies. He advised that the crucial investment decision was not current valuation and yield but buying the shares of companies capable of growing earnings and dividends and avoiding at all cost "decadent enterprises which ... appear to have reached their maximum earnings." Both investment creeds eventually would have their days in the sun, but there were difficult years ahead.

In the late 1930s and early 1940s the New York Stock Exchange was still mired in deep depression. The so-called "financial district" was a wasteland of half empty buildings, shuttered restaurants, and dull days. Investment activity was in the doldrums. Volume averaged slightly less than a million shares a day, down from one and half million in 1936 and 1937 as scandals cast a pall on sentiment. So listless was activity that on August 19, 1940, only 129,650 shares traded. The brokerage and investment banking business were dying a slow death, and the threat of war raised the prospect of even more uncertainty, even higher taxation, regulation, and profitless prosperity.

Once-wealthy, supposedly patrician men like the blue-blooded Richard Whitney were defaulting on loans and embezzling money, and J.P. Morgan, his august self, was humiliated both by the Senate committee investigating Wall Street and by a dwarf who perched on his lap in the hearing room. For a sense of the social stress of the times in New York and Long Island, read Louis Auchincloss' wonderful novel

The Embezzler, which sensitively chronicles the rise and fall of Richard Whitney. FDR's egalitarian New Deal and liberal cries for reform had not materially altered the top-heavy structure of wealth in the United States with 61,000 shareholders in 1939 receiving 50% of all dividends. The New York Stock Exchange was still an aristocratic, "old boys" club, and Morgan Stanley accounted for 23% of all underwriting volume.

On September 1, 1939, Hitler invaded Poland and Prime Minister Neville Chamberlain, his voice quavering, announced Britain was at war with Germany. The next day the New York Stock Exchange experienced a three-day mini-buying panic with a 20 point or 7% gain in the Dow. Volume was the busiest in two years as investors anticipated defense orders would create an economic boom. However, as 1939 drew to a close, the market was becoming more and more sensitive to war worries even though military orders were helping to revive the economy and increase employment. A rally that year was aborted by growing worries about the situation in Europe, and from 1940 on, war news dominated market action. At first investors believed Hitler could be stopped and that a successful war in Europe would be bullish. Then they began to fear that a long war would impede trade and cause another depression.

In the months that followed, the market stalled. Orders for ships, equipment, and armaments were boosting the economy, but the market was unsettled by the ease with which the Germans took Poland and annexed Eastern Europe. In four and a half years Hitler, this bizarre corporal, this Austrian peasant, had transformed a disarmed, chaotic, nearly bankrupt Germany from the weakest of the big countries in Europe to the most powerful with hardly the loss of a German life. His vision of *Lebensraum* for the German people frightened many, and Jewish refugees were recounting horrifying stories of pogroms and concentration camps. The aggressive activities of Italy and Japan were also ominous. The world seemed a dangerous, uncertain place that was full of hatred and rage. There were no enduring themes in the 1939 market in New York. Trading was listless, and for the first time since 1923 average volume fell below one million shares a day. (See Figure 3.3, and compare these prices with those in Figure 3.2, from two years earlier.)

Stock and Dividend	Price ($)			
	High	Low	Close	Change for Year
American Telephone $9	171	148	171	+21
Bethlehem Steel $1.50	100	50	81	+2
Chrysler $5	95	54	90	+7
General Electric $1.40	45	31	41	−3
General Motors $3.50	57	36	55	+5
U.S. Steel $1	83	42	66	−3

Figure 3.3   Price Changes Selected Issues, 1939
DATA SOURCE: *New York Times,* January 4, 1940.

1940: Global Markets Hit New Lows

Over the winter of 1939–1940, the armies in Europe appeared stalemated in what was dubbed "the phony war" and the *Sitzkreig* by those who didn't understand the buildup of German military power that was under way. While the Germans planned and trained, the French and Belgium armies went home on Christmas leave. During those months stock prices in both London and New York moved sideways on increasing volume as shown in Figure 3.2. On May 9, 1940, Hitler launched his so-called "Low Country Blitz," and on May 10 the British pound hit a new low. The next day Churchill replaced Neville Chamberlain as prime minister. There was no celebration. Churchill was viewed by many as a loser who as a military strategist had been a dismal failure in World War I. In the days that followed, the French and Belgium armies collapsed, the Netherlands surrendered after four days, and the British Expeditionary Force (BEF) appeared to be cut off and trapped by the German *Panzers.* By May 27, the Dow had fallen from 150 to 114 and then to 112 in early June, a stunning decline of 25% (see Figure 3.4).

However, inexplicably in May in the face of the horrendous news from France, the U.S. market bottomed. After the successful evacuation from Dunkirk of the BEF, the Dow staged a sharp rally which recovered about 40% of the ground lost. Nevertheless, there was much pessimistic commentary in newspapers in New York, Washington, and

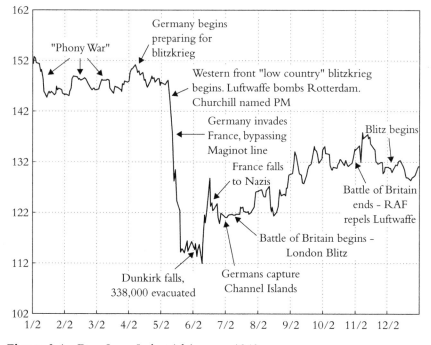

Figure 3.4   Dow Jones Industrial Average: 1940
DATA SOURCE: Dow Jones & Co.; Global Insight.

Chicago on England's dire predicament. A cross-channel invasion of Britain was anticipated at any moment, and the experts pointed out that so far no one had stopped the Germans. Hanson Baldwin, of the *New York Times,* the leading military commentator of the time, argued that the *Luftwaffe* had consistently proved itself superior to the Royal Air Force (RAF) both in terms of aircraft and pilot skill. He noted that the RAF had reduced flight school training schedules and had nowhere near the core of experienced pilots that the *Luftwaffe* had amassed. He also repeatedly pointed out (as did the editorials in the *Times)* how woefully under-trained the U.S. Army and Navy were and noted that most of their aircraft, tanks, and ships were obsolete.

The U.S. stock market weakened after the fall of Paris and the surrender of France, and when Germany seized the Channel Islands invasion fears increased. Meanwhile, William L. Shirer, reporting for CBS and Universal News was warning of the magnitude of the Nazi military buildup and the extraordinary charisma of Hitler. He wrote:"Hitler may be the last of the adventure conquerors in the tradition of Alexander, Caesar, and Napoleon." One commentator who still kept the faith was Edward R. Murrow with his dramatic radio broadcast that began each night with the tolling of Big Ben and Murrow intoning, "This is London . . ."

In face of all this bad news and despair, that summer stock prices in New York showed some resilience. Even before the air war began, the world seemed to sense that the Royal Air Force (RAF) was capable of denying the Luftwaffe the air superiority required for the Germans to mount a cross channel invasion. As the appalling prospects of a German invasion of the British Isles were diminished, stocks in both New York and London rallied. "Never in the history of human endeavor," said Churchill of the Spitfire pilots, "has so much been owed by so many to so few."

In late 1940, as the war news steadily got worse and the dimensions of England's peril unfolded, New York weakened again. Could a vast metropolitan city such as London long endure nightly attacks that were destroying its infrastructure not to mention the sleep of its people? The market declines came in spite of signs in the United States of growing economic strength and substantial gains in manufacturing employment. Hiring was up 10% on the year while payrolls gained 16%. Then as now, war was good for commodity prices with raw material prices soaring 25% in September alone. Gross national product and corporate profits in 1940 were both still slightly below the $104.4 billion and $9.6 billion, respectively, of 1929, but equities were one-third of their 1929 value. Average daily volume fell even further to a mere 751,000 shares. For the year 1940 the Dow Jones Average fell 12%.

The British stock market reacted similarly. As the German army raged triumphantly across Europe in the spring and summer of 1940, and it appeared that an invasion by air and by sea was imminent on the next moonless, misty night, stock prices collapsed back to the secular bear market lows of 1932. London's fall from its 1929 high was only 43%, far less than that of New York, and London actually had set a new high in late 1936. Then, with the country's very survival threatened in 1940, it fell 56% from that high to the low in the late spring of 1940 when even the evacuation from Dunkirk was in doubt.

Take a look on page 44 at an epic low. No double bottom. One final panic and a buying opportunity for the ages.

Moreover, in the early 1940s British investors were suffering an additional, albeit patriotic, indignity. The Bank of England was desperately short of dollars for the massive purchases of war materials from the U.S. government and companies. At that point, before Lend-Lease, it was a cash and carry operation. To meet this need, the Chancellor of the Exchequer decreed that British citizens who owned U.S. securities must report them to the Bank of England. The bank then combined them and secretly sold them through Morgan Stanley. The dollars raised were then used for munitions purchases. The sellers received a credit in pounds for the proceeds of the sales.

It was a delicate operation as any news of it could have triggered sharp price declines on the New York Stock Exchange. Of course it was absolutely necessary, but in a way it was a violation of the investment rights of British investors. At the time, it would have been unpatriotic to complain, but some were not forthright in reporting their holdings. It does show that even in a capitalist democracy, in a time of great national emergency and mortal peril, the freedom of capital can be imperiled. In 1940, with the Huns 20 miles away across the channel, if you were a wealthy Englishman, you would certainly have wanted to have some money in the United States.

It is impressive that the London market bottomed just after the humiliating route of the British army in France which must have seemed a national disaster of epic proportions (see Figure 3.5). Churchill himself warned that Dunkirk was an evacuation and that it must not be mistaken as a victory. Somehow investors sensed that it was a watershed event that the core of the British army had been saved and was on British soil to defend the homeland. Moreover, the upturn began months before the Battle of Britain had been won and at a time when it was expected there could be a cross-channel invasion at any time.

It was not evident until October that the Germans could not establish air superiority, but the market realized early on that they could not mount an invasion without control of the air. There were many dark days that summer as the battle raged overhead, and as will be recounted later, when even Churchill feared the RAF was finished.

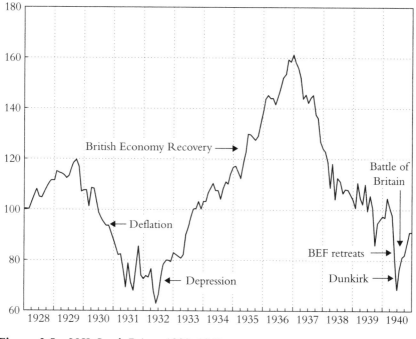

Figure 3.5 U.K. Stock Prices: 1928–1940
DATA SOURCE: Citigroup; *Financial Times;* Global Financial Data, Inc.

1941: U.S. and British Markets Respond to the Alliance

Although the U.K. market faltered in early 1941 under a deluge of more bad war news, from that secular low point in mid-1940 it labored higher, enduring much pain but never again testing the lows of 1932 and 1940 (see Figure 3.6). It almost seems that throughout 1941 the London stock market intuitively sensed and responded to the growing and deepening alliance between Britain and the United States. It was more confident of America's entry into the war than even Churchill. Certainly there was no good war news to celebrate because Britain was suffering defeat after defeat. More on this later, but by comparison, the U.S. market didn't bottom until a year later after the United States' equivalent of the Battle of Britain—the Battle of Midway.

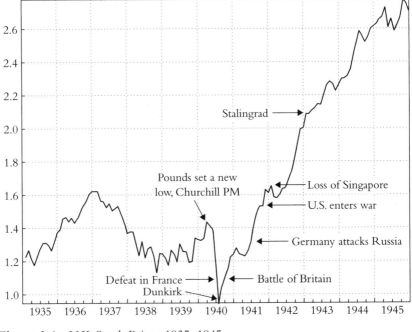

Figure 3.6   U.K. Stock Prices: 1935–1945
DATA SOURCE: Citigroup.

Once again, as shown in Figure 3.6, stocks proved that the bottom of a bear market by definition has to be the point of maximum bearishness, and from that point, the news doesn't actually have to be good, it just has to be less bad than what has already been discounted in prices. (The story of 1940 and the vicissitudes of the London stock market over that perilous year are told in Chapter 4.)

Meanwhile, as the fateful year of 1941 began, Churchill fretted about FDR's political problems with the America First clique and worried about that country's isolationist tendencies. Churchill desperately wanted the U.S. to enter the war on the British side, but feared the Japanese were too clever and too rational to provoke her. Although he never admitted it, he must have wondered whether Britain and what remained of her empire could stand alone. The U-boats were exacting a fearful toll on the island's seaborne lifeline, and it appeared very possible that even if Britain could not be successfully invaded, she could be starved and bombed into submission. Here is what Churchill wrote in *The Grand Alliance* of his thoughts at the time:

> It had seemed impossible that Japan would court destruction by war with Britain and the United States. A declaration of war by Japan could not be reconciled with reason. I felt sure she would be ruined for a generation by such a plunge, and this proved true. But Governments and peoples do not always take rational decisions. Sometimes they take mad decisions . . . I have not hesitated to record repeatedly my disbelief that Japan would go mad.

In the same book cited above, Churchill wrote that on the night of December 7, 1941, after hearing of the attack on Pearl Harbor he "went to bed and slept the sleep of the saved and thankful. He knew Britain would still have to endure many unexpected defeats and grievous losses, some in the very near future, but with the United States in the war, he no longer doubted England would survive.

It is well to recall how grim were the circumstances the Allies found themselves in during this dark period of mortal danger:

- Germany occupied almost all of Europe.
- The Italians, Hungarians, and Rumanians had joined the Axis powers.
- The Finns, a tough and determined people, had been attacked by Russia, had mauled the Red Army in a winter war, and would fight with anyone who fought Russia.
- By the spring of 1941, after fierce resistance, Greece had fallen to the Italians but only after the Germans had diverted forces to rescue Mussolini's legions.
- As a result, the German invasion of Russia, Operation Barbarossa, was delayed three crucial weeks, which as we shall see, may have made all the difference. (Chapter 6 recounts this invasion in more detail.)
- Elsewhere, the slashing attacks of Rommel had driven the British back to within 75 miles of Alexandria, Egypt. U.S. Army intelligence told Roosevelt that Rommel would be at the Suez Canal in three weeks.

Although the Royal Air Force in the Battle of Britain had denied the Germans the air superiority they needed for an invasion, England was in a perilous state. Her army was decimated and exhausted. The German bombing of London and other British cities, the Blitz, came at dusk and left at dawn leaving shattered buildings and hundreds of casualties behind. With the U-boats wreaking havoc, food and other essentials were in desperately short supply. In one week the Allies lost 40 merchant ships to submarines in the Atlantic. Meanwhile, the Royal Navy was suffering crushing losses in the Mediterranean and the Pacific.

By December of 1941, the panzer and storm trooper divisions had driven 500 miles into Russia, and it seemed only the onset of winter had averted the capture of Moscow. In fact, in early December of 1941, German patrols looked down on the spires of both Moscow and Leningrad. As will be recounted in Chapter 4, the Germans had not been issued winter uniforms, and their tanks and artillery were not winterized, so the Russian counterattacks were able to blunt the offensive and force a withdrawal. Nevertheless, in six months a million Russian soldiers had been killed, and an equal number taken prisoner in perhaps the most spectacular military campaign in world history. Once again, Hitler's military judgments had been proven prescient, and only the stubborn recalcitrance of his field marshals denied him the capital that could well have been the *coupe de grace.*

The truth is that Hitler's intuitions about military and political events from 1935 until 1943 were original, unconventional, and almost infallible. He correctly calculated the weakness and reluctance to fight of his adversaries, and his tactical decisions and audacious gambles succeeded time and time again. A surprising number of eminent people in both London and New York, when in their cups, would confess to a secret admiration of Hitler, for what he had done for Germany and for his attack on the Soviet Union. Many of them had met Hitler and been charmed. They seemed willing to turn a blind eye on his pogroms.

The rest of the saner world was also terrified by Hitler's murdering ways, his book burnings, his poisonous racial hatred, and his ability to manipulate the psyche of the German people. W.H. Auden expressed it lyrically in these lines. Linz is the town in which Hitler was born. The reference to evil being done is to the reparations imposed on Germany at the end of World War I, and the consequent devastating hyperinflation that followed that had contributed to Hitler's ascendancy.

> Accurate scholarship can
> Unearth the whole offence
> From Luther until now
> That has driven a culture mad,
> Find what occurred at Linz,
> What huge imago made
> A psychopathic God:
> I and the public know
> What all school children learn,
> Those to whom evil is done
> Do evil in return.

The Markets Hit Bottom

Wall Street was in no mood for poetry. Figure 3.7 shows the course of the Dow Jones Industrial Average in 1941. The attack on Pearl Harbor ignited heavy selling but there was no one-day panic. From December 5 to December 9 the market fell 5.7% but it had been in a steep decline since late summer. The newspapers attributed the losses to the sneak, surprise attack, and there was a sharp rally at year end. Investors recognized that the U.S. had been a "belligerent neutral" for two years, but the conventional wisdom was that war meant nothing good for the stock market. Throughout 1941 individual issues were grimly pummeled, as shown in Figure 3.8, and as we shall see, continued Japanese successes depressed sentiment in early 1942.

The year 1941 ended dismally for the Allies (and for their stock markets) but at least the lineups on both sides were now apparent. As one now reads the commentary in the American and British press at that time, it is striking how discouraged and depressed the elite, the talking heads of the time, in both countries were about the ability of the Allies to wage war successfully against the Axis forces. That doesn't mean they had given up; they just were skeptical about prevailing and as to how long it was going to take.

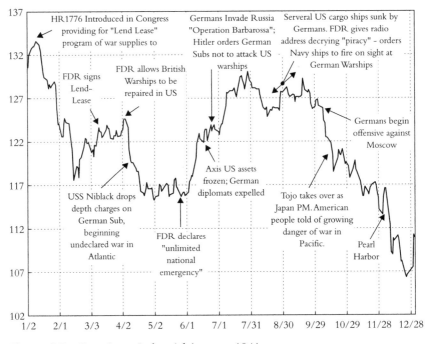

Figure 3.7   Dow Jones Industrial Average: 1941
DATA SOURCE: Dow Jones & Co.; Global Insight.

Stock and Dividend	Price ($)			
	High	**Low**	**Close**	**Change for Year**
American Telephone $9	169	115	129	−39
Boeing Aircraft $-	25	12	20	+2
Bethlehem Steel $6	90	51	65	−21
Du Pont de Nemours $7	164	126	143	−21
General Electric $1.40	35	25	26	−7
General Motors $3.75	49	23	31	−17
U.S. Steel $4	71	47	53	−16

Figure 3.8   Selected Stocks: 1941
DATA SOURCE: *New York Times*, Jan. 2, 1942.

However, as the year unfolded two great battles would be fought: one in the sea off Midway Island in the Pacific, the other in and around the Soviet city of Stalingrad. Although neither Robert Sobel who wrote *The Big Board,* the definitive history of the New York Stock Exchange, nor financial commentary at the time mentions either as important market factors, these two magnificent allied victories both halted the advance of the Axis powers and changed the momentum of the war. In Europe the Nazis were fighting off their back foot after the surrender of a huge army at Stalingrad, and Midway was high noon for the Land of the Rising Sun. As Figure 3.9 dramatically shows, the U.S. stock market instinctively understood the significance of Midway, well before expert opinion or the conventional wisdom grasped its importance.

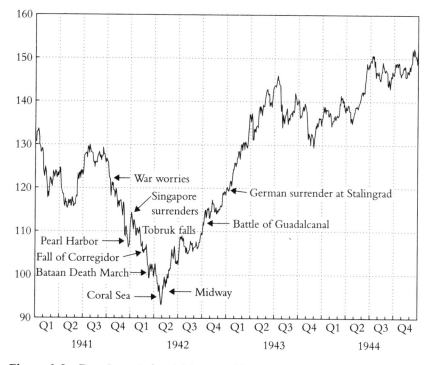

Figure 3.9   Dow Jones Industrial Average: 1941–1944
DATA SOURCE: Dow Jones & Co.; Global Insight.

In fact, the bottom that American stocks made in the second quarter of 1942 was really the end of the great *secular* bear market that began in 1929. A new *secular* bull market was born that spring that would last for almost 20 years and would take American stocks to unimaginable new highs in the burst of post-war prosperity. Of course there would be intermittent *cyclical* bear markets, but only the big, dumb, clumsy stock market somehow dimly understood that the long bear market was over and that a new era had dawned.

Chapter 4

"1940: The Most Splendid, Most Deadly Year"

The Time of England's Greatest Peril

As Churchill so succinctly put it, "1940 was the most splendid, most deadly year in our long English and British story." It was the time of her severest peril. Although many of her most crushing defeats in the war came in the first half of 1942, the year 1940 was when England stood alone and faced an invasion and the full force of the Axis onslaught. Her very survival was in doubt, but her people were united and resolute as perhaps never before or since. "If the British Empire lasts for a thousand years, men will still say: This was their finest hour. The citadel of the Commonwealth and Empire could not be stormed."

To be even more precise, with the benefit of after-sight, Lukacs in *The Duel* vividly argues that the key moment, the tipping point of the war between Nazism and Britain, was condensed into the eighty days between May 10 and July 31, 1940. This was the make or break moment for Germany and for Britain. Hitler knew he had to establish air superiority over the Channel and the southern English coast to make the invasion. In many ways, it became a personal contest, a duel between two extraordinary men—Churchill and Hitler. In the end, Hitler blinked. Observing the long-term chart of the *Financial Times* Index from 1929 to 1945 (see Figure 4.1), it is amazing how much the London stock market understood of all this. In the late spring of 1940, it fell steeply as the German *Blitzkrieg* smashed through the Allied armies in France and the Low Countries. The Netherlands, Belgium, and Denmark surrendered in a matter of days, and the panzer spearheads and the Stukas

Figure 4.1 U.K. Financial Times, 30 Industrials: 1930–1945

DATA SOURCE: *Financial Times;* Global Financial Data, Inc.

chewed up the demoralized French army. The BEF, consisting of the most the elite divisions of the British Army, was badly mauled in the rout, and at one point was on the verge of being surrounded and destroyed. Only the miracle of the evacuation from Dunkirk saved the BEF from extinction.

In June, as Britain gathered back from France its shattered expeditionary force, and the island braced itself for an invasion, the stock market fell to the lows it had reached during the darkest depths of the Great Depression in 1932 and traced out, in technical terms, a massive and perfect double bottom. Then, with the Battle of Britain raging in the summer sky, and the Germans assembling an invasion armada, stocks steadied. As August and September stretched on, prices rallied as the air battle continued and in spite of the desperate straits of the RAF. Perhaps British investors were inspired by Churchill's rhetoric or maybe it was just a visceral reaction that Britain was not going down, that it would not be conquered, but prices rose jaggedly higher.

Being bullish on England was certainly not the conventional wisdom that summer and fall. Many supposedly wise and sophisticated commentators in London and the United States despaired, but the market understood. As noted previously, in the summer of 1940, a great many people in occupied Europe believed, with good reason, that Germany was the greatest military power in the world, and that Hitler would rule Europe for the indefinite future and placed their bets accordingly.

Looking again at Figure 4.1, the chart of the London stock market, it is also fascinating to observe how prices rallied again in the fall of 1941 and after Pearl Harbor, but fell with the defeats and losses of early 1942. There is no question that 1942 was also a very harrowing year, but by then the United States was in the war and fully committed, and there was no doubt about England's survival. The issue was more of how long and how costly the eventual victory would be. The market was right to be worried. The struggle to subdue the Axis powers would be extended, and the war itself had opened huge cracks in the British Empire. Furthermore, the price of winning the struggle was so high that by the end of the war, Britain was impoverished and virtually bankrupt.

Churchill Becomes Prime Minister
At the Darkest Hour

After the dreary winter of 1939–1940 and the stalemated "phony war," in the late spring of 1940, the full force of the German onslaught across the so-called Low Countries and then France swept all before it with a speed that stunned the world. Winston Churchill ascended to prime minister on May 10, and the British pound made its low that very day. Since the early 1930s this pugnacious and romantic, yet prophetic, man had warned of the danger of Nazi Germany. For years, he had sat in the House of Commons like the conscience of England as the big clock above the speaker's chair ticked away the wasted hours. Auden captured his somber mood.

> In the nightmare of the dark
> All the dogs of Europe bark,
> And the living nations wait,
> Each sequestered in its hate.

However, Churchill's warnings of catastrophe looming from a Germany obsessed with vengeance, and of the need for Britain to rearm were not popular. The love of glory and the pride of patriotism had expired in the damp and bloody trenches of Flanders, and sometimes Churchill was heckled by crowds when he delivered his gloomy message. In the 1930s, there were debates at Cambridge and Oxford titled: "Resolved: We will not fight again for King and Country." Victorian England's anthem of imperial conquest that Churchill loved to sing no longer thrilled hearts.

> It's the soldiers of the Queen, my lads,
> Who've been the lads, who've seen the lads,
> In the fight for England's glory, lads,
> Of her worldwide glory let us sing!

Churchill's Own Financial Problems

In the meantime, Churchill had become renowned for his eloquence but had offended many with his acid tongue and repartee. Once, when he was seated at dinner and had argued politics with the very beautiful but very liberal Lady Astor, in exasperation she told him: "Churchill, if I was your wife I would put arsenic in your coffee." He replied: "Astor, if I was your husband I would drink it." His wit could be cutting and acerbic. At another dinner, Bessie Braddock, a corpulent Labor Member of Parliament who Churchill disliked and who had heckled him, said loudly: "Winston you are drunk again and what's more you are disgustingly drunk." Churchill surveyed her and replied: "And I might say, Mrs. Braddock, that you are ugly, but tomorrow I shall be sober and you will still be ugly."

On another occasion, Aneurin Bevan, a leader of the Labor party and a committed Socialist, was standing at a urinal in the Members Only House of Commons Men's Room when Churchill entered and went to the urinal furthest away from Bevan. "Feeling a little standoffish are we today, Winston?" asked Bevan. "No," replied Churchill, "it's just that whenever you Socialists see anything big and robust you want to nationalize it."

Bevan was not amused by Churchill's brand of humor. "He is an adolescent . . . an extrovert, a picture thinker. He really has the values of a boy of 17 or 18, but he makes them sound like mature judgments by his sophisticated speech." Another Labor rival, Clement Atlee (who Churchill once described as "a sheep in sheep's clothing" and as "a modest man with much to be modest about") said, "Fifty percent of Winston is genius, fifty percent bloody fool."

To make ends meet between the wars, Churchill had been forced to resort to speaking tours in the United States and Canada. He abhorred the endless receptions and sometimes had one cocktail too many. At one event in Canada after a long day he found himself in a group chatting mindlessly with a stiff-necked but loquacious Methodist bishop. An attractive young waitress approached them with a tray of sherry glasses. Churchill took one and then she offered another to the bishop. He was aghast at the prospect, and said huffily something to the effect of: "Young lady, I'd rather commit adultery than take an intoxicating beverage." Thereupon Churchill, or so the story goes, beckoned to the girl: "Come back, lassie, I didn't know I had a choice." Of course he was fooling, but the story gained currency.

Beyond the witticisms, Churchill was suffering severe financial distress as detailed by William Manchester in his biography *The Last Lion*.

His life style was extravagant, he was careless with money, and by 1938 his lecture fees and writing royalties were nowhere near meeting his expenditures. Although he had been Chancellor of the Exchequer, he was a babe in the stock market woods. In late 1937, he had been lured by the rally into putting his savings into the American stock market on margin. On a speaking tour in the United States he wrote this incredibly naïve and gullible note to his wife:

> Fortune attended me lately in finances. Sir Harry Gowan asked me rather earnestly before I sailed whether he might, if an opportunity came, buy shares on my account without previous consultation. I replied that I could always find 2,000 or 3,000 pounds. I meant this as an investment limit, i.e. buying the shares outright. He evidently took it as the limit to what I was prepared to go in a speculative purchase on margin. Thus he operated on about ten times my usual scale. . . . So here we have recovered in a few weeks a small fortune. . . . It is a relief to me to feel something behind me and behind you all.

By March of 1938, with the New York market plummeting, he was not only wiped out, his broker, Vickers Da Costa, informed him that he owed them 18,000 pounds, an immense sum of money in those days. Dismayed, he considered resigning from Parliament but instead put up for sale his family's beloved country home, Chartwell, with its 80 acres of land, hoping to realize 25,000 pounds. London's infamous "yellow press" leaped with glee on the story, pointing out that Churchill, who was often critical of the government's inability to balance its budget, was unable to balance his own and was on the verge of bankruptcy himself.

In the end Churchill gifts survived what W.H. Auden described as "the parish of rich women" and his own physical decay from the lifestyle he lived. Wealthy friends loaned him the money with the property as collateral and Chartwell was saved. Royalties from his new book *A History of the English Speaking Peoples* eventually paid off the debts but it was a near thing. Churchill earned 20,000 pounds (about $2 million dollars in today's money) from the book. Ten years later, with his six-volume history of World War II, he earned the present day equivalent of almost $40 million, making him the best paid author in history for a single work. The record still stands! President Clinton earned $12 million for his memoirs; Alan Greenspan got an advance of $8.5 million.

Churchill's Personality: Caustic, Colorful, and Magnanimous

Churchill's ascendancy to prime minister was not particularly popular. Churchill's wit and his caustic pen had offended many powerful members of the House. On occasion he seemed to revel in his acid one-liners, oblivious to the enduring animosity of the recipient. Of Stanley Baldwin, once a prime minister from his own party, Churchill had said: "Occasionally he stumbles over the truth but hastily picks himself up as if nothing has happened." On another occasion during a long session in Parliament, a member was droning on in a tedious discourse. Churchill reacted by slumping in his seat and closing his eyes. The speaker, noticing the nap, asked, "Must the right honorable gentleman fall asleep when I am speaking?" Churchill opened his eyes and replied, "No, it is purely voluntary."

There were others, notably Lord Halifax who was favored by the king, who many thought were better suited to be prime minister at this crucial moment. Halifax was approached but declined believing he could not be an effective prime minister from the House of Lords. Peter Drucker wrote that in 1940, Churchill was "a might have been; a powerless old man rapidly approaching seventy, a Cassandra who bored his listeners in spite (or perhaps because) of his impassioned rhetoric; a two-time loser who, however magnificent in opposition, had proven himself inadequate to the demands of office." William Manchester relates that some members of his own Conservative party felt the deposed prime minister, Neville Chamberlain, had been badly treated in the debate when jeers and insults flew like shrapnel across the chamber. At the end, Chamberlain had walked out a beaten, broken man.

The public and the press recalled Churchill's miscalculations as First Sea Lord in World War I and particularly the bloody disaster at the Dardanelles. Many families in Scotland and England were still bitter at the needless sacrifice of their sons, and the Foreign Office's R.A. Butler called him "a half breed American whose main support was that of inefficient but talkative people of a similar type." At the elaborate dinner parties of the ruling class, it was sometimes said he was just an eloquent loser who drank too much brandy. In fact, Sumner Welles, a confidant of FDR, told the President in March 1940 that Churchill was "unsteady and drinking too much."

Churchill did drink. He sipped from before noon until he retired deep into the evening—sherry in the morning, whiskey at lunch, Johnny Walker Red in the evening, and champagne and brandy into the night. Liquor did not seem to dull him or leave him tired, and he never got drunk. In fact, he despised those who did. All this alcoholic consumption was augmented with Havana cigars as well—about 10 a day, although most were only partially smoked. Some he just chewed, and he never inhaled. Later his longtime personal physician, Lord Moran, was to say: "Winston Churchill is 80 years of age today—a remarkable achievement for a man of his habits. A fine disregard for common sense has marked his earthly pilgrimage."

Churchill was not exactly your ordinary, aristocratic Englishman. For one thing he didn't laugh at anti-Semitic jokes. For another, his wife, Clementine, was outspoken and sometimes verged on the radical. Winston himself was never a true-blue Tory, and other patricians occasionally felt uneasy with him and his liberal ideas.

Although Winston and Clementine claimed to have adored each other, they never dined alone, slept in the same bedroom, or took vacations together. Clementine loved sightseeing and leisurely gallery viewing, both activities Churchill loathed, and as she grew older she went on long tours. On one of them, a five month voyage to the South Seas in the late 1930s, she met a kindred spirit, Terence Philip, a handsome, wealthy art dealer who was considerably younger than she, and they fell deeply in love. Upon returning to London they apparently maintained their relationship, and she suggested to Churchill another trip. He emphatically said "no" and the affair seems to have faded. Churchill, according to his great biographer, Martin Gilbert, was "weakly sexed." Once in Parliament, another MP whispered to him that his fly was open. "It makes no difference," he replied, "the dead bird doesn't leave the nest."

It is generally believed that Hitler also was under sexed. Lukacs cites anecdotal evidence that many beautiful women admired him and were anxious "to bed him" but to no avail. It is fascinating that the two most dynamic leaders of the twentieth century were not in any sense "womanizers."

As for Clementine, except for this one incident, she was devoted to Churchill and was convinced that he was destined for great things. As will be recounted later, during the war years she was fiercely protective and did her best to insulate him from the anguish of his wayward and often embarrassing children. Winston and Clementine always used their affectionate names for each other. He was "pug," she was "cat." However Churchill, the self-indulgent night owl, was not an easy man to live with. Clementine gave Lord Moran this insightful and not entirely flattering sketch of her husband:

> Winston has always seen things in blinkers. His eyes are focused on the point he is determined to attain. He sees nothing outside that beam. . . . He knows nothing of the life of ordinary people. He's never been in a bus, and only once on the Underground. Winston is selfish; he doesn't mean to be; he's just built that way. He's an egoist, I suppose, like Napoleon. You see, he has always had the ability and force to live his life exactly as he wanted.

During the war, Churchill's schedule as he described it in his memoirs was to wake around eight in the morning and then for the next several hours read and dictate messages from his bed and bath. Both Churchill and FDR were such self-assured men that they were perfectly comfortable receiving subordinates propped up in bed or while emerging "in the pink" from a bath. When possible, Churchill liked to take a brief nap in midafternoon, preferably in pajamas and then work most evenings until well after midnight, often till two or three in the morning. Like Hitler, he often scheduled meetings with his senior advisers for late in the evening which wreaked havoc with their metabolism, sleep, and family lives.

Later in the war, as the prime minister rallied "the race" (as he proudly referred to the English people), he had a private train that transported him around "his island" with an office, switchboard, dining room, sleeping compartment, and for the man who liked to bathe, a large bathtub.

Churchill enjoyed the effect of appearing in bizarre costumes, uniforms, and hats. Clementine joked that he owned more hats than she did.

An imp still lurked within him. General Sir Alan Brooke describes in his memoirs a morning visit with the prime minister in bed propped up on pillows in his oriental dressing gown, a cigar sticking out of his mouth, the remains of a breakfast tray beside him, and the bed littered with papers and dispatches. "The red and gold dragon dressing gown in itself was worth going miles to see, and only Winston could have thought of wearing it. He looked rather like some Chinese Mandarin. The bell was continually being rung for secretaries, typists, stenographers, or his faithful valet, Sawyers."

As Prime Minister, Churchill was into everything. Almost every day he dispatched 10 to 20 "personal minutes" to various ministers, generals, and government officials requesting action or information. Invariably they began "pray tell me why" and "this day respond" (they became known as "Churchill's prayers.") as this dominating personality that had waited so long for power and knew the terrain and the personages of the British government so well masterminded the conduct of the war and civilian life. In fact, he had known many of the principal players (because England was still a closed plutocracy) since his anxious, unhappy, bullied boyhood at Harrow and then at Sandhurst. No detail was too small, no event too minor to escape his relentless scrutiny as he alternately harried, meddled, and inspired his subordinates.

Reading his personal minutes for 1941 and 1942, when the war was at some of its darkest moments and he was facing votes of confidence in Parliament, the following gems of detail were striking. The unlucky First Sea Lord seems to have received more than his share.

Prime Minister to First Sea Lord
6 July 1942
(Copy to Minister of Works and Planning)

1. The Horse Guards Parade is not Admiralty Property, and you should have obtained permission from the Cabinet before erecting the bicycle sheds which cover so large a space.

2. As to the buildings used for the construction of the Admiralty fortress that you wish to keep, you should ask the Minister of Works and Planning to prepare a plan, and make your case and bring it before the War Cabinet.

Prime Minister to First Sea Lord
27 January 1942
Is it really necessary to describe the "Tripitz" as the "Admiral von Tripitz" in every signal? This must cause a considerable waste of time for signalmen, cipher staff, and typists. Surely "Tripitz" is good enough for the beast.

Prime Minister to Chancellor of the Exchequer
28 August 1941
How much gold have we actually got left in this island or under our control in South Africa? Don't be alarmed: I am not going to ask you for anything."

Prime Minister to Minister of Agriculture and Fisheries
12 January 1943
Pray make me a plan this day to have more eggs. I am told that 67,000 tons of oats or barley out of the million produced on the farms would suffice to restore the ratio of all the garden hens, and this would make a large difference in the number of eggs produced. When you have done so well in other directions it seems a pity to have such a large and obvious failure.

Prime Minister to First Sea Lord
27 December 1942
These names for submarines are certainly much better than the numbers. Pray see my suggestions. I have no doubt a little more thought, prompted by the dictionary, would make other improvements possible.

Now please get on with it, and let them be given their names in the next fortnight.

Hitler and Churchill: A Study in Contrasts

It is interesting to contrast the warlord styles of Churchill and Hitler. Both were intimately involved in masterminding their country's military activities. Churchill operated out of London, the capital, and he lived the life of an English lord with numerous servants and aides. As John Keegan comments in *The Mask of Command,* his daily breakfasts of partridge or pheasant cheerfully exceeded the weekly protein of British schoolchildren.

Keegan notes that Hitler's style was very different. Hitler was not an extrovert who could effortlessly work a crowd, and he had studied hard and long at becoming a gifted and charismatic orator. Always a driven man, in the late 1930s and early 1940s, he was relatively amiable and sociable. He enjoyed dining with political associates, his aides, and often his generals in surroundings similar to a senior officer's mess. During the campaigns of 1939 and 1940, he circulated among the troops, personally decorated the heroes, and often invited them to his dinners where he enjoyed holding forth and reminiscing.

Eva Braun, his mistress, was fascinated with the then-new moving picture cameras, and recently Hitler's home movies have been discovered. Most of them were filmed (presumably because the light was good) on a terrace at his weekend retreat and do not appear staged. Hitler is always nicely but casually dressed in a sports jacket and slacks and invariably wears a hat. He is seen petting his dogs, playing with the young children of his staff, and greeting and then chatting amiably with aides over drinks. There are scenes of Eva sunbathing with other women, doing gymnastics by a lake in a rather scanty bathing suit, and hanging fetchingly from a small tree.

The movies are silent, so an expert lip reader was employed to decipher the conversations, most of which it turns out were innocuous. The most interesting insight was a scene where Hitler and Braun are talking animatedly to one side of the group. Her back is to the camera, but apparently she has just told Hitler she can't find the dress she wants to wear to dinner. Hitler rather grouchily tells her: "You are complaining to me about a dress when I have to worry about whether one of my armies is surrounded!"

Watching the films is an out of mind experience. The man in them is not the familiar ranting, raving demagogue, gesturing to his audience, his voice rising, provoking an hysterical response from the crowd. Instead it is like seeing the apparition of a normal, middle-aged man nattily dressed in a coat and tie and wearing a hat, like Humphrey Bogart, emerging reassuringly from the fog of the past. Abruptly, he removes the hat and out of it's shadow the trademark small, black moustache becomes apparent, but the apparition is the face of the Devil incarnate. He gestures, pirouettes grotesquely, and raises an eagle's talon rather than a hand. Then he turns, swivels, and lifts the back of his jacket to show a tail that is powerful, dark, and thick with spines to prove that he is Lucifer before mincing off into the future on cloven feet.

After the debacle at Stalingrad with the humiliating surrender of his generals, the real Hitler became reclusive and spent the last years of the war in remote command posts where he ate a miserable vegetarian fare in wooden barracks or concrete bunkers. He insisted that the menu be the military field meal. He neither drank nor smoked, and to light a cigarette in his presence was bound to draw a baleful stare.

Although he exterminated millions of people in cold blood and cruelly sacrificed his own armies, he was extremely considerate of the welfare and feelings of the people around him. He was deeply moved by deaths of those in the conference room on June 20, 1944, when the bomb assassination attempt against him aborted, weeping with their widows. His secretaries were also his companions and confidantes with whom he often ate and chatted. Their diaries report that he shared his aspirations with them, discussed art, and even confided in them about his generals. There is no evidence of physical intimacy. Keegan says that his "sexual life remains a mystery . . . he had a strong inclination towards *schwarmerei* in his relations with the opposite sex—that sort of semi-physical sentimentality more characteristic of friendship between a young man and an older woman than of passion between lover and mistress."

It is hard to imagine this man, Adolph Hitler, the most murderous, ruthless bully in the history of the world, after a coarse meal of potatoes and vegetables in austere quarters at his command post, finding his relaxation chitchatting over tea and stale cakes with a gaggle of female secretaries and assistants, but that apparently is what happened. Eva Braun, except at the end, was never allowed in those remote command posts, although her light and frivolous personality was, in fact, quite similar to that of his secretaries. She was certainly not Nancy Reagan, no schemer or wielder of power behind the scenes.

Waging War "Against a Monstrous Tyranny"

But to return to Churchill. As he assumed power the press was critical, and it was noted that on May 13 when Neville Chamberlain, the former prime minister, first entered the House of Commons after he had been deposed by Churchill, Chamberlain received an enthusiastic standing ovation, particularly from the Conservative benches. By contrast, the new prime minister's reception was muted, especially from Churchill's own party. However, Churchill was not dismayed. He wrote later that assuming the leadership of his country at this moment of "mortal peril" was what he had prepared for all his life.

And it was a time of mortal peril. On May 10, 1940, world opinion was that the French army was the finest in the world, that its Maginot Line was impregnable, and that Britain with its powerful navy was the pre-eminent military power in the world. As allies they, after all, had won the First World War. A week later, France was a beaten, almost helpless nation, its Maginot Line a farce, and the English army was fighting for its life at Dunkirk. It was one of the most stunning reversals in history, and stock markets everywhere staggered under its consequences. On Monday May 13, 1940, Churchill for the first time as prime minister addressed the House and asked for a vote of confidence in the new administration. It was then he made his famous proclamation: "I have nothing to offer but blood, toil, tears, and sweat." He went on:

> You ask what is our policy? I will say: "It is to wage war, by sea, land, and air, with all our might and with all the strength that God can give us, to wage war against a monstrous tyranny never surpassed in the dark, lamentable catalogue of human crime. That is our policy. You ask, What is our aim? I can answer in one word: Victory—victory at all costs, victory in spite of all terror; victory however long and hard the road may be; for without victory, there is no survival."

He got the vote of confidence he wanted, and for the rest of the war, for almost five years, Winston Churchill in sickness and in health was not only prime minister but minister of defence (sic). And across those years through his eloquent, passionate, and resolute radio addresses and speeches, he mobilized the English language and sent it as a weapon into the battle to hearten and inspire his people, and in fact all free people around the world.

But that spring of 1940 was a grim time. The *Blitzkrieg* (or lightning war) in Western Europe began on May 14. The world had never seen anything like it. It employed new tactics, new technology, and superb planning and training. However, it should not have been a surprise.

In 1937, General Heinz Guderian had published *Achtung–Panzer!*, a book advocating combining tanks and motorized infantry with air power into a "spearhead" to puncture an enemy's defenses. The attack on the Western Front precisely followed this model. First waves of Stuka dive bombers blasted the deeply entrenched French positions. Combat engineers followed throwing up pontoon bridges across which stormed panzer divisions, each with its own self-propelled artillery and a motorized brigade of infantry. Special forces in gliders landed silently at dawn far behind the Dutch frontiers and seized bridges and canals before their surprised guards could throw the switches that were supposed to blow them up.

Germany Takes Holland in Only Five Days

The Dutch had maintained that their sluices were so efficient that with one phone call they could in moments present an invader with an impassable wall of water. It was all "nonsense," wrote Churchill. In the event their dyke and border guards were either betrayed or killed, in a single day the Dutch basic defense line could be breached. For example, at the Gennep Bridge over the Maas, three men in Dutch uniforms— two Dutch Nazis and one German—took the border post guards by surprise and murdered them. Eleven German commandoes in an unmarked ambulance immediately joined them and held the bridge while an infantry battalion hidden in a freight train crossed.

As the train proceeded into Holland, it would stop in town after town and 10 to 20 commandoes dressed as priests, businessmen, farmers or ordinary citizens would unload. The commandoes, taking advantage of their disguises, shot policemen and attacked army posts. In other locations paratroops, gliders, and even sea planes (to land on the canals) were used. Panic and chaos resulted as dark rumors of treachery and parachutists spread in the Dutch cities. After Rotterdam was heavily bombed, resistance collapsed. Tough little Holland surrendered in five days.

The Fall of Belgium

Much the same fate befell Belgium. The wide, level gateway into the country was defended by a series of ultramodern fortresses, and Belgium had a formidable army of 700,000 men. During the winter of 1939–1940, the Germans had built for training and rehearsal purposes an exact replica of the Belgian bridges and the great fortress of Eben Emael, which guarded the entrance valley. All during the winter of 1939–1940 the Germans had rehearsed the attack while the Belgian officers and guards were celebrating the holidays. Sited high on a peak of solid rock with deeply imbedded, reinforced gun emplacements, Eben Emael was believed to be impregnable, and from it 1,500 elite Belgian troops had commanding fields of fire over the bridges. Hitler himself had taken a special interest in the operation and had suggested a hollow charge demolition device be used that would explode inside the gun turrets killing the crews and filling the underground galleries with choking fumes.

In the final assault, 80 German commandoes did what was thought to be impossible and landed on top of the fortress in gliders. They killed the guards on the roof, and began cramming explosive charges into gun slits and tear gas into the ventilators. They inserted Hitler's hollow-charge devices into the massive gun turrets. Gas seeped into the chambers below, and portable flame throwers were used at other gun portals and observation posts. Parachute reinforcements landed, and after fierce hand-to-hand fighting in the underground tunnels, the Belgians hoisted a white flag at noon and 1,000 dazed defenders filed out. From the fortress with its commanding fields of fire, the Germans routed the Belgian forces on the bridges.

Both Holland and Belgium had rigorously held to a neutral position in the run-up to the war in the vain belief that by placating Hitler he would ignore them. They hoped, as Churchill put it, that "if they fed the tiger, he would eat them last." Both countries suffered long and brutal occupations. In a bizarre miscue by the usually methodical Germans, several weeks before the attacks, two German officers who had had too much too drink got lost on the flight home and crashed their light plane on Dutch soil. One of them was a messenger who was carrying the detailed plans for both attacks. The Dutch and Belgian high commands gave them no credence because they seemed so unconventional and exotic.

Another imaginative idea of Hitler's that worked was outfitting the new German dive bombers with sirens. The Stukas were terrifying apparitions. The dreaded, gull-winged Junker 87 dive bombers with their strange dihedral wings flying at 15,000 feet would suddenly peel off in sequence, port wings dipping sharply as they half rolled, half turned and then fell out of the sky plummeting arrow-true for their targets in a near vertical dive. But what froze men with their hands on triggers, what was so demoralizing, what left them shattered and trembling uncontrollably afterwards was not the big underslung bomb but the ear-piercing, shrieking death-signifying scream the Stukas' sirens emitted as they dived. By June of 1940, French infantry that had endured a Stuka attack, would panic and run for the nearest ditch at just the sound of the siren.

France Is Overrun and Retreats

Within a few weeks of the launching of the *blitzkrieg,* the entire front in France was irretrievably broken with the supposedly impenetrable Maginot Line either breached or outflanked. The French army of over two million men, considered to be highly disciplined and well-trained, was in desperate retreat. The elderly and dyspeptic French High Command, sodden with defeatism and despair, had no stomach for hard fighting. At the time, the French military leaders were thought to be among the most sophisticated military thinkers in the world, and its officer corps was steeped in tradition. They had fought the Germans to a standstill in World War I.

However, once serious combat began, the French High Command's obsession with fixed defense emplacements and cavalry, its disdain for tanks and mechanized vehicles, and its lack of strategic reserve was a recipe for disaster. In the open ground the shrieking Stukas dive bombed, strafed, and terrorized the French infantry, and then the panzers chewed them to pieces. The retreat became a rout. The French tanks were slower, had shorter fuel range, and lacked radio communication. Nevertheless, some French units resisted fiercely against overwhelming armor and airpower but to no avail.

The Evacuation at Dunkirk

As for the British Expeditionary Force (BEF) in France, it was being relentlessly strafed by the *Luftwaffe* and was in desperate straits. The RAF had lost 268 of the 474 aircraft sent to France and was unable to provide air cover. Churchill, within six weeks of becoming prime minister, was faced with a major catastrophe. England stood alone, much of its military equipment abandoned in France, and with an outnumbered air force facing an invasion of the homeland by sea and air. He immediately recognized that at all costs the BEF's 400,000 men now had to be evacuated. They were the cream of the British army. Without them the defense of the homeland would be perhaps fatally diminished.

The BEF began fighting its way back toward the port city of Dunkirk (in the far North of France), pursued and harried by the Germans. The roads were choked with refugees and Belgium and French soldiers. It was chaos. Units became separated and discipline broke down. There was considerable looting by marauding bands of French and English soldiers. As they neared the sea and the potential evacuation port of Dunkirk, this huge, disorganized mass of men was partially surrounded by the five panzer divisions under General Heinz Guderian that were closing in to cut them off and then destroy them.

In the late afternoon of May 24, 1940, Hitler, in a big black Mercedes with the top down wearing a brown jacket and riding breeches, arrived unexpectedly at the headquarters of General Gerd von Rundstedt of Army Group B whom Guderian reported to and headed for the map room. Panic ensued at the commandeered villa because Rundstedt and his staff smoked and drank, and Hitler could not abide either, particularly the former. Windows were thrown open, but fortunately the Führer was in a jovial and tolerant mood. A council of war followed.

The minutes of that meeting suggest that the cautious Rundstedt and his staff argued the panzer spearheads supply lines were overextended, and that the tanks themselves were in need of maintenance after their long, hard run. The terrain was marshy and difficult, they said. Paris, not Dunkirk, was the primary objective of the offensive. Besides, Air Marshall Hermann Goring was promising that the *Luftwaffe* would kill most of the British troops on the trip back to England. By contrast, Guderian strongly urged pressing the attack. This was a priceless opportunity to destroy the cream of the British army, he said. One more day of advance and his tanks would have them surrounded. It was easier to kill them now than fight them later.

Hitler himself made the decision to halt and not press the encirclement but to continue to harass the evacuation with artillery and with strafing from the air. It is unclear whether he did this for military or political reasons. Some historians believe he may have been reluctant to give his Prussian generals, with whom he had an uneasy relationship, this great victory. Or had Goring convinced him the *Luftwaffe* could destroy the BEF more economically from the air. In any case there is no question it was one of the major strategic errors of the war. If the BEF had been wiped out in France, the British Isles would have been almost defenseless in terms of frontline troops.

Over 350,000 English and French soldiers were now being squeezed into a seven-mile perimeter around the port of Dunkirk. The evacuation was an epic event. The royal Navy had only 41 destroyers available, so the call went out for help. The British are a sea-faring nation, and fishing trawlers, fireboats, tugs, barges, river steamers, and hundred and hundreds of yachts and motor boats sallied forth. The harbor at Dunkirk was not deep enough for troopships, so shallow bottomed vessels were needed. The flotilla that was assembled included such exotic craft as the Yangtze River gunboat *Mosquito,* the Thames barge *Galleon's Reach,* the cross channel ferry *Canterbury,* the island ferry *Gracie Fields,* the launch *Count Dracula,* and the one-time America's Cup challenger *Endeavour.* Even the 100-year-old open sailboat *Dumpling* made a few trips. The skippers of the civilian boats often were amateur yachtsmen, some of very advanced age. It is estimated almost 900 vessels of one character or another were involved in the evacuation and that 243 of them were sunk or destroyed.

By the time the BEA got to Dunkirk, much of the city was on fire, and as the troops approached they were dive bombed and strafed. A huge pall of smoke hung over the city, and the beach itself was littered with burnt-out vehicles and at the end, corpses. Looking at the pictures today one can see the long serpentine lines of gaunt, exhausted men waiting to be rescued stretching far back from the piers. Other photographs show soldiers wading through chest-high water to reach boats that are already jammed to the gunnels. One picture shows a harbor that is a jumble of everything from World War I four-stack destroyers to an antique paddle wheeler, the *Empress of India.*

By the second and third day, ships that had been partially sunk while loading men cluttered much of the harbor. The paddle steamer *Crested Eagle* was set on fire by a Stuka, and most of the 600 men aboard died before the burnt-out hulk drifted onto the beach. The destroyer *Grenade,* loaded with troops, was another Stuka victim and for a while blocked the harbor entrance. A loaded hospital ship, despite its Red Cross, was dive bombed by a Stuka and exploded just outside the harbor. The dead and wounded drifted in to the beach. The RAF by this time was so debilitated there was not much it could do, so the *Luftwaffe* had almost total air superiority. The British soldiers, when they arrived back in England, cursed the RAF.

The trip back across the channel was no picnic either. The Germans had long-range artillery, which fired on the ships as they cleared the harbor, and air attacks continued. From fear of the Royal Navy, the Germans did not commit warships, but if they had the British destroyers were so jammed with men that their main armament could not have been fired. Darkness, fog, and some inclement weather assisted the crossing, and in the end 338,226 fighting men, 123,000 of them French, were rescued from Dunkirk.

"We Shall Go on to the End"

But, as Churchill told Parliament on June 4, 1940: "We must be very careful not to assign to this deliverance [at Dunkirk] the attributes of a victor. Wars are not won by evacuations." Then he went on to give one of his greatest fighting speeches.

> Even though large tracts of Europe and many old and famous states have fallen or may fall into the grip of the Gestapo and all the odious apparatus of Nazi rule, we shall not flag or fail.
>
> We shall go on to the end. We shall fight in France, we shall fight on the seas and oceans, we shall fight with growing confidence and growing strength in the air, we shall defend our island, whatever the cost may be.
>
> We shall fight on the beaches, we shall fight on the landing grounds, we shall fight in the field and in the streets, we shall fight in the hills, we shall never surrender.
>
> And even if, which I do not for a moment believe, this island or a large part of it were subjugated and starving, then our Empire beyond the seas, armed and guarded by the British Fleet, would carry on the struggle, until, in God's good time, the New

World with all its power and might, steps forth to the rescue and the liberation of the Old.

When he had finished, the House of Commons, inspired and thrilled, rose as one and cheered him wildly. His Elizabethan phrases and eloquence still echo across time. However within a few weeks, France had surrendered. Eighteen months later, by the spring of 1942, the empire he so cherished was much diminished.

Germany's Occupation of France

The Germans had achieved a state-of-the-art military innovation with their panzer divisions and motorized infantry. No one had seen anything like it. The retreat had become a rout. French civilians, some in horse drawn carts, many pushing handcarts, in wild flight from the *chars allemands* choked the roads and impeded movement. Meanwhile, the panzers stormed across the open country towards Paris facing little resistance. Crowds of French prisoners marched sullenly but docilely along dusty roads, many still carrying their rifles, which the Germans collected from time to time and broke under the tanks. German officers, stylishly dressed and wearing sunglasses in open staff cars, nonchalantly waved to the inhabitants as they rolled through French towns.

Both U.S. and British embassy officials believed a pernicious influence on the leaders of France at this crucial moment was Premier Paul Reynaud's mistress, the Countess Helene de Portes, who had fantasies of ruling France from her *boudoir* in the manner of the mistress of Louis XV, the Marquise de Pompadour, 200 years earlier. At times it appeared she was already running France. H. Freeman Mathews, the first secretary of the American Embassy, later remarked to the author that he called at the Premier's office on one of those fateful days only to find him "resting" in another room and the countess sitting at his desk "surrounded by generals and high officials and doing most of the talking and making decisions." An admirer of Hitler, she was convinced Germany would rule Europe and France for centuries. She favored immediate capitulation on the assumption Reynaud would then be installed by the Germans as the premier of occupied France, and that she would be the premier of Reynaud.

Although he does not comment on the countess, Churchill's remarks about the French leadership in his chapter, "The Battle of France" in *Their Finest Hour,* are withering. He was dismayed by their inaction and defeatism. Even the German High Command found their successes hard to believe, but they nevertheless ruthlessly exploited the 60-mile wide wedge that had been created in the French front. Every available motorized vehicle was thrown into the attack and in 10 days they had gone further into France than the Kaiser's World War I armies had in four years. As the news reached Hitler, General Alfred Jodl reported that he was "beside himself with joy." It was no wonder. It was his daring plan that had severed the Allied forces and annihilated the huge French army.

The Collapse of the London Stock Market . . .

Meanwhile, as shown in Figure 4.2, the London stock market was collapsing back to the secular bear market lows of 1932. To understand the London stock market and the depths it reached at that time, one has to appreciate the desperate atmosphere of the summer of 1940. An invasion by the Huns either by sea or by air was expected on the first dark night, and although resolute, the English people like the rest of the world were awed by the Nazi conquest of Europe. They watched newsreels of endless processions of tanks, motorized guns, and trucks with arrogant German stormtroopers goose-stepping through the streets of Paris while huge black bombers and transports with Germanic hooked crosses swarmed overhead. Then there were the pictures of pitiful refugees staring at the rubble of their wrecked homes. Pessimists predicted a similar fate awaited England.

The stunning thing about the market low in late June was that it came even as pessimism in England about the war was at its peak. Even Churchill at the time was somewhat glum. While he was defiant and resolute, his speeches had a realistic and even pessimistic tone. On June 4 he cautioned the House of Commons that parachute landings were possible and "we have found it necessary to take measures of increasing stringency" against aliens, "suspicious characters," and even British subjects. On June 17, in a radio broadcast on BBC he warned that "the

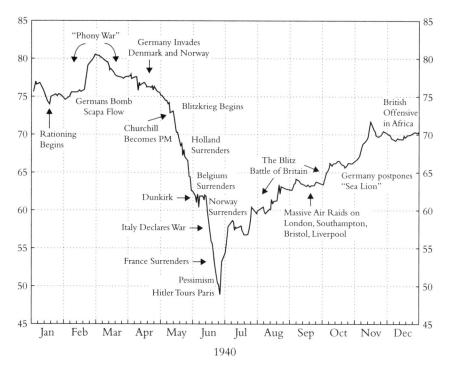

Figure 4.2   U.K. Financial Times, 30 Industrials: 1940
DATA SOURCE: *Financial Times;* Global Financial Data, Inc.

news from France is very bad," and spoke of the "disastrous military events of the past fortnight." The next day in the House of Commons he described "the colossal military disaster" in France. On July 4 he told the House of the destruction of the French fleet and warned that officers or officials "who are found to be consciously exercising a disturbing or depressing influence and whose talk is calculated to spread alarm and despondency" should be reported and would be removed. These speeches, although dramatic and stirring, do not seem to provide the fuel for a stock market rally.

. . . And the Rise of the Berlin Stock Market

Throughout May, as the German army stormed across Europe, the Berlin stock market climbed. Then in late May, at the moment of Dunkirk the market had a short but sharp correction. The *New York Times* on May 30, 1940, had a three-column banner headline:

ALLIES ABANDONING FLANDERS, FLOOD YSER AREA; A RESCUE FLEET AT DUNKERQUE; FOE POUNDS PORT; ONE FORCE CUT OFF FROM THE SEA AS LILLE FALLS

Also on the front page that day a headline in smaller type read: **Berlin Exchange Slumps As Optimism Is Decried.** The story said "that in what was an apparent reaction to warnings against over-optimism generally among the population following German victories in the West, the Berlin Borse today took a sudden nose dive. Shipping and metal works in the Rhineland had the biggest declines with most issues falling 5%." The reaction is interesting because Dunkirk in many ways marked the high-water mark of Germany's war against Britain.

The conventional wisdom is that Hitler's decision not to send his panzers against the BEF when he had them trapped may well have been his fatal miscalculation. However, there are those to this day that maintain he pulled his punches because he had always regarded Russia and Communism as the real enemy that had to be destroyed and still hoped for a separate peace and an alliance with Britain. If that had happened, Germany waging only a one-front war would have crushed Russia in 1941. Then the rich, "black belt" of Eastern Europe, the Ukraine, and western Russia would have become "Germany's India" to be occupied and exploited in the imperial style. Certainly the history of the world in the second half of the century would have been very different. For one thing, Britain would have kept its empire.

France Surrenders and The Battle of Britain

Back in London, Churchill was appalled by the passivity of the French population and their lack of resistance. He believed deeply in the stalwart, patriotic nature of the British people, and to harness that spirit, appealed for volunteers for a newly created self-defense force to be called the "Home Guard" with the sinister recruiting slogan, "You can take one with you!" A half million older or unfit men immediately stepped forward and were armed initially "with shotguns, pistols, sporting rifles, and even pikes and maces." Housewives kept pitchforks handy. Eventually the Home Guard reached a million and a half men, and they were issued old World War I American Springfield rifles. People turned to building "pill boxes" on the beaches and digging antitank ditches. The British nation, inspired by Churchill's rhetoric and exhortations, were united as never before and determined to fight to the end.

With the swastika flying from the Eiffel Tower and Europe won, Hitler now began to think of offering England a negotiated peace under which Germany's control of Europe would be acknowledged and certain overseas possessions would be received. He admired the British, knew an invasion would be long and bloody, and would like, he said, "an understanding" that would enable Germany to concentrate on "other enemies." In retrospect, it becomes increasingly evident that Hitler believed (as did many others in both the United States and Britain) that the real enemy was the Soviet Union and Communism. He wanted Britain as an ally or at least neutral. At that time he rejected Jodl's recommendation of terror bombing London, and after a meeting with him, Goebbels wrote in his diary: ". . . but the Fuhrer does not want to destroy the Empire." In mid June he authorized Mussolini's foreign minister and son-in-law, Count Ciano, to make the approach.

In the secrecy of the five-member War Cabinet, Lord Halifax, supported by Chamberlain, suggested Britain should consider the offer. There were a number of prominent members of the government who were already disenchanted with Churchill's sentimental romanticism and bluster, and they agued that, as Chamberlain put it, terms should be considered that "although grievous, would not threaten our independence." In effect, it would be a conditional surrender. These events are discussed in detail by John Lukacs.

Churchill was outraged. "Nations that went down fighting rose again, but those which surrendered tamely were finished." England would rather go down fighting than negotiate with a man like Hitler. Immediately thereafter, when he spoke to the full cabinet of 25 he was all defiance, and the cabinet rallied around him. There was to be no negotiations, no surrender. All these conversations were highly secret, but again, it is intriguing that as this was going on, the British stock market was in the process of putting in a bottom for the ages.

This cold British reaction resulted in the Füehrer ordering plans for Operation Sea Lion, an amphibious and parachute invasion of Britain that because of weather would have to take place no later than September 15. The Nuremberg Documents record his first directive: "As England, in spite of the hopelessness of her military position, has so far shown herself unwilling to come to any compromise, I have therefore decided to begin preparation for, and if necessary carry out an invasion." He went on to say it would be one of exceptional difficulty because "a defensively prepared and utterly determined enemy faces us and dominates the sea area which we must use." Hitler, at least during "the duel" in 1940, was a realist.

Nevertheless, German hubris was running high. June 21 was a lovely summer day in France with the sun casting long shadows between the stately elms, oaks, and pines in the forest of Compiègne where Germany had surrendered at the end of World War I. The German leadership was all there, be-medaled and bizarrely dressed in ornate uniforms. Now in the same antique railroad car with Hitler sitting in the very chair from which Marshal Ferdinand Foch had humiliated the Kaiser's generals, Hitler accepted the French surrender and danced another little jig of joy. The stab in the back at the end of World War I that had so long enraged him was now avenged. The terms of the treaty were harsh. Among other things, any Frenchman caught fighting for another country would be treated as *francs-tireurs* and immediately shot.

Anything now seemed possible to the inflamed German imagination. Other countries including Italy and Rumania were pledging their eternal fealty. The Aga Khan and the Khedive of Egypt, both volunteered to drink a celebratory bottle of champagne with Hitler at Windsor Castle. The latter also proposed himself as the ruler of India. However, Hitler realized England still had to be dealt with and pondered the details of an invasion. His Air Minister, Hermann Goering, bulging and greedy for more power, assured Hitler his *Luftwaffe* could destroy the RAF and establish overwhelming air superiority. A huge fleet of landing barges was assembled, and practice began for large amphibious landings over a wide front. Ninety thousand men would be the first wave, and by the second day 260,000 men would have been landed.

However, from the beginning, the German navy was very doubtful it could protect such an undertaking in the face of the superior numbers and firepower of the British fleet unless "absolute daylight mastery of the air" could be guaranteed. Hitler understood that without control of the air, the invasion fleet would be incredibly vulnerable. Goring promised he would destroy the RAF in time to permit a September invasion. No one seems to have mentioned his earlier boast that his aircraft would deny the BEF a successful evacuation from Dunkirk. The Prussian General Staff were uneasy about an amphibious landing, but Hitler had proved them to be to cautious and wrong so often that they remained silent.

Thus began "The Battle of Britain." The German air campaign, code named *Adlerangriff* (Eagle Attack) was programmed to commence on July 10 with intense attacks on shipping and concentrated bombing to soften the southern port cities, which were the initial objectives of the invasion, and to lure the RAF into combat. Then, from August 24 to September 27, the offensive would be broadened and massively intensified with heavy bombing of London in preparation for the invasion itself. Over this 11-week period, the RAF was to be eliminated and total air superiority established. It was not an unreasonable calculation considering that in July of 1940 the Germans could deploy roughly 2,000 aircraft; the British 700 to 800.

As it turned out, the latter period was the time of maximum stress. Some days a thousand German aircraft were involved with three or four hundred German bombers and fighters over England at one time! On August 15, a huge sky battle was fought over an area of 500 miles. Many British pilots flying Spitfires and Hurricanes flew three combat missions that day. Seventy-six German planes went down compared to 34 Spitfires lost, but the RAF simply did not have the deep inventory of experienced flyers that the *Luftwaffe* possessed.

On the other hand, the *Luftwaffe* had some severe handicaps compared to the RAF flying and fighting over their own country. The German fighters had a fuel limit of about 90 minutes of flying time of which 70 were consumed getting to and from England. That meant that after 20 minutes over England they had to break off contact or risk running out of fuel and ditching over the English Channel. Because of their limited range, the German fighters were limited to the southeast corner of England and London. The rest of England was relatively safe because unescorted bombers were vulnerable. If a German plane was shot down or damaged, the pilot had to bail out over England and was inevitably captured. A Spitfire pilot in the same circumstances could live to fight another day, and if he could crash land his damaged machine it could be salvaged.

By mid-September the RAF had lost a quarter of its pilots, and airplanes, and extensive damage had been done to its airfields and support facilities. Five airfields were completely down, and the entire Fighter Command communications network was on the verge of collapse. In the crucial two weeks of battle between August 23 and September 6, the RAF casualties were 466 fighters destroyed or damaged and the German losses were 385 of which 138 were bombers. The RAF was so depleted that inexperienced pilots were being taken from flight school before their training was complete and inserted into combat. Churchill admitted in his notes that a few more weeks of this and the RAF would be finished. That September an unknown RAF pilot tacked to his ready room the W.B. Yeats's poem "An Irish Airman Foresees his Death" "somewhere among the clouds above" fighting those that I do not hate guard those flot that I do not love.

Those two weeks were so crucial because both sides knew that from September 8 to 10 conditions for the moon and tide on the southeastern coast of England were almost perfect for an amphibious landing. "We must regard the next week or so as a very important period in our history," Churchill told the British people in a radio address on September 6. "It ranks with the days when the Spanish Armada was approaching the Channel and Drake was finishing his game of bowls; or when Nelson stood between us and Napoleon's Grand Army at Boulogne." Hitler replied in another radio address on September 14: "If people in England are asking 'why doesn't he come,' I can put their minds at rest. He's coming."

The truth was that the German military planners knew that they had still not established daylight air superiority and that they weren't coming until they could. Then inexplicably Goering, on September 10, suddenly changed tactics and turned to night bombing of London. For 10 nights the *Luftwaffe* blasted London's docks and railway centers, killing many civilians. The RAF was not prepared for night combat, and the bombers were unmolested. However, the diversion provided the RAF with the respite it needed to rest its pilots and service its aircraft.

Experts with the benefit of hindsight later maintained categorically that by abandoning the first principle of offensive warfare and not pressing his advantage by persisting in the daylight fighter war, Goering lost his opportunity to gain daylight air superiority without which there could be no invasion.

With perfect hindsight, it now appears that by September 10, Goering and Hitler had reached the conclusion that they were incapable of supporting a successful invasion and changed tactics. It was probably a wise decision. At the time it was widely believed that one Germans trooper was worth two to three British or French soldiers. The Huns were a race of warriors, and the average German was better trained, armed, in superior physical condition, and more highly motivated. But on British soil, the invasion force would have been outnumbered by an aroused people, and probably would have been consumed after a bloody struggle.

With access to the *Luftwaffe's* records, it is now known that the RAF was inflicting such heavy losses on the *Luftwaffe* that it was questionable whether air superiority could have been established with the daylight fighter war. For the period July 10 to October 31, the time of the Battle of Britain, the RAF lost 915 planes; the *Luftwaffe,* 1,733. Churchill told the House of Commons: "Never in the course of human conflict was so much owed by so many to so few."

The Bombings of London: The City Is Pummeled . . .

In late September, Hitler postponed the invasion until the following spring. The Germans now turned their full attention to London with the objective of breaking the spirit of its people or at least rendering it uninhabitable. Every night until November 3 an average of 200 bombers hit London. At that time, techniques of night fighter interception were undeveloped so there was not much the RAF could do, and the English antiaircraft fire made a lot of noise but was ineffective. For example, in one major raid, 437 Heinkel-111s dropped 450 tons of high explosive and incendiary bombs with only one bomber shot down. In time, the antiaircraft technology and night fighting skills of the British improved, but initially London was an unprotected city and it took a tremendous pummeling.

People lost their homes and their businesses, and this raised compensation issues. Children were uprooted and sent out of the city to families in the safer countryside. At the same time the city's complex sewage system was being destroyed and waste was being pumped into the Thames creating a health threat. The inhabitants of London were spending almost every night in cold, damp subway tunnels where sleep was almost impossible and they were vulnerable to epidemics. In October 1940 a survey showed that only 15% of Londoners were getting more than six hours sleep a night; 22%, four to six hours; 32%, less than four hours; and 31% reported they were getting virtually no sleep at all.

Conditions in the subway tunnels were so horrendous that it was no wonder that each night only about half of the population of London went into the Underground. The bathrooms in the tube stations were not equipped for permanent crowds and were rudimentary and filthy. The tunnels were infested by mosquitoes and rats. Nevertheless, as dusk fell and the sirens sounded, people would arrive with some food, drink, blankets, and babies and camp on the train platforms. The trains kept running until midnight so travelers had to pick their way through the sleeping bodies. After a night trip a woman named Rosemary Black wrote in her diary:

> Horrified by ghastly sight in the Tubes. Seeing every corridor and platform in every station all along the line crowded with people huddled three deep, I was too appalled for words. The misery of that wretched mass of humanity sleeping like worms packed in a tin—the heat and smell, the dirt, the endless crying of the poor bloody babies, the haggard white-faced women nursing their children against them, the children crammed and twitching in their noisy sleep . . . why if I wanted to torture my worst enemy, I could think of no better Procrustean bed for the purpose.

Even the tunnels of the Underground were not perfect protection. On October 14, 1940, a bomb dropped just short of the Balham tube station smashed the elaborate infrastructure above the platform where 600 people were sheltering. The lights went out, and water, sewage, and gas poured in. Panic erupted and although 350 escaped, 250 drowned in the ghastly sewage. Another night at Bethnal Green Station during a raid, a woman tripped and fell on the stairs. Those directly behind her fell over her, and the rest stampeded. That night 250 people were either trampled or suffocated to death.

However, as 1940 passed into 1941 and the Blitz continued, the Londoners adjusted. Families began to have permanent patches of platform, and a neighborhood atmosphere developed. There were community sings, and wandering minstrels performed. People knew each other and shared food and drink. A "we're all in it together, mate" atmosphere developed. At Aldwych in the center of the theater district, famous stars would come down after their evening appearances and perform. Amazingly, when the Blitz ended some Londoners missing the convivial atmosphere continued to sleep on the platforms.

Nevertheless, the raids terribly disrupted the life of the city. Getting to and from work in the midst of air raids was an endless ordeal. Would the city's workforce be able to continue to function? Later in the year the *Luftwaffe* introduced a new and even more terrifying weapon. The parachute mine, packed full of high explosives, was eight feet long, two feet in diameter, and weighed two and a half tons. Some were delayed action bombs that had to be identified and dug out, leaving large areas uninhabitable. Some were booby-trapped, which made defusing them even more hazardous. One unexploded parachute bomb hung swaying in the breeze by its fraying parachute from the biggest gas storage tank. Another landed and became entangled on Hungerford Bridge, which spanned the Thames. These were followed by incendiary bombs that also wreaked havoc. But as Churchill famously said, "London can take it."

Unfortunately the bombing had some very chilling side effects, namely a huge increase in crime, particularly in the cities. Bombed houses were looted, theft increased markedly, minor crimes and pick pocketing soared, and murders in England and Wales increased by 22% between 1939 and 1942. War unravels the bonds of civil society, and the wealthy suffered as priceless heirlooms went missing from clubs and private properties. The rich literally either had to take physical possession of their valuables or hide them to prevent them from being stolen. It obviously was a lot easier to safeguard jewelry and silverware than antique furniture. Pictures and sculptures were not of much interest to thieves as they were too difficult to transport, but on the other hand, they were more vulnerable to destruction from the bombing. An ancient and very rich old lady confided to the author many years ago that she had "slept with my jewelry instead of my husband for four years. England will never be the same again."

Another consequence of the bombing was the evacuation of women and children to the countryside and a dramatic rise in the divorce rate of middle-aged men and women.

On the other hand, the arrival of the American forces in 1942 with cigarettes and nylon stockings revitalized the black market and created wealth—for the wrong kind of people. Thus two patterns that were repeated across Europe throughout the war emerged in England. Jewelry was the most portable, liquid, and easily protected form of wealth, and the only people that got rich during the war were those connected in one form or another to the black market.

. . . But the London Stock Market Prevails: the British Are "Invincible"

At year-end 1940, London was a city under siege and in great distress. The London stock market prevailed in spite of all this. As shown in Figure 3.5 in Chapter 3, in the mid-1930s, the U.K. economy seemed finally to be on the mend, and the Financial Times Index had a huge surge, which, by the end of 1936, saw it triple from its 1932 low. It was the only major market in the world to exceed its 1929 high. Note the double top formation. Then as the international situation deteriorated, it fell again and by January of 1940, was down almost 40% from the 1937 high. The first half of 1940 was virtually straight down and back to the 1932 lows. The lows occurred after Dunkirk and the fall of France in the early summer as the Battle of Britain raged in the skies overhead. Over the course of the rest of the year as the Battle of Britain and the Blitz took place in the sky above, prices rallied. Churchill wrote later that he was most worried in late August but the stock market lows were earlier. Why? Probably because the bottom of a bear market by defini-tion has to be the *point of maximum bearishness*. The *new* news doesn't have to be good; it simply has to be less bad than what has already been discounted. In May and June of 1940 most stocks in London were selling at 20% to 40% discount to book value, and the faint-hearted pessimists sold to the resolute. In fact, buying shares was viewed almost as an expression of confidence and defiance. The nation was now totally engaged, and as Churchill wrote in *Their Finest Hour,* "The soul of the British people and race proved invincible."

In *A Treasury of Great Reporting* five correspondents, Robert Bunnelle, Helen Kirkpatrick, Edward R. Murrow, Robert Casey, and S.N. Behrman vividly describe the atmosphere of the time in London and throughout England. A country that had been riven by hard times and class warfare was suddenly united as never before. The danger from the bombing and the invasion invigorated people and they forgot class warfare and their grievances. For the time being they ignored the hardships. Everyone wanted a weapon. The common enemy was the Germans, and both men and women wanted to contribute to the defense of their island. It was a stirring time.

Churchill tells in *Their Finest Hour* of visiting a beach defense near Dover. The brigadier in charge informs him that he has only three anti-tank guns covering four miles of prime landing beach. Furthermore, he has only six rounds of ammunition for each gun. He asks whether Churchill thinks it's okay if he allows his men to fire one single round for practice so they might at least know how the weapon worked. Churchill told him they "couldn't afford practice rounds, and that fire should be held until the last moment at the closest range." The English people realized that they were in a life and death struggle and were focused on one thing: defending their island at all costs. The Home Guard also developed a bomb that would stick to the steel on German tanks. The concept was that devoted soldiers or civilians would run up close to the tank and thrust this "sticky bomb" on it even though the explosion would cost them their lives.

The Battle of the Atlantic

From July 1940 until July 1941 another life and death struggle, the Battle of the Atlantic, was being waged. The British knew that if their island's supply lines were severed, they could not long survive much less wage war.

Churchill later wrote "that the only thing that really frightened me during the war was the U-boat peril. Our lifeline, even across the broad oceans and especially in the entrances to the island, was endangered." The Germans employed U-boats, surface raiders, and Henkel 111 bombers to attack the convoys. In the week ending September 22, 1940, 27 ships totaling nearly 160,000 tons were sunk. A few weeks later, an Atlantic convoy was massacred by a pack of U-boats and 20 of 34 ships were sunk in two days. Nicholas Monseratt's novel *The Cruel Sea* is a superb description of the long battle against the U-boats, the bitter cold, and the remorseless sea itself. In the North Atlantic in the winter a man could survive in the water for only about two minutes.

In October of 1940 six German surface raiders broke out into the North Atlantic and began attacking the convoys. Destroyers and converted freighters armed with six-inch guns and with Royal Navy crews were the shepherds against U-boat, but they lacked the firepower and armor to slug it out with a German cruiser. One of the most dramatic incidents occurred when the pocket battleship *Scherer* came upon a convoy of 37 ships escorted by the armed merchant cruiser *Jervis Bay*. The captain of *Jervis Bay* immediately realized he was hopelessly overmatched, but he determined to attack the German battleship and engage her as long as possible in order to give the convoy time to scatter in the gathering darkness. Hoisting a huge battle flag, he closed at full speed on the powerful German ship. The *Scherer* opened fire at 18,000 yards with her 14-inch guns while the *Jervis Bay* armed with old six-inch guns still was well out of range.

On charged the *Jervis Bay*, and as she closed some of her rounds began to have effect. As the uneven battle raged on, the *Scherer* was forced to turn to maneuver away from torpedoes. Meanwhile the convoy was fleeing in all directions. As darkness fell the *Jervis Bay* wracked with fires and completely out of control continued to fire until she sank about 8 P.M. with her battle flag still flying. Two hundred officers and men including her captain (who was posthumously awarded the Victoria Cross) went down with the ship. The *Scherer* now turned to the convoy, which had scattered into the wintry night. She was able to overtake and sink four, but worried that her position was now known, she broke off the engagement and fled into the South Atlantic. This heroic engagement was captured in Alistair McLean's wonderful novel *H.M.S. Ulysses.*

What Might Have Happened

After the war, documents were discovered that revealed Germany's plans for an occupied England. On September 9, 1940, the commander in chief of the Whermacht had signed a directive that stipulated, "The able-bodied male population between the ages of 17 and 45 will . . . be interned and dispatched to the Continent." Within 24 hours after the surrender, anyone who had not turned in firearms and radio sets would be liable for immediate execution as would anyone resisting the occupation. Hostages would be taken. The administration of the occupied land would be conducted by the SS and the Gestapo. It would have been a cruel and harsh occupation. In such an environment, British wealth, the accumulated riches of the centuries, would have been confiscated or destroyed. Not exactly a friendly environment for equities.

The blitz and the U-boat war did not break the will of the British people. Churchill recounts an anecdote that captures their determined, resolute, yet fatalistic mood. A subaltern says to a downcast superior: "Anyhow, sir, we're in the Final, and it's to be played on the Home Ground."

However, as the next chapter relates, there was more pain and suffering to be endured interspersed with moments of the highest drama and heroism in the years to come.

Chapter 5

Besieged and Alone:
England in 1941

The year 1941 was another perilous year for England. The issue of her very survival was still very much in doubt. As the year began the stock market rally off the June 1940 secular low aborted (refer back to Figures 4.1 and 4.2 in Chapter 4). The winter of 1941 was a hard, dreary time in a London that was still reeling from the Blitz and the privations of the U-boat blockade. Along with everything else, January and February were even wetter and colder than normal, and in a country short of coal and food with so many houses destroyed by the bombings, the weather added to the general misery.

It is amazing that at this time of the home island's mortal peril, the British had diverted troops to Africa and in effect were fighting a two-front war. In January spirits were buoyed by victories over the Italians in the desert at Bardia and Tobruk with almost 70,000 prisoners taken. The following months there were more victories over the Italians in Ethiopia,

Kenya, and Somaliland, and the British and Indian forces acquitted themselves with great distinction, but against a less formidable foe. By April, an Italian army of more than 220,000 men had been either captured or destroyed, and Mussolini (who had famously remarked that he "wanted to make history, not endure it") had seen his dreams of establishing an African empire to be built by conquest and colonized in the spirit of ancient Rome evaporate. Haile Selassie, the emperor of Abyssinia (now Ethiopia) had been restored to his throne, such as it was.

Churchill, however, given his low opinion of Italian military prowess was not impressed. A year earlier, when informed that the Italians had entered the war on the German side he commented: "Well, that's fair. Last time they were on our side." However, now he worried that the Germans might decide to rescue Mussolini from his North African misadventures. "This whipped jackal, Mussolini," said Churchill disdainfully, "who to save his own skin, has made all Italy a vassal state of Hitler's empire, comes frisking up by the side of the German tiger with yelps not only of appetite—that could be understood—but even of triumph."

Meanwhile, British intelligence believed that Hitler was pondering his next move. Would he risk a channel crossing to invade Britain, or would he find less hazardous worlds to conquer and expand eastward or south to Greece, the Balkans, or even North Africa? At this time British intelligence did not contemplate a German attack on the Soviet Union.

In late January, Wendell Wilkie, who had been FDR's opponent in the 1940 election, visited Churchill. He brought with him a handwritten note from the president with these lines from Longfellow, which deeply moved the prime minister.

Dear Churchill,
Wendell Wilkie will give you this. He is truly helping to keep politics out over here. I think this applies to your people as it does to us:
"Sail on, O ship of State!
Sail on, O Union, strong and great!
Humanity with all its fears,
With all the hopes of future years,
Is hanging breathless on thy fate!"

German U-Boats versus the British Royal Navy

Meanwhile, the desperate Battle of the Atlantic to keep England's supply lifeline open against the U-boats and occasional surface raiders continued with heavy British shipping losses. The Germans had several pocket battleships and heavy cruisers that were more than a match for anything the somewhat antique Royal Navy had available. However, the Royal Navy had far more capital ships so the Germans could not risk a pitched battle. Therefore they used their fast and powerful warships as raiders, thus effectively pinning down the Royal Navy to convoy duty.

At this stage of the war, the U-boats were very effective as the Royal Navy's antisubmarine warfare skills and sonar were still rudimentary. The German submarines were manned by elite crews, and after each cruise they went on leave to exclusive resorts complete with wine, women, and song where they were treated like heroes. Morale and esprit de corps was high. Furthermore, the U-boats began to employ "wolf pack" tactics devised by the head of the U-boat service, Admiral Karl Dönitz, a decorated World War I submarine commander, and refined by Captain Günther Prien of U-47.

The latter, a ruthless and highly intelligent officer inspired his fellow captains to surface at night, stalk a convoy, and then attack from different angles. Prien and other captains acquired reputations for invincibility, and their subs were regarded as "lucky" ships. In late March, however, Prien's boat was sunk with himself and all hands, and a week later U-99 and U-100, both commanded by outstanding officers, were surprised on the surface and destroyed by Royal Navy destroyers. Thereafter, the U-boat captains were less daring, and as the losses of experienced crews increased, the quality of the service inevitably deteriorated.

More London Bombings

Then, as spring came the Blitz resumed. In January and February the *Luftwaffe* had been frustrated by the foul winter weather, but as visibility improved the intensity of their bombing of not just London but of cities across the country increased. These raids caused great damage, and considerable disruption of the economic life, war effort, and civil society of the country. Since factories were specifically targeted, many family businesses were so damaged they had to be shut down or were destroyed.

In the long run, business interruption compensation was paid by the government but it was usually inadequate to restore the properties to operating condition. Business owners complained that the Hun has ruined them when even the Great Depression couldn't. In essence, wealth was wiped out.

However, perversely from the German point of view, they brought the war home across England and Scotland and made the people even more united and determined. Churchill made it his practice to visit the blasted cities and he described a visit he made to Bristol, which had just been heavily bombed. "At one of the rest centers a number of old women whose homes had been wrecked and who still seemed stunned were sitting there, the picture of dejection. When I came in they wiped away their tears and cheered wildly for King and Country."

On May 10, 1941, London was subjected to a massive air raid with incendiary bombs. This was the first time that fire bombing and terror was used against a residential city, and it took war between two supposedly civilized western countries to a new level of total involvement. More than 2,000 fires were started, and five docks and many factories were leveled. The historic building of the House of Commons was destroyed. The principal water mains of London were knocked out so the fires could not be extinguished and civilian casualties were heavy. It was the worst, and last, attack of the 1941 Blitz.

Hitler's Deputy Führer Tries to End the War on His Own

A bizarre incident occurred on May 10, 1941, when Rudolph Hess, deputy führer and the leader of the Nazi Party, secretly and acting on his own volition parachuted onto the estate of the Duke of Hamilton whom he knew from before the war. Hess had left a letter to be hand delivered to Hitler informing him that he was going to England to negotiate peace. He then flew across the channel by himself in a stolen ME 188 fighter and surrendered to a Scottish farmer. When Hitler received the letter, he flew into a towering rage and had Hess' adjutant who had delivered it immediately arrested and charged with treason. In addition

Hess' astrologer and clairvoyant were detained. Because the British had not yet disclosed the arrival of Hess, the Germans announced that the deputy führer was missing and presumed dead after an unauthorized plane flight.

Thus the Germans were further embarrassed when the British announced that Hess had turned himself into them. The British transferred him to the Tower of London where he was extensively examined by psychiatrists and interviewed by senior Foreign Office officials. It was determined he was perfectly sane but hallucinatory. Back home he had consulted frequently with a clairvoyant and astrologer (both of whom were now experiencing the tender ministrations of the Gestapo) who had confirmed his intuition that he, and he alone, could prevent needless German and English bloodshed.

Rudolph Hess was an attractive man of about 40 who worshipped Hitler and who, at one time, had been his closest confidante and friend. At early Nazi Party rallies he had been a formidable brawler with Marxists and others who attempted to disrupt Hitler speeches. Later Hitler and Hess had been cell mates at the Landsberg Fortress prison, and Hitler had dictated *Mien Kampf* to Hess. In 1939, Hitler designated Hess to be, after Goring, his successor. In the early years after Hitler came to power, they dined together two or three times a week and exchanged confidences. No one knew Hitler as intimately, he told the British, or better understood his inner mind: his hatred of Bolshevism and Soviet Russia, his admiration of Britain and her empire, and his wish to reestablish the historic ties between the two countries and their royal families.

According to Hess, Hitler believed that deluded and evil warmongers led by the "ambitious criminal Churchill had poisoned the minds of the British people." The current government's policies were blocking Britain from her natural alliance with Germany against Bolshevism, which was the real threat to the world. Hitler apparently particularly resented Churchill's lack of respect and his demeaning descriptions of him as "Corporal Hitler" and as "this bloodthirsty guttersnipe" and "the repository of evil."

However, as time went on Hess became queerer and queerer. He began to grate on Hitler, and besides Hitler was developing new confidantes, and increasingly he enjoyed dinners with party personages. Even though he was still the Deputy Führer, Hess' power diminished and he began to feel his contribution was inconsequential. He came to believe that his greatest contribution to the Führer would be to somehow contact the English king and convince him of Hitler's true feelings. Hess believed that Britain had no chance now that she was alone, and much needless suffering would be endured by both countries if the war continued.

He, Hess, he passionately explained, had been horrified by the air raids on London and the killing of innocent civilians, particularly children. The senseless slaughter must stop. Hitler would never negotiate with Churchill, but if the king would dismiss the present government, a peace treaty could be worked out where England could keep her empire and leave Europe to Germany. He stressed he was proposing all this for idealistic reasons and had not discussed it with anyone much less Hitler himself. "If only England knew how kind Hitler really was, surely she would meet his wishes," he said.

The affair created a sensation. Churchill himself wrote later that he thought Hess sincerely meant well and wanted to end the war. He described him as "a lunatic benevolent." In the end, Hess was harshly treated. He never got to speak with Churchill or the king, and after being imprisoned in the Tower until late 1945, he was transferred to Nuremberg and later tried for war crimes with the other Nazi leaders. Testifying at his trial through the mist of his madness, Hess, loyal to the end, said that Hitler "was the greatest son whom my nation has brought forth in a thousand years. If I were standing once more at the beginning, I should once again do as I did then, even if I knew that at the end I should be burnt at the stake." He wasn't burnt by the tribunal but he was sentenced to life imprisonment and in 1987 he committed suicide at the age of 93.

Stalin, always suspicious, was very curious about the Hess incident and suspected a plot between Germany and Britain to act together in an invasion of Russia. In 1943 at a dinner in Moscow, Stalin in his imperious and bullying way demanded Churchill tell him the true story. Churchill replied, "When I make a statement of facts within my knowledge I expect it to be accepted." Stalin, he wrote, "received this somewhat abrupt response with a genial grin."

General Rommel's Command of the German Army

As the year 1941 progressed, the Axis armies continued to drive east into Yugoslavia, Iraq, Syria, and Greece. Great battles were fought at Crete and in the Mediterranean war in the air and on the sea. In Libya, Hitler inserted the elite Afrika Korps to bolster the bedraggled Italians, and General Rommel took command and immediately went on the offensive. For the most part, throughout 1941 the German forces prevailed and gained ground. Churchill complained that when the opposing sides were anywhere near equal in number, the Germans always won.

General Edwin Rommel was not a political man; he was a professional soldier who had won the Iron Cross First Class twice in World War I. He was an innovative military leader of great daring, and he became a master at handling mobile armored formations. His officers and men had immense confidence in him. Time and time again he outthought and outmaneuvered superior Allied armies. In the Battle of France in 1940, he commanded the spearhead 7th Panzers, nicknamed "the Phantoms" because they appeared where their opponents least expected them, in the breakout across the Meuse. Churchill in the House of Commons said of him: "We have a very daring and skillful opponent against us, and, may I say across the havoc of war, a great general."

Rommel came to despise Hitler and hate what he was doing to Germany with the Gestapo and the SS. In 1944 he took part in the conspiracy to overthrow Hitler for which he was subsequently secretly murdered. Because of his heroic stature with the German people, Hitler ordered a state funeral with full military honors. *Rommel: The Desert Fox* by Desmond Young is a superb biography. *The Eagle Has Landed* by Jack Higgins is fiction but it graphically describes the growing disgust of the Army's elite officer corps with the SS and its brutal activities.

Germany Attacks Russia

In late June (as recounted in detail in Chapter 6), the Germans launched Operation Barbarossa against Russia. Since early in the year, British intelligence had been reporting to Churchill that Germany was massing troops on the Russian border. In April, Churchill instructed the British ambassador in Moscow, Sir Stafford Cripps, to deliver a personal message to Stalin warning him that an attack was imminent. Cripps, thin, tweedy, stubborn as well as self important, believed he had already warned the Russians and much to Churchill's irritation never did directly deliver the message to Stalin. Churchill later mused that perhaps if Cripps had given the warning, at the very least the Russian air force would not have been caught lined up in orderly rows on the ground on the first day of Barbarossa.

The British weren't the only ones to warn Stalin of a German attack. The Soviet Union for years had employed a German journalist, Richard Sorge, as a spy in Tokyo. Sorge grew up in Berlin, was wounded in World War I, and in the chaotic aftermath became a dedicated Communist. As a foreign correspondent for German newspaper, *Frankfurter Zeitung,* he had natural cover for his espionage. After assignments in Scandinavia and London, he was sent to Tokyo in 1933. Sorge was an attractive, sociable man, and in Tokyo he became friendly with the German ambassador. He learned of Barbarossa from the German military attaché and on May 12, 1941, he informed Moscow the attack would come on June 20. Three days later he changed it to June 22, the exact date. Even though Sorge was a trusted, longtime agent, inexplicably his messages were ignored. In late 1941, he was betrayed under mysterious circumstances and arrested by the Japanese. He was tortured and then hung.

After the initial attack, Stalin demanded aid, and Churchill graciously offered all the help that could be spared. His aide, John Colville, asked how he could do this when he had for years preached that Bolshevism, Stalin, and Soviet Russia were the mortal enemies of free societies. Churchill memorably replied: "If Hitler invaded the realms of Hell I would at least make a favorable reference to the devil in the House of Commons."

However as time passed, Churchill became less gracious. Unless massive aid was forthcoming, Stalin warned, he might make a separate peace leaving England to face the Nazis alone. Churchill, angered at this threat, pointed out to the Soviet ambassador that Russia had never lifted a finger to help Britain or any of the other European countries that had been assaulted by Hitler. Instead, Stalin had attempted to take advantage of the world chaos by attacking Finland, an adventure that resulted in a very embarrassing bloody, Soviet nose.

In November of 1940, Stalin had used a pretense provocation to launch 36 infantry and 6 tank divisions in a surprise attack on Finland. Russian planes heavily bombed Helsinki, hitting residential as well as industrial areas and killing many civilians. Finnish reports of these raids were dismissed as fabrications by the Soviets who claimed that the Russian air force had been dropping bread for the starving Finnish people. The Finns called the bombs Molotov Breadbaskets, but no one in the West thought the fantastically outnumbered Finns had a chance against the Red Army.

They were wrong. In the late 1930s, Stalin had ruthlessly purged the Red Army officer corps, and the million-man army he sent into Finland was poorly led and inadequately equipped for the Arctic winter. The Finns had a tough 300,000 man army that knew the terrain and how to fight a winter war on skis. They had no antitank guns to speak of, but they devised the Molotov cocktail to compete with the breadbasket. The lethal cocktail was kerosene, potassium chlorate, and a detonator in a bottle, and the Finnish ski troops would ambush tanks with it, set them on fire, and kill the crews when they came out.

The Finns and the fierce winter slaughtered the Soviets, and the world cheered. Sweden sent antitank guns, howitzers, medical supplies, and an 8,000-man volunteer brigade. Other nations promised aid and men as well, although the men and much of the aid never materialized. The aristocratic and athletic Finnish Field Marshal, Carl Gustav von Mannerheim, became an instantaneous world celebrity. However, when spring of 1941 came, an enraged Stalin poured massive resources across the border, and in the warmer weather Finland was overrun in a few months. Finland ceded its second largest city and 16,000 square miles to Russia in a humiliating capitulation. Hitler studying this episode came to the conclusion that the Red Army was an inferior fighting force and that the Soviet Union was ripe for the picking.

The London Stock Market Rallies

As shown in Figure 5.1, the *Financial Times* Industrials rallied in early January 1941 after victories over the Italians at Tobruk and in Abyssinia. However, that winter the market fell again with the grim war news,

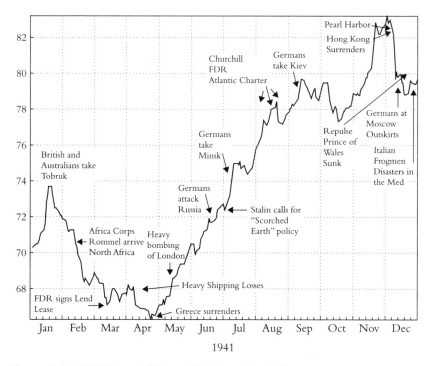

Figure 5.1   U.K. Financial Times, 30 Industrials: 1941
DATA SOURCE: *Financial Times;* Global Financial Data, Inc.

and as shortages and shipping losses disrupted industry. The vibrant patriotism of the previous summer was beginning to fade. In April Greece surrendered. London newspaper columnists were carping about the government's mismanagement of the war, and the mood of the British people was resolute but resigned to more hardships and privation, hardly an atmosphere to make one want to buy stocks.

In the midst of the barrage of bad news and heavy bombing of London, the stock market perversely but intuitively rallied. Was it anticipating Operation Barbarossa, the German attack on Russia? Even though the *Wehrmacht* bit off great chunks of the Soviet Union, once Russia was involved, Britain no longer stood alone. The chances of a German landing in Britain had to be much diminished. After the late winter sinking spell, London stocks staged a resolute rally for most of the rest of the year. From the low in April the Index rallied 24% to its mid-December high. It's interesting how well the stock market performed after mid-October in spite of another avalanche of very bad war news.

Unquestionably it was buoyed by the growing alliance between the United States and Britain, and it must have sensed the rising odds of the United States being drawn into the war. Another example of the wisdom of markets.

The British Destroy *The Bismarck,* Germany's Greatest Battleship

Meanwhile, British and Australian forces under General Claude Auchinleck were enduring defeats and retreats in Africa. Once again there was squabbling between the Australian government and Churchill, which resulted in a costly evacuation of Australian troops from Tobruk. A disastrous battle in Crete with German paratroops, the collapse of Greece, the occupation of Syria, and the rise of a pro-German faction in Iraq all were negative and unsettling developments. The war news was consistently bad, but nevertheless stocks worked higher.

But in June there was the dramatic chase, battle, and destruction of the *Bismarck* to lift British hearts. This great German battleship, displacing 45,000 tons, was a masterpiece of naval construction and design with an intricate system of watertight compartments. She was unquestionably the most powerful, fastest, and most heavily armored ship in the world. *Bismarck* was 25% bigger than any battleship the British possessed, and there were no illusions in London or Scapa Flow about the quality of her crew and the precision of her gunnery and fire control. "You are the pride of the navy," said Hitler when he visited in early May.

On May 23, 1941, *Bismarck,* a new heavy cruiser *Prinz Eugen,* and six escorting destroyers left port in Norway with the objective of wreaking havoc on convoys in general and in particular to attack a British troop convoy carrying 20,000 troops to the Middle East. There was no Royal Navy battleship or cruiser that could single-handedly stand up to *Bismarck* so a convoy would be easy prey. The British immediately dispatched *Hood,* the Royal Navy's largest and fastest capital ship, plus the modern battleship *Prince of Wales* and two cruisers, *Manchester* and *Birmingham,* to intercept the German ships.

The initial encounter took place in the Denmark straits, a grey, ice bound, misty stretch of water between Greenland and Ireland. Both sides began firing at a range of 25,000 yards. *Bismarck's* fire control was superb, and her first salvo struck *Hood* and set some fires. The *Hood* was heavily armored, but she had an Achilles' heel. There was a small area between her two funnels where there was little protection. The Royal Navy knew this and had intended to correct this chink in her armor but had not gotten around to it. The chance of a direct hit in such a small area seemed remote.

However, in the next exchange, one of *Bismarck's* heavy shells hit that vulnerable spot, penetrated through six decks, and exploded in *Hood's* magazine among 300 tons of high explosive ammunition. Suddenly a volcanic flame shot up a thousand feet from the heart of the ship. It flashed for several seconds high in the sky, and then the ship was shrouded in smoke. As the cloud parted awestruck observers saw that the ship had been split in two by the explosion. The entire bow structure and then the stern rose and then plunged into the black sea. *Hood* literally disintegrated and sunk with the loss of 1,419 men who were either blown up, trapped in watertight steel compartments deep in the bowels of the ship, or froze to death in a minute and a half in the ice cold, oil choked sea. There were only three survivors.

The shock to the Royal Navy at the sudden destruction of their most powerful and finest can only be imagined. The *Prince of Wales,* a newly commissioned battleship that had just completed her sea trials a week earlier, also received several direct hits, one of which destroyed her bridge, and she began to take on water. What was not known was that *Bismarck* in the intense fire fight had been hit below the waterline as well and was leaking fuel. At 5:56 A.M. the *Prince of Wales,* badly mauled, retreated to the southeast, and the smaller two British cruisers also wisely withdrew. The battle had lasted 17 minutes.

In retrospect, the German commander, Admiral Gunther Lutjens, knowing his ship was wounded and discovered, should have broken off the engagement and retreated to Brest. Instead, possibly elated by the damage he had inflicted, he headed straight for the troop convoy. The Royal Navy had already dispatched all available capital ships in the North Sea to seek out the Germans and protect the convoys. Several hours later, *Bismarck* realizing she was in trouble, turned for her base at Brest. The problem for the British was that no two or even three of their battleships or cruisers could hope to prevail over the German super-ship and her consort. By now, the weather was rotten with pack ice and snow squalls, and the big ships were laboring, butting into heavy rolling swells from the north. Glistening sheets of ice were beginning to coat their forecastles and their rigging. It was all very beautiful but very dangerous because it made the top-heavy warships roll through long arcs.

For a while the pursuing British force lost *Bismarck,* but they had been joined by the aircraft carrier *Ark Royal,* and on the afternoon of the May 26, she launched 15 Swordfish torpedo bombers. In the icy mist they mistakenly attacked the British cruiser *Sheffield,* which was shadowing the Germans from 40 miles away. The *Sheffield* dodged the attack, and the chastened Swordfish returned to the carrier. Suddenly the wind blew itself out, the snow stopped, and the last bank of heavy black clouds drifted away to the south.

The Swordfish were immediately turned around, and this time they found the right ship, and late in the day on the 26th, in the fading Arctic light, they bravely pressed their attack coming in at 10 feet above the sea. At least two of the torpedoes hit *Bismarck,* but she was so sturdy that she could easily have withstood them. However, by chance one of the torpedoes sheared off her rudder, and she began to steam at high speed in circles. Throughout the night, four British destroyers surrounded and attacked the stricken ship, lit by the flickering, pulsating ribbon of the northern lights, with more torpedoes.

On the morning of May 27, the weather abruptly deteriorated again. Though unable to maneuver or even steer straight, *Bismarck's* massive firepower was intact, and she was still a very dangerous opponent. Determined to save her, the Germans sent bombers and U-boats to drive away her tormentors. Furthermore, her Royal Navy pursuers were running out of fuel and they reported to the First Sea Lord in London that they might have to abandon the chase. Churchill intervened and furiously ordered them ignore their fuel shortages and to close and sink her even if they had to be towed home afterwards. The *Prinz Eugen* now was detached to save her, and raced toward Brest. Admiral Lutjens radioed Berlin: "Ship unmaneuverable. We shall fight to the last shell. Long live the Führer!"

The battleships *Rodney* and *King George V* and several cruisers now approached and began to fire on the wounded super-ship. The ships were pitching and plunging in the heavy seas that were longer now in their crests, deeper in their gloomy troughs, and visibility was poor. *Bismarck* absorbed the punishment and fought back, initially keeping her adversaries at long range with accurate shooting. However, her gun crews were utterly exhausted after four days at battle stations in freezing turrets and were falling asleep at their posts. Her salvoes became increasingly erratic, and *Rodney* crossed in front of her and poured in fire at the point blank range of 4,000 yards.

Still the magnificently constructed *Bismarck* fought on until she was just a burning hulk. It seemed as though she was unsinkable. Finally the cruiser *Dorchester* closed in and hit her with three more torpedoes, and at 10:40 A.M. she rolled over on her side, hesitated a moment with men scrambling on her side and then jumping into the huge black, icy seas, and floundered taking with her 2,000 souls. The British rescued only 110 exhausted and sullen sailors. When it was over, the sea surged on— immense, eternal, and indifferent. Henceforth, the convoys would be safe from giant surface raiders, and the Royal Navy's North Sea fleet was no longer tied to Scapa Flow. This was an important victory for Britain in that long year of agony and travail.

A U.S.-U.K. Alliance Inspires Hope . . .

However, the two major events of the second half of 1941 were the German attack on the Soviet Union and the increasingly close alliance and cooperation between England and the United States. The London stock exchange amazingly seems to have anticipated both events. Despite the tremendous victories of the Nazi armies and the huge chunks of Russia they had consumed, commentary at the time shows that British investors believed that they had gained an important ally in the Soviet Union and even more important, it was extremely unlikely that Hitler would mount an invasion of the British Isles while his armies were engaged in mortal combat with a formidable adversary on the Eastern Front. In fact, German documents later revealed that prior to launching Barbarossa, Hitler was repeatedly cautioned by both military and political advisers that the English will would be strengthened and morale lifted by his Russian adventure. However, Hitler would have none of it, and his judgments had been so infallible in the past and he was so intolerant of dissent, that few dared to press their case.

As for the alliance with the U.S., Churchill and FDR had been in close and friendly contact for years. The two men, both twentieth century aristocrats, seemed genuinely to like each other and enjoy each other's company. Both were voluble, sociable, and FDR cherished his cocktail hour almost as much as Churchill did. (Of course Churchill's cocktail hour extended from lunch to bedtime.) Beginning in 1940, arms and destroyers were being "loaned" to Britain, and by 1941 the U.S. navy was becoming increasingly involved with protecting convoys and even depth charging U-boats. U.S. merchant ships were being sunk, American citizens were being drowned, and the odds were increasing that the United States would eventually be drawn into the war.

All this cooperation climaxed in August when the prime minister and the president journeyed by warships to a secluded bay in Nova Scotia and met for three days. Camaraderie flourished both between the leaders and their staffs. There is a wonderful picture of the Sunday church service on the afterdeck of the *Prince of Wales* with 500 British and American sailors singing *O God Our Help in Ages Past*. FDR can be seen with his head up and mouth wide open singing lustily while Churchill, who disdained singing hymns as a waste of time, is looking over his spectacles to see who else is singing. The final joint declaration had language that made it clear that the two countries were of one mind about Hitler. To wit, Article Six of the document itself: "After the final destruction of the **Nazi tyranny** they hope to see established a peace . . ." This was not the language of a belligerent and a neutral; these were the words of allies. A grand alliance had been forged.

The risk in 1940 had been that the Germans would invade and conquer Britain before the United States fully committed to the war, and that Japan would cherry pick Britain's possessions in the Far East. Churchill and many others were seriously worried that this dire outcome could happen, and there is much evidence that FDR was also. However, as noted previously, there was still substantial isolationist and pro-German sentiment in the United States, which FDR was very cognizant of. There was an American Mothers' Crusade Against Lend-Lease, which lobbied for votes against the Lend-Lease bill arguing the policy was just a prelude to American intervention. Remember that in the spring of 1941, the House of Representatives passed by only one vote the bill to extend compulsory military training. Another isolationist was Father Charles Coughlin, a fiery Catholic priest, who preached rabid antiCommunist, antiSemitic propaganda to a Sunday afternoon radio audience of 40 million. In the 1940 Presidential election, when FDR stood for an historic third term, under pressure from the isolationists and the mothers, he promised he would not commit America to war unless the U.S. was attacked.

. . . and the London Markets Respond

As the second half of 1941 unfolded with more and more hostile acts by Germany and military responses by the U.S. Navy, the course of events was such that the United States' direct involvement began to seem increasingly likely. The Lend-Lease program already was supplying England with arms and ammunition. As noted, the London stock market seems to have grasped this in the early spring and despite an onslaught of bad war news, rallied about 25% by December, peaking almost precisely the day after Pearl Harbor.

The Dow Jones Industrial Average reacted in exactly the opposite manner with prices steadily declining as the prospects of war became more inevitable. In retrospect, this was a perfectly logical reaction. A U.S. entry into the war was a godsend for Britain. For U.S. companies and investors it meant wage and price controls, higher taxes, and excess profit taxes. No one knew what the unintended consequences would be of a war economy.

The sharp setback in the London stock market in the last three weeks of December reflected the losses that both the United States and England were suffering in the Pacific, and the German advances to the outskirts of Moscow. The British stock market had been for months eagerly anticipating America's entry into the war, and when suddenly news came of the staggering losses at Pearl Harbor and the Philippines, investors began to worry that the United States was a paper tiger. Newspaper stories indicate that the market on a day-to-day basis also reacted sharply to reports of specific British losses in Asia and in the Mediterranean.

The British Navy Suffers Great Losses

The most devastating disaster may have been the sinking in deep water off Singapore of *HMS Repulse* and *HMS Prince of Wales* by Japanese naval aircraft in mid December of 1941. Not only did England lose its two most modern, technologically advanced capital ships, but the experienced crews of both, over 2,000 men, were nearly all drowned. Their loss raised questions about the fate of Singapore, and whether Britain's navy was obsolete and ineffective against Japanese airpower. What were these two great ships doing wandering around without air cover? In reality it was a far greater Japanese victory than Pearl Harbor where the battleships were sunk in shallow water and thus were able to be raised fairly quickly and repaired. *Repulse* and *Prince of Wales* were at the bottom of the ocean and gone forever.

The British had also suffered other losses at sea; a domain where it had been previously thought Britannia ruled supreme. In early December of 1941 German U-boats sunk four major British capital ships in the Mediterranean with a huge loss of life. Then on the night of December 18, 1941, six Italian frogmen riding on three motorized torpedoes stealthily entered the harbor of the British naval base at Alexandria when the boom-gate was opened for the passage of a ship. They fixed these time bombs to two major battleships, *Valiant* and *Queen Elizabeth,* severely damaged both, and escaped into the darkness. It was a great and daring feat, and it particularly vexed Churchill as he had low regard for Italian valor. He ruefully told the House of Commons: "In a few weeks we lost, or had put out of action for a long time, seven great ships, or more than a third of our battleships and battle cruisers."

But further disasters were still to come. On the same day, another British squadron of three cruisers and four destroyers sorted out of Malta after a large Italian convoy heading for Tripoli. Approaching Tripoli, the ships ran into a minefield. All three cruisers were damaged, and one, *Neptune,* sunk with the loss of over 700 men. One destroyer also was sunk. These disasters temporarily cost the British the control of the

Mediterranean, and for the first time Hitler was able to resupply the Afrika Korps by sea. Then in February of 1942, the two powerful German battle cruisers, *Scharnhost* and *Gneisenau,* successfully broke out from Brest, which was another embarrassment to the Royal Navy.

Even when Britain struck back, she was dogged by bad luck. On November 23, 1941, as the beleaguered British Eighth Army in the desert outside of Tobruk was about to launch a counteroffensive, a carefully planned raid behind the German lines was organized to kill the brilliant General Rommel and destroy the command and communications center of the Afrika Korps. Fifty men of the Scottish Commando under Colonel Robert Laycock were carried by submarine down the coast to a beach far behind German lines.

However, the sea was very rough and only 30 of the commandoes could be landed. Nevertheless, they did achieve complete surprise and stormed into the house where Rommel was supposed to be sleeping. Unfortunately British intelligence was faulty, and Rommel and his chief of staff were in Rome. Nevertheless, a fierce fight, some of it hand-to-hand combat, ensued in the dark complex, and 20 Germans and 8 commandoes died. The remaining commandoes returned to the beach where they were to embark onto the waiting submarine, but the sea had become so rough it swamped their rubber boats. Laycock ordered them to disperse into the countryside in groups of two. Harried, under fierce pursuit, and with minimal food and water, they were hunted down. Only Laycock and a sergeant eventually regained Allied lines after 36 days behind the Afrika Korps.

All in all, 1941 was a difficult year that the British were glad to see the back of. Unfortunately, the first half of 1942 was to be even worse.

Chapter 6

Operation Barbarossa: Germany Attacks Russia

The German war with Russia is often described as the War of the Century, and the greatest battle of this war took place at and around the Russian city of Stalingrad. Operation Barbarossa, the surprise German attack on Russia in June 1941, was the classic reflection of the magnetic and violent personality of Hitler, the ultimate warlord. He alone conceived of and planned Barbarossa. First, he lulled Stalin into complacency and then struck with coordination and force inconceivable to his adversary at a time and place of his choosing. Hitler described it as "the battle of annihilation" against "the Judeo Bolshevik conspiracy, commissars, and the Communist intelligentsia."

In *Mein Kampf*, Hitler had clearly identified the Soviet Union as the ultimate enemy. Strategically, the accomplishment of *Lebensraum* or "open space" in the East would insure the "Thousand Year Reich" against economic want and military threat. Hitler told his skeptical generals "smash in the door and the whole rotten structure will come crashing down" and that was exactly what Barbarossa was designed to do. It was both audacious and contrarian, and superbly planned and executed.

There are some historians who adhere to conspiracy theories and still believe that just as FDR deliberately for good and sufficient political reasons ignored warnings of the Japanese strike on Pearl Harbor, the Soviet leadership deliberately allowed the Germans to surprise attack Russia. The correspondent-historian Harrison Salisbury argues that it was partly the absolutism of Stalin. Then he maintains it is also possible that the triumvirate of Malenkov, Beria, and Molotov, who had full access to the intelligence warnings and who opposed putting Soviet forces on alert, did so to permit the Germans to achieve tactical surprise for devious political reasons. If so, they certainly grievously underestimated the force with which the Germans would strike and the successes they would achieve.

Salisbury maintains Stalin was locked in his room in a state of nervous collapse as the German armies raged across the border, and perhaps the triumvirate thought they could seize control of the government and then execute a coup and behind Stalin's back negotiate a separate peace. No one knew the Kremlin's political intrigues and complexities better than Salisbury, and he wrote in *The 900 Days: The Siege of Lenningrad:* "Kremlin politics bars nothing—nothing in the realm of possible goals, nothing in the realm of possible means." However, this conspiracy seems unlikely.

Hitler's Uneasy Relationship with his Generals

The German General Staff, still a Prussian old-boy club, had repeatedly cautioned the Führer that it was too dangerous to strike at Russia while England still survived. They cited the inexorable military truths of superior numbers, vast distances, extended supply lines, the early and brutal winters, and the lack of paved roads for Germany's mechanized army. Hitler's relations with his stiff-necked Prussian generals had always been uneasy. He never fully trusted them—and with good reason. At the time of Barbarossa, the average time of active service for senior generals was 36 years. All had battle experience from World War I and most had commanded divisions in combat in 1940. They came mostly from the Prussian aristocracy or from middle class, long-established German military families.

The army's senior officer corps was deeply imbued with the sacred tradition of *uberparteilichkeit*, the army above politics and total obedience to the ruler—be he called the Kaiser or the Führer. However, their tradition also required they express their opinions to the sovereign whether he asked for them or not. Hitler sensed they viewed his military strategies with contempt, although they knew from his World War I record that he was a brave man. After all, he was not a professional soldier, an amateur—a corporal, not even a gentleman. Behind his back they scoffed at his imaginative innovations such as fitting the Stuka dive-bombers with sirens and lengthening the gun barrels of tanks. They obviously did not believe Napoleon's famous assertion that in war as in prostitution, amateurs are often better than professionals.

But there was a far more profound reason for Hitler's distrust of the generals. In September 1938, General Ludwig Beck, the army's chief of staff, believed Hitler was flirting with disaster with his audacious plans to attack the Czechs. He asked for a meeting with the Führer, and at it he pointed out that between 30 and 40 Czech divisions were deploying on Germany's eastern frontier and that the French army outnumbered the German divisions facing it by a margin of eight to one. Russia might attack, and the British had mobilized their navy. The Czechs could hold out for at least three months, which would give the French and the British time to intervene with power.

Furthermore, the German army was under strength. Beck estimated that for combat effectiveness no fewer than an additional 48,000 officers and 100,000 senior noncommissioned officers were necessary. Finally, he apparently told Hitler that less than a fifth of the officers of *Reichswehr* believed in the possibility of a victory for Germany. It was madness to proceed with this aggression. Hitler listened, his penetrating, all-seeing eyes boring into Beck, never leaving his face. When Beck was finished Hitler told him in effect: I'm not in love with your Prussian traditions, and as far as I am concerned the *Wehrmacht* (the German Army) is an instrument of the state, and I am the head of the state and I expect you to follow orders. Beck resigned on the spot.

Beck was widely respected within the army, and 10 generals, including the commander of the Berlin garrison and Graf von Helldorf who was in charge of the Berlin police force, gathered to plot a coup to remove Hitler. The commander in chief of the army, General von Brauschitsch also was in on the plan. Meticulous arrangements were made, and an elite panzer division, commanded by one of the plotters, was moved close to the capital. Hitler and the other Nazi leaders would be arrested and held for trial on charges of murder. A nonaggression statement would be issued, the army would stand down from the Czech border, and an interim army government would be installed prior to elections. All that was required to activate the plan was for Hitler to come to Berlin where he could be captured.

On the morning of September 14, 1938, Hitler arrived in Berlin from Berchtesgaden. The plotters quickly convened and decided to execute the plan commencing at 8 P.M. that day. All units were in position when late that afternoon Graf von Helldorf, the police commandant of Berlin, was notified that Prime Minister Chamberlain suddenly was flying to Berchtesgaden to meet the Führer, and that Hitler's motorcade had just left Berlin for Berchtesgaden. The plan had to be aborted. The opportunity had passed. The next day the panzer division was ordered to the frontier.

The pressure on Hitler at this time must have been intense. Could he, in the face of unfavorable German public opinion and the solemn warning of his generals that not only was the army not ready but that the risks were too high, launch this attack? If it failed he could well be out of power. His confidence in his own judgment was astounding.

The rest is history. Chamberlain suckered for Hitler's line, and Hitler, against the advice of all his experts, plunged into the abyss and achieved astounding military success in weeks, not months. His mystique and legend were now firmly established in the German psyche. There were to be other coup attempts in the years to come, but one cannot help wonder what the history of the world over the next seven years would have been if this early one had succeeded.

Planning the Attack on Russia

By mid-1941 not just Czechoslovakia but all the Führer's previous military judgments had been masterful, and he brushed aside the General Staff's reservations about attacking Russia. For the onslaught he assembled

3,050,000 German troops in 154 divisions and a 140,000-man vassal army consisting principally of 14 Rumanian divisions, 18 divisions of tough, battle-hardened Finns, and a collection of Hungarians, Poles, and Italians who had old scores to settle with the Russians. The attackers had 3,350 tanks, 7,000 artillery pieces, and over 2,000 aircraft. Even though it was the middle of the twentieth century, the *Wehrmacht* also relied for transport on an amazing 600,000 horses to pull artillery, tankers, and even troop transports. On the dirt roads of Russia, which were often muddy, horses worked. Furthermore, cavalry was effective and was used by both sides in the scrub forests and for lightening raids on interior camps.

The attack was originally scheduled for late May to provide enough time for the invaders to reach winter quarters in Leningrad, Moscow, Kursk, and Karlov before December when the fearsome Russian winter descended. This was essential because of the burden of carrying winter clothes and de-icing equipment; moreover, Hitler wanted to motivate his generals to be aggressive. However, that spring Hitler was forced to divert forces to rescue Mussolini in Greece, and wet weather on the border delayed the launch of Barbarossa by three to four weeks.

A bizarre incident occurred on June 17. A German master sergeant with a front-line unit struck an officer, and that night fled across the border. To save himself he volunteered to the Russian colonel who interrogated him the exact date and time of the attack. The colonel reported it up the chain of command but it was dismissed as fanciful. Figure 6.1 shows the plan of attack.

On the border, the principal armored strength of the German army, 10 *Panzergruppens,* each of 200 tanks supported by motorized infantry, were concentrated in three widely separated sectors. Army Group North's objective was Leningrad, Army Group Center was to blast through the heartland to take Moscow, and Army Group South had the longer and harder task of seizing the Caucasian oil fields and going all the way to Stalingrad. On the first day, June 21, 1941, with perfect surprise and overwhelming superiority in numbers, mobility, and fire power, these spearheads followed by a train of motorized infantry, more tanks, divisional artillery, and then more infantry slashed through the Russian defensive membrane on the frontier, penetrated 20 miles into the interior, wheeled around, isolated, and cut off the mass of the Russian army as it faced the frontier in the opposite direction.

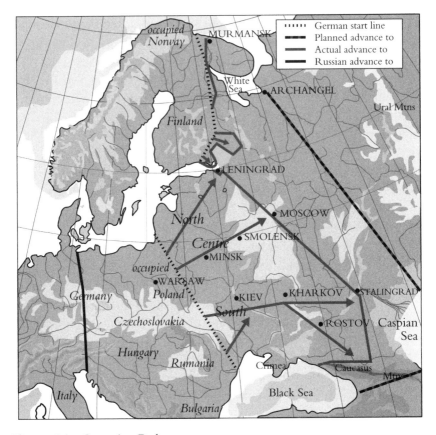

Figure 6.1   Operation Barbarossa
SOURCE: naval-history.net

In addition, there was brilliant coordination of close air support from the *Luftwaffe* through forward air controllers attached to the panzers. This lethal combination of massive armored firepower on the ground and ubiquitous airborne artillery from above devastated and demoralized the lightly armed peasant troops arrayed against them. The objective of this onslaught, both on the ground and in the air, was to deliver a knockout blow and to prevent the escape of battle-worthy forces into the interior of Russia. The speed and penetration of the German armored spearheads resulted in gains in the initial week of the battle of as much as 250 miles and yielded a stunning two million Russian casualties and prisoners. On that first day alone, Manstein's 56th Corps had advanced over 50 miles by sundown. In five days, his Panzer Corps had crossed the Dvina River and was halfway to Leningrad.

"There Are No Russian Prisoners of War"

In previous campaigns across Europe, the response of surrounded troops to the German *Blitzkrieg* had been perfunctory efforts to escape and then to surrender. In fact, in France so many demoralized French troops had surrendered that they became a burden. By contrast the reaction of the trapped Russians was to try to fight their way out. Their officers simply assembled them in uncoordinated formations, marched them toward the firing, and then the formations were cut to pieces by the panzers and from the air. Individual units that were caught in hopeless positions would seldom surrender, and often the Germans took casualties in rooting them out and killing them.

Although the Russian soldier had always been brave and resolute, a ruling reason for their "fight to the last man" mentality was that Stalin immediately after the attack had announced that anyone who surrendered would be considered a traitor. "There are no Russian prisoners of war," he announced in a general order issued June 25, 1941. A POW's children would be deprived of their food ration, and his parents sent to the gulag. If a man who had surrendered escaped, he was immediately sent to the work camps or shot. As a result of this harsh policy, Russian POWs were amenable to fighting for the Germans in return for better living conditions. The Russian Liberation Army of 50,000 POWs fought for the Germans at Stalingrad under the command of a Russian general.

The map in Figure 6.2 shows the complexity and dimensions of the German onslaught and inroads into the Soviet Union in 1941. By December 5th, the front was 1,600 kilometers wide and a 1,000 kilometers deep. At that point Hitler controlled more real estate than any of the great conquerors of all history. Imagine the complexities of the evacuation of wounded and front-line supply, almost all of which had to be done by rail through sullen if not downright hostile areas. Note that Stalingrad was still 400 kilometers further east.

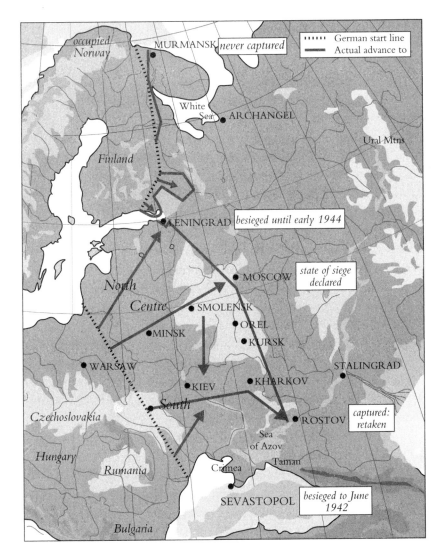

Figure 6.2 The Eastern Front
SOURCE: naval-history.net

The incredible fact is that of the 3.2 million Russians taken prisoner in 1941, 2.8 million were dead by the summer of 1942. Hitler ordered that all political commissars and officers were to be shot immediately. All armies on the offensive have great difficulty in dealing with prisoners, and in this case, the numbers were overwhelming. However, the Germans made no attempt to preserve lives, and in the end it would have been more humane to kill them. The captured soldiers were herded into barbed wire enclosures surrounded by towers manned by SS guards with heavy machine guns. The prisoners had no shelter from the elements other than their filthy trench coats, and they were given virtually no food or water. When the ferocious winter came, they died where they stood. It is estimated another 2.5 million Russians were captured in subsequent years, but only about a million of them died in captivity. As the war progressed, the Germans became much more inclined to work their Russian prisoners rather than kill them.

Soviet field commanders, including general officers, who failed to achieve objectives or who retreated, were removed from command and often executed on the spot by the field commissars. Stalin's dictum as published in General Orders was "No Retreat and No Surrender Under Any Circumstances." From his dacha, the dictator practiced what he preached. He had always had a difficult relationship with his oldest son, Yakov, but nevertheless he was his first born. When Yakov was captured near Smolensk, the Germans thought they had a prize and offered to exchange him for an imprisoned German general. Stalin disdainfully rejected the offer and instead arrested and imprisoned Yakov's wife Yulia. Yakov later died in a German concentration camp when in despair he threw himself against an electrified fence and was then shot by a guard.

The Russian Air Force and Infantry Are Destroyed

By the afternoon of the second day, aircraft from airfields all over central Russia began to appear over the battlefields in tight, obsolete formations. It was, as one German pilot put it, "infanticide." In the first two days of battle, the Russians lost over 2,000 aircraft and the numerically largest air force in the world had been virtually destroyed. A day later the commander of the bomber group committed suicide, and within a week Stalin had ordered the commander of aviation on the front arrested and sentenced to death for "treasonable activity." In the first three weeks of the war, the Russians lost two million men, 3,500 tanks, and more than 6,000 aircraft.

The loss of air cover was catastrophic for the Russian frontier armies. Staggering defeats were inflicted by the invaders at Smolensk, Kiev, Bryansk, Vyazma, and almost the entire Ukraine was overrun. By December the Russian losses were estimated at five million men, 14,000 aircraft, and 40,000 tanks and artillery weapons. In one epic, weeklong struggle at Kiev in the Ukraine, a million Russians died and 600,000 were taken prisoner. At the end, the Russian infantry charged the German tanks with arms locked and four rounds in each rifle as loud-speakers endlessly brayed Stalin's exhortations to fight to the end for Mother Russia. The battlefields were later described by one observer as charred landscapes of steel and ash "where the round shapes of lifeless heads caught the light like potatoes turned up from new-broken soil."

Over 30 million Russians were mobilized by the end of the war. Eight million of them died compared to a quarter of a million British and Americans. Thirty-five percent of all Russian officers were killed. Of course, Stalin alone murdered almost as many of his own people as did the Germans. The average frontline tour of duty for an infantryman before he was killed or seriously wounded was three weeks. Did the Russian soldier fight to the death because of his Russian soul or spirit, or did he fight because he had no alternative?

The Russians even used dogs as suicide bombers. The dogs had been trained to search for food under large vehicles. They had a pack strapped on their backs loaded with explosives with an upright stick that would detonate their bomb when it caught on the underside of the German vehicle.

One reason the Red Army performed so poorly in the first months of the war was its lack of experienced senior officers. Years earlier, the German intelligence chief, Hans Heydrich, knowing that Stalin was a murderous paranoid, ingeniously through double agents fed that suspicion until the dictator became convinced his general staff had been infiltrated by German agents. In late 1936, Heydrich skillfully allowed 32 documents to be "discovered" that confirmed Stalin's fear of treachery. They included letters that implicated the Soviet chief of staff, Marshal Tukhachevsky, and other senior generals as having been in direct correspondence with the German military. In a three-year reign of terror, Stalin liquidated 35,000 field grade officers, or about half of the Red Army's officer corps. He had executed or imprisoned three out of five marshals, 14 of 16 military commanders in chief, all Russian admirals of Ranks I and II, 60 of 67 commanding generals, 136 of 199 divisional commanders, and 221 out of 397 brigade commanders. All 11 deputy defense commissars also were liquidated.

Soviet Hatred Causes the Ukrainians to Welcome the Germans

In the first months of the attack, the local people in the overrun and occupied western provinces were not hostile to the invaders. In most towns in the Ukraine, the inhabitants greeted the Germans with bread and salt, the traditional Slavic welcome to strangers. The Ukrainians hated the Soviets, who had harshly treated them and felt little affinity toward the Communist regime. The Soviets had purged local officials, persecuted school teachers, and enforced collectivization. The Ukrainians regarded the Germans with curiosity and a certain sense of relief. They thought of themselves as white Russians. Often, statues of Lenin and Stalin were toppled by the locals in village squares.

The frontline German troops were disciplined and generally well-behaved, and they released jailed Ukrainians and reopened churches. There were relatively few incidents of lootings and rape as the panzers churned ahead. The Ukraine was a fertile agricultural area with large cooperative farms, but since it was Soviet there was no real accumulated wealth, and the people that lived best were the commissars. They were ejected from their homes and roughly handled by the locals but ignored by the Germans. In the early days of the war there was little sabotage or partisan activity in the German rear.

However, Hitler wanted the Ukraine to provide *Lebensraum*—living space. The Ukraine was also a major industrial center, but he wanted the farms and vast stretches of rich agricultural land for Aryan settlers. As a result, three things happened. First, Hitler imposed a brutal campaign of pacification of the occupied areas by "racial cleansing" and extermination. To accomplish this he inserted the SS into the occupied territories as the administrative arm of the occupation. The SS were bigots, sadists, and often perverts as well, and their governance was indescribably brutal. Bull whips and savage Doberman Pinschers were routinely used, even on children. Sometimes in the long summer evenings for sport, "people hunts" were organized with the SS hunters often inebriated and with the grisly objective to shoot as many civilians as possible in the stomach to create slow, agonizing deaths over a certain time period.

Second, as the war continued, the Germans realized they were going to need workers to build the arms and equipment their armies required. The conquered territories were a vast source of labor that must be exploited. Families were wrenched apart. Villages were burned to the ground, women were dragged off as sex slaves, and men were sent to Germany as laborers. They were jammed into rail cars with no food or sanitation where they stayed for days in the heat of the summer as the "slave" trains were shunted from siding to siding on the way back to Germany. Often a third of these unfortunates died on the trip. These inhuman and repressive measures led not to pacification but to hatred and a fierce resistance.

Third, as the *Blitzkrieg* roared forward, groups of Russian soldiers and deserters that had been cut off found themselves far behind the front lines. They knew that if they rejoined the regular Russian army they would either be shot or assigned to penal battalions. These bands roamed the countryside, living off the land, looting and pillaging. Local officials and commissars who had accumulated possessions and lived in relative luxury were easy targets. Lightly armed, these outlaws had no interest in attacking the powerful Germans. Initially, the indigenous populations were reluctant to support them, but as the locals were brutalized, curiosity about the Germans turned to a deep, sullen hatred. In time, these guerilla bands became a major and implacable adversary, attacking truck convoys, blowing up railroads, and attacking German garrisons. By the end of 1942, it has been estimated that there were 30,000 partisans behind the German lines. By December of 1943 that number reached 150,000, and Moscow was providing them with arms through air drops.

Hitler believed the so-called white Russians in all the western provinces and not just the Ukraine would rise against the Communists. He misjudged the intensely patriotic, long-suffering Russian people whose devotion to Mother Russia had survived the persecution of both czars and commissars. The partisan groups went from being viewed as wandering brigands to national heroes and an instrument of revenge.

Soon, an underground movement developed that harried the German rear. It was a cruel, no-holds-barred guerilla war with German hospital trains attacked and the wounded mutilated in their stretchers.

Life in the woods behind the lines in Eastern Europe was not exactly as depicted in Ernest Hemingway's great novel *For Whom the Bell Tolls,* with a bunch of sturdy partisans drinking wine and toasting hot dogs with Ingrid Bergman look-alikes climbing into their sleeping bags. The terrain was a maze of pine and birch forests intersected by streams and marshes. It was impenetrable to tanks. There were Soviet partisans, Jewish bands, Polish groups, and then there were common bandits. As Alan Clark wrote in his epic history *Barbarossa,* "All of them preyed on the Germans, and most of them preyed on each other." They had no respect for private property, and they stole anything that they could get their hands on. The partisans were as much a threat to wealth as the Germans.

In 1942, the German high command issued this warning: "We Germans make the mistake of thinking that if neither offensive nor defensive operations are in progress, then there is no war going on. But the war is going on . . . when we are cooking potatoes, when we lie down to sleep. A soldier must carry his weapons always and everywhere." Stalin also was always suspicious of independent guerilla bands, particularly if they were Ukrainian. In 1944, he invited the leaders of three of the biggest Ukrainian groups to Moscow. They never returned.

Germany Presses on to Take Moscow: "One Final Heave and We Shall Triumph"

By mid-October, the Germans were driving relentlessly toward Moscow with a three-pronged attack. Now on the central Russian front there was the first mist of snow and the *rasputitiza,* the autumn mud time, had begun. On the 14th, the 1st Panzers reached Kalmin, took the key bridge over the Volga, and severed the Moscow to Leningrad train line. At the same time the 10th Panzers were a mere 70 miles from Moscow in the rolling farm land of Borodino where Napoleon had fought a great battle. By mid-October, Moscow was being flooded with refugees and deserters, and riots and looting broke out. On October 16, Stalin, panicking, ordered the evacuation of key government departments, and civilians began fleeing the city. That day the secret police, the NKVD, began burning their files, and thick black smoke rose from the chimneys of the Lubyanka. Stalin himself contemplated fleeing to Kuibyshev some 600 miles away, and a special train and his personal Douglas DC-3 were readied for departure.

But Stalin didn't flee, although he went to the station and paced up and down beside his train. Instead, he steadied and vowed to remain. On October 19, he declared martial law, and NKVD units were ordered to shoot to kill looters and deserters. Many civilians were murdered in the chaos that followed, but order was restored and the city was not abandoned. If Moscow, the communications center and the spiritual capital of Russia, had been deserted and had fallen to the Germans, their winter would have been much easier and tactically the course of the Russian war would certainly have been altered.

However, as the weather deteriorated, the German onslaught began to lose momentum and strategy became an issue. The generals in the field all wanted to concentrate on reaching Moscow, arguing it was the nerve center for communications and the armaments industry, and that to capture the city would break the Russian morale. Hitler, on the other hand, was obsessed with the Caucasian oil fields and was determined to divert resources to this objective even if it meant not reaching Moscow by Christmas. As discussed, the Prussian military tradition was that the king must listen to and consult with the nobility when a crucial decision was about to be made.

Hitler's Prussian generals picked Heinz Guderian who had always been a favorite of the Führer as their spokesmen. He went to see Hitler at his war quarters and they met in a plain room furnished in Spartan fashion with an oak table, straight back chairs, and maps on the walls. Guderian recounts that Hitler was friendly and open and listened attentively as he made his case. When he had finished, Hitler, speaking in his high-pitched, earnest voice, explained how desperately Germany needed the oil of the Caucasus and that economic considerations must come first. He told Guderian that the generals did not fully comprehend the whole geopolitical picture. At this point Guderian, probably thinking of what had happened to Beck and of the estate in Poland he had selected for himself, did not press his case.

Guderian then told Hitler of the growing effects of winter from the lack of warm clothing for the troops on the army's efficiency. Incredibly, Hitler even then refused stubbornly to provide his armies with winter gear, perhaps believing they would press on more resolutely to winter quarters if they didn't have it. Equally serious, the mechanized equipment and artillery were not winterized and antifreeze was in short supply. The ironic part of all this is that if Barbarossa had been launched in mid-May as originally planned instead of six weeks later, the army easily would have been in winter quarters by early December. Hitler said he would see to it, but supply lines were extended and ammunition was more important than antifreeze. He told Guderian to press on.

As it was, the troops in the field still in their summer gear without boots, gloves, and great coats suffered terribly from the cold, and by November mud, fatigue, and shortages had slowed the German advance to a crawl. The tanks, mechanized artillery, and trucks were bogged down on the muddy, snowy, wild plains, and were in desperate need of maintenance. The terrain, a mixture of scrub pine and birch forests, was poorly suited for tanks. A third of the frontline soldiers were suffering from frostbite, with 50,000 cases severe enough that amputation of an appendage was necessary. Hitler had failed to grasp that in a vast country like Russia (unlike his lightning strikes in the much smaller European countries) logistics would be a decisive factor in the battle. "The vastness of Russia devours us," wrote Field Marshall von Runstedt to his wife even as his armies achieved great victories in the fall of 1941. He spoke of the huge distances, bad roads, and extreme weather, and how this combination grinds down a modern army.

By early December of 1941, the advance German patrols had reached the outskirts of both Moscow and Leningrad, the two historic cities of Russia. On December 2, five days before Pearl Harbor, a reconnaissance battalion of the 258th infantry division penetrated to a Moscow suburb and saw the spires of the Kremlin reflecting in the pale afternoon sunlight. That night the temperature fell to 31 degrees below zero. The reconnaissance unit was driven back the next day by a half dozen tanks and a rabble of home defense troops. A few days earlier the advanced guard of 41st Panzer group saw Leningrad (now St. Petersburg) under similar circumstances. No Germans as conquerors would see either of the two cities again even though the siege of Leningrad lasted 900 days.

Although no one knew it at the time, the glimpses of those two great cities were the high-water marks of Barbarossa, and although there were other great victories to come in the summer of 1942, the German advance had finally been blunted. The following year, at Stalingrad, the tide turned.

The Russian Winter Overwhelms the German Army

But in early December 1941, the Führer Hitler staring at the maps could see that his armies had advanced 500 miles and that there were only 20 left to go to reach, the ultimate prize, Moscow. "One final heave," he told General Jodl, "and we shall triumph." However, it was not that simple. Stalin was desperate and determined to hold Moscow. In early December the Russians began to prepare to commit their strategic reserve by moving their elite Siberian divisions from the Far East. These fresh troops were equipped with padded, white uniforms, fur caps, and winterized equipment. Stalin, realizing the symbolic importance of show, marched these reinforcements through Red Square past the Lenin mausoleum and what was left of the population of the city, straight to the front lines. On December 4th and 5th, on a 100-mile perimeter in front of Moscow, the Russian launched a massive counterattack and achieved complete surprise. Clark writes that "The Russian recovery and their winter offensive of 1941 remain one of the most remarkable achievements in military history." At the same time, partisan units harried the German rear and disrupted their supply lines.

The winter of 1941–1942 was the most severe in a hundred years with blinding blizzards, bitter winds, and temperatures dropping to 40 degrees below zero, congealing men, guns, and equipment. Without antifreeze, the panzers wouldn't start; without salve, gun breeches were frozen solid; 200,000 Germans became casualties of frostbite; men died when their anuses froze while defecating; and self-inflicted wounds became common. Overnight, the Germans lost their mobility and firepower.

Even more serious, the élan, the myth of the absolute invincibility of the German army, was shattered. Suddenly cold, hungry, and frightened men began remembering what had happened to Napoleon and his *Grande Armee* in 1812 and cursed the supply officers in Berlin who had neglected to provide winter gear. Goebbels organized an emotional Christmas collection, and by February, shivering, gloomy soldiers of the mightiest army in the world wearing ladies coats, sweaters, and boas huddled around fires on the desolate plains under the dim, low, Russian sun.

Better equipped for the weather, the Russians pushed the invaders back a hundred miles from Moscow along a broad front. At this point, Hitler dramatically intervened and probably saved the German army. He absolutely forbade any further retreat. His response to commanders who wanted to fall back was the sardonic question: "Is it any less cold fifty miles back?" General Günther Blumentritt, no admirer of Hitler, later expressed it succinctly:

> Hitler's fanatical order that the troops must hold fast regardless in every position and in the most impossible circumstances was undoubtedly correct. Hitler realized instinctively that any retreat across the snow and ice must within a few days, lead to the dissolution of the front and that if this happened the Wehrmacht would suffer the same fate that had befallen the Grande Armee. . . . The withdrawal could only be carried out across the open country since the roads and tracks were locked with snow. After a few nights this would prove too much for the troops, who would simply lie down and die wherever they found themselves. There were no prepared positions in the rear into which they could be withdrawn, nor any sort of line to which they could defend.

Generals who retreated for whatever reason were stripped of their rank and relieved of command on the spot and forbidden to wear the uniform. In one case, General Hans Count von Sponeck, a winner of the Iron Cross for leading the airborne landings at The Hague, was imprisoned, court-martialed, and sentenced to death for pulling back after Russian troops landed by sea behind him in the Crimea. Hitler is alleged to have told another general who had retreated that he had "so disgraced the uniform" that he would be discharged wearing nothing but his underwear. Finally, Hitler had broken the will and spirit of the Prussian officer corps, and for the remainder of the war he was the sole commander.

Yet the German Army Persists

But the fanatical, draconian measures worked. The retreat did not become a rout; the German army did not suffer the fate of the *Grande Armee*. Instead it dug in across the snow-choked, open countryside and endured. The men learned how to build snow caves, and hunkered down across Russia, they fought off the elite Siberian divisions. Behind them they still held the major towns they had seized earlier and where they had established supply dumps. Airlifts were organized to bring in reinforcements and weapons and to evacuate wounded. Morale began to improve. Now they organized an interlocking system of what they called "hedgehogs" linking these fortified towns and farms. The line held.

By early February 1942, the Siberian fighters were exhausted and decimated by the ravages of the winter campaign. The Russian counter-offensive was over, but a cruel and brutal war raged in the endless cold. Both sides routinely executed prisoners, and the Germans regarded most civilians as partisans and shot them for their clothes in the struggle for survival. Both sides lived off the land, and since the Russians had executed a scorched-earth policy, millions of their own civilians died of frostbite and starvation. "It is like living in the horrors of the thirteen century," wrote a German soldier in his diary. "We are chipping at the frozen carcasses of horses for meat to eat."

The Berlin Stock Market Senses a Change in Hitler's Luck and Power

Figure 6.3 shows the Berlin CDAX Index adjusted for inflation from 1930 to 1950. From the 1932 bottom until the 1937–1938 high, Germany was the best market in the world as the domestic economy enjoyed a strong recovery from the horrors of the 1920s. Unquestionably the strong leadership and charisma of Hitler were also important factors. Then from the late spring of 1938 until the end of 1939 German investors experienced the same misgivings as the aristocracy and the Prussian generals about the risks Hitler was running with his aggressive actions in Europe. In fact, the German people displayed little of the enthusiasm for war that was evident in 1914. They remembered all too

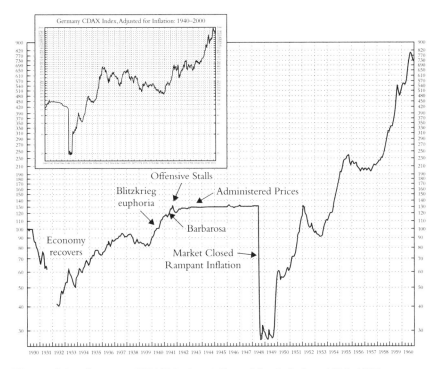

Figure 6.3 Germany CDAX Index, Adjusted for Inflation: 1930–1950
DATA SOURCE: Credit Suisse; Global Financial Data, Inc.; Traxis Partners LLC.

well the hardships and aftermath of that first world war, and there was certainly some uneasiness about the strong arm tactics of the Nazis and their treatment of the Jews. Rumors about coups and concentration camps were circulating.

In late 1939, however, well ahead of the *Blitzkreig* stock prices began to anticipate the overwhelming victories of 1940. By 1940 and throughout 1941 the German economy was booming from military production. Food was plentiful as Germany stripped the occupied countries, unemployment was almost nonexistent, and profits were soaring from low-cost forced labor from French, Polish, and Dutch prisoners.

The ascent of prices was steep until January of 1941 when the market paused, but three months later there was another final vertical surge that began prior to Barbarossa. The interesting insight is that by the late fall of 1941, the Berlin market was somehow sensing that Hitler's luck, his infallibility were fading and that Germany's military momentum had crested. The *Wehrmacht* was **about** to be bloodied. The Soviet counterattack, the withdrawal, the winter of 1941–1942 with its horrible privations had not yet occurred.

How did the news of the stalling offensive and the sense of the vastness of Russia reach the Fatherland? Frontline troops were allowed to write letters home, but the mail was strictly censored. There was virtually no unit rotation back to Germany for leave until the spring and summer of 1942, and war news in newspapers and on the radio was strictly controlled. The newspapers and the official radio made no mention of the offensive in Russia stalling, the lack of winter uniforms, or the difficulties that the bitter cold, even in October and November, was causing for men and equipment.

Quite to the contrary. The press described heroic deeds and continuing military successes both in Russia and in the desert campaigns. Life in Berlin and the other big cities was rich and full as the Christmas season began. There was plenty of money and food, and Germans were exhorted to write their brave soldiers and to remember their valor at Christmas. Did anyone know the tide had turned except the stock market? Certainly a few of the generals suspected. As will be discussed subsequently, a year later Berlin became a sterile, administered stock market under state control.

Throughout 1940 and 1941 some non-Jewish, German wealth, appalled by what was going on, was exiting the country. It was a tricky thing. There was no difficulty in transferring gold and jewelry to Switzerland, but getting serious amounts of money out was another matter. For one thing there were exchange controls and taxes. For another it was considered to be unpatriotic and virtually treasonous. There was corruption in the central bank and the ministry of finance, and you were taking your life in your hands when you made the approach. Nevertheless, Swiss bankers say capital did exit to interest-bearing bank accounts in Zurich, Buenos Aires, Madrid, and Santiago where is stayed for the rest of the war. The postwar records show that by 1943 some Nazis—*just in case*—were also surreptitiously sending money to South America.

By February of 1942, the Russian counterattack had expended itself. The Siberians had taken heavy losses, and the bitter cold had exhausted even them. When warm weather returned in the spring of 1942, the

German army would go on the offensive again, and the panzers, with battle pennants flying, would rampage across the steppes. But the invincibility that was seemingly so precious to the German stock market expired in the bleak winter of 1941–1942, never to return.

Meanwhile on the other side of the world, the great war with Japan was about to begin with the launching of the most dramatic, audacious, and successful surprise attack in history.

Chapter 7

Miracles at the Coral Sea and Midway: Japan and America

On the other side of the world, Japan had been following the events in Europe with close attention. She had long felt vulnerable from her lack of an empire and of a secure raw material base. She resented the rich possessions of the colonial powers in Asia and believed it was her destiny to dominate the Far East. Now, with the European powers distracted and the United States apparently profoundly isolationist, she believed the opportunity presented itself to seize the territory and resources she needed.

The Japanese prime minister in January 1941 was Prince Konoye, a sophisticated man whom Churchill describes as "a wise statesman." He was widely traveled and he believed it would be a grave mistake for Japan to go to war with the United States. The emperor himself and the royal family were not enthusiastic about a war with the West. They admired and felt great empathy for the English monarchy and copied British traditions. For example, on Imperial Navy ships, a Western style lunch was served by stewards in white mess jackets while a band played. Furthermore, Japan had a close relationship with the Morgan banks, which the aristocracy was loath to sever. Morgan had underwritten large international bond issues for Japan at difficult times after earthquakes.

Admiral Isoroku Yamamoto, a powerful and influential thinker who knew the United States well, was also skeptical. He conceded that Japan had designed and built the most modern navy in the world, and its army was battle-tested and superbly trained, but as an industrial power, he argued, Japan was no match for the U.S. In some respects, the Japanese economy was almost medieval. For example, Japan's new aeronautical marvel, the Zero, was the best fighter aircraft in the world, but it was delivered from its factory in ox carts.

Japan's navy, its traditions, and even its naval academy, Eta Jima, had been modeled on the British Royal Navy. The regime at the academy and the character of officers it produced is described in detail by Evan Thomas in *Sea of Thunder*. The midshipmen were tutored by English instructors in table manners and making toasts. They were told they must always travel first class and never be seen carrying packages. The academic and seamanship programs were very demanding, and above all unswerving loyalty to the emperor, obedience, and readiness to die in battle was enforced.

However, midshipmen were also brutalized. The smallest infraction of a rule resulted in a beating and guard duty punishment. Every Sunday freshmen stood at rigid attention in the yard for four hours and were slapped and pummeled by upperclassmen. The physical training program was intense and unrelenting. British officers observing the program questioned whether it didn't produce narrow-minded robots whose creativity and independence had been beaten out of them. Despite its Spartan regimen, Eta Jima had 30 applicants for every one it accepted.

Once graduated, officers followed a strict code of impassivity, discipline, and a stern chain of command. However, off duty their release was *sake* parties where they stayed out all night drinking and sometimes sat in one another's laps and wept.

In fact, throughout the Imperial Navy, violence was employed to enforce discipline and blind obedience. Although it had conducted sophisticated planning and maneuvers and was less xenophobic and more cosmopolitan than the army, it cherished ancient traditions. Just as the samurai warriors of the past could kill an impudent commoner who failed to get out of their way in the road, Japan's naval officers in 1941 were required to strike five times with their fist any enlisted man who failed to salute or who disobeyed a direct order. Petty officers on Japanese ships carried thin, but heavy sticks called "spirit bars" with which they hit enlisted men who did not respond fast enough to orders. The practice was effective but understandably engendered hatred.

In the early 1940s most of the Japanese military and industrial elite believed the United States was a decadent society that was ripe for the taking. However, at a strategic planning conference in early 1941, a logistics specialist, Colonel Iwakuro, delivered a cautionary message to the assembled military leaders who were eager to challenge what they believed was "the American paper tiger. He pointed out that in 1940 Japan produced only 48,000 automobiles while U.S. assembly lines had turned out 4.5 million. With half of its population still involved in agriculture, Japan had a severe shortage of trained assembly-line workers and mechanics. Its munitions output was one-tenth that of the United States, and its coal and steel production one-thirteenth. Japan in 1940 produced only 20% as many airplanes, had half the ship building capacity, and had an industrial workforce one-tenth the size that of the United States. After hostilities began, the United States could construct ships and planes far faster than Japan. Colonel Iwakuro wondered if it was wise to attack such a country.

A History of Japanese Aggression

However, Japan in the 1930s and early 1940s was a schizophrenic combination of the impulses of sophisticated capitalism and Shinto barbarism, which maintained that the Japanese were *the* superior race who had not lost a battle in 2,600 years. Honor and courage were the dominant forces in Japanese public life, and the army generals in particular did not like the pacifists' message. Admiral Yamamoto was given a sea command to keep him safe from assassination, and Colonel Iwakuro was packed off to Cambodia.

There was a very dark and sadistic side to Japanese politics with the murders in the late 1920s of a prime minister and a senior adviser to the emperor. In 1932 there were assassinations that were almost ritual in nature of the prime minister, the finance minister and leading industrialists. In December 1933 the emperor himself was nearly murdered. Three years later the most serious coup occurred with far right army officers armed with swords and submachine guns breaking into the homes of the leading members of the government at dawn. Four cabinet ministers were ceremonially murdered. Prime Minister Admiral Okada, who had just announced the return to parliamentary government, was saved by the heroism of his wife who locked him in a cupboard and defied the assassination squad, which killed his brother instead.

Ironically, the army was the least prepared of the Japanese services for modern warfare. Its success against larger forces in the Sino-Japanese war of 1894 and the Russo-Japanese conflict of 1904–1905 had convinced the generals that the Japanese fighting man was inherently superior because of his racial purity and training. They believed in the dominance of spiritual factors such as loyalty, faith in victory, and fighting spirit over numbers and weapons. Officer training emphasized aggressiveness and the offense. In the Japanese army manual there was no chapter on how to conduct a retreat.

The most influential figure in Japan from 1931 to 1934 was the War Minister, General Sadao Araki, whom the great historian Paul Johnson describes as "a ferocious bushido ideologue, who ran a Hitler-style youth movement and was one of the leading exponents of the new totalitarian Shinto." Later the principal planner of Japan's grand strategy was a fanatical, Shinto-indoctrinated staff officer, Colonel Masanobu Tsuji. Tsuji was so pure in his doctrines that he tried to assassinate the prime minister with his sword and actually burned down a brothel full of fellow officers out of sheer, passionate moral indignation.

An Attempt to Avert War with the U.S.

The Japanese navy had performed brilliantly against the Russians, but the officer class had fewer illusions about war with the United States. Admiral Yamamoto, in particular, was a serious and realistic man. He had fought and been wounded in Japan's great victory over Russia at Tsushima and was the leading apostle of naval air power. He believed the aircraft carrier would be the key piece in the next naval war, and that extensive ship to ship gunfire exchanges like those that occurred in the Battle of Jutland in World War I were a thing of the past. He had opposed the building of super-battleships saying they would be about as useful in the next war as a samurai sword. As mentioned, he knew the United States and had traveled widely across the country. He argued that with no natural resource base, Japan was not yet a developed industrial economy capable of fighting a long, modern war. Unlike many of his fellow officers, he was not a drinker and preferred the company of his favorite geisha to drinking binges.

As recounted by Churchill, Yamamoto confided to Prince Konoye in early 1941: "If I am told to fight regardless of the consequences, I shall run wild for the first six months or a year, but I have utterly no confidence for the second and third years." However, the *zaibatsu* (the businessmen and bankers who controlled the big companies) and the powerful army generals were demanding that Japan take advantage of the chaotic events in Europe to secure a natural resource base in southeast Asia while the colonial powers were engaged in fighting each other. They insisted it was essential for Japan's future as an industrial nation and they were right. In July 1941 the U.S., Britain, and Holland imposed embargoes that cut Japan off from all supplies of oil. Those that knew Japan warned that this was a dangerous move as the navy, which had been opposed to war, ran on oil.

As relations deteriorated and well aware of the bellicose nature of the Japanese military establishment, Konoye desperately searched for a way to avert war. In the fall of 1941 through diplomatic channels, he offered to go to Honolulu to meet with FDR to negotiate some kind of *modus vivendi*. He proposed to bring his military chiefs with him and thus bind them to whatever agreement could be reached. FDR summarily rejected his overtures and refused to meet with him. It's hard to understand why unless the president knew the United States eventually had to ally with England and wanted to provoke a war to jar the country out of its isolationist tendencies. In October, Konoye, discouraged and disgraced by the rebuff from Washington, resigned, and the planning for war accelerated.

Japan's Strategy to Take Control
of Southeast Asia

The destruction of the U.S. Pacific fleet by a surprise attack on Pearl Harbor was the cornerstone move in Japan's complex offensive to take control of Southeast Asia. At Eta Jima, Yamamoto had practiced *kendo* (the martial art that disables a dangerous enemy with a single, violent blow) and he now proposed to do this in the war. The strategic concept was that the U.S. fleet would be destroyed at anchor at Pearl Harbor, and in the interim while it was being rebuilt, Japan would seize Southeast Asia. The plan was conceived of by a still-reluctant Admiral Yamamoto and perfected at the Tokyo Naval College in September 1941. The Pearl Harbor strike was very risky. It involved sneaking, undetected, a huge carrier task force across thousands of miles of ocean in total radio silence. To accomplish the objective, new technologies had to be developed in torpedoes, intelligence, and tanker refueling at sea. It also required perfect coordination, tactical surprise, and complete secrecy when probably a thousand Japanese would know of it.

In the event, the plan was executed masterfully, and at first blush it seemed a spectacular success. However it had less strategic impact than the Japanese expected and had dire unintended sociological consequences. First, it aroused and united the American people. FDR depicted December 7, 1941, as a "day of infamy" and portrayed the attack as a cowardly and treacherous act (which it was). Second, although 18 warships were sunk or badly damaged, most rested in shallow water and nearly all were raised and repaired in months not years. Japan's window of naval supremacy was closed six months later. In addition, losses of trained men were small, and the U.S. carriers were out at sea when the attack occurred and remained unscathed. Little damage was done to the oil storage tanks at Pearl Harbor or to the submarine pens.

However, none of this was fully appreciated until later, and as 1942 dawned Japan was well along in the process of conquering most of Southeast Asia with its vast resources of food, raw materials, and oil. Japan's takeover of the Dutch Indies had been successful, and even more disconcerting, in several countries, the locals had welcomed the conquerors as liberators from the yoke of European colonialism. Ronald Spector in his classic history of the war in the Pacific, *Eagle Against the*

Sun, relates how the Japanese spoke of their "sacred mission to retake Asian territory and free it from the white man's yoke." They maintained they were not taking the Philippines from the Filipinos but from the Americans; nor Singapore and Malaysia from the Malays and the overseas Chinese, but from the British; nor Borneo, Java, and Sumatra from the Indonesians but from the Dutch. They were waging a war of liberation from colonialism to create the government's vision of a Greater East Asia Co-Prosperity Sphere for Asians, not Europeans. All this, as was noted earlier, struck a responsive chord in many bleeding hearts across Asia.

Hong Kong surrendered on Christmas day, Manila on January 2. Shortly after came the loss of Britain's two newest capital ships, *HMS Repulse* and *HMS Price of Wales* to Japanese aircraft. These two great ships, after searching in vain for a Japanese troop convoy, were caught without air cover by Japanese aircraft off the coast of Malaya and sunk with the loss of most of their experienced crews. Churchill later confessed that the news of this catastrophe was the greatest blow he suffered in the entire course of the war.

Then Malaya was overrun, and shortly thereafter the supposedly impregnable fortress of Singapore ignominiously surrendered with 100,000 soldiers of the British Empire doomed to an incredibly harsh captivity, which few would survive. Another disaster came in late February when in the Battle of the Java Sea, the Japanese sunk five Allied cruisers and four destroyers. Britain's Southeast Asian empire was gone, and important elements in India were speaking of rebellion and a separate peace. The Dutch East Indies (what is now Indonesia) had been lost, and China was reeling from years of Japanese domination.

Advantages and Strengths
of the Japanese Military

Furthermore, the Japanese soldier was proving to be a skilled jungle fighter, mixing *banzai* frontal attacks with clever flanking maneuvers through seemingly impassable jungle. In the advance down the Malaya peninsula to Singapore, the British and colonial forces often outnumbered the Japanese two to one but were repeatedly outflanked, ambushed, and decimated by night surprise attacks. For years every young Japanese man had experienced two years of compulsory military service. The army regimen was probably the harshest in the world with 14 hours a day, 6 days a week, of infantry training. The Japanese soldier was capable of walking 25 miles a day for weeks on end carrying a rifle and a pack that was two-thirds of his weight. Maneuvers often occurred at night. "Our men already know how to sleep," the field manual said. "They need training in how to stay awake." The Japanese soldier was expected to follow *Bushido* "the way of the warrior." Aggressive small unit tactics were stressed, and above all surrender to the foe was forbidden.

As Spector so succinctly wrote the Japanese navy in 1942 as personified by its carrier strike forces "was probably the finest naval weapon in the world." For years it had been training for night fighting and carrier warfare whereas the English and U.S. navies were reliving the daytime, battleship-dominated Battle of Jutland. Flight training for Japan's carrier-based air crews was 700 hours versus 325 for U.S. naval aviators. Many of the flight crews had seen combat in China, and, in fact, the pilots of the torpedo planes in the strike on Pearl Harbor were all combat veterans.

In addition, Japan's aircraft were superior. The Zero was lightly armored, but it was the fastest, most maneuverable fighter plane in the world, and Japan's torpedo bombers were speedier and better designed. Japan's torpedoes ran faster and truer, and they exploded on contact while those of the United States did not and often ran deep and malfunctioned. Japan kept its best, most experienced pilots flying combat until they were killed. The United States rotated its frontline pilots between combat and training. As a result, by the end of the war Japan's pilots were far inferior, but in 1942 American rookies were flying against skilled aces in superior aircraft. In 1942, the Japanese war machine seemed invincible.

The Effect of Japanese Military Success on Global Stock Markets

As 1942 unfolded, it was no wonder there was gloom on the stock exchanges in New York as well as London. The United States had just seen most of its battleships sunk or disabled at Pearl Harbor. Perhaps even more devastating was the loss of the Philippines, the surrender of the fortress of Corregidor, and the subsequent Death March. On April 9, 76,000 U.S. and Filipino troops had surrendered to the Japanese at Bataan and a month later, the last 13,000 capitulated at Corregidor. The Bataan Death March was about to begin. The battered U.S. navy along with the remnants of the British and Dutch Asian fleets were suffering setbacks and losses in every encounter with the Japanese in the Philippine Sea.

The mood in Tokyo, by contrast, was euphoric. By early 1938, Japan had converted to a war economy with strict rationing. The army was making great progress in China, but Japan's lack of raw materials was constricting domestic consumption. There were shortages of toothpaste, chocolate, chewing gum, golf balls, and anything made of iron. In fact, crews of carpenters were sent to dwellings to extract surplus nails. Nevertheless, stock prices in Tokyo climbed throughout 1939 and much of 1940 as investors sensed the rise of Japan as a great power. Throughout most of 1941, stocks languished as investors worried about the embargo imposed on Japan by the Western powers, but then surged again after Pearl Harbor and with the conquests in Southeast Asia.

The U.S. Strikes Back

In mid-April, the U.S. struck back, at least symbolically. Sixteen Army B-25 bombers commanded by Colonel James Doolittle were loaded onto the aircraft carrier *Hornet*. The small carrier task force sneaked to within 650 miles of Japan where radar detected Japanese picket boats. The range was 150 miles further than planned and meant ditching at the end of the flight rather than landing on Chinese airfields as planned. Nevertheless, Doolittle elected to launch and take his chances. No one had ever taken off in a B-25 from a carrier, but all the planes labored into the air.

The bombers reached downtown Tokyo undetected and came roaring in at treetop level causing consternation and panic. There was no antiaircraft fire. Doolittle himself flew directly over a packed and startled baseball stadium. The bombing started fires, but the physical damage was slight. About 50 people were killed. The Americans followed their escape route to China where, out of fuel, they crash landed either in China or the ocean. Doolittle was awarded the Medal of Honor.

The psychological consequences of the raid were immense. The American press and population were elated; the Japanese were appalled. Eight out of the 80 men on the raid had been captured, and the Japanese public demanded revenge on these "war criminals." They were summarily tried, and three were executed, and the other five brutally imprisoned where one died of malnutrition. Admiral Yamamoto, according to Spector, regarded the raid "as a mortifying personal defeat." The navy had failed in its sacred duty to protect the emperor and the homeland from attack.

Planning to Control the Pacific Ocean

Immediately, the Naval General Staff that ran the war and reported directly to the emperor demanded revenge, and plans were finalized for Japan to conquer the key island of Midway in the central Pacific. (Midway is an atoll almost exactly midway around the world from the Greenwich Meridian/International Date Line: It is 2,800 miles west of San Francisco and 2,200 miles east of Japan, situated near the northwestern end of the Hawaiian Islands archipelago.) The largest fleet in Japanese history would lead the attack, which would culminate in an amphibious landing.

Meanwhile in late April, the Japanese launched a long planned offensive aimed at extending their sphere of influence in Asia in preparation for an invasion of Australia. The objective was to capture Port Moresby (the capital of Papua New Guinea, located on its southern shore, across the Coral Sea from the northernmost point in Australia), for use as an airbase against Australia and to seize Tulagi opposite the large island of Guadalcanal (both part of the Solomon Islands, also in the Coral Sea, east of northern Australia), which was later to be the scene of a long and grinding battle. Australia had sent its only four well-trained divisions and all its best officers to fight in the Middle East, and, stripped bare, was preparing panic plans to withdraw from the coast and fight an invasion from the outback. Its government, rife with partisan politics, was making life miserable for Churchill with its complaints of desertion. Thus the Allies felt the Japanese thrust must be repulsed, and a makeshift U.S. task force was pieced together commanded by Admiral Frank Jack Fletcher.

The Battle of the Coral Sea

From May 4 to May 6, 1942, the American task force intercepted and fought a series of running engagements with the Japanese invasion force and a major fleet consisting of three carriers with elite air wings and numerous cruisers and destroyers as it steamed towards Tulagi and Port Moresby. This came to be called The Battle of the Coral Sea. The weather was changeable with fog, mist, and occasional strong thunderstorms with heavy rain, and it affected air operations and the outcome. Fortune also was a major factor in the skirmishes, and this time it smiled on the Americans. Although at times the two fleets were only 60 miles apart, they never saw each other or came into direct contact.

The Japanese had substantial numerical superiority both in carriers and heavy cruisers and vastly more experienced air crews. However, from the onset, Admiral Fletcher was the aggressor. In the first encounter he launched three air strikes against the Tulagi Japanese invasion force which sunk a destroyer, two patrol boats, a troop transport, and severely damaged another troop transport. The Japanese invasion force was caught in the open without air cover because the main fleet was hundreds of miles away delayed by refueling in high seas. The Japanese losses were such that the Tulagi invasion was aborted until the next day.

On the next morning through a break in the clouds, an American scout plane sighted the Port Moresby invasion force, which had separated from the main Japanese fleet. Fletcher struck immediately with everything he had. His planes sunk *Shoho,* the carrier providing air cover for the landing force, compelling a further delay of the invasion. Fletcher's aircraft returned to his carriers, but as they were refueling, aircraft from the carriers in the main Japanese battle fleet appeared. Fortunately for the Americans, at the most perilous moment a heavy rain squall enveloped the U.S. carriers and hid them from the Japanese aircraft and Fletcher was able to recover and refuel his planes. The weather was so bad that a squadron of Japanese planes became disoriented and mistaking the American carriers as their own, attempted to land on them and were shot down. Others crashed into the sea. Less than a dozen of the 27 Japanese planes dispatched returned safely to their carriers.

In subsequent action, another large Japanese carrier was so severely damaged it became inoperable. The next day the two large American carriers came under heavy attack by 70 Japanese bombers and torpedo planes. The carriers' combat air patrols were handled badly, and the Japanese bombers were able to press their attack. The largest U.S. carrier, *Lexington,* was badly damaged and eventually sank although the Japanese did not realize this until after the Battle of Midway. The other carrier attacked, *Yorktown,* was roughed up and was sent back to Pearl Harbor for major repairs. The U.S. also lost a fleet tanker and a destroyer. As was to be the case at Midway, the American torpedo bombers proved to be totally ineffective death traps. Their torpedoes were so slow the Japanese ships could actually outrun them, and in the few instances they did hit, proved to be duds. By contrast, the Japanese torpedoes were fast and seldom misfired.

After these inconclusive engagements, without the close air support they felt they needed, the Japanese postponed (as it turned out, forever) the invasion of Port Moresby. The Battle of the Coral Sea was the first major naval engagement in history in which the two battle fleets never exchanged direct surface fire. It was entirely carrier-based warfare. American aircraft losses were 33 planes; Japan lost 43 planes with their elite aircrews. The Japanese thought they had won the battle, but strategically, the United States, for the first time had repulsed a Japanese expansion move, and the American navy had proven it could fight a carrier-oriented sea battle with inferior equipment and thwart and bloody superior forces.

Miracles at Midway

Meanwhile the raid on Tokyo had so enraged the Japanese that they accelerated the timetable for the invasion of Midway. They always rehearsed their battle plans with an elaborate table war game with unforeseen circumstances accounted for by rolling dice. The Midway game did not go well in rehearsal because the dice indicated there was a chance of discovery and a trap by the U.S. fleet. However, Yamamoto's chief of staff reversed the adverse decisions of the umpires saying that the Americans "have suffered heavy losses and have lost the will to fight." Japanese naval officers were so confident of their naval supremacy and a great victory at Midway that they brought back onto their ships their intimate personal possessions that had been left behind during the Pearl Harbor operation.

Because of the accelerated schedule, Japanese communications were vulnerable to cryptanalysis. American cryptographers had partially broken the Imperial Code so by mid-May Japan's intentions to attack Midway could be pieced together. At first Washington rejected the intelligence, questioning that Japan would send its main battle fleet against a remote coral atoll. They didn't understand the honor factor. Eventually the evidence was conclusive. Reinforcements were rushed to Midway, and a major, albeit patched together, fleet was assembled at Pearl Harbor. On May 22, *Yorktown,* which had been badly damaged in the Battle of the Coral Sea, limped into Pearl Harbor. The original estimate was that it would take three months to repair her. The dockyard crews were given three days. On the fourth day, she sailed with workers still on her.

The U.S. fleet that had been so hastily assembled was far less powerful than the Japanese armada. It consisted of 8 cruisers, 15 destroyers, and 3 carriers. The U.S. Navy's battleships were still in dry dock and not combat ready. Its biggest carrier, *Yorktown,* was barely seaworthy, its aircrews were mostly inexperienced and unfamiliar with their planes, and many had just left flight school. The torpedo planes and their torpedoes were antique. The Japanese sent two fleets. The Invasion Force had 16 warships while the Main Force had 32 ships including two battleships one of which, *Yamato* was Yamamoto's flagship and the world's largest battleship, four heavy cruisers, and two heavy and two light carriers. The aviators were veterans of China and Pearl Harbor.

The U.S. battle plan was for the fleet to sneak into position southeast of Midway, and then to surprise the Japanese and attack their carriers while their planes were off striking Midway in preparation for the invasion. The U.S. fleet was so hopelessly outgunned that there was no thought that it could take on the Japanese in a surface-to-surface naval gunfire battle. For the plan to work, the elements of secrecy and surprise were essential. If it didn't succeed, Japan would rule the Pacific, and Australia, Hawaii, and the U.S. West Coast were at risk. As it turned out luck and courage were the major factors in the battle.

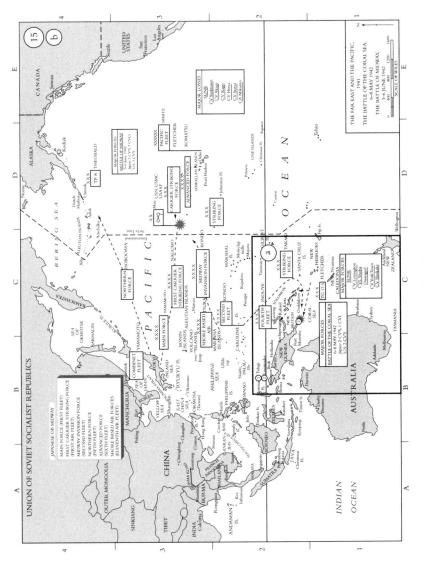

Figure 7.1   The Battle of the Coral Sea; The Battle of Midway

SOURCE: United States Military Academy, Department of History.

Japan Sails into an Ambush

As the Japanese fleets steamed toward Midway adhering to strict radio silence and believing the U.S. did not know their objective, the Japanese detected an unusual amount of radio traffic out of Pearl Harbor. As a result, Yamamoto ordered an aerial reconnaissance of Pearl Harbor by two long-range flying boats to ascertain if the fleet was still there. The planes needed to refuel to make the extended flight, and it was arranged that two submarines would meet and refuel them at the anchorage at French Frigate Shoals, a remote and uninhabited atoll. When the submarines arrived, by sheer chance, an American destroyer was anchored there. The Japanese waited three days, but the U.S. ship remained, and the reconnaissance flights had to be cancelled. Yamamoto never learned that the U.S. fleet had left Pearl Harbor.

Meanwhile another Japanese submarine scouted Midway. The captain surfaced at night, and observed frantic activity with numerous aircraft landings. It appeared that Midway seemed to know it was about to be attacked. He relayed this intelligence to Tokyo, but it also did not reach Yamamoto or Admiral Nagumo, the operational commander, because of the rigid enforcement of radio silence. As a result the Japanese commanders at sea never learned Midway knew it was going to be attacked. Even more serious Yamamoto did not know that there was a major fleet stalking him until it was too late and so he blithely sailed into an ambush.

On the morning of June 4 the Japanese carriers counting on the element of surprise launched the first wave of over a hundred bombers and fighters to soften up Midway for the invasion. These planes were flown by the cream of the Japanese naval air force. Unfortunately for the Japanese and again by chance, on the way in they were sighted by an American patrol plane and Midway was warned and was ready with every gun manned and everything that could fly in the air when the Japanese arrived. The Marines were flying obsolete Buffaloes and outclassed Wildcats, but they and the antiaircraft fire shot down a stunning total of 38 Japanese planes and 30 others were too heavily damaged to fly again. More serious still was the loss of skilled pilots. The Marines lost 15 of the 25 fighters deployed, their highest casualty rate of the entire war, but they had inflicted a crushing loss on the Japanese naval air arm. The whole air battle was over in 20 minutes.

Midway counterpunched against the Invasion Force with six torpedo planes and four Army B–26 bombers. The old torpedo bombers were cut to pieces on the way in, and the B–26s hit nothing. Seven of the attackers were shot down. Then 16 Marine dive bombers attacked. The dive bombers were brand new, and most of them had crews that had not flown them before. On one of them, the tail gunner was a mechanic who had never fired his machine gun. Half of them were shot down and again no hits were made.

Admiral Naguno now elected to land his planes that were returning from Midway and his covering Zeroes. He was confident he could handle anything that Midway could throw at him, and he began to refuel and rearm his aircraft with bombs for another attack on Midway. Suddenly he received a belated report from one of his patrol planes of the appearance of the American fleet. Quickly he made the decision to forget the bombs and rearm with torpedoes for an attack on the American fleet. Normally this would take half an hour, but his operations officer, Commander Minoru Genda, allowed the planes returning from Midway that were running low on fuel to land first. The timing turned out to be fatal. Genda, a graduate of Princeton who later became postwar chief of Japan's Self-Defense Forces, bitterly blamed himself for not immediately sending the Midway planes circling overhead to attack the U.S. fleet. He knew they lacked the fuel to return, and he was close friends with many of the pilots in the air above him. Afterwards he believed friendship had influenced his decision, and he was tortured by remorse.

U.S. Torpedo Bombers Fail, but Set Up Spectacularly Successful Attack by Dive Bombers

Meanwhile, the U.S. had launched the torpedo bombers from *Hornet* and *Enterprise*. There was little coordination, and they arrived unescorted. These old planes could only make around 100 knots an hour, and with the Japanese fleet steaming away from them at 25 knots, there was no element of surprise. Soon the Zeroes were all over them. Their courage impressed even the Japanese. "They are true Samurai," commented Yamamoto. Every one of the 15 planes of Torpedo Squadron Eight was shot down, and only 1 of the 30 crewmen survived. That one pilot,

Ensign George Gay, crashed into the ocean in the midst of the Japanese fleet. Floating in his jacket, he was almost run down by a destroyer that never saw him. For the remainder of the battle he had a front row floating, albeit perilous, seat and was picked up the next day by an American seaplane.

Next to arrive was the squadron of 14 torpedo bombers from the *Enterprise*. The Zeros now turned on them. Only four managed to get close enough to launch their torpedoes, and their torpedoes were either duds or else went under the target. However these losses were not in vain. The two uncoordinated low level torpedo plane attacks had distracted the Zeros from the arrival at high altitude of 54 dive bombers from *Yorktown*. The entire Japanese fleet was spread out below them with the flight decks of the carriers jammed with refueling and rearming planes.

The dive bombers came out of the sun, catching most of the Zeros at sea level chasing the hapless American torpedo bombers. In a few minutes the dive bombers wrecked the three Japanese carriers with multiple hits on flight decks packed with airplanes, fuel, pilots, and ammunition. Fires and secondary explosions rocked the huge carriers and they began to lose way and settle. Captain Mitsuo Fuchida, the aviator who had led the Pearl Harbor raid, was on *Akagi* preparing to climb into his plane. Suddenly he heard the scream of the dive bombers and a terrific explosion rocked the ship. He was knocked to the deck, and then staggered to his feet.

"Looking around I was horrified at the destruction that had been wrought in a matter of seconds. Deck plates reeled upward in grotesque configurations. Our planes stood tail up belching livid flames and jet-black smoke. Reluctant tears streamed down my checks as I watched the fires spread." All three Japanese carriers sank by midafternoon. Other ships were hit and damaged as well. The radio message from one elated American pilot as he came out of his dive was "scratch one carrier."

In retrospect it was almost a war crime for the U.S. Navy to send those slow, obsolete, totally helpless torpedo bombers carrying virtually useless, ancient torpedoes against the Japanese fleet and the Zeros. All 15 planes of Torpedo Eight went down, and 26 of the 29 of the two flights were lost. Fifty-one of the fifty-two naval aviators flying them perished. The few torpedoes that hit were duds. The letters home from the pilots reveal they knew what they were getting into. It was even worse than the *kamikaze* attacks later in the war, because at least the *kamikaze* planes were loaded with explosives that worked. There is a photograph of the 30 smiling young pilots of Torpedo Eight standing casually on the flight deck of the *Enterprise* grinning with their arms draped over each other's shoulders. It was just as Alfred, Lord Tennyson had written almost 100 years earlier, in 1854, about Britain's courageous yet tragic attack in the Crimean War, which he immortalized in his epic poem, "The Charge of the Light Brigade"

> "Their's not to reason why,
> Their's but to do and die: . . .
> Into the jaws of Death,
> Into the mouth of Hell . . ."

What made these young flyers do it? All were college men who had graduated from the likes of Yale, Rice, Michigan, and UCLA in 1939 or 1940. Jobs were hard to get at the time. Wall Street was moribund and aristocratic. Training programs were nonexistent. A new "customers' man" had no chance without connections, and the big industrial companies were not hiring. The Navy's Officer Training Program, flight school, and then Navy Wings of Gold seemed an intriguing alternative. The program instilled patriotism, invulnerability, and intense group loyalty.

With their ships sinking, the anguished captains of the Japanese carriers lashed themselves with their sashes to the bridges of their ships and prepared to go down with them. On *Soryu*, Chief Petty Officer Abe, who was the Navy's heavyweight wrestling champion, was sent to save the beloved Captain Yanagimoto in spite of himself. As Abe approached Yanagimoto on the burning bridge he said: "Captain, I have come on behalf of all your men to take you to safety. They are waiting for you." The captain stared coldly at him, drew his sword, and began singing the national anthem. Abe saluted and left.

The U.S. Destroys the Last Japanese Aircraft Carrier

Now only one Japanese carrier, *Hiryu,* was left. At midmorning she launched two waves of dive bombers and torpedo planes against the

American fleet. They concentrated on *Yorktown,* and pressed their attack in the face of fierce fighter defense and antiaircraft fire. Planes fell out of the sky, but the carrier was hit with bombs, and then as she became sluggish, took two torpedoes. With fires raging and threatening to capsize, the decision was made to abandon ship. Nevertheless she still stayed afloat although listing badly.

Meanwhile, *Hiryu* was absorbing a tremendous pounding. She was hit by both bombs and torpedoes, and at dusk began to take water and list. Fires raged in her pagoda-like superstructure. The commander of the carrier division, Admiral Tamon Yamaguchi, called the crew together, turned them in the direction of the Imperial palace, and led them in three cheers for the emperor. He handed his black cap to his senior aide as a memento for Mrs. Yamaguchi and ordered the crew to abandon ship. Then he turned to the captain of the sinking carrier, Tomeo Kaku, drank a toast of *saki,* and said, "There is a beautiful moon tonight. Shall we watch it together as we sink?" Shortly thereafter *Hiryu* rolled on her side and with battle flags flying sank.

Yamamoto, although distraught and disconcerted, still had hopes that even without carriers he could close on the American fleet and fight a night surface battle. The American admirals wisely (since they were seriously outgunned) decided to withdraw. However, as twilight fell, another air strike battered the carrier *Hiryu,* and she also had to be abandoned. Without any air cover, Yamamoto knew that when daylight came and with his carriers gone his fleet would be terribly vulnerable to air power. To try to proceed with the invasion would be suicidal, and around midnight he ordered withdrawal. In the process, two of his four heavy cruisers, the largest and fastest in the Japanese Navy, collided at high speed while trying to avoid an American submarine. One was finished off the next day by aircraft from *Hornet* and *Enterprise* and the other, heavily damaged, limped back to Yokuska.

In the fog of war, Midway initially was at first not perceived as the great victory it was. An inexperienced, bedraggled, out-gunned American task force had beaten the best navy in the world at its own game and nobody could believe it. After a long succession of defeats, exaggerated combat reports, and incompetence, the U.S. Navy had proven it could fight and win. At Midway the Japanese had lost four carriers, one heavy cruiser sunk, and one severely damaged compared with the loss of one carrier and a destroyer for the U.S. The Japanese had lost 322 planes versus 150 for the American fleet, but most of the American planes that went down were obsolete and should never have been flying in combat.

Most serious were the staggering and irreplaceable losses that had been inflicted on Japan's elite carrier aircrews with the veterans of China, Pearl Harbor, and the Coral Sea, missing and presumed dead. Japanese naval aviation never recovered. Bad luck, over-confidence, and a few poor decisions had doomed their effort. The courage of American aviators flying inferior airplanes, and the United State's ability to read the Imperial Code were also major factors.

In five minutes on that perfect May morning, the course of the battle, the war, and probably history had been changed. At 10:25 A.M., the Japanese seemed to have accomplished one of the greatest naval victories in history, one that would make Japan the master of the Pacific and in all probability of Asia for at least a generation. Five minutes later, the Japanese admiral, Nagumo, was faced with disaster. Not only had the Japanese lost four carriers, 2,200 highly trained officers and seamen, and 250 aircraft, but 150 pilots were gone, many of whom subsequently were forced to ditch in the ocean because they had no carriers to land on. The loss of the pilots, according to the great military historian John Keegan, was as devastating as the destruction of the carriers.

The spectacular and abrupt change of fortune was the result not of an exquisitely synchronized American attack, but of two fortuitous accidents. The timing of the arrival of the American torpedo bombers, which inadvertently lured the Zeros down to sea level was accidental, as was the bad luck for the Japanese that they were caught refueling and rearming aircraft by the dive bombers. The second was another chance event. At 9:45 that morning, the formation of American dive bombers had become separated from the torpedo planes and was lost and unable to find the Japanese fleet. Just before 10:00 A.M., the lead pilot spied in the distance the white wake on the blue Pacific of a Japanese destroyer that had been sent to investigate a sonar intercept of an American submarine that was not where it was supposed to be. The American pilot guessed the destroyer must be racing to rejoin the fleet, and the formation followed it to the carriers, arriving at the exquisite moment.

Japan's Defeat at Midway
Creates Doubt about the War

The Japanese commanders at Midway, Admirals Yamamoto, Nagumo (who appears to have a nervous breakdown as his flagship was sinking), and Kondo, were the men who had planned and carried out so ruthlessly and skillfully the bold and skillful operations that in four months had destroyed the British, Dutch, and American fleets in the Far East and given Japan command of the seas from the Indian Ocean to the Pacific. Their captains and crews were battle-hardened veterans with tremendous pride in the Samurai naval tradition and the inherent superiority of their race. Midway shook their confidence. After Midway they were never to be the same again.

In the weeks after Midway, the Japanese government announced that a "great victory had been won." They even told their ally, Hitler, that Midway was a triumph, and the official German war diary records his elation. However, within the officer corps the truth could not be concealed. In his wonderful book, *Sea of Thunder,* Evan Thomas writes, "All the senior officers who survived had been deeply shamed by Midway."

A veil of denial had been dropped over the defeat. To disappoint one's superior, to fail in one's obligation was unbearable to the duty bound Japanese. It was more acceptable to cover up and to dissemble. Prime Minister Tojo was not told the extent of the disaster for a week, and the public was informed that while Japan had lost a carrier, America had lost two. The actual totals were four Japanese carriers sunk to one American carrier. Officers from the sunken ships were confined to base; the sailors were sent back to the South Pacific, not even allowed to see their families.

Yamamoto himself was deeply depressed. However, he felt compelled to reassure his staff at a secret strategy conference in June at the Navy War College. "There are still eight carriers in the combined fleet. We should not lose heart. In battle as in chess it is the fool who lets himself be forced into a reckless move out of desperation." In the following months as the Japanese people who had believed in the invincibility of their navy learned about the losses, some began to have doubts about the outcome of the war. For the first time there was malingering and even some sabotage, although it was relatively minor.

Churchill in his thoughts on Midway in his memoirs comments on the rigidity of the Japanese leadership and planning and the Samurai tradition. When events did not follow their planned schedule, he believed they tended to become confused and make bad decisions. He wrote that part of this was "due to the cumbersome and imprecise nature of their language which rendered it extremely difficult too improvise by means of signaled communications."

Japan's offensive moves both at the Battle of the Coral Sea and at Midway had been repulsed with heavy losses. Despite the loss of Singapore, after the two sea battles Australia finally felt safe from invasion. Yamamoto had said from the beginning that Japan had to deliver a knockout punch in the first year of the war, and she had utterly failed to do so. After Midway, in a letter to his beloved geisha, Yamamoto expressed his depression. Among other things, the bravery and self-sacrifice of Torpedo 8 must have disabused the Japanese leadership of the idea that they had engaged a soft and inferior nation.

Chastened by the defeat, from July 1942 onward, Japan's offensive moves were over even though she still had the naval firepower to challenge and perhaps beat the U.S. fleet. Instead she reverted to defensive tactics, which resulted in a long war of attrition that she could not hope to win against a superior industrial power. Already the United States was laying down modern new battleships and carriers at a high rate. Less than a year later Admiral Yamamoto died when his plane was ambushed and shot down by a U.S. fighter plane that knew its location, again because of the cryptographers. His ashes were interred in Tokyo at a state funeral in June 1943, ironically on the first anniversary of Midway.

Even if nobody else did, both the U.S. stock market (as will be discussed in the following chapter) and Winston Churchill perceived the dimensions of the victory. In *The Grand Alliance,* he wrote: "The moral effect was tremendous and instantaneous. At one stroke the dominant position of Japan in the Pacific was reversed. The glaring ascendancy of the enemy, which had frustrated our combined endeavours (sic) through the Far East for six months was gone forever. From this moment all our thought turned with sober confidence to the offensive."

Chapter 8

Stock Markets Understood: Nobody Else Did

W orld War II was about freedom and democracy, but it was also about the survival of capitalism, and, in a way, the future existence of stock markets with all the beauty and ugliness attached to them. Functioning, free equity markets working as suppliers of capital with independently determined prices are simply not compatible with either authoritarian Socialist dictatorships or Communism. In the chaos and turmoil of the early 1940s, stock markets around the world occasionally dimly but brilliantly most of the time comprehended the ebb and flow of the war. It had to be the inherent wisdom of crowds because both sides controlled the war news reaching the civilian population and used propaganda as a weapon.

At the turning points, stock markets were positively prescient. The only big miss was Tokyo's failure in May and June 1942 to grasp the significance of the two naval battles in the Pacific. As noted in Chapter 7, the Japanese official battle reports and the Japanese press reported the Battle of the Coral Sea as a great triumph, and Midway was portrayed as a victory, not a defeat although some losses of aircraft and ships were admitted. Although the casualties must have been noted and grieved, Japanese society at the time was so united behind the war policy and believed so totally in the invincibility of the Japanese military, that defeat and economic failure were virtually inconceivable. It would have been unpatriotic to sell stocks because of unconfirmed rumors about losses at sea.

By mid-1942 Japan was virtually a planned economy with control of labor, prices, wages, and industrial decisions. Prime Minister Tojo had centered overall economic policy in the Ministry of Munitions run by Vice Minister Kishi Nobuske. Although the reorganization was theoretically successful in that it simplified the table of organization, it failed completely to increase production because Japan was totally dependent on imports of raw materials and the U.S. sea blockade was becoming increasingly effective. Industrial production fell steadily from the fall of 1942 until the surrender in 1945. The U.S. economy expanded by about two-thirds from 1940 to 1944 while Japan's grew by only 25%.

Not every investor in Japan misread the battles at the Coral Sea and Midway. Food was in short supply, and railings in the parks around the Imperial Palace were being dismantled for their iron. The Nomura family and Nomura Securities in mid-1942 began to suspect the eventual defeat of Japan. Although the newspapers and radio broadcast only good news about the course of the war, the Nomuras apparently picked up information in the elite tea houses of the upper class. Many of the naval officers and aviators involved in the battles at Midway and the Coral Sea had geishas, and when they failed to return, rumors began to circulate. The Nomura family, sensing something was amiss, began gradually to sell its equity holdings, and even sold short. Later they purchased real assets, probably reasoning that land and real businesses would be the best stores of value in a conquered country. These protected assets allowed the family to have the capital to finance the rapid expansion of Nomura Securities & Research in the immediate postwar years and eventually emerge as the dominant securities firm in Japan.

The U.S. and London Stock Markets Got It

By contrast, the New York stock market perceived almost immediately the significance of the battles of the Coral Sea and Midway despite the fact that the official communiqués initially did not portray Midway as a victory because the War Department had been severely criticized for proclaiming defeats as victories in the first months of the war. In the spring of 1942, the stock market was depressed. After the steep declines of 1941, prices had steadily fallen through the first months of 1942 as the war news continued to be desperate. German submarines infested the East Coast preying almost at will on America's shipping lanes, and the carnage was frightening. Churchill worried that England's vital seaborne supply lifelines might be strangled. On the other side of the world, Singapore capitulated, the Battle of the Java Sea was a disaster, Burma and the Dutch East Indies were taken by the Japanese, and Corregidor, the last bastion in the Philippines, finally surrendered. America's war effort was faltering, and, as the press repeatedly pointed out, its military management was inept.

The mood in 1942 in both Britain and the United States was of resolution but also of despair and deep disillusionment about the future of mankind. Mathew Arnold's magnificent poem *Dover Beach* was much circulated with its message of: "Ah, love let us be true to one another! For the world . . . hath really neither joy, nor love, nor light, nor certitude, nor peace, nor help for pain; and we are here as on a darkling plain swept with confused alarms of struggle and flight, where ignorant armies clash by night."

In the war years when so many were dying at sea, on land, and in the air, a short poem was often tacked to bulletin boards in British officer's messes.

There is an old belief
That on some distant shore,
Far from despair and grief
Old friends will meet once more.

In the late winter and spring of 1942 as Japan threatened to invade Australia, and the Japanese onslaught continued across Southeast Asia by land and sea, stock prices in New York and London dropped sharply.

Defeat followed defeat. The Japanese seemed invincible. Investors were also unnerved by the success of the new German offensive in Russia and continued British setbacks in the desert. The Dow Jones Average rallied only briefly after the Doolittle raid, despite the vociferous propaganda hoopla, and by the end of April, was down 20% for the year. The low for the entire era was on April 30, 1942, at 92, 31% below the early 1941 high of 132.

As 1942 began with more losses and defeats, the sluggishness and declines in both the London and New York stock markets continued. In fact as Robert Sobel (who wrote the definitive history of the New York Stock Exchange, *The Big Board*) describes, February 1942 was the slowest month at the exchange since 1915. On February 14 there were only 320,000 shares traded and there was one hour with a total volume of just 30,000. A seat on the Exchange changed hands for $17,000, the lowest price since 1897 and 97% below the record high of $625,000 in 1929.

The listlessness affected real estate. A New York hotel could not be sold at one times its annual earnings, and rents in Wall Street office buildings were as low as a dollar a square foot. According to James Grant in his wonderful book *The Trouble with Prosperity,* some called it a "dry panic." Remember that these declines were occurring at a time when war production was surging, huge budget deficits were occurring, and corporate profits were strong.

However the stock market had other things on its mind. The U.S. Treasury had proposed a corporate tax rate of 60%, and a Renegotiation Board to recover excess profits was looming, which made forecasting earnings and dividends impossible. Individual income tax rates of 85% on earnings above $50,000 were imposed. The Roosevelt administration seemed determined to use the mobilization to level incomes and wealth, and these policies, combined with bumbling and incompetence in fighting the war, further sapped the confidence of the investor class.

Every right thinking prognosticator with a head on his shoulders was bearish. In 1939, a famous Harvard professor (who out of decency shall remain nameless) published an influential essay in which he argued that America's economy was doomed to an inevitable secular decline because of the depressed birthrate and because there were no more uninhabited territories to develop. Furthermore, he said, new industries and inventions were in short supply. Even as he wrote, the birthrate was turning up, and the war was to spawn a thousand new industries and technologies.

The bearish mood of early 1942 was attributable in part to the inept performance of America's armed forces in the Pacific. Pearl Harbor, the destruction of MacArthur's air force on the ground, and the defeats of Britain and the United States across Asia were initially described as heroic encounters with an overwhelming enemy. As the public in general and investors in particular learned that the upbeat news reports were either false at worst or misleading at best they lost faith in the military and the news media.

In early February Admiral Bill "the Bull" Halsey lead a sortie against the Japanese in the Marshall and Gilbert Islands. In the battle, the Navy pilots claimed to have sunk 16 Japanese ships. Halsey's dispatches described a great victory, and he told of the vibrant radio traffic of the attacking pilots. "Get away from that cruiser, Jack, she's mine!" and "Bingo! Look at that big bastard burn." "Revenge by the Bull" screamed the *Herald Tribune*. "Pearl Harbor Revenged!" Evan Thomas recounts how when Halsey returned to Pearl Harbor with his flagship, the carrier *Enterprise*, flying a huge stars and stripes battle flag, sirens blew and sailors and workmen on the damaged docks cheered themselves hoarse. It turned out Halsey's report was mostly bull. One transport and two small barges were all that was sunk.

In February 1942, one Leon Henderson, an administrator in the Office of Price Administration, cheerfully predicted that the cost of the war would throw American living standards back to the levels of the Great Depression. With prime corporate bonds yielding 2.75% and stocks yielding between 8% and 9%, the chairman of the Metropolitan Life Insurance Company intoned that stocks had no role in the portfolios of life insurance companies, and the State of New York Insurance Commission concluded they were "an inappropriate investment" and banned them from insurance company portfolios. This costly edict stayed in force until the mid-1950s when the great postwar bull market was already fully entrenched.

But God knows stocks were cheap. Not only were dividend yields three times greater than bond yields (today it's almost just the opposite), but in April 1942 30% of the stocks on the new York Stock Exchange sold at a price earning multiple of less than four times 1941 profits and many sold at a discount to net cash. Over two-thirds of this beleaguered crew were quoted at a price between 4 and 6. W.E. Hutton, with tongue firmly in patrician check, remarked that perhaps FDR "should give more attention to the ill-housed, poorly clothed, and inadequately fed third of the stock market." The median price earnings ratio of 600 representative stocks was 5.3 times, and only 10% of all stocks traded at more than 10 times the previous year's earnings.

However, there was one bull left. Harry Nelson of *Barron's* who on April 13, 1942, wrote:

> In late 1928 and early 1929 there were those who could see the grief that lay ahead, but it seemed as if the market never would or could break. Today the logic is just as much in favor of the buyer only it seems as through the market will never turn up.

The Wise Old Stock Market Bottoms

Then in May 1942, just before the United States' military fortunes in the Pacific improved, in the midst of the gloom and the bargains and at the point of maximum bearishness, the U.S. stock market made a bottom for the ages. There was still a steady stream of bad news from other parts of the world, but *the market crowd* sensed the turn of the tide in the war with Japan. At the Battle of the Coral Sea in early May, although it was more of a draw than a victory, for the first time Japan had been denied what it wanted, which was Port Moresby, the stepping stone to Australia. For the first time, the Japanese advance in Asia had been halted, and the U.S. Navy had shown it could hold its own even against superior Japanese forces. Then came the outright victory at Midway, and although the market stumbled in June when Tobruk fell to Rommel, the late April early May pit was the bottom of the long, secular bear market of the 1930s and early 1940s, as shown in Figure 8.1.

The April to May 1942 bottom was an epic bottom, and it spawned a new, cyclical bull market that ran for four years with only minor corrections, peaking on May 29, 1946. 1945 was a tremendous year with large company stocks up 36.4% and small stocks up 73.6% climaxing an incredible run off that 1942 bottom. Small stocks, according to Ibbotson Associates, rose 44.5% in 1942, 88.4% in 1943, 53.7% in 1944, and 73.6%

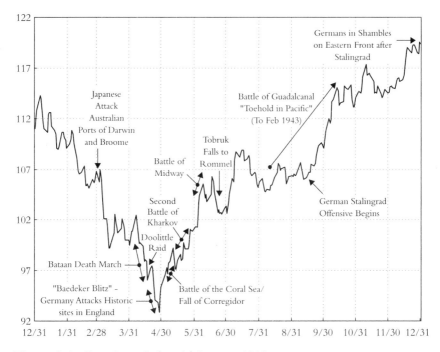

Figure 8.1   Dow Jones Industrial Average: 1942
DATA SOURCE: Dow Jones & Co.; Global Insight.

in 1945. Once the gloom lifted, stocks were propelled as though a compressed spring had been released.

Postwar Blues in the U.S. Markets: 1946–1949

In fact, the first real setback occurred in February of 1946 with a classic "warning crack" decline of 10% in the Dow. From that low on February 26, the Dow surged 14.2% in 78 trading days (the market was open six days a week then) in a classic blow-off pattern to the May 29 peak which was the highest level since 1930. The market then drifted down for a couple of months, and then fell almost 20% in a month.

U.S. stocks then got a bad case of the postwar blues and drifted sideways for almost three years. The blues descended because the European economies were struggling, the Cold War was under way, and the U.S. economy was having trouble adjusting. The consensus was that without

Figure 8.2   Dow Jones: 1935–1950
DATA SOURCE: Dow Jones & Co.; Global Insight.

the stimulus of defense spending, the United States would drift into stagflation with high unemployment. Inflation soared to 18% in 1946 and 9% in 1947 but then abruptly fell to deflation of 1.8% in 1949. Stock and bonds languished until the malaise of the postwar world began to clear in mid-1949, as shown in Figure 8.2.

Japan's Markets: Bullishness in 1942: Then Illusion and Disillusion

The Japanese stock market was a very different story. In the first six months of 1942 as the Japanese military colossus bit off rich chunks of Southeast Asia, the stock market soared. A mood of euphoric bullishness swept the Tokyo Stock Exchange as investors began to believe that Japan now was at last acquiring an empire, a vast raw material base, and the secure oil supply it so desperately needed. Japanese companies would dominate not only the new Greater East Asia Co-Prosperity Sphere but all of Asia. The deeply engrained belief in the racial superiority and warrior characteristics of the race of Nippon—the people of the Rising Sun—surfaced. This mood of national euphoria was not to be repeated again until almost half a century later, just prior to another stock market bust.

But to return to 1942. Early that year the Japanese Ministry of Finance (MOF) became concerned about how the war was to be financed, and a smart young deputy minister conceived of a plan to make the country richer by elevating stock prices. The MOF (whose word then as now was law to the financial community) encouraged the big brokerage firms to create and then market to the public investment trusts. The people bought the story of the "New Japan," and stock exchange volume soared, as the market continued to climb throughout 1942 and 1943 in *nominal* terms. Presumably investors were still optimistic because they thought Japan would at least be able to keep its new empire, but just as in Germany, the economies apparent prosperity was artificial because of massive deficit financing and a rising inflation rate.

By 1944 the war situation had become more desperate. School children were put to work making balloon bombs that were supposed to drift 5,000 miles across the Pacific to set fires and kill Americans on the West Coast. A seven-day workweek was imposed, women were doing heavy manual labor, and there were rumbles of unrest. Inflation soared in 1944 as the government printed more money and issued bonds to finance the war. Black markets and barter exchanges sprang up across the country. In March, stocks were subjected to rigid MOF price controls, and, for all extents and purposes, prices were frozen and artificial, but in *real* terms prices were falling. Trading volume declined precipitately. After the surrender in 1945, both the Tokyo and Osaka stock markets were officially closed.

In 1945 as defeat, unconditional surrender, and the uncertainties of the occupation loomed, the Japanese economy and stock market totally collapsed. From 1944 to 1946, GDP as calculated fell by 46% although that figure has to be a wildly inexact estimate. From 1940 to 1949, Japanese stock prices fell a staggering *25.7% a year.* The money illusion factor is best illustrated by the fact that in nominal terms from 1930 to 1949 prices rose 3,280% but in real terms they fell 75%. Government bonds weren't much better with the total return falling 17.0% a year over the same period. In other words, for the 20 years that Japan was in its aggressive, militaristic stage, long-term financial assets were an utter disaster. These are imprecise figures for both stocks and bonds since calculations involve the London Business School linking three different indexes. However the numbers are much more reliable from May 1949 on, because the data is for the Nikkei 225 and then in 1995 for the TOPIX.

The swapping of stocks resumed as early as the autumn of 1945. Since the floor of the Tokyo exchange had been taken over by the American Army for use as a gym, and the Osaka Stock Exchange building was a hospital, informal markets were opened by traders in the backrooms of restaurants near the closed exchanges. Capitalism, the cult of the equity, and speculation is deeply imbedded in the Japanese psyche. From 1945 until May 1949 an informal over-the-counter market developed in shares for which an index was constructed called the Nikkei-Dow Jones Average.

Initially quotations fell sharply from the totally artificial, MOF-controlled prices of the war years. No records were kept of dividend payments but the numbers cited include "interpolations," whatever that means. This informal market began to develop a life of its own as businessmen' and investors' confidence about Japan's future grew, and activity began to revive. There must have been some huge fortunes begun prior to 1948 as farsighted speculators who foresaw the eventual resurgence of Japan as an economic power bought shares at deeply depressed levels.

After the war, the old, blue chip companies desperately needed money to rebuild their shattered factories, so to finance their capital spending they sold new shares to the banks to the insurance companies, and to anyone who had some capital. These issues were hard to sell to individuals because the potential buyers surmised they would be diluted by future issues. As it turned out, they were right. But the dilution was actually favorable because the capital infusions made these companies world class competitors. The first issue was New Japan Chemical in April of 1946, and two dozen more followed the following year, according to Albert Alletzhauser in *The House of Nomura*.

By 1947 the public was again becoming interested in shares. The brokerage firms began to hire young salesmen (most of the old ones had been killed in the war) and these new recruits beat the proverbial bushes. "Buy a share instead of a pack of *Peace*" was their pitch. *Peace* was the leading brand of cigarettes, and a pack sold for 50 yen, which was big money in impoverished Japan. This chain-smoking race averaged one or two cigarettes per person per day in the early postwar years. Those who bought shares made a fortune; those who smoked presumably suffered the consequences.

General MacArthur's Plan to Reform Japan's Economy

Following the surrender, General MacArthur was installed as virtually the viceroy of Japan. The complex decisions he made about whom to prosecute for war crimes, ways to reform Japan, and how to govern the country are covered in great detail in James Webb's *The Emperor's General* and in William Manchester's epic biography *American Caesar: Douglas MacArthur 1880–1964*. MacArthur wanted to **reform** Japan to ensure her survival as a modern nation, not punish her for what she had done. A key decision he made was not to indict the emperor for war crimes as many Americans and most of the Allies wanted. Instead, a number of generals and high government officials were tried and executed. The principal crime of at least one of whom, Tomoyuk Yamashita, was fighting too well, surrendering too slowly, and thus angering MacArthur. The reforms that MacArthur conceived of were liberal and democratic. The subsequent economic success of Japan and its commitment to Capitalism rather than Communism speaks for their wisdom. However, the changes posed a serious threat to existing wealth. MacArthur, was an aristocrat, an elitist, but not a wealthy man. He was determined to destroy the *zaibatsu* (the historic corporate monopolies), end feudalism, and effect a drastic reduction of ancient, inherited privileges. Specific programs included land reform, abolition of the nobility, and steep taxation of the rich. Banks that were judged to have financed the war effort and imperialism were suspended and their assets seized.

As for land reform, in 1945 there were about 160,000 wealthy, absentee land owners, each of whom owned on average 36 small farms. They controlled 89% of the arable land in Japan. Around 10 million peasants labored on miniscule tracts of land on these farms either as outright serfs or share croppers. MacArthur ordained that all land held by the absentee owners was to be sold to the government at an administered price that was ridiculously low. The land would then be sold back at the same price in small lots to the peasants with a 30-year repayment clause and the proviso that the buyer had to work the land himself.

This was society transforming reform, and MacArthur wanted this radical measure to be approved by the Diet. However, Japan's parliament strenuously resisted because most of its members were landowners themselves. After a year of complaining, the Diet finally acquiesced to the general, and the legislation was reluctantly enacted. There were a few exceptions made, but by 1950 five million acres had been redistributed. This resulted in an enormous redistribution of wealth from one class to another that altered the wealth profile of Japan forever.

There were some unintended consequences, however. It was difficult to enforce the provision that the land had to be worked by the original buyer. European and American families who knew Japan saw the land sales as fantastic bargains. The winters in the early postwar years were unusually cold, and people were hungry and cold. Speculators bartered warm clothes, diamonds, food, anything they could lay there hands on with the farmers for land, and some great fortunes were eventually made. Land was being sold so cheaply you could buy one *tsubo* (about one acre) for the price of a cup of coffee. People involved in the black market and the sourcing of construction materials for rebuilding the bombed out cities made fortunes in those early postwar years.

MacArthur also was determined to dismantle the monopolies that were at the heart of the *zaibatsu*. The big conglomerates (of which there were about 80) were broken up into individual companies run by their prewar managers. Holding companies with interlocking family directorships were abolished. In addition the 11 richest families in terms of corporate equity were required to exchange the majority of their stock holdings for government bonds that were nonnegotiable for 10 years. Graduated taxes on income were introduced, and the inheritance tax was dramatically increased, eventually rising to 75% which meant that 95% of an individual's wealth was taxed away in three generations. The effective inheritance tax in Japan is still around 60%.

Obviously all these measures had a dramatically destructive impact on the wealth of the upper class, and the reforms transformed Japan from being probably the most **unequal** of the major industrial countries in terms of wealth and income to what it is today, the most **equal.** Of course the wealthy dragged their feet, obfuscated, concealed assets, and ingeniously resisted the reforms. To some extent they succeeded, and the *zaibatsu* ended up still having control of their companies but with diluted equity stakes. Furthermore the *doyens* of Japanese business, who were known as the Four Heavenly Kings, for years to come controlled Japanese politics, even to the selection of the prime minister and finance minister. Thus, wealth and power were partially retained by the aristocracy of the old Japan.

Nevertheless, MacArthur's reforms were probably almost as *destructive of wealth,* although not as bloody, as what the Soviets did to Eastern Europe. The difference is that Japan emerged immeasurably stronger from the occupation's reforms; Eastern Europe emerged weaker and far less stable. The reforms also explain MacArthur's immense popularity to this day with the Japanese people, and why Japan never had a serious internal Communist movement.

Creative Destruction in Japan

Over the course of the 1940s in Japan, brains, an entrepreneurial spirit, and owning industrial land or a small business that had the potential to become much bigger ones were the best wealth protectors. The bombing had incinerated factories and destroyed production machinery, but the underlying land and the franchises were still there from which to rebuild viable commercial enterprises. The postwar boom and the end of shortages also spawned completely new businesses, banks, and brokerage firms. Just as in Germany, defeat caused "creative destruction" of the old ways. Even the giant conglomerates like Hitachi, Toshiba, and Komatsu were energized, and dynamic new companies producing technology and consumer products of which Sony is the most prominent example sprung from the ashes.

Nomura Securities rebuilt itself, and in the late 1980s, a 40 years after the end of the war, had a market capitalization bigger than General Electric and the combined value of every other investment bank in the world. The Industrial Bank of Japan (IBJ), which was really a merchant bank, rose from the ashes and in 1989 with revenues, earnings, and employees equal to those of Morgan Stanley had a market capitalization 10 times larger. That year in the height of the Japanese bubble, a grand merger of Deutsche Bank, Morgan Stanley, and IBJ was discussed, but the plan had to be discarded because IBJ's market capitalization was so disproportionate that it would have totally controlled the new company. The Japanese commercial real estate market became so inflated that in the late 1980s the real estate in the heart of Tokyo on which the Imperial Palace presided was worth more than all the land in California. Obviously values were grossly distorted.

Without the MacArthur reforms, postwar Japan would have remained a feudal society and none of this might have happened. On the other hand, a vast amount of inherited wealth, accumulated by hook or by crook in the old Japan, was destroyed. Of course there were exceptions. One of the richest families in Japan today has owned for a century and a half coal mines in remote areas of Japan that were untouched by the war and escaped the reforms. These mines are worked in a more enlightened manner today than they were 70 years ago, but the family still owns them. How they have escaped the confiscatory inheritance tax is a mystery. Also in the late 1930s, priceless Chinese antiquities, art, and enamel were shipped back to Japan as the spoils of war by Japanese army officers serving in China, and those collections have become very valuable. The occupying Americans were not interested in precious Chinese collectibles; their desire was for swords, flags, and war memorabilia.

Japan's Perception of Invincibility

It is important to understand how Japan emerged from the ashes and how the country laid the foundations on which it would become far more prosperous and richer than before. The key was the very surprising acquiescence of the Japanese people and the emperor to surrender and occupation, and the benevolent and enlightened reaction of the occupying forces. At the time, no one foresaw how well it would go. Douglas

MacArthur may have been a pompous, vain, egomaniac, but in many ways, he was the father of the great nation that is the modern Japan.

Even by the summer of 1945, the Japanese government had not told the common people the dimensions of how badly the war was going and of the defeats they had suffered although they must have had some sense of the losses. The news reported only heroic defenses by outnumbered outposts. The Japanese had always been a proud and fighting race, and a long succession of victories over the centuries had convinced them of their invincibility and racial superiority. They had an almost mystical belief in the strength and wisdom of the warrior caste. Defeat was inconceivable. As noted, in the Japanese Army Field Manual, there was no chapter on retreat. At the time of the surrender in 1945 there were 6,983,000 troops under arms around what was left of their empire. On the home islands alone there were 2,576,000 solider comprising 57 divisions, 14, brigades, and 45 regiments.

Although the emperor and the ruling class realized after the two atomic bombs were dropped that surrender was the only sane course, there were still a number of fanatics left in Japan. In protest of the emperor's broadcast announcing the surrender, the outgoing class of *kamikaze* pilots mutinied and invaded the grounds of the Imperial Palace, killed several Imperial guards, and fired on the house of the prime minister before being subdued. There was considerable concern on the American side that the landing of MacArthur and U.S. troops in Japan would be resisted.

In the event, the Americans were astounded by their docile reception from the Japanese people. One Marine's diary written just after the surrender and cited in *The Spirit of Semper Fidelies* by Rick Sooner tells of an advance Marine regiment moving down a street in Yokahama in a column of files with slung but loaded M-1s and fixed bayonets.

> The scene was one of complete devastation. Japanese civilians and a few soldiers lined the route of march. They stared but showed no animosity or emotion. Their faces were ashen and their expressions blank. They surprised us by courteously bowing low as we passed. They were quiet and docile. Was this the vicious, brutal, fanatical enemy that we had fought for so long? How could this be possible?

The key to understanding Japan's docile acceptance of surrender and subsequent acquiescence to occupation seems to have come from the respect the Japanese had for MacArthur and from Emperor Hirohito. MacArthur treated Hirohito with dignity, and Manchester maintains that this consideration was deeply appreciated by the Japanese people. James Webb, in his marvelous and historically accurate novel *The Emperor's General*, describes how the emperor at a meeting of the Diet in the first months of the occupation made it clear that he expected the Japanese people to *peacefully* abide by the terms of the Potsdam Declaration just as the other side would be careful in its enforcement. "Then it will be possible," he said, "for us to rebuild in all areas and to keep our national structure." At the end of his speech he announced: "I have written a poem for our people." The members of the Diet buzzed with anticipation. It was customary for the emperor to communicate his sincerest emotions through such 31-syllable tankas.

> Courageous the pine
> That does not change in color
> Under the winter snow
> And truly the men of Japan
> Should be a forest of pines.

The members of the Diet murmured their admiration, rose as one, and bowed deeply to the emperor. His coded message was that the Japanese people were like the forest pines and the American occupiers were the winter snow bringing a temporary whiteness to the pines. However, spring would come and the snow would melt and be gone. Japan, however, was like the trees. It would endure and be stronger and become a forest. That, of course, is exactly what happened. There was no resistance to the occupation, and Japan rose from the ashes healthier and stronger than before.

Japanese Stocks Prevailed over the Very Long Term

Equities have been a fine store of value and wealth enhancement over the long term in Japan. Economic growth in Japan since the Meiji Restoration in 1867 has been more rapid than in any major Western economy including the U.S., but it has also been very volatile and cyclical. As noted earlier, from 1944 to 1946 GDP fell sharply, and then from 1950 to 1990 it soared. Since then growth has stagnated, and now it is generally agreed Japan's future trend line real GDP growth is probably not much more than 1.5% because of its declining population and workforce. We shall see if the demographic gloom-sayers are correct.

For the full span of the twentieth century, despite total defeat, occupation, and three very severe and long-lasting bear markets, Japanese equities provided an annual *real* return of 4.6% as calculated by Smithers & Company or 5.0% as reported by the London School of Business and ABN Amro's *Millennium Book II: 101 Years of Investment Returns.* For the last half of the twentieth century, stocks had a return of 9.1% *real* per year despite ending the century with a 10-year, secular bear market. In the first part of the twentieth century, from 1899 to 1942, stocks posted an annual real return of 6.5% but then from 1942 to 1946 fell 32% a year in real terms.

Andrew Smithers, in a paper written in 2004, argues that rapidly growing economies tend to have rising real exchange rates because of the Balassa-Samuelson effect—whatever that is. He calculates that from 1899 to 1942 the real return for a Japanese investor in yen was 6.48% a year but for a foreign investor, the appreciating yen added about 0.90% a year so the real annual return for a foreigner was 7.38%. Then from 1942 to 1946 as the economy withered and declined, the yen fell and the real return reversed to a minus 31.81% a year for the local investor and a minus 43.68% for a hypothetical foreigner. From 1950 to 2000 the real return for locals was 9.1% annually and the yen added another 1.10% per annum so the total real return for an international investor was 10.2%. Don't be fooled by the apparent precision of these numbers.

What matter is that the returns for Japanese stocks for the full century and particularly for the second half are spectacular. However, as in Germany in modern times, there was one four-year period in Japan from 1943 to 1947 when stocks were at first effectively subject to price controls, and then in the initial years of the occupation there was no market. Because of the long price breaks when the market was closed after 1945 and the inaccuracy of the inflation data, Figure 8.3 is far from precise, but it does convey the divergence and illusion of nominal and real returns during the war years.

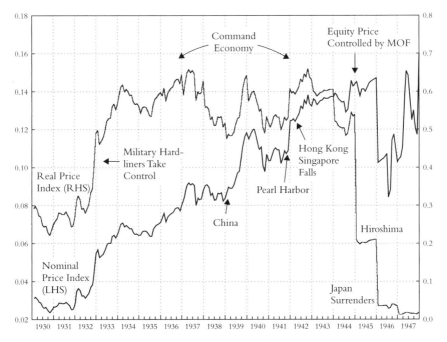

Figure 8.3   Japan Stock Market Price Index: 1930–1947 (Real and Nominal)
DATA SOURCE: Citigroup; Credit Suisse; Traxis Partner LLC.

Can stocks be considered a true store of value if you can't sell them at any reasonable price for several years, particularly since those periods coincide with the most extreme distress and therefore are the times of an investor's greatest need for liquidity? The answer seems obvious: In those dark circumstances they fail the liquidity test, but the truth is so does everything else except maybe gold and jewelry.

Could you have swapped even gold for food in Japan in those first bitterly cold postwar winters? Those that were there say that warm clothes and food were the most desirable barter items. People wanted to first cure being cold and hungry before they became greedy for possessions. One European family that lived through the war in Japan found that the exchange rate for clothes was much higher than that for jewelry, and they survived the hungry years by bartering their large inventory of sweaters and overcoats for food.

There was one other asset class in Japan that functioned to preserve wealth during the war years and enhance it afterwards: commercial and residential land. Japan is the only major industrial country where homes are a depreciating rather than an appreciating asset. The average Japanese house has no value after around 30 years because it is built principally of wood and because new houses can be built cheaply and quickly. Prior to World War II about 20% of the population owned homes, and well-maintained houses were regularly bought and sold, held value against inflation, and were a store of wealth.

But the total destruction of so many cities during the war and the desperate need for shelter in the early postwar year compelled the government to implement measures to encourage home building. This resulted in massive construction of cheap dwellings and an oversupply of houses. Thus old, depreciating homes had little resale value. Even today the ratio of existing home transactions to housing starts is only 0.25 in Japan versus 3.8 in the U.S. and 7.5 in the U.K. Six-tenths of 1% of the Japanese stock of existing homes is traded, as compared to 10 times that in both the U.S. and the U.K. Thus the percentage of household net worth in nonfinancial assets is far less in Japan, and the average Japanese has to rely solely on pensions and financial assets for his or her old-age nest egg. This unquestionably fosters insecurity and perhaps is why the *Momma-sans* are such speculators.

By contrast, in postwar Japan, commercial and residential land has been a magnificent investment. From 1950 to 1990, while nominal income rose 50 times, land prices climbed 330 times. Since 1990 when the bubble burst, prices have had a major decline but recently have begun to rise again. Thus, if in 1940, you had your wealth in land, you preserved your wealth, albeit in an illiquid form, during the war years. Then, after the war, as described previously, if you owned agricultural land, you were forced by the MacArthur administration to sell your acreage to the government at a deeply distressed price so farm land didn't work as a wealth preserver.

However commercial, industrial, and residential land especially in Tokyo and Osaka was a different story. You had to hang on, even as the structures on it were incinerated by the firebombing, and believe that Japan would rise from the ashes. After the war, you didn't have to sell it to the government, and when the post-war boom came you became incredibly rich as property values soared to unimaginable heights. Indeed, the guys who bought (and top-ticked) the trophy art masterpieces were mostly real-estate lucky tycoons. Land! Land! Land! But who could have foreseen that farm land was not going to work and that commercial real estate was.

After all is said and done, considering the enormity of the calamity that was World War II, Japanese equities and land did an impressive job of preserving and enhancing real wealth *over the long run*.

Chapter 9

The Four Horsemen
of the Apocalypse
Ride Again

*What Happened to Wealth in the Countries
Germany Occupied*

According to the Book of Revelation, the Four Horsemen of the Apocalypse are War, Famine, Pestilence, and Death. In the fifth decade of the twentieth century they rode again. Their previous appearance was during World War I, which caused millions of senseless, trench warfare deaths, hyperinflation in Germany, and an aftermath of hatred and revenge that led to World War II. The Book of Revelation, written 2,000 years earlier, could not foresee that the secondary consequences of the Four Horsemen's second ride would be the greatest onslaught of killing, an even longer war, more extensive occupation, persecution, famine, pestilence . . . and massive wealth destruction.

A Comparison of Global Stock Markets in the Twentieth Century

One way to look at and study wealth destruction is to take a big-picture look at various stock markets in different countries, over the very long-term—such as the entire twentieth century. Several years ago, William Goetzmann of the Yale School of Management and Philippe Jorion of the University of California did exactly that, when they published an article entitled, "A Century of Global Stock Markets." The study focuses on the countries for which they could find good stock market and inflation data back to 1921. Of these, only five (the U.S., Canada, the U.K., New Zealand, and Sweden) experienced no interruption in trading in that 85-year period. Nine had a break in trading that lasted at least six months, and seven suffered a long-term closure lasting years related to war, invasion, or revolution. In addition, there were 11 other occurrences of permanent breaks, or what the authors call a "death." They define a death as being when a stock market is closed and never restarted again in its existing form. Hungary, Czechoslovakia, Romania, Poland, and Finland are all markets that died when they were controlled by the Soviet Union (although all have since been reincarnated).

Such private wealth havens as Hong Kong and Singapore (occupation by Japan in 1942–1945) also suffered deaths. The Argentine stock market, the darling of emerging market investors throughout much of the first half of the twentieth century, was shut for 10 years between 1965 and 1975. Spain was down for four years during its civil war, and Austria for eight years. In addition, the equity markets in Norway, Denmark, the Netherlands, France, Belgium, Greece, Czechoslovakia, and Poland were shut when their parent country surrendered. Although they were reopened subsequently by the occupying authorities, they were barely functional and had virtually no liquidity. In each case the equity market had already had at least a 20% decline and usually more in the 12 months before they were closed.

Using the *Millennium Book*'s calculations of *real* (after inflation) returns for the period 1900 to 2000, the real return from equities markets in countries that were not defeated or occupied during World War II and that did not have hyperinflation episodes was 6.5% per annum in local currency terms and 6.2% in dollars. These are total returns including reinvested income. Over the century, U.S. equities are calculated to have had a 6.9% real return. Providing confirmation of this number, Shiller has updated the S&P 500 Index for new data and historic revisions to the Consumer Price Index and calculates an almost identical 7% real return for the twentieth century. A seven percent real long-term is a very impressive return number. It means that the purchasing power of money invested in stocks doubles every 10.5 years and quadruples in a little over 20 years. Spectacular!

However, Andrew Smithers argues that using 1900 as a starting date is misleading because the years immediately before 1900 were very lean. From 1871 to 1900 in the U.S. the real return for equities was only 3.02% per annum. Inflation for those years was minus 1.57%, which means equity had a nominal return of a mere 1.45% annually. As a result, as calculated by Smithers the linked real return from 1871 to 2004 was 5.75% real and 7.81% nominal. Good but not spectacular. However, I question whether the data for the nineteenth century is accurate and where you start measuring from is always a problem.

Figure 9.1 shows that for the century, the long-term real annual return from equities in the *stable and lucky* countries was about 6.5%. What does "stable" mean? It means that the country has all the usual cyclical slings and arrows of outrageous economic fortune but did not lose a war, was not occupied by a conqueror, did not have an episode of hyperinflation, and was not ravaged by a civil war. In the 1930s every country had at least a whiff of the world-wide deflation.

As for the future, the countries that posted these results in the twentieth century are now bigger and more mature economies. Furthermore, many of them currently are demographically challenged in that their populations and workforces are declining instead of growing. Realistically unless these demographic plagues reverse (which is certainly possible), these countries can expect only trend line real GDP growth of perhaps 1.5% to 2% derived from 2% to 2.5% productivity growth and a labor pool that is flat to down 0.5%. Thus long-term real corporate profits and dividends could expand 2% to 3% per annum, which suggests it will be difficult to have stock markets that are solving for 7% real returns.

	Equities	Bonds	Bills	Inflation	Equities Std Dev
Australia	7.6	1.0	0.4	4.0	17.7
Canada	6.4	1.8	1.7	3.1	16.9
Ireland	5.5	1.6	1.3	4.5	24.3
Switzerland★	5.0	2.8	1.1	2.2	20.4
Sweden	8.2	2.3	2.0	3.7	23.4
UK	5.9	1.3	1.0	4.1	20.0
USA	6.9	1.5	1.1	3.2	20.4
Average	6.5	1.8	1.2	3.5	20.4

Figure 9.1   The Stable Lucky Ones: Annualized Real Returns per Year (%), 1900–2000
★From 1911
SOURCE: *Millennium Book II; ABN Amro.*

In the future, the high-growth economies of the world will be what are now called "developing countries" or "emerging markets." With rapidly growing populations, workforces, and rising productivity, they have the ingredients to be the best stock markets. It is hard to argue with the arithmetic of real GDP growth and real earnings growth. In other words, the country lineup will have to be periodically refreshed with successful, stable emerging market entries. But just being a developing country does not mean you will automatically be able to produce the required success and stability.

The individual country total returns (including dividends and interest) on stocks, bonds, bills and the inflation rate for the century are shown in Figures 9.1 and 9.2. The data is derived from the *Millennium Book II* by Elroy Dimson, Paul Marsh, and Mike Staunton and copublished by ABN Amro and the London Business School. It is *the* study of financial asset returns in the twentieth century and a monumental work. All returns in Figures 9.1 and 9.2 are expressed in local currency terms adjusted for inflation. They do not correspond to the returns that would have been achieved by an unhedged foreign investor. Figures 9.1 and 9.2 are derived from the book, but the groupings, calculations, and the conclusions (and errors) are mine. Figure 9.1 shows the results for those countries that could be called the Stable Lucky Ones.

Figure 9.2 reveals the same data for countries that were defeated, occupied, and in some cases had hyperinflation episodes. Spain was not

	Stocks	Bonds	Bills	Infl	Std Dev Eq
Belgium	2.7	−0.5	−0.4	5.6	17.7
Denmark	5.1	2.8	2.9	4.0	21.4
France	4.0	−1.1	−3.4	8.0	23.2
Germany	3.7	−2.3	−0.6	5.2	32.2
Italy	2.7	−2.3	−4.1	9.2	29.4
Japan	5.0	−1.6	−2.1	7.7	30.3
Netherlands	5.9	1.1	0.7	3.0	21.0
Spain	4.7	1.2	0.4	6.2	21.7
Average	4.2	−0.3	−0.8	6.1	24.6

Figure 9.2   The Losers: Annualized Real Returns per Year (%), 1900–2000
Source: *Millennium Book II; ABN Amro.*

a victim of World War II, but it did have a long, bitter, and brutal civil war that disrupted the society and was really a prelude to World War II. Both Japan and Germany generated strong gains in the second half of the century and dim or minimal real returns in the first half.

Figures 9.1 and 9.2 clearly demonstrate the superiority of stocks over bonds and bills over the course of the last century. Equities in the Lucky Countries (refer again to Figure 9.1), in addition to earning 650 basis points a year of real returns, returned almost 500 basis points more than government bonds. Equities in The Lucky Countries returned 230 basis points a year more than those in "The Losers" (refer again to Figure 9.2) and had less volatility in their returns (20.4% versus 24.6%).

Make no mistake, 230 basis points a year compounded over a century is a huge deal. Losing wars and being occupied is deleterious to the long-term real returns of domestic equity investors, and plunges financial markets into secular bear spasms. It is also debilitating in that as the table shows, it results in negative returns for government bonds and bills. Conversely, the Luckies' government bonds and bills had positive real returns over the course of the century. These real returns in government-issued financial assets nourished investor confidence, which made the financial and economic management of those countries much easier and less expensive.

As you would expect, the standard deviation of the Luckies' bonds was less than that of stocks, but in most countries, not dramatically less.

For example, in Australia the standard deviation of equities was 17.7% and of bonds 13.0%. The U.K. relationships are somewhat similar. Only in the U.S. did bonds have a significantly different standard deviation (9.9% versus 20.4%).

The Losers and the Vanquished paid a high price for their misadventures and sins. Their lower equity returns speak for themselves, but it is intriguing to see that the stock markets of dynamic countries like Germany and Japan, despite enormous national tragedies, had spectacular surges after the bad times were over. Neither resisted their occupations and instead concentrated on rebuilding their shattered economies. As a result, wealth creation began all over again. As Iraq has demonstrated, resistance and internal factional warfare can prolong the agony. However, in general, the investment world is mercenary, has a short memory, and forgives quickly.

All these numbers show the rewards of political stability, of winning wars and of not having hyperinflation episodes. Inflation was almost twice again as high in the Losers as in the Luckies. Who would have thought that Sweden, a perpetually neutral and profoundly Socialist country, would be the best equity market of the twentieth century? But perhaps staying neutral at all costs and avoiding political upheaval and unrest by a drift left to benevolent Socialism are the recipe for stock market prosperity.

Diversification Is Always Critical

The Crash of 1929 and the Great Depression of the 1930s affected almost everyone, but if you kept your nerve, hung onto a diversified portfolio or an index fund, and if you had not been a speculator, you at least preserved some wealth. However, you had to have staying power and **patience.** Ambrose Bierce in *The Devil's Dictionary* describes patience as "a minor form of despair disguised as a virtue," and certainly the despair at the wealth losses in the long depths of the Depression must have been almost overpowering.

Notice the reference above to owning an index fund to insure you are going to capture the secular real return seemingly embedded in equities. The rewards of active management are spotty, its costs are high, and an index fund that charges eight or ten basis points is a great alternative for everyone but the professional investor. Stock market history every time, everywhere warns of the obsolescence factor in corporate life and that no business is forever and that no portfolio is eternally diversified. There were stocks that were blue chips in the 1920s that never emerged from the Depression because time and progress had rendered obsolete their business models. Index funds are periodically refreshed. The average life of a company in the S&P 500 Index has gone from about 35 years in the 1950s to 10 to 15 years today.

The other cataclysm was World War II, which was a far sterner test for financial assets than even the Great Depression. The record is clear. The Winner countries in the end did fine particularly with stocks but also with bonds, although there were some anxious moments. The U.S. and British stock markets were amazingly prescient in sensing the precise turning points in the long war struggle. However, the real test for financial assets as a purchasing power haven was what happened to the Losers (Germany, Japan, and Italy) and the Occupied Vanquished (Belgium, Denmark, France, the Netherlands, and Spain). Here the record is less clear. Of course there were other countries that were surrendered both in Europe and Asia, but solid data on returns is not available from them.

Occupation and Exploitation of the Countries Germany Conquered

In late 1940, with most of Western Europe subjugated and plans for an attack on Russia hatching in the back of his mind, Hitler convened a meeting in the Great Hall of the Reich Chancellery. The splendor of the vast chamber conveyed the power of the state; its wealth and strength expressed in immense chandeliers of glittering crystal, marble walls hung with heroic Teutonic art, vast red drapes, and acres of thick brown and rose oriental carpet. Stationed by the door, foot men dressed in black with gold braid, white stocking, and black pump slippers (who in actuality were members of the SS) respectfully but with a vague menace checked identification. Two hundred of the Nazi leadership elite, bedecked with medals, were present, each in a seemingly more elaborate uniform. Who couldn't believe in a Thousand Year Reich in this, the temple of the Master Race?

The Führer, Adolph Hitler, dressed in a plain brown uniform which stood out in its simplicity, entered the chancellery when all were seated. No national leader in modern times with the possible exception of Ronald Reagan has had his sense of theater and his ability to project himself as a visionary. His deep blue eyes fascinated his audience. At first he spoke quietly and then, gesticulating, his voice rising with passion, he laid out his grand vision for the new Germany and Europe. The Greater German Reich would be a European empire. Germany must have living space, the *lebensraum,* and she would achieve her destiny by expanding to the east and annexing vast regions of the Soviet Union, specifically the Ukraine, the Volga Basin, and the Crimea, which were rich in raw materials, food stuffs, and oil.

During World War I, the Kaiser's government alienated the German people by neglecting the welfare of soldiers' families. With their provider at the front, family welfare payments were below the subsistence level. Food prices soared because of meager harvests, and the obliviousness of the Wilhelmine government to the agony of the working class resulted in a deep antagonism that contributed to the post war social chaos. Hitler vowed this would not happen again and that the conquered lands would be looted not just riches and industrial materials but also for food.

These new territories would have to be purged of the their present populations, the despised, subhuman Slavs, the *untermenschen,* who would be prohibited from propagating and educated only enough so that they could understand German orders and "learn traffic signals." These regions would be populated by peasant soldiers of Aryan blood from the West, much the way the American West was settled. Sexual relations between a Slav man and an Aryan woman would be punished by death by hanging for the Slav and humiliation for the Aryan. (Presumably sex the other way round was okay.) Eventually, he said, these new territories would have a population of one hundred million Germans served by perhaps twenty five million *untermenschen* slaves. He ended dramatically, almost in a whisper: "It will take a generation to accomplish all this. I know I will not live to see it."

But Hitler's grand design also envisioned expansion to the West. He had become convinced that the people of Norway, Denmark, Finland,

Holland, and Flemish Belgium had some Aryan blood and so were racially related to the Germans. Their language was somewhat similar to German, and often their physical appearance was Germanic. In his speech to the Nazi leaders he noted that Nazi ideals already had taken some root in these countries, that their men were volunteering for military duty with the German army, and that many of their towns and cities had German names. The Reich should also encourage Germans who had migrated to North and South America and Australia to return to the Fatherland to participate in the new empire.

The conquered countries, he said, should be occupied and *exploited* but always bearing in mind that at some time in the future they would become part of the Greater Germany Reich. A commissioner and a small cadre of administrators would be inserted to supervise economic activities, and the SS would run civil services such as the police. Compliant national puppets would be installed and allowed to have the appearance of ruling, and the existing order in these countries should not be left alone as much as possible.

The English, he added, because of their native recalcitrance, would be subjected to a harsher regimen.

At this meeting and in informal chats thereafter, Hitler let it be known that "the nobles" of the Third Reich would be granted by the state large estates in the occupied countries that would be worked by slave labor. Although Hitler was always suspicious of the Army officer corps, he told certain of his favorite generals to look around for a spread they would like. One of Hitler's favorites, General Guderian—between commanding an army on the Eastern Front and becoming panzer inspector general—spent several months touring the occupied territories looking for a suitable estate. This program presumably purchased the loyalty of officials and generals by making them rich and was a direct expropriation of the property of the landed wealthy in Eastern Europe.

Moreover, by early 1941, Air Marshal Goring, puffed up with the glory of the exploits of the *Luftwaffe,* was preaching a far harsher occupation message. At the time, Goring had been anointed by Hitler as his most senior deputy and was even challenging the Führer on certain issues. While speaking to a meeting of the Occupation Commissioners, the air marshal bulging out of his ornate, custom tailored uniform with a chest-full of decorations, called a spade a spade and unleashed the jackals of the SS. He specifically said that he "scorned the word *exploitation*." "It used to be called *plundering*," he said, "but today things have become more humane. In spite of that, I intend to *plunder*, and to do it thoroughly." The manpower, the production of the private economies, the wealth, and the precious possessions of the occupied countries were to be seized and used to support the German war machine and for the personal enrichment of the Nazi leaders, including the commissioners. The wealth of Jews was to be expropriated without mercy. This mandate from on high sanctioning looting created an extremely perilous environment for wealth in the occupied countries.

As will be discussed, financial asset prices in some of the countries that were occupied by the Germans suffered, but in other cases equities were reasonably effective wealth preservers—under the circumstances. The small stock exchanges in Austria, Czechoslovakia, Greece, Poland, Romania, and Hungary suffered steep declines as war loomed and than were closed, and simply disappeared, in some cases forever. Equities obviously failed to preserve wealth in these countries, and in the countries that ended the war as Soviet satellites behind the Iron Curtain, even privately owned equity stakes became worthless.

The Dutch Economy: Food Was the Best Currency

The Dutch market was a different matter. The Amsterdam Exchange had a long tradition, and by 1940 there was a strong equity culture in Holland. After declining steeply in the worldwide depression and bear market of the early 1930s, the 50-stock weighted CBS Index rallied throughout the late 1930s and right into the spring of 1940. The Dutch believed Hitler would leave them alone because they had been pro-German in World War I, and because their system of dikes and water sluices made Holland a tough nut to crack. They were terribly wrong, but they were relatively lucky after the surrender as Holland was favored with a form of civilian rule—at least for a while.

Hitler remembered that the Dutch had been neutral in World War I and at the end of that war had adopted many young Germans who were suffering from malnutrition. He saw the Dutch as a fellow Aryan race to be integrated into the Reich, and there were a number of pro-Nazi

Dutch. Two of the most prominent were Anton Mussert who schemed to run Holland as an enlarged German province, and Meinhoud von Tonnigen who shamelessly cooperated with the SS and argued to settle Dutch farmers in the rich agricultural lands of the Ukraine.

Both Mussert and von Tonnigen above all wanted to enrich themselves, and the two men competed to expropriate wealth. They used trumped up charges to seize businesses of prosperous Dutch families, particularly Jewish families. Prominence of wealth was a real liability. Holland had always treated Jews decently, and the SS's arrests and deportation to death camps of Jews aroused resistance from the Dutch. The most famous sheltering, of course, was the case of Anne Frank. However, it is estimated that of the 120,000 Dutch Jews, about 100,000 were exterminated and their possessions stolen by the Germans and unscrupulous Dutch.

Because of Hitler's objective of integration, initially the German administration of Holland was perhaps the most enlightened of that of any of the occupied countries. Arthur Seyss-Inquart, an Austrian who was appointed as Reich Commissioner in May of 1940, was an accomplished and experienced bureaucrat. He was thrilled to learn of his appointment. He jubilantly told his wife: "Trude, the Führer wants me to go and plant tulips!" Seyess-Inquart permitted political freedom "within reason," and established a system of parallel control where a small number of German administrators worked side by side with Dutch civil servants.

However as time went on, the Dutch resistance movement grew. In February of 1941 a nationwide strike was called that briefly paralyzed the country. The Germans brutally broke it with troops, and the Gestapo, aided by von Tonningen, arrested the instigators, brutally tortured them, and then sent them to the camps in Poland where they were worked to death in a month. As the Resistance grew and sabotage and murder increased, Seyss-Inquart, implemented a policy of executing a hundred Dutchmen for every German solider murdered, and he became known as the "Butcher of Holland."

Holland in 1939 was a huge net exporter of food stuffs, but the Germans stripped the country of its crops, and throughout the war years food was scarce in the Netherlands. By 1944 agricultural inventories were nonexistent, and that fall the entire harvest went to Germany.

In the brutal winter of 1944–1945 a desperate famine ensued. It is estimated that more than 100,000 Dutch civilians literally starved to death, and the food shortages lasted into the late 1940s.

The Amsterdam stock market was shut for four months from May 1940 until September when it was reopened. Trading during the war was limited, and the index was flat in nominal terms until the exchange was closed in August 1944. However, according to ABN Amro in real terms it fell about 15% during the war years, and this figure is probably understated. Nevertheless in real terms Dutch equities were higher in August 1944 when the market was closed than they were at their 1929 peak or than they were during most of the 1930s.

However, you couldn't eat stock certificates, and food was what people had to have to survive. To that extent, stocks didn't work. Food was the best currency in the latter years of the war. The stock market was reopened in April 1946. Dutch government bonds also were decent investments. They had small, regular negative real returns but they were far better than the government paper of the other occupied countries.

Owning a business in the German occupied countries worked fairly well. Many families in Holland were able to keep their homes, land, and small enterprises during the occupation years and emerge from the war in reasonably good financial shape. The trouble with owning real assets was that if you were a Jew, a member of the resistance, or "an enemy of the state" the first thing the Nazis or the Soviets did was to seize your properties. Sometimes you were able to recover them after the war; often there was nothing left or your ownership was hard to prove.

Occupation by the Nazis was a searing experience and there were secondary consequences that resulted in personal distress and even wealth destruction. For example, a Dutchman known as Jan to the author had a prosperous farm machinery business. In January of 1944, a German soldier was killed at night in an adjacent village. Early the next morning, a squad of Germans under the command of a sergeant suddenly appeared in Jan's neighborhood. Although he was not aware of the killing, sensing trouble, he hid upstairs in an attic loft while his wife went to meet them.

"A German soldier has been murdered. A hundred hostages are to be taken. Where is your man?"

"He's away," she told him.

"Of course. So we will search your house, Fraulein."

To make a long story short, Jan's wife invited the sergeant in for coffee and then seduced him. As her intent became apparent, the sergeant sent his men to the next house, and after a passionate morning neither he nor his men came back. A hundred men were shot that afternoon, but Jan was saved. But he had heard and virtually been witness to the whole affair, and he and his wife were never able to put it behind them: nightmares, guilt, obligation, and so forth. After the war, Jan began to drink heavily and his once prosperous business collapsed. He later asphyxiated himself in his car.

Denmark and Belgium: The Stock Market Survives

The Danes, realizing the futility of resisting, surrendered quickly and accepted Germany's lenient occupation terms. As a result, Denmark had a relatively enlightened military government under a career diplomat, Cecil von Renthe-Fink, and a staff of only one hundred. The market was closed for only two months in 1940, but as was the case in the Netherlands, had a steep decline just prior to the shutdown as fear of the occupation spooked investors.

However, after reopening, Danish stocks rose about in line with published inflation during the occupation years so investors didn't lose purchasing power value and equities worked as wealth preservers. In fact, in real terms Danish stocks in 1950 were about where they were in 1930. As in other countries in occupied Europe, there was an active black market during the war years, and in all probability stocks did lose purchasing power value versus the really scarce essentials such as food and medicine.

Belgium was another story. The commissioner, General Baron Alexander von Falkenhausen disliked the Nazis in general and the SS and the Gestapo in particular. He and his administrator ran a reasonably gentle, hands-off government. Unfortunately he became involved in one of the unsuccessful conspiracies against Hitler, and ended up in a concentration camp. During the occupation years, the Brussels market was flat in nominal terms but declined steadily in real terms. Over the long run, equities in Belgium have been volatile and have not been particularly good wealth enhancers.

Next we turn to France, which is a far more complicated saga.

Chapter 10

France Declines Financially, Economically, and Socially

Neither the French people nor the French stock market were wise in the 1940s. Both were suckered by the Germans. As shown in Figures 10.1 and 10.2, along with the rest of the world, the Paris stock market had a steep decline in the early 1930s, but unlike most other markets there were no sustained rallies to speak of. In fact, the market drifted lower, and as war loomed in the late 1930s, prices were considerably below their 1930 highs both in nominal and in real terms. This insipid performance reflected the malaise, the mood of national self-doubt, which had been brewing in France for a long time and had been deepened by 20 years of political chaos and disappointment with the supposed spoils of the victory in World War I.

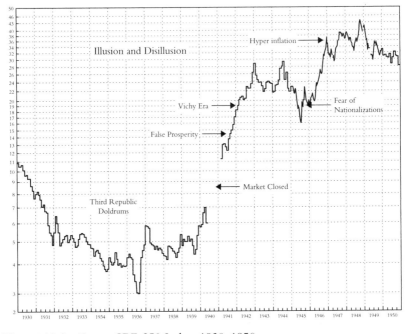

Figure 10.1   France SBF-250 Index: 1930–1950
DATA SOURCE: Global Financial Data, Inc.

The Third Republic, as the government that ruled France during the 1930s was known as, was an unhappy, failed government of "flaccid parliamentarism." [sic] It was disparaged as "the regime of palaver" that was "too spineless and too indulgent to narrow self interest" to ever address the great national issues that plagued France, specifically slow economic growth, unemployment, and a plunging birth rate. France still remembered the two million dead in the mindless slaughter of trench warfare, and the horror of farm boys maiming themselves with self-inflicted wounds and then being staked out between the lines. The legacy of war was strikes in the factories, mutinies in the army, and Socialist politics. Manufacturing productivity was abysmal, and German soldiers in 1940 were astounded to see French farms using agricultural methods that were 50 years out of date.

So France, like its stock market, sulked listlessly through the 1930s. The Catholic middle class was appalled by the degenerate, sordidness of

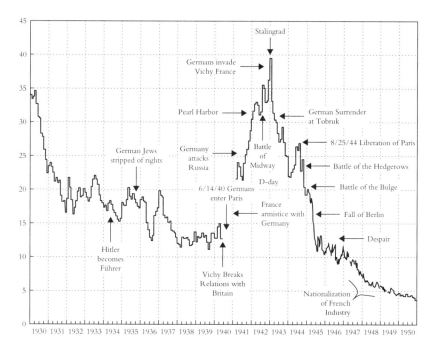

Figure 10.2   France SBF-250 Index, Adjusted for Inflation: 1930–1950
DATA SOURCE: Global Financial Data, Inc./Traxis Partners LLC.

Paris nightlife with its jazz, drunkenness, short skirts, promiscuity, birth control, and the general moral depravity. They despised the new intellectuals such as Leon Blum who had ridiculed marriage; Jean Cocteau, whose play *Les Parents terribles* undermined the authority of parents; and Andre Gide and his concept of libertine self-fulfillment. Paul Valery, a prominent journalist, wrote that the irony was those very features that had made France so delightful and artistically creative had ill-fitted her for the new harsh age she now lived in.

As for the wealthy aristocrats and the Catholic Church, both felt desperately threatened by Communism in general and the Soviet Union in particular. They had watched with more than a touch of envy the success of National Socialism and the rise of authoritarian rule in Germany and Italy. Dictators might be a little rough around certain edges, but they created order and at least they made things work. There was a strong anti-Semitic strain in French life, and the elite rationalized away events like the Nuremberg Race Laws, enacted on September 15, 1935, which stripped German Jews of their civil rights.

The crushing defeat of 1940 brought all this dissatisfaction with the existing order of French life—social, economic, and political—gushing to the surface. That summer it was estimated 10 million people, 25% of the French population, was wandering aimlessly across the country, scavenging for food like nomads, trying to escape the Germans, and stealing and looting. There was no government, no police, or respect for property. Disbanded groups of French soldiers were among the worst offenders. By contrast, the German soldiers appeared fit, disciplined, and their behavior was invariably "correct." At that time they were under strict orders to do no looting and to pay for everything with German Marks. The soldiers agreeably accepted higher prices at stores, and merchants welcomed their business.

France in Chaos Welcomes the German Occupation

The great mass of the French people now were thoroughly frightened by the social and economic chaos. As they tried to sort out the wreckage of their lives, they were ready to accept discipline and even some loss of liberty in return for normalcy and order. They came to believe Hitler and Germany represented order and stability, and in addition there was the prospect of substantial business from the surging German economy. After all, General Maxime Weygand, commander of the French army, in a widely cited remark, had said: "England will have her neck wrung like a chicken." "Ah," remarked Churchill quoting the comment in a speech in December 1941 to the Canadian parliament, "some chicken!" Then pausing for dramatic effect as the audience laughed: "some neck!" The crowd roared!

Of course Germany was France's historic enemy, but it appeared that Germany would dominate Europe for the foreseeable future. It was questionable if England would even survive much less be able to liberate Europe. The joke in France in 1940 was, "*les Anglais?* Have you seen the English?" Of course the punch line was that no one had because the English had run back to their boats and fled to England. What kind of an ally was that?

Simone de Beauvoir quoted this witticism in her journal. She also commented admiringly on the German soldiers in their *beaux uniformes* that matched their *belles autos*. She scornfully remarked that the English were in such a hurry to flee that they had left behind masses of everything from cigarettes to petrol. So logically the French asked: Was an alliance with Germany collaboration or was it the acceptance of reality? In July 1940 André Gide, ever the cynical social observer, commented that if German dominance meant abundance, 90% of all Frenchmen would accept it, 75% with a smile.

There is nothing to be gained from recounting the sordid political machinations that surrounded the armistice and the creation of Vichy France with Marshal Philippe Petain, the aged hero of World War I, as the new dictator. In the long debate, Pierre Laval, the shrewd architect of the new Vichy era and a French Mussolini, bluntly told the deputies of the new reality and warned that the old system of a multiparty, democratic form of government was over.

> We are going to destroy the totality of what was. We're going to create something entirely different. Either you accept what we demand and align yourself with a German or Italian constitution or Hitler will impose it on you. Henceforth there will be only one party, that of all the French. We are paying today for the fetish which chained us to democracy and led us to the worse excesses of capitalism, while all around us Europe was forging, without us, a new world.

Marshal Petain was a figure steeped in French history. Born in a peasant family, he had spent his entire life in the army. The "hero of Verdun," in 1917 he had restored discipline and morale to the shattered French army by refusing to execute frontal attacks against machine guns to gain a few hundred yards of mud. As a result he was a beloved by the army and by the people and became a national icon. By all accounts he was a stupid man. His military books had been ghostwritten by junior officers. One officer, Colonel Charles de Gaulle, had refused "the honor" of ghostwriting for Petain because he despised him. However, in 1940 when de Gaulle formed his Free French brigade only 35,000 soldiers joined him.

The marshal was an imposing, dignified figure; straight as a ramrod with a bushy white mustache and a firm, paternal gaze. Although he was almost 90 in 1940, he was still vigorous, alert, and lecherous. He had famously remarked that "in life sex and food are the only things that matter." Petain also had an immense ego. He believed he was indispensable, and in June 1940, in a radio message to the French people pompously announced that he had given France "the gift of my person to alleviate her misfortunes." The French people, tired of paunchy politicians, loved it! Paul Johnson later wrote that "he quickly became the most popular French leader since Napoleon. He was treated like royalty. Women held out their babies for him to touch."

Under the Armistice of 1940, the Germans had agreed to a certain amount of economic freedom for the French economy. French employers ran their own companies and paid their workers. Lucrative contracts for armaments were dangled by the German government. By the fall of 1941, 900,000 Frenchmen were working for the Germans either building the Atlantic Wall Defense System or in arms and ammunitions plants. Another 250,000 were working in Germany for nominal wages. Everything seemed as before—only better, and for the first few years of the occupation, French businesses thought they could not only live but prosper from their association with their new military governor and German occupier. When it reopened in February of 1941, the Paris bourse quickly responded to the new optimism. France and French industry would be an important part of the new Europe run by Hitler and Germany. It was preferable to the chaos of the Third Republic and what choice had they anyway? At least corporate France was working for the winner and not only was old French wealth being maintained but finally, at last, new wealth was being created.

In the first two years of the war, life in France both in the occupied and Vichy zones was relatively serene. The Germans were model conquerors—at first. In the summer of 1940 when Paris' food supply was disrupted, they opened soup kitchens to feed the hungry population. The German troops were polite, well-disciplined, and went out of their way to be friendly. People began to think that being occupied wasn't so bad after all. An editorial proclaimed: "Vichy has done more reform in one year than the former regime failed lamentably to do in more than a century."

However, there were many who were disgusted. One writer described the atmosphere in the countryside as the Germans arrived and then in Paris as follows:

> The population gave the victors a hearty welcome, the girls waving their handkerchiefs and scarves at the athletic young men on motorcycles, handsome as gods, with laughter in their eyes.
>
> Things were not much different in Paris, I felt. The Opera and the Comedie-Française were playing to stalls packed with officers in full-dress uniforms. The cafes were crowded with shaven square skulls and Frenchmen unconcernedly drinking cheek by jowl. In the automobile-less streets, German soldiers, smartly dressed French women, and corpulent businessmen let themselves be towed in cycle cabs, there being no taxis. I could not bear the sight of my own fellow creatures reduced to beasts of burden, even with their own consent to this degradation.

In July of 1941 the Vichy government proposed to Germany that the armistice be rescinded and that a new treaty be written that provided for French sovereignty and military and economic cooperation with Germany. Marshal Petain (the 90-year-old hero of WWI who had been installed as dictator of the newly created Vichy France) and his deputies were clearly elated by the German attack on the "menacing evil" of the Soviet Union, and the destruction of the French fleet at Oran the year before by the British still rankled. Some of the German high command began to conceive of France as a budding ally and the "military western wall" of the German empire. Would Britain and her allies ever dare invade a France that was militarily allied with Germany with a combined population of almost 100 million? Wasn't England the historic enemy of both?

However, for whatever reason Hitler was not tempted. It was perhaps racial. The French were not Aryans. He had never spoken of France racially as part of the Greater German Reich, and there was no official response to the French proposal. It was a major mistake, similar to the error he made in treating the White Russians so harshly. If France and Germany had become allies, the Axis powers would have been greatly strengthened.

Confiscation of Property and Wealth from French Jews

Although many French people seemed complacent about the German occupation of France from the outset, there was nothing subtle about the treatment of the French Jews. All Jewish-owned property was summarily confiscated. Those wealthy Jews who could, fled. The three Rothschild brothers, Edouard, Robert, and Maurice, managed to get to the U.S. or to Britain. The French authorities blocked all transfers of money, but Maurice on his flight to London carried a satchel of antique jewelry worth about £300,000 in 1940 money (at least £4 million today), which he sold off to support his lifestyle and for working capital. The others had to rely on family charity, which inevitably wore thin after awhile.

In some cases wealthy Jews were able to bribe their way out. Georges Levin, a prominent and very wealthy French Jew, was picked up in a raid on a synagogue and found himself in a cell with 10 Jewish Socialists. A few days later when the Gestapo discovered who they had, Levin was moved to a relatively comfortable private cell in a Gestapo prison. His rations improved considerably. Then a man named Otto Weber who identified himself as an associate of a Dr. Gritzbach who in turn was an adviser to *Reichsmarschall* Hermann Goring came to see him. Weber told him that the Gestapo knew he had on deposit a substantial sum of money in the Zurich branch of his French bank. If the German state received a transfer of $2 million, he would be freed. However, said Weber, he needed an additional $200,000 in cash to compensate Goring for his trouble.

The deal was agreed to, but for a month nothing happened. Then one morning, Levin was visited by Heinrich Himmler. Himmler offered him a cigarette, and asked whether he had any complaints about his treatment. Himmler apologized for the delay and told him that Herr Weber had been arrested. He, Himmler, was now in charge of the case. The terms would be the same, and Himmler guaranteed his transfer to Spain from where he could easily travel to London or the United States. This time the money was transferred and Levin was transported to Madrid. Levin never unraveled what had happened between Goring, Himmler, and Weber but apparently the Nazis were settling some internecine struggle. In any case, Levin had done the right thing by keeping a large deposit in Switzerland.

After 1941, the Gestapo and the Vichy regime employed the French police as an enforcement tool in the rounding up of Jews. In Bordeaux an aristocratic, elegant, and pleasant French civil servant, *un fonctionnaire,* named Maurice Papon ruled. In his office with the tricolor furled behind his desk, he efficiently and dispassionately carried out the orders from Berlin and Vichy. In 1942 and 1943, he "dejudaised" more than 600 businesses and quietly arrested 1,700 Jews including 223 children who were then shipped out in sealed trains to a staging camp at Drancy in northern France. Where they went from there was not his affair. Establishing a *modus vivendi,* getting along, collaborating with the Germans was more widespread than was admitted after the war. If you fled France to save your skin, all your assets were summarily seized by the state just as in Germany, choosing exile was an expensive decision.

In fact, if you were a wealthy and conservative Frenchman, collaboration and a blind eye were the way to protect your assets and your status. After all, murmured many, weren't a lot of the Jews Socialists or even Communists and besides there was no proof the Germans would mistreat them. In one of the most shameful acts of police collaboration, 4,000 Jewish children of 12 and younger were brutally torn from their parents, loaded onto freight trains, and shipped to Auschwitz. The *gendarmes* later claimed they didn't know what was going to become of the children. A notorious anti-Semite in Vichy identified thousands of Jews and had them deported to death camps.

On the other hand, many French were courageous in their support of the Jews. Gentile students at universities wore the yellow star, papers were forged for Jews, Jews were hidden during searches, and many were sheltered for years in remote villages. Such bravery was very dangerous. In the end, Richard Vinen, author of the *The Unfree French: Life under the Occupation,* says that nearly 80% of the Jews in France survived the occupation.

France Profits from German Military Contracts

In the fall of 1940, French companies received from Germany what appeared to be lucrative orders for machine tools, tractors, trucks, milling machines, and capital goods. By 1941, unemployment had changed to labor scarcities, and production was rising. However, the two million French prisoners of war taken in the summer of 1940 had not been returned and were still working under grim conditions in Germany. Hitler and the Nazis remained determined to loot France, but at the outset it was done subtly.

In early 1941, senior management representatives and accountants from the large German firms like I.G. Farben, Siemens, and Krupp began visiting and studying the major French firms. Patents, equipment, and skilled workers were "temporarily" transferred to German companies. Nevertheless some French companies prospered mightily from their military contracts. Renault's factories were converted to building tanks for the Germans; Marius Berliet, a pioneer of the automobile industry, got a large contract for trucks for the German army. The price of these companies' shares climbed although it was noticed that German officers who had been tipped bought prior to the announcement of the contracts.

French businesses that needed funds were urged to raise capital. Bank loans were "not appropriate," but companies were encouraged to issue equity. The catch was that the new shares had to be sold at a discount to the occupation authorities, German companies, or officials of the SS and Hitler's cronies. The new stock was paid for with confiscated French francs or with Reich marks whose value had been arbitrarily and dramatically revalued upward versus the franc. A few French companies such as the locomotive manufacturer, Campagnie de Batignolles, and the automobile company, Peugot, were prosperous enough to avoid this fate, but most were not and had their equity diluted.

French investors were initially unperturbed as they believed having the Nazi officialdom with them as investors was a plus. The bourse (i.e., the stock exchange) soared; by the end of 1942 it had almost tripled in nominal terms. It still appeared that Germany was going to win the war or at least rule Europe for many years, and the reports of the German advances in the summer of 1942 toward Stalingrad and the oil fields was regarded as very good news: 50,000 French solders were fighting with the German army inside the Soviet Union. The French investor class had a deep aversion to and fear of the Soviet Union and Bolshevism. In addition there were rumors of gifts of stock to German officials of the occupation including the SS., and investors felt that this insured further gains for the shares. In the early years of the occupation, *stocks were the place to be* and there was rampant exchange of tips and inside information about German business interests.

France in 1942: Famine, Poverty, Inflation

However, all the illusions faded in time. It became apparent Hitler and the Nazis were planning not to partner with France but to plunder her. Forced labor laws were implemented that virtually compelled 600,000 more Frenchmen to go to Germany to work in factories under abysmal conditions for minimal wages. As a result of this forced exodus and the loss of several million soldiers in World War I, there was a severe shortage of young and middle-aged men in France to do manual labor and work farms. Food became in desperately short supply, and inflation began to rise astronomically.

With the population of France primarily female and the Germans controlling the food supply, young French women scrabbling to survive were vulnerable to the advances of German soldiers. It is estimated that 200,000 children were fathered by Germans during the occupation. After the liberation, their mothers suffered brutal punishments during *l'epuration*,"the sunset of blood" as Vinen calls it in *The Unfree French.* Their heads were shaved, they were paraded through the streets, spat on, manhandled, and physically abused. For the rest of their lives they were pariahs.

By 1942 most of France was hungry. The Germans were exporting massive amounts of food to Germany and to their armies on the Eastern Front and on the Western Wall. Vinen tells of 2,000 Parisians lined up to buy just 300 portions of rabbit. In other cities people stood in line at 3 a.m. only to find there was no food in the shops. A daughter of a judge married a peasant farmer from the Loire not for his money but for his food. Criminals masqueraded as German soldiers to extort food and fuel from their fellow citizens, and many people had to resort to the black market for food. Understandably, farmers sold what excess food they had to the highest bidder, and in effect the countryside benefited at the expense of the cities.

In the early 1940s in France, by most accounts, having wealth enabled you to obtain food, medicine, cigarettes, liquor, and clothes on the black market. You still could sell shares, still withdraw money from a bank, and you could *fence* possessions and use the money to buy some of what you needed. By 1944 and the winter of 1945 this was no longer the case. Food, warm clothes, perhaps a prewar bottle of wine were the items with the maximum purchasing power.

As shown in Figure 10.1, the stock market *in real terms* peaked at the end of 1942 and began a steep decline as investors were shocked by the surrender of an entire German army at Stalingrad. That news combined with England's growing strength and the United States' victories in the Pacific worried French stock market riders that they had signed on with the wrong side. From then on it was all a steep fall downhill. We concede that there was not much intuition or wisdom demonstrated by the Paris Bourse!

In 1943 the occupation and the Gestapo became even harsher, the resistance fiercer, and eventually the German army invaded Vichy. By 1944 much of France was a police state with the sadistic maniacs of the Gestapo brutally torturing anyone that aroused the slightest suspicion. The French economy was barely functioning, and food was in desperately short supply. Inflation and the black market sapped incomes. Stocks fell steadily in real terms but listed prices limped along and masked some of the pain. After France was liberated, the Index continued to decline as the economy stagnated, inflation soared even higher, and Socialism once again reared its ugly head. Then in 1945 and 1946 came the nationalization of insurance companies, banks, coal mines, and the electric and gas utilities. In real terms, stocks collapsed.

After the liberation, there was a messy period where scores were settled with those who had collaborated with the Germans. Liberation for some was a nightmare. The Vichy police, the *milice,* were hounded and often killed in cold blood. Collaborating journalists were given harsh jail sentences, but the contractors and suppliers who worked for the Germans received little attention. A few businessmen were imprisoned as criminal collaborators. Berliet was convicted and forfeited his company. Renault died in jail, but most French businessmen who trafficked with the Germans escaped unscathed and retained their equity holdings. As cited in Robert Paxton's classic *Vichy France: Old Guard and New Order*

1940–1944, one sardonic wit described this paradox, as a collaborator went free if he had built the Atlantic Wall defenses, but went to jail if he had written that the Wall was a good idea.

Petain and Laval were tried for treason, convicted, and sentenced to death. Laval was executed by a firing squad on October 15, 1945. Petain's sentence was commuted to life imprisonment on the Island of Yeu by the Provisional President Charles de Gaulle, where he died on July 23, 1951, at the age of 96. De Gaulle said of him: "His old age was a shipwreck."

The Postwar French Economy

In the first years after the war, provisional French governments tilted towards the left. The Russian model had become widely admired, and perhaps a third of the country was Communist. In the agricultural sector, *meteyage* (where farm profits were split evenly between the land owner and the farmer) had long been the practice, and there was the tradition of a strong *l'etat.* Many of the big businesses and banks were nationalized. By 1950 the stock market was a disaster in real terms, but in nominal terms as shown in Figure 10.1 still had a pale false glow of wealth. In fact in 1944, even as it was collapsing in real terms, France's SBF index actually set a new high, admittedly by a small amount, and then in 1948 amidst roaring inflation set another new high.

Were investors in French stocks fooled by this false glow of prosperity? It is unlikely! Measured inflation was around 20% for most of the occupation, and then in the aftermath of the war soared to 60% by the second half of the 1940s. Some of this may have been a delayed black market effect. With all this statistical confusion, precise real purchasing power calculations become somewhat meaningless but Figure 10.2 (shown earlier in this chapter) is what the *real* stock market looked like.

We do know that for the full decade from 1940 to 1950, French equities rose in nominal terms but fell 7.6% a year or more than 50% in real terms. This sounds bad but don't forget that in 1982 the Dow Jones Industrial Average was selling at the same price that it first reached in 1966, a decline of over 50% in purchasing power. Admittedly, in that span the United States had lost the Vietnamese war and experienced serious inflation but it hadn't been occupied. However the tough statistic in France is that equities in 1950 were some 20% below where they had been in real terms 50 years earlier.

Did public equities do their job in France? Even a skeptic would have to say that for the war years (1938–1940), the occupation (1940–1944), and then the turmoil of liberation and nationalization (1945–1950) they could have been a lot worse considering what happened to France during that period. From 1938–1945 they actually were flat in real terms and up in nominal.

Stocks were certainly better than the alternatives. The franc fell like a stone, and bonds and bills declined *by more than 20% a year* in real terms for the decade. Ironically, it was after the liberation that financial assets had their most severe falls. For the first half of the century, equities certainly failed to be wealth preservers or enhancers, but so did equities in many other countries. It was a tough 50 years.

Were French equity investors perceptive and wise? The answer is that after the fall of France in 1940 they weren't in that they gave up on England, thought German occupation was going to be both benign and profitable, and made the ghastly mistake of thinking the Germans were going to rule Europe for a long time. The steep climb in prices that lasted through 1941 was a sucker rally if there ever was one. On the other hand, they correctly interpreted the significance of the Soviet victory at Stalingrad.

Wealth Preservation only via Real Assets and Gold

The best place for wealth in France between 1940 and 1950 was in real assets and gold. The wealthy families of 1940 were still wealthy in 1950 because their holdings of farmland, property, and their businesses had appreciated hugely in nominal terms, and as best I can tell were up about 20% from 1940 levels in **real** terms. In other words, real assets were excellent inflation hedges but were only modest wealth enhancers.

For example, wealthy French families for generations had hoarded gold. Swiss private bankers say that in 1939 most family fortunes were 20% or so in gold bars that were either in Switzerland or were buried in the chateau's backyard. They had hardly anything invested in equities or bonds in London or New York. The price of gold was fixed to the dollar, and so as inflation accelerated and the franc fell against the dollar, the price of gold in francs soared. The *real* price of gold must have risen significantly more than property or business assets but it's hard to know now how much more.

There were three problems with gold as a disaster hedge during those horrendous years. First, in order to sell some of your gold hoard, you had to find either a real buyer or a black market dealer. Both were dangerous in that in a savage society rife with informers and treachery, anything could happen, and you might end up in an alley with a knife in your back or in a cellar with the Gestapo. Second, with either buyer you had to accept a significant discount from the true value of your gold, but that was just a fact of life in an environment in which there was no open market.

Third, you had to hide your gold if you lived in occupied France. As of the fall of 1940, every French bank had to report to the Germans the contents of all safe deposit boxes. The occupation authorities used this knowledge to "borrow" the gold by issuing a promissory note. The gold was then shipped back to Germany. At the end of the war, the promissory notes were not honored because the Nazi government's files were destroyed in the fighting for Berlin. As the allied armies got closer to Paris, any gold that remained was expropriated by German officials to finance their escape from the disaster they knew was approaching. Nevertheless, in the chaos of the last years of the war, gold buried in the backyard was a less dangerous, less expensive sale than any of the other alternatives like property or a business.

The people that got rich in France during the war were the black marketers. That was where the serious money was made. These sleazy entrepreneurs were adept at converting their profits into real assets, and they used their black money to buy and hoard gold. They bought gold because as the war went on and Germany's fortunes flagged they worried about the aftermath. Buying property or ostentatious displays of wealth would be dangerous after liberation. During the occupation, the operators involved in the black market were hated and despised as leeches on society. In fact, with liberation known black marketers were physically abused and their property seized. However, many black marketers converted their new ill-gotten wealth to gold and then bought businesses several years after liberation. Gold was a fine place to have wealth from 1945 to 1950 as inflation soared.

Incidentally, the story was the same in Italy. The 20 or so wealthy families maintained their wealth with their holdings of real assets through all the trauma of Mussolini, German occupation, and the Allied invasion of Italy. But again it was the black market dealers who made the big money and discretely converted it into legitimate businesses whose wealth soared in the 1950s. The black market in Italy was a dangerous, life-threatening game, but the rewards were huge. Some of the great European companies of the second half of the century were financed with black market money.

In occupied Europe during World War II, all things considered, gold was the best asset to hide in, preserve wealth, and maintain some liquidity. Stocks, land, real estate, and businesses worked only if you had a very long-term horizon. The black market was the most lucrative profession.

Chapter 11

Gone with the Wind: Preserving Wealth in Italy and Germany

Study the past if you would divine the future.

—Confucius

I taly from 1930 to 1945 is a tragic story from every point of view. As a country and a people, the Italians suffered grievously for their empowerment of Mussolini. His dreams of creating an empire led to disastrous military adventures, and the alliance with Hitler brought down the wrath of the Allies and an invasion. By 1944, civil society was wracked with ferocious strife that was tantamount to civil war.

Over the course of the twentieth century, equities in Italy had the lowest real return of any major market. Even after the war, stock market returns have been volatile and relatively poor compared to every other country in Europe so the malady has lingered on. The Italians are a great and dynamic people, but the country has simply failed to get its act together. But what we are interested in is how Italian equities did during the 1930s and 1940s as the country suffered through a disastrously incompetent dictatorship. If you just look at the Italian stock market index (the BCI), it appears the returns were all right. But if you strip away the superficially flattering effect of inflation, they were terrible.

Italy in the early 1930s was wracked by inflation, a high birth rate, and pervasive poverty, and was an unhappy, poorly governed country afflicted with rampant corruption. Benito Mussolini had begun as a Marxist but then had clawed his way to power using a mixture of violence, oratory, and guile. He thought of himself as a new Caesar, and, in fact, his profile in the right light was classic Roman. He told his followers: "If I advance, follow me; if I retreat, kill me; if I die, avenge me."

Mussolini was a physical fitness fanatic. A stocky, powerful man, he some days didn't shave believing that it made him look tougher and more menacing. One of his mistresses once gave him a solid gold razor and shaving kit of which he was very proud. Like Hitler he didn't smoke, drank very little, and derided overindulgence. He was vain, ambitious, and endlessly lecherous. According to Paul Johnson, who quotes Lenin as his source, in the course of *Il Duce's* sexual career, he had 169 mistresses, the last of whom shared his humiliating roadside demise in March 1945. "One would have thought that the Duce's vulnerability of blackmail was so enormous as to make him immune," wrote Malcolm Muggeridge.

Once in power, Mussolini installed himself at Rome in an enormous, high-ceiling chamber that was approached through a long corridor that ended in golden oak doors. *Il Duce* held forth behind an ornate sixteenth century desk that had belonged to a Pope. To advertise his intellectualism, heavy antique wooden tables were littered with maps, and the walls were lined with high floor-to-ceiling bookshelves stacked with leather-bound old books with the engraved nomenclatures of Cervantes, Plutarch, and Dante.

A passionate and romantic speaker, given to hyperbole, Mussolini could arouse a crowd, and for a while he even inspired the tired men in baggy suits with disillusioned faces who populated the bureaucracy of the Italian government. Beginning in 1936, Hitler began to court him, and although initially skeptical, *Il Duce* succumbed to Hitler's flattery and came to believe that Germany would be the great power of the future. By 1936, Mussolini was having delusions of grandeur. Thomas Lamont, the most famous of the JP Morgan partners, visited him in Rome, and there was an extended discussion of a major international debt issue to be underwritten by the House of Morgan. In 1939, amidst immense fanfare, Mussolini signed The Pact of Steel with Germany that committed each to support the other.

Mussolini's Effect on the Italian Stock Market

As shown in Figure 11.1, Italian equities (along with the rest of the world's) fell sharply in the early 1930s but then rallied as Mussolini consolidated his power. However as time went on, investors grew skeptical about Mussolini's grand plans for the creation of a "New Roman Empire." Conquests in Africa derived from spraying Abyssinian tribal villages with mustard gas didn't exactly exalt investor spirits. Although Italian stocks soared in nominal terms from 1939 until 1947, inflation was climbing just as fast so there were no sustainable gains in purchasing power. The Italian government was as corrupt as ever, and the military build-up was being financed by printing money. It was as though the stock market knew that the conquests in Africa, the appearance of better health for the Italian economy, and Mussolini's bluster were all a sham, which indeed it was. The chart that follows (Figure 11.1) looks good, but it is a total illusion.

Italian stocks did rally in 1940 as Mussolini, salivating over the spoils, belatedly declared war on France. In one of his more cynical comments, he remarked that he needed several thousand Italian war dead to justify to Hitler his claims for the French Riviera. When his troops faltered in the face of French resistance, he blamed the failure on the quality of their leadership. "Even Michelangelo had to have marble to make statues," he said.

The Italian stock market surged again in the summer of 1941 as Italy, now fully committed to the war, seemed to be on the right side. The Italian press was closely controlled, and the official line was that Italy was going to be Germany's partner in ruling the New Europe in a Thousand Year Reich. Italian stocks in both nominal and real returns set

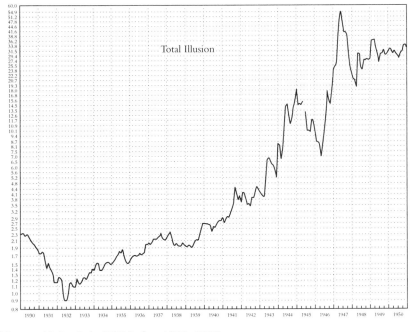

Figure 11.1   Italy BCI Index: 1930–1950
DATA SOURCE: Global Financial Data, Inc.

new all-time highs in the summer and fall of 1941 as the German juggernaut roared across Russia and Northern Africa.

However, by the summer of 1942, unrest was growing. The attack
on Greece had been a disaster, and the Italian people had never much
cared for the Germans. When the four Italian divisions fighting with the
Germans in Russia began to take heavy casualties, active, open dissent
for the first time appeared. The opposition political parties began to say
that Italy's participation in the war as an ally of the Germans was a bad
idea, and that Mussolini had picked the wrong side. A hundred thousand
Italian soldiers surrendered to the Soviets at Stalingrad, most never to be
seen again, and another hundred thousand were captured by the British
in the desert. The pictures of sullen, bedraggled Italian prisoners at
El Alamein, Egypt, are striking.

After drifting in 1942 and the first half of 1943, stock prices collapsed in July 1943 about the time that the Allies invaded Sicily and it

was apparent that Italy was next. On July 25, 1943, Mussolini's critics summoned the Grand Council, and after a heated debate, the council ordered his arrest and imprisonment. On September 1, 1943 Italy surrendered to the Allies.

Although Italy was now officially at war with Germany, Hitler refused to turn his back on Mussolini, and ordered German commandos to rescue *Il Duce* from his mountaintop chalet prison. One of the enigmas of Hitler's character was his loyalty to Mussolini, who himself was strictly a fair-weather friend. In 1941 Hitler had diverted troops from Barbarossa to extricate Mussolini, from Greece, and he consistently expended resources to save him. Why?

In any case, the German commandoes spirited Mussolini away to a warm reunion with Hitler who installed him in power in northern Italy. However Mussolini's charisma was shattered, and neither he nor the Italian stock market took any comfort from the Germans propping him up as a puppet dictator. He was a broken man, depressed and apathetic but brutal to the end. Once he was back in control, Mussolini executed those who had voted against him in the Grand Council, including his son-in-law, the cosmopolitan Count Galeazzo Ciano, who had been his foreign minister and who was married to his daughter.

Not surprisingly, stock prices continued to fall as the noose around Mussolini and Italy tightened. Italy became a country split apart and in total chaos. In the North, there was virtually a civil war, with old scores settled and summary executions of Fascists. From 1944 to 1945, there was no law and order, and no respect for personal property. Desperate groups wandered the countryside searching for food and loot. Around Lake Cuomo, families that had some wealth banded together, moved their prized possessions to the most defensible villa in the hills, and stood ready to fight for their lives. It wasn't worth the bloodshed for roving bands of brigands to storm such resolute groups.

As time went on, the Italian Resistance became more and more active and grew in power. In northern Italy it became a serious disruptive force behind the German lines. It was a partisan band that eventually caught Mussolini and his last mistress, Clara Petacci, outside of Milan, executed them on March 15,1945, and then hung them together—upside down at a crossroads. Petacci's dress was tied firmly to her legs to avoid any final impropriety.

Churchill had low regard for Mussolini. To the prime minister's dismay his daughter, Sarah, had married a music-hall comedian, Vic Oliver, of whom he was not fond. The irrepressible Oliver did not further endear himself by persistently referring to his father-in-law as "Popsy." Once, after the war at a dinner at Chartwell when the Black Dog of his periodic bouts of depression was plaguing Churchill, Oliver, in an attempt to draw out the great man asked:

"Popsy, who was the greatest statesmen you have ever known?"

"Benito Mussolini," was the unexpected reply.

"What? Why is that, Popsy?" asked the surprised Oliver.

"Mussolini is the only statesmen I know of," grumbled Churchill gazing at him dourly, "who had the necessary courage to have his own son-in-law executed."

For the decade of the 1940s, Italian stocks declined a staggering 11.5% a year in real terms as inflation soared. The soaring BCI index shown earlier in Figure 11.1 was strictly an illusion. Inflation consumed all the gains and more, as shown in Figure 11.2. Government bonds were even worse, losing an almost inconceivable 27% a year over that decade according to ABN Amro, and government bills had a staggering annual decline of 30%. In other words, financial assets in Italy as a repository of wealth were almost totally destroyed and became virtually worthless in the carnage and confusion of the war. But in the published prices on the stock exchange, that disaster was mostly concealed.

After 1945, however, as optimism grew about the postwar world and with equities so depressed in real terms, stocks rallied. By the end of the first half of the century Italian stocks had compounded at 11.8% annually in nominal terms but were virtually unchanged in real terms from where they had been 50 years earlier. Amazingly, the Italian stock market in the 1940s never closed, although there was little trading from 1943 to 1945.

Bonds and bills did far worse. For the first half of the century the total return from bonds and bills in real terms fell 6.2% per annum and an astounding 27.6% respectively for the decade of the 1940s. In the 1940s there was no place to hide in Italy in financial assets—not in stocks, bonds, bills, or the lira. Buildings and houses of any substance were mostly destroyed, pillaged, or commandeered during the war years.

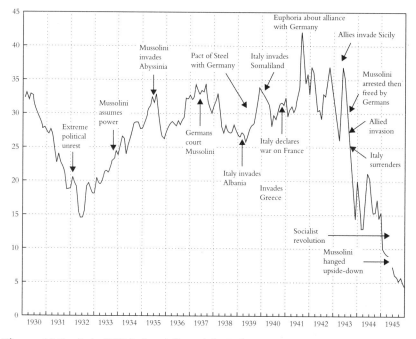

Figure 11.2 Italy BCI Index, Adjusted for Inflation: 1930–1945
DATA SOURCE: Global Financial Data; Traxis Partners LLC.

But in the end, the land itself was still there. As for making money, the career of choice was to be in the black market. The only Italians with wealth in 1940 that still had it in 1945 were involved with the black market or owned land.

One ironic footnote to the saga of Italy and Mussolini is that the war saved the Mafia. Mussolini hounded the Mafia relentlessly. The Fascist regime was extremely corrupt, but they wanted to be the only organization preying on Italy. By the early 1940s, the Italian Mafia was virtually out of business. The invasion of Italy by the Allies ended their harassment by the Fascists, and presented the Mafia with lucrative opportunities. The Mafia dons learned the names of Italian-American officers and quickly moved to ingratiate themselves with the naïve and gullible Americans. By 1945, the Mafia controlled the black market and local governments, and become once again a major force in Italy. It was not the U.S. Army's finest hour.

Preserving Wealth in Germany

Germany from 1914 to 1950 was an almost impossible place to preserve and enhance wealth. Over that period, the country lost two wars, was occupied by its enemies, had crushing financial reparations imposed on it, suffered hyperinflation, became a Fascist state, experienced the assumption of total power by arguably the most evil dictator in the history of the world, and was bombed and shelled almost into oblivion. What does a rich person do to preserve wealth in the midst of such total national catastrophes, particularly if you belong to a minority race that is the object the most intense pogrom of all time?

If you were a German Jew, there was nothing you could do except anticipate the pogrom and get out with whatever you could. What could you do in 1944 if you were a non-Jewish German, particularly if you lived in the eastern part of Germany on the eve of an occupation by hordes of a revengeful enemy whose homeland your countrymen have ravaged and with whom you have just fought to the death? For thousands of years, this has been the excruciating question faced by people with wealth, first around the Mediterranean, and then in Europe, and even in the United States at the time of the Civil War. Once every couple of generations, an epic event occurs that destroys accumulated wealth. A few countries such as the United States, Sweden, and Australia have been lucky—so far—but in Europe, the apocalypse has happened in one form or another on a regular, generational basis.

The conventional wisdom has always been that owning property (houses, farmland, timberland) are the best safe havens in the apocalypse. Remember in *Gone with the Wind,* how Scarlet O'Hara's dying, aged father, as the Union Army approached and the countryside was in flames, tells her at all costs to hold on to the property of Tara. "It's the land, it's the land, it's the only thing that really matters." The history of World War II (with the exception of agricultural land in Japan) generally supports this thesis. Estates and buildings were expropriated, converted, depreciated, or destroyed, and getting them back or obtaining compensation after the hostilities were over was problematical at best.

On the other hand, the underlying land was always there, and even if the local property records had been destroyed, the locals knew who the owners were. Of course, sometimes, if the original owner was Jewish or a hated landlord, the locals conveniently couldn't remember who owned the land In any case, the land, whether it was farmland, timberland, or a plot in town, maintained its value. By 1947 as Germany began to rebuild and recover, land prices rose. Of course land did not meet the instant liquidity test. In the dead of the winter of 1945–1946 when your family was starving, it was no consolation to be land rich and food poor.

In the case of Germany (and Japan), it turned out their conquerors' occupations were relatively benign and enlightened—unless you were in East Germany. (In fact, it could be argued that the U.S. occupation and its reforms were the best thing that had ever happened to Japan; refer back to Chapter 7 for details.) In the case of Germany, since the United States, France, and the U.K. were also involved in the occupation, property rights were respected and eventually restored in what became West Germany. As a sanctuary for wealth, it was crucial that your property not be in the Soviet zone, although after the Wall came down, values in the East recovered. In cities that were bombed, no compensation was ever received for destroyed homes or property, but title to the underlying land was retained.

A Prewar History of the German Economy

To understand the trauma of German wealth in the first half of the twentieth century, you have to go back to 1914. One of the most dangerous scourges of wealth and well-being is hyperinflation. This horribly debilitating economic disease occurs when, for whatever reason, a country prints money, which leads to inflation and then, because of lack of political courage, continues to run the printing press, and the addictive process spirals out of control. As always, the development of hyperinflation has complex causes, but in Germany's case, losing World War I was the primary driver. In 1914, the German Mark, the British shilling, the French franc, and the Italian lira all were about on a parity with each other and all fluctuated between four or five to the dollar. Since Otto von Bismarck's administration at the end of the previous century, Germany's military adventures had been financed by borrowing and were subsequently paid for by paying off the debt with the spoils of the war. In 1914, Germany was a prosperous, rich country, and its army was thought to be the best in the world. In addition its ruler, Kaiser Wilhelm, had constructed a formidable navy. The Kaiser and the Ministry of Finance confidently expected to win The Great War (as WWI was called at the time) relatively quickly, and they assumed the historic financing pattern would continue. The only outspoken skeptic was the stock market, which fell like a stone as war loomed. From January to December 1914, the Berlin market dropped in real terms 41% and at year-end, the exchange was closed.

However, after the armistice in 1918, there was no loot for the loser—Germany. By the end of the war, she had a huge amount of public debt in the form of government bonds that had been sold to the people, which caused a massive increase in the money supply and an extremely weak currency. The result was that the German economy was on the verge of hyperinflation even before the first reparations payment was due. After the armistice, but well before the terms of reparations had been determined, the Berlin stock exchange reopened, rallied briefly, and collapsed. In May of 1921, the amount of reparations that Germany must pay was set: scheduled payments amounted to 10% of GNP and 80% of exports—a crushing burden that JP Morgan and others maintained could not be borne.

The German economy plummeted into hyperinflation, and by late 1923, inflation was completely out of control. The Mark traded at literally around one trillion to one dollar. Banks were charging 35% a day, and housewives went marketing with a wheelbarrow full of Marks and returned with meager food. The ordinary people who had bought government bonds to support the war effort and bank depositors lost everything. Walter Levy, a German-born oil consultant in New York, told the author George J.W. Goodman (Adam Smith) how his father had planned for his retirement: "My father was a lawyer and he had taken out an insurance policy in 1903, and every month he had made payments faithfully. It was a 20-year policy, and when it came due, he cashed it in and bought a single loaf of bread."

The only winners from the hyperinflation were a few sophisticates who had hedged the Mark in 1918 or earlier, landowners who paid off their mortgages, and businessmen who repaid their loans and became unencumbered owners of real property. "It was," wrote Paul Johnson in *Modern Times*, "one of the biggest and crudest transfers of wealth in history."

Hitler and the German public blamed the Versailles Treaty and Jewish speculators.

No chart can capture the stupendous ascent slope of true hyperinflation. Numbers actually do a better job. From 1919 to 1921, German CPI inflation was gradually rising from virtual price stability to a 2% annual rate. By June of 1922, inflation was at an annual rate of 4%; by September, 22%; and by December, 68%. Then it really took off: in March 1933, it hit 285%, then 765% in June, 1,500,000% in September, and finally 152,221,670,000% in December.

Across the long gap of time, it is not easy to determine what stocks did during the hyperinflation. The index that was used from 1917 to 1923 was measured in gold Marks rather than paper Marks. As Figure 11.3 shows, from catastrophically depressed levels, the index soared fourfold in purchasing power terms into the teeth of the hyper-inflation storm and then fell and did nothing for the rest of the decade. The problem is that beginning in 1924, a new broader index of 213 shares

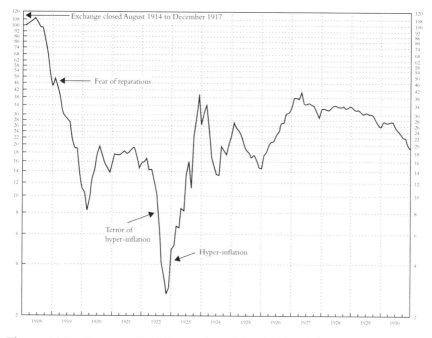

Figure 11.3   Germany Gold-Denominated Stock Price Index: 1918–1930
DATA SOURCE: Global Financial Data, Inc.

was introduced, so the performance of the two linked indexes is not strictly comparable. Stocks seem to have been a good place to hide in the last, most cataclysmic stages of hyperinflation but mostly because they had already fallen so much that they had discounted the economic disaster. However, in general German equities were very smart in that they perceived in 1914 that Germany was going to lose the war. Then in 1918, they anticipated that the victors would impose reparations that would bankrupt the country, and finally in 1921, they foresaw the coming hyperinflation.

The message for wealth preservation is important. Hyperinflation occurs from time to time, and basically it is one of the Four Horsemen in drag. To survive much less prosper, the wealth holder needs to own, with borrowed money, property, real estate, or a business. Then you pay off your debts with depreciated currency and own outright the real assets. Of course, if you bet wrong and conversely deflation is the outcome, the debt destroys you and the lender is the winner.

The sequence of events climaxing in hyperinflation created the environment of extreme social disorder and disillusionment that led to the rise of Hitler. Germany was still a rich country, but with wheelbarrows being used to transport money, the price of food and milk changing twice a day, and petty thievery rampant, people sensed something was terribly wrong. Farmers refused to sell food for worthless paper; and workers when they were paid rushed to the nearest store. Food riots broke out. Middle-class Germans were forced to sell or barter jewelry, furniture, pictures, anything in order to obtain something to eat. Businesses, hospitals, and institutions closed. In June 1922, the moderate, charismatic, and very able foreign minister, Walter Rathenau, was assassinated by right-wing fanatics. That such a man could be murdered in a supposedly, stable law-abiding society shocked the middle class. People wanted order and stability at any price. Communism or Fascism seemed the alternatives.

The rise of Hitler has been endlessly chronicled. By the late 1920s, Hitler was in jail dictating *Mein Kampf* to Rudolph Hess, and Dr. Hjalmar Schacht had become the president of the Reichsbank. Earlier, John Maynard Keynes had advised the Reichsbank that the budget must be balanced and the money supply stabilized. Initially, he was ignored, but now Schacht followed his advice (although he never admitted it and took the credit for himself). A new Reichsmark backed by gold was introduced, the money supply was stabilized, and the budget was brought into a semblance of balance. The result was a steady economic expansion, moderate inflation, and a measure of political stability. Stock prices rallied, but then the equity market declined sharply again, 74% to be precise, between 1929 and 1932 as the Great Depression afflicted all world equity markets.

With the ascendancy of Hitler to power and a semblance of order, stocks climbed again, albeit from a deeply depressed level as investors dreamed of a new German empire. Hitler himself was both ignorant of and bored by economics, but he knew enough to leave the conduct of the economy to businessmen, so he turned the management of the economy over to the brilliant Dr. Schacht. With confidence restored, Schacht was able to print money and cleverly manipulate the currency. He implemented measures to enforce savings and devised new methods of government finance. It all worked. From 1932 to 1936, unemployment was reduced from 6 million to less than 1 million. Industrial production rose 102% from 1932 to 1937. Wages were essentially frozen, strikes were *verboten,* tourism was promoted, and margins and profits boomed.

The impetus for this growth came partially from the rearming of the German military. But it also derived from the intrinsic strength and rigorous management of German industry itself. By 1938, the German economy was, if not booming, at least healthier than that of any other major industrial country. After the United States, it was the second largest economy in the world. By the early fall of 1941, with the German armies roaring across Russia and vast riches pouring into Germany from the occupied countries, German stocks soared, and in *real* terms, German equities finally surpassed the highs of 1910.

It is fascinating that stocks peaked just before, or really as, the German onslaught into Russia reached its high-water mark in the suburbs of Moscow on that early December afternoon in 1941. Although there were great Axis victories in 1942, German investors had lost their enthusiasm. Was it the stories of the soldiers returning from the Eastern Front? Was it Hitler's dictatorial powers that worried them? Or was it that the German aristocracy who owned the equities were becoming increasingly disenchanted with Hitler and the Nazi regime? We now know that even as early as the fall of 1941, the senior officers of the army were once again beginning to plot Hitler's removal from power. Nevertheless, broad-based disillusionment didn't begin until after Stalingrad in 1943.

Recently, another interpretation of economic events in Germany has been put forth by Adam Tooze in a formidable 832-page book, *The Wages of Destruction: The Making and Breaking of the Nazi Economy*. Tooze is an erudite and well-regarded economic historian at Cambridge, and he has done an immense amount of research. He argues that by 1939, Germany was still not a "recovered, prosperous, powerful economy" but instead had been drained by years of frantic rearming and was starved for natural resources and foreign exchange. Furthermore, it was crippled by an oversized and inefficient agricultural sector that relied on men and horses. In effect, he discounts the efficiency and creativity of German industry. Tooze cites figures that show the standard of living in Germany in 1938 was half that of the United States and only two-thirds of Britain.

His case seems a little far-fetched. In 1939, all the European countries had labor-intensive agricultural sectors, which was one reason wars were fought in the spring and early summer. German industry, with its precision manufacturing, has always been and still is the best in the world, but on military arms, Tooze may be right. As early as the fall of 1941, German field commanders on the Eastern Front were complaining that the Russian tanks were superior. After the spring of 1940, French industry became an additional manufacturing source for German tanks, trucks, and munitions.

By the early 1940s, according to Tooze, even as the Nazi juggernaut was at the peak of its power, the underlying economy was on the brink of collapse. It lacked the steel, coal, oil, and even manpower to fuel its military, and for the remainder of the war, "scarcity management" was the order of the day. These longstanding economic deficiencies, Tooze maintains, shaped Hitler's thinking on political and military strategy.

On the political issue, Tooze says Hitler was fascinated with the economic power of the United States because of its vast territory, natural resources, and huge domestic market. He had intensely studied the manner in which the U.S. Army, cavalry, and pioneers had quite ruthlessly conquered the Indian population. This was the basis of his grand design to colonize the East by creating a huge 100-million-person German *volk* in Eastern Europe by first starving and working to death the local Slavic populations and then settling the area. Hitler believed that the American extermination of the Indians justified what he planned to do to the Slavs. Tooze argues this *lebensraum* theory explains Hitler's obsession with attacking Russia in 1941, even when England was not yet subdued.

As for the military influence, Hitler knowing that the German economy was basically weak and short of resources, recognized that Germany could not fight a long war of attrition against more populous, better-endowed adversaries. Therefore, he was compelled to follow a quick strike, *blitzkrieg* strategy in his offensives against the West and against the Russians.

The Perilous Value of Art

Returning to how to protect Jewish and German wealth during the 1930s and 1940s, if equities were inadequate, was art an alternative? Art could be hidden, but that was a risky proposition with a marauding, looting, barbaric army—be it German or Russian—on the loose. The Nazis were certainly into plundering, particularly of art. Alfred Rosenberg, the head of the *Einsatzstab,* was charged with confiscating enemy property and he exercised his mandate with enthusiasm. In the case of art (and it has been well documented, in many other books), the Nazis looted museums and the private collections of the wealthy and shipped their treasures back to Germany. Hitler knew very little about fine art, although he considered himself to be an artist before he became a politician, and he was really not interested in collecting. The Nazi's culture ministry encouraged raw Germanic art that featured handsome, powerfully built, naked Aryan-looking men and women.

In the full flush of his glory, Hitler envisioned a gigantic Führer Museum at Linz, Austria, his birthplace, whose vast collection would surpass in quality the Louvre in Paris, the Tate Gallery in London, and the Metropolitan Museum in New York. He told Rosenberg to get the very best pictures and sculptures from all over Europe for this project. The other big acquirer of art was Air Marshal Goring, who, by contrast, thought of himself as a connoisseur with a far more refined and cultured taste. He particularly favored the works of the seventeenth century Dutch masters, but he was eclectic and acquired the best of other schools as well. He shamelessly used his power to browbeat lesser Nazis who might have acquired a piece that he desired to trade their acquisition for a picture he owned of far less value.

Rosenberg had the difficult and delicate task of balancing these two demanding clients and in addition dealing with requests from generals and high government figures who wanted specific styles and objects. Goring was by far the most involved and the greediest. He went to Paris from time to time and directly intervened to obtain certain pictures, sculptures, tapestries, and porcelains which he had sent to the huge estate he had seized in Germany. Thus, between 1940 and the summer of 1944, several hundred pieces of the finest art in Paris, Brussels, and Amsterdam were transported to Germany for Hitler and Goring. The collections were meticulously inventoried and photographed and were recovered after the war. Thousands of other, less famous *objects d'art* were just plain stolen by the occupiers, and many were never recovered.

The stories of the plundering of art in the countries conquered and occupied by the Nazis are manifold. Hector Feliciano's book, *The Lost Museum,* relates the indignities and the travails of recovering masterpieces. The two Bernheim brothers had an elegant gallery located in Faubourg Saint-Honore in Paris, and when the Germans came, they immediately split their collection of sculpture, Monet, Renoir, Pissarro, Sisley, Cezanne, and Matisse. One brother sent his pictures to Monaco for storage where they survived the war. Misreading the intensity of the occupation, another moved his art to his fine Paris home. When the Germans billeted officers there, his collection was discovered and expropriated—in other words, stolen.

However, the best of the gallery's collection was taken off their frames, rolled up in brown paper bags, and taken to the chateau of a close friend in France's rugged and remote Dordogne region in the Free Zone, where the brothers assumed the Germans would never come. The paintings were hidden under the eaves of the chateau that had been built in 1811 in the model of the U.S. White House. Unfortunately, when the Germans occupied the Free Zone in 1943, perhaps angered by the White House imitation, they pillaged the chateau, carted off all the furniture, Flemish tapestries, antique Persian rugs, and linens, and then deliberately and methodically burned the chateau to the ground. The priceless, undiscovered paintings presumably were destroyed, hence the title of Felicano's book.

Thus it would appear that art in the occupied countries was not a good haven for wealth. In 1940, as the German armies drew ever nearer to Paris, many wealthy art collectors surmised that the conquerors might expropriate their possessions. Besides, they questioned whether fine art or antique furniture could be swapped for food if ordinary people were starving. They were right to wonder. As I have recounted earlier, the wealthy Hong Kong Chinese found that all their money and homes on the Peak were worth very little when the Japanese occupied the city in 1942. Instead jewelry was the best wealth preserver under dire circumstances, because it could be readily swapped for necessities such as food and medicine with the Japanese officers who wanted to curry favor with their girlfriends. In the occupied countries of Europe, legends are still told about the magnificent pieces of jewelry that were swapped on the black market during the occupation years, for a fraction of their value.

When the Nazis invaded Poland, the famous Czartorski collections of more than 5,000 paintings, antiquities, porcelains, and jewelry were taken to a country house in Sieniawa, in southeastern Poland. But other wealthy people could not be bothered: for example, Prince Drucki-Lubecki buried his silver in his basement, and Count Alfred Potocki packed away his best things in hiding places and left the rest where they were. Unfortunately, all three families were betrayed by informers, and their collections were seized. As the Germans advanced across the countryside, the big houses were ransacked.

In desperation, Countess Matgozata Radziwill sent her daughter-in-law back to Warsaw from their country house near Bialystock, with instructions to retrieve the family jewels from a safe-deposit box. When she arrived at the bank, German officers were methodically opening every safe-deposit box. As she stood there, the bank manager carefully laid out the Radziwill's fabulous jewelry collection in front of them. "What a pity," he told the Germans, "none of this is real." The Germans, not knowing the difference, waved the box on. "Ah," whispered the bank manager to his client, "we have saved the countess's jewels!" The countess and her daughter-in-law fled with their jewelry to Cracow, where they lived for two years by selling pieces from time to time.

But there were many ways to lose your fortune. And unfortunately, the story has an unhappy ending. A man calling himself a Dutch diplomat persuaded the countess to let him act as her agent and take most of the jewelry to her cousin's in the West for safekeeping until the countess also could escape and reclaim it. The so-called diplomat then fled and sold off the jewelry while the countess remained trapped in Poland. This episode illustrates how vulnerable frightened, wealthy people were to con artists in the chaos of war.

Some art escaped the Nazi's grasp. The *Luftwaffe*'s headquarters in Paris was in an expropriated mansion of the Rothschild family at 23 Avenue de Morigny. Goring must have gone there on his frequent trips to Paris to acquire art, but little did he know that behind the bookcases in the elegant, paneled library, a secret room had been built in which were concealed the finest pictures of the Rothschild's fabulous collection. Another French family that owned Hera, the wife of Zeus, one of the finest classical statuettes in existence, successfully disguised its value from the Germans by junking it up with doll clothes.

Other Parisians in the late spring of 1940, as the panzers drew ever closer to Paris, opted to sell. Dealers were flooded with first-class paintings. It was a spectacular time to be a buyer. John Maynard Keynes on a mission to Paris in the spring of 1940 bought, to the sound of howitzers, two Cézannes and two Delacroixs that, if he had lived, would have appreciated forty-fold over the next 40 years.

The Loss of a Family Fortune

In the case of Germany, with hyperinflation in the 1920s, then the rise of Hitler in the 1930s, and finally war, surrender, and occupation, much wealth was lost. One of the odder stories is that of Fritz Thyssen, the German steel magnate, who was one of the richest men in Germany. In the early 1930s he supported Hitler with massive amounts of money and had access into the upper reaches of the Nazi party. He assumed he had paid his dues, and that his family holdings would be protected by a grateful Führer. Instead, in 1938 the Nazis nationalized his company and replaced the management, citing the national emergency. Thyssen was outraged, powerless, and much poorer but by no means impoverished.

However, unwittingly he got his revenge. Thyssen was on the boards of a number of international companies, and he circulated in world business circles. Nursing his grudge, he complained long and loud about Hitler. In 1938 he mentioned to the English businessman William Stephenson, who was actually an intelligence agent, that hundreds of units of a superb new, portable cipher machine called "Enigma" were being built in one of his factories near Berlin and that Thyssen was not being fairly compensated for their manufacture.

The Enigma was a model of German technology, Thyssen boasted. The machine had a keyboard like a typewriter with the keys linked through a system of drums. The relationship between the drums could be changed swiftly in a multitude of ways. The sender of the message would type the message routinely but the machine switched each letter to a different one thus anyone intercepting the signals would get junk. The receiving Enigma with its drums adjusted to the prearranged setting would respond by translating the message back into clear language. The drum relationship would be continually changed. The code was called the ULTRA and the Germans believed it was unbreakable.

Stephenson immediately recognized that a new cipher machine that was designed to be simple, secure, and easy to use yet totally secure would be a huge advantage in a fast-moving global war. The *blitzkrieg* strategy depended on surprise, speed of execution, and swift, secret communications.

Forewarned, Stephenson created a team of mathematicians and cryptologists at a remote manor house, Bletchley Park, to break the ULTRA code. It was a monumental task, but eventually the team unraveled the code. The ability to read the German transmissions proved to be an incalculable advantage.

What Happened to the Wealth of German Jews

It is always startling when talking with prosperous, elderly Europeans to learn how conscious they are of protecting their wealth, especially if they are Jewish. They have a deep-ingrained "refugee mentality," an insecurity that compels them to perpetually question prosperity and always worry. It's obvious why they are so sensitive, particularly the latter group. In the last century they experienced two wars, hyperinflation, a pogrom, and a depression. Americans have led incredibly sheltered lives compared to the citizen-investors of other countries. It's only the markets that threaten us.

The most tragic saga was the plight of the German Jews. Prior to the rise of the Nazis in the 1920s, the Jews had long been an integral part of German society and the economy. Many German Jews could trace their ancestors in Frankfurt back to the late Middle Ages. Their position in Imperial Germany was respected, and no one was closer to Bismarck than his financial adviser, Arnold Bleichroder. During World War I, many German Jews had fought on the Western Front, and some such as Otto Frank (the father of Anne Frank) were decorated for heroism and promoted to be officers. His father, a loyal German, had in 1916, supported the war effort by buying government bonds, and, in fact, the family's wealth had been wiped out by the subsequent hyperinflation, which rendered the bonds worthless. However, for many years there also had been an undercurrent of German anti-Semitism spawned by envy and the age-old prejudices. The hyperinflation of the 1920s was used by the Nazis to fuel this animosity by shrilly alleging that the "Jew shylocks" had engineered the inflation and were reaping immense profits from the agony of the people even though as lenders they were the biggest losers from the inflation.

The aristocratic German Jewish community in the early 1930s considered itself Germans and felt secure. They knew there were anti-Semitic elements in Germany but they believed their position in German society had steadily improved over the previous 50 years. They could not accept that a cultured, educated country that had produced so many great musicians, philosophers, and writers would empower a man like Hitler who seemed to be preaching ethnic cleansing. Many aristocratic Germans agreed with them.

They pointed out that the Warburg firm in Hamburg and Mendelssohn & Co. in Berlin, although controlled by Jews, were the bankers to many of the largest companies in Germany, and that in 1930 their partners held seats on the boards of over a hundred corporations. Many Jews had served in the Kaiser's army and navy in World War I.

However in the early 1930s, middle-class Jews—i.e., those who owned stores and businesses in the smaller cities and towns—began to experience increasing pressure and prejudice. On March 30, 1933, in Frankfurt, a city that had a Jewish mayor, a manifesto was published. It said in part:

> To Members of the Community
> Nothing can rob us of a thousand years of traditional links with our German homeland; no distress or danger can estrange us from the faith we have inherited from our fathers. We will stand up for ourselves with circumspection and with dignity.
> If no one else will speak for us, then let the stones of this city speak on our behalf; it owes its prosperity in large part to Jewish achievements, and contains many institutions bearing witness to Jewish public service. Relations between the Jewish and non-Jewish citizens have always been particularly close.
> Do not lose heart! Close ranks! No honorable Jew should desert his post at this time. Help us preserve our father's inheritance.
> Executive Committee of the Israelite Community in Frankfurt

The Executive Committee was clearly not recommending emigration. At the same time the Nazis were accusing the German Jewish bankers of "plundering the *volk*," the regime was granting them special dispensations because it needed their assistance to finance Germany's exports. Without exports, Hitler could not deliver the job growth he had promised, and he required foreign exchange to buy raw materials and munitions for his rapidly expanding armed forces. By 1933, Jews were being roughed up on the street by Nazi hoodlums, arrested on trumped up charges, and in some cases disappearing after the arrest. Financial persecution was becoming intense. The smaller Jewish German banks outside of the big cities were ostracized and compelled to sell out to German banks at a fraction of book value. A wealthy Jew who owned apartment houses would be told that Aryans could no longer be tenants in Jewish-owned buildings, thus forcing him to sell his properties at half of their true value. Foreign exchange controls resulted in a tax of 78% on money transfers unless a Jew was going to Palestine.

Throughout the 1930s, daily life for Jews deteriorated. If you were a Jew, you never knew when you would be assaulted on a street for no reason by a gang of thugs, or when an arbitrary but crippling new rule would bankrupt your business. A Jew who had for generations owned and run a general store in a small town suddenly would find windows broken at his home and picketing in front of his store with signs urging his customers to not patronize the "Jew bloodsuckers" anymore. Often these small-town merchants were upstanding, highly regarded members of their community, but suddenly their neighbors and friends were afraid to continue to do business or socialize with them.

These middle-class Jews had less to lose than the wealthy, and often they were more amenable to emigrating. Many of them faced with this cruel dilemma of a persecuted minority opted to sell and get out. Of course when they went to sell their businesses and homes, they found that it was a buyers' market and the proceeds they received were half of what the true value was. Nevertheless they took what they could get and fled Germany as virtually penniless refugees but still having one priceless possession, their brains.

On September 15, 1935, the Nuremberg Laws stripped Jews of citizenship, deprived them of the vote, and barred them from public office. Jews were also prohibited from having sexual intercourse with or marrying Aryans. As Ron Chernow wrote in *The Warburgs:* "In one stroke these laws repealed Jewish emancipation and transported the community back to the Middle Ages." Rumors were circulating about what was happening in the concentration camps, and the handwriting was clearly on the wall. Then there was the terror of the assaults of Jews on *Kristallnacht* November 9, 1938.

By the end of 1935, 100,000 Jews had left Germany but 450,000 still temporized. For example, Max Warburg, the leading Jewish investment banker, continued to stay and do business, and from 1936 to 1938 M.M. Warburg & Company made money facilitating the exodus of Jews and servicing their German industrial clients. Wealthy Jewish families still lived very well, and to some extent their servants insulated them from harassment. However their social life became increasingly constrained. Still they kept thinking and hoping that the worst was over, and meanwhile the price of leaving continued to go up.

These elite German Jews with property and wealth were faced with a terrible dilemma: emigrate and leave most of their wealth behind or stick it out and hope for the best. Max Warburg for one argued that Nazism was a temporary disease and that to flee the Fatherland where they had such deep roots and to sell at deep, distress discounts their assets and businesses that they had built up over generations was a cowardly, impoverishing, overreaction. Things weren't that bad, he argued. Besides, the Nazis seemed to need them. Even by the late 1930s the Warburg firm's partners were still on the boards of the big German companies, and they continued to do banking business for those companies. From 1935 to 1938 M.M. Warburg booked profits of more than a million Reichsmarks a year.

Help from an Unusual Source: Hitler's Economist

Dr. Hjalmar Schacht, Hitler's economic czar, was friendly with the German Jewish elite, and he was supportive and sympathetic. He enjoyed socializing with them, and often attended elaborate dinners at their homes. They in turn favored him with shares in hot new stocks, and in the custom of the times, passed on inside information. Schacht maintained to Hitler that persecuting Jews only complicated his effort to obtain raw materials and foreign exchange. In the mid 1930s he consistently reassured Jewish bankers that Hitler was not as menacing as he seemed, and that once he had restored order and prosperity, persecution of Jews would end.

Schacht was a fascinating character. With advice from John Maynard Keynes, he had cured the hyperinflation of the 1920s. In 1935, he was at one time president of the Reichsbank, Minister of Economics, and Hitler's economic czar. Schacht was an economist, but he had no economic religion. Basically he played each situation by ear and intuition. Germany was the only major industrial country to recover quickly from the Great Depression, and Schacht got most of the credit. He had supervised the construction of the autobahn and overseen the public works programs of the Nazi era that had stimulated the economy. He was an old-school, aristocratic banker and looked the part, sporting rimless spectacles, fine white hair parted down the middle, and invariably attired in suspenders and pinstripe suits. He smoked endless cigars, which no one else dared to do in the Führer's presence.

Schacht had close personal relationships with the titans of world finance. The great British central banker, Montagu Norman, was a close personal friend and held him in high regard. He also was well known to the senior partners of JP Morgan. Apparently Hitler and Goring regarded him with some awe. He never joined the Nazi Party, but was given free rein from Hitler to run the Reichsbank. "He [Hitler] understood nothing whatever about economics," Schacht wrote later. "So long as I maintained the balance of trade and kept him supplied with foreign exchange he didn't bother about how I managed it." He seems to have completely bamboozled Norman who told Tom Lamont of JP Morgan that the Nazis are "fighting the war of our system of society against Communism. If they fail, Communism will follow in Germany, and anything may happen in Europe."

Schacht was self-confident and arrogant. As Ron Chernow wrote, Schacht "took liberties with Hitler that would have cost others their heads." Schacht was not afraid to argue with the Führer, and once when Hitler gave him a painting as a gift Schacht returned it, saying thanks but it's a forgery. He skillfully orchestrated the repudiation of Germany's external debt and used Germany's Jewish bankers to finance the war economy that was being built. In the late 1930s he worked diligently to keep family banks like Warburgs from taking flight, and he continued to tell them Hitler's intentions were benign. By then he must have known better. At the same time Chernow says he was bragging to Hitler about how the Jewish bank accounts he had blocked from transferring money out of the country were financing German rearmament.

However, as time passed Schacht and Hitler had substantive disagreements. Schacht argued civilian production and consumption should be allowed to grow rather than channeling all resources into rearmament. He warned Hitler that he was starving domestic spending and of the dangers of an economy built almost entirely on military demand. Hitler had promised in speeches to smash the big Jewish-owned department stores, and Schacht argued that destroying them would cost 90,000 jobs and damage the economy. Hitler listened and tempered his rhetoric, but nevertheless, the stores eventually were assaulted by Nazi hoodlums and in the end their Jewish owners had to sell them for a pittance.

After a legendary shouting match with Hitler at Berchtesgaden in the fall of 1938, Schacht was replaced as finance minister by Goring although he stayed on at the Reichsbank. That year he was involved with the Berlin officer's coup that was described in Chapter 5. In December 1939, at the Reichsbank Christmas party, perhaps having consumed too much holiday cheer, he vehemently criticized the excesses of *Kristillnacht* with its burnings of Jewish shops and synagogues, and proposed a plan for the emigration of 50,000 Jews. When, a few weeks later, Hitler heard of his comments, he fired him from the Reichsbank but miraculously did not throw him into prison as he did so many others and Schacht survived the war.

German Takeover of Jewish-Owned Companies

By 1937 the new catchword was "Aryanization," which meant the Nazi government wanted Germans to own all substantial business enterprises. The policy encouraged Germans to buy Jewish companies at whatever discount they could negotiate, and if the discount wasn't big enough, the Nazi government would intervene with not-so-veiled threats of a long visit to a concentration camp for the recalcitrant owner. A Jewish businessman would be lucky if he could sell his business for half its fair value. If he decided to leave the country, and needed to sell his home, again it was a buyer's market with huge discounts. After paying the exorbitant foreign exchange tax, a middle-class Jewish family left Germany with virtually no wealth whatsoever.

The beneficiaries of all this, of course, were the German buyers who acquired businesses and real estate at very attractive prices. Large as well as small transactions took place. The Berlin and Hamburg department stores were sold for a fraction of the value of their real estate alone. Friedrich Flick bought a wonderful business jewel that he had long lusted for, the Lubeck Blast Furnace Company, at a 50% discount on its market value. One bizarre story concerns a Jew who was forced to accept 10,000 canaries instead of money for his business. He took the first 5,000 canaries to New York, sold them to pet stores, and then returned to Germany and did the same with the second 5,000. He then stayed in New York and built a huge business selling pets.

As time went on, discounts on sales often rose to 70%. For the Jewish seller who then wanted to get his money out of the country, the exchange control tax took at least 75% of the remainder. When the Warburgs finally sold their bank in late 1938, the cash purchase price of 3.4 million Marks was a fraction of the book value of 11.6 million Marks. Then there was a Reich Flight Capital Tax of 850,000 Marks and a stamp tax of one million Marks for the approval of the Aryanization Commission leaving 1.55 million Marks. After the now 90% foreign exchange tax, the Warburgs left Germany with 155,000 Marks. Talk about wealth confiscation!

A similar fate befell the Bleichroder family. Gerson von Bleichroder was the great Otto von Bismarck's financial adviser, investment manager, and confidant. Jew and Junker built the German Empire, and Bleichroder's firm, founded in 1803, was arguably the most powerful investment bank in Germany around the turn of the century. Bleichroder's heirs thought they were fully incorporated into German society, and in 1936 when one of them sought to marry a young woman from an old Prussian family, he filed for an exemption from the Nuremberg Laws that forbade a German to marry a Jew. His petition was summarily denied, and the young man shortly thereafter became ill and died supposedly of a broken heart. In 1938, the Bleichroder firm collapsed, and the other family members fled to Switzerland and then to New York where some established a new and successful firm, Arnold and S. Bleichroder.

But at least they got out. In May 1939, the German liner *St. Louis* left Hamburg with 900 affluent but not super-wealthy Jews bound for Cuba where they were to receive entry permits to the United States. Many of the passengers had jewelry and unframed canvases in their luggage. Tragically Cuba reneged on its commitment to the refugees, and the United States also refused to issue entry permits even though the issue was taken directly to FDR. It was never clear why. The ship had to return to Europe. A few of its passengers were eventually given asylum in Britain but most were forced to go back to Germany, to concentrations camps, and the Holocaust.

While the German Jews and the wealthy of the occupied countries were being stripped of their wealth, much of it was being transferred to the Nazi leaders. Hitler himself was not interested in aggrandizement, but he had no objection to his henchmen accumulating wealth as long as it stayed in the main Nazi gang. Most desired country estates, and many wanted art. The more financially astute acquired shares in German and French companies that they knew would be arms contract beneficiaries. Corruption and conflict within the leadership was rife. Hitler, according to Paul Johnson, promoted internal battles. "People must be allowed friction with one another," the Führer liked to say. "Friction produces warmth, and warmth is energy. It's institutionalized Darwinism."

After the German surrender in 1945, there were reparations negotiations that dragged on for a number of years. The present value of confiscations and distress sales were hard to prove, and most of the payments were small. In the case of the Warburg family they eventually got a 25% interest in their still existent firm and some cash. They also received a five-year option to increase their interest to a controlling 50%, but when the time came they didn't have the money to exercise the option.

Just recently, in March 2007, another case was finally settled. Gunther Wertheim owned the elegant and prosperous Berlin retailer, Wertheim & Company, on the *Kurfurstendamm,* the prime shopping promenade. In 1939 his store and a five-acre parcel of land on the edge of Potsdamer Plaza were expropriated, and he and his family fled to New Jersey where this once wealthy man ran a chicken farm. After the war, the five-acre plot became part of East Berlin and seemed to have little value in a divided city. A con man persuaded Wertheim to sell him the rights to the store and the land, and he in turn sold them to a large German company, KarstadtQuelle. When the Wall came down, suddenly the five acres was hot property. It is now the site of glittering luxury apartments, office buildings, and a Ritz-Carlton. After extended wrangling, KarstadtQuelle in March 2007 paid the children of Gunther Wertheim, now in their mid-70s, $117 million for the land, roughly one-third of its current value. Not full restitution but better than nothing.

To Preserve Wealth, Move It out of the Country

What is the message for owners of wealth who have lived in a country for generations but are a minority—particularly a prosperous minority? It seems obvious. The Germans Jews call it *shtetl,* literally the ghetto mentality of always looking over your shoulder. The rich overseas

Chinese in Indonesia and the Philippines have always kept a nest egg in Singapore or Hong Kong because they know their indigenous business empires are only a pogrom away from confiscation and destruction. The message for anyone who has either created or inherited big money is don't flaunt it, and no matter how secure and integrated you feel, always keep an escape hatch open and maintain some substantial wealth outside the country. Just be very sure the legal entitlements to that overseas wealth are utterly, incontrovertibly clear.

Meanwhile, pay homage to the wisdom of the Berlin stock market.

Chapter 12

Stalingrad: The Battle of the Century

Avenge not yourselves, but rather give place unto wrath for it is written, Vengeance is mine, I will repay, saith the Lord.

—ROMANS 12:19

The Allies who had been fighting off their back foot from the beginning of the war began to gain some traction in the second half of 1942 not only in Asia but in Europe as well. This chapter describes Stalingrad, the "Battle of the Century" within "The War of the Century." The eventual Soviet victory at Stalingrad reversed the course of wealth destruction in Europe and turned it back on Germany. The unraveling of the Nazi empire had begun.

In March of 1942 the front in Russia stretched 1,500 miles from the Gulf of Finland just outside Leningrad south of a point west of Moscow, and then south through the Ukraine to the Black Sea. At a meeting in early March at Hitler's East Prussian headquarters, the General Staff emphasized the extended supply lines and advised a passive strategy of holding what they already had. In private the generals sometimes whispered about possibly suing for an armistice. As the warlord, Hitler was becoming increasingly pathological and paranoid. The Chief of the General Staff, General Franz Halder, at the time wrote in his diary:

> Once when a quite objective report was read to him [Hitler] showing that still in 1942 Stalin would be able to muster from one to one-and-a-quarter million fresh troops in the region north of Stalingrad, not to mention half a million men in the Caucasus, and which provided proof that Russian output of frontline tanks amounted to at least 1,200 a month, Hitler flew at the man who was reading with clenched fists, and foam in the corners of his mouth and forbade him to say any more of such idiotic twaddle.

Perhaps Halder should have kept his thoughts to himself. He ended up in a concentration camp.

Instead, Hitler launched his armies on new offensives. He was still obsessed with taking Stalingrad, the manufacturing center of Russia's arms industry and the "model" city of Communism, occupying the oil fields of the Caucasus, and inflicting a crushing defeat on the Soviet armies that would break them once and for all. The battle plan was named "Code Blue." Rather than frontal attacks, both Moscow and Leningrad would be outflanked, cut off, and starved into submission.

Forward into Battle Once More . . .

By the spring of 1942, the number of German panzer tank divisions had been increased from 19 to 25 although their tanks remained the 1941 model and were still inferior to the Russian T 38. The German army had been augmented by three Hungarian divisions, twelve from Romania, three from Italy, two from Finland, and three from Slovakia, although the Hungarians and Rumanians sometimes seemed more interested in quarreling with each other than fighting the Russians. Surprisingly,

50,000 Russians who, disenchanted with Soviet rule, had either mutinied or deserted, were formed into a separate division although the Germans were loath to provide them with much firepower.

However the morale and confidence of the core groups of the Germany army, the field level officer corps and the senior noncommissioned officers, had been severely damaged by the disappointments of the 1941 campaigns and the horrors of the dreadful winter. There were now two million German soldiers in Russia, and their letters home reflected discouragement and in some cases despair. "You can't believe Ivan is dead just because his legs are blown off or someone has stuck a bayonet through his guts," one *Wehrmacht* officer wrote his family. "If he has an arm left and a rifle within reach, he'll roll over and shoot you in the back as soon as you're past him." At home the German people were beginning to realize that being sent to the Eastern Front was almost a death sentence.

Nevertheless, in the spring of 1942 the *Wehrmacht* girded its loins and went forth to battle as Hitler ordered. It was still the finest army in the world, and that summer it achieved another high-tide moment as it fought its way south, pennants fluttering from the command tanks, along the Don and the Volga rivers to Grozny, the oil fields in the Caucuses, and above all, toward Stalingrad. Initially, as the German columns hurtled across the steppes, victory followed victory, and it was a repeat of the summer of 1941. The Russians were outgunned, outmaneuvered, poorly-trained and suffered stupendous casualties. That year 500,000 prisoners were sent back to Germany as slave laborers. In August, Hitler confidently told Field Marshal Erich von Manstein: "The Russian is finished." As Alan Clark describes the offensive:

> The progress of the German columns could be discerned at thirty or forty miles distance. An enormous dust cloud towered in the sky, thickened by smoke from burning villages and gunfire. Heavy and dark at the head of the column, the smoke lingered in the still atmosphere of summer long after the tanks had passed on, a hanging barrage of brown haze stretching back to the western horizon. War correspondents with the advance waxed lyrical about the "Irresistible Mastadon," the "mot pulk" or motorized square which these columns represented on the move, with the trucks and artillery enclosed by a frame of Panzers.

"It is the formation of the Roman Legions, now brought up to date in the twentieth century to tame the Mongol-Slav hordes."

Stalin, however, still believed that Hitler wanted Moscow above all, and he was convinced that the offensive toward Stalingrad was a ruse. A bizarre incident occurred on June 19, 1942, when the operations officer of the 23rd Panzer Division, a Major Reichel, in a Storch light aircraft was shot down in contested territory. Against all operating procedures, he had with him the master plan and Order of Battle of the entire southern operation, which showed that the objective of the German campaign was Stalingrad.

Reichel survived the crash, and with a Russian patrol approaching, armed only with his Luger, tried to fight them off and inexplicably missed the opportunity to burn the plans. He was killed and the patrol recovered his charred briefcase. It was immediately read and then sent to Stalin. When told of this breach, Hitler was enraged and ordered that Reichel's division commander be court-martialed. However, the ever-suspicious Stalin refused to believe the papers were genuine and ordered that they be ignored.

But the Tide Was Beginning to Turn

As the Germans approached Stalingrad, the ferocity of the resistance rose exponentially. German communiqués begin expressing dismay at the willingness of the enemy to trade seven or eight lives for that of one German soldier. In them phrases appear like "insane stubbornness," "wild beasts," "barbarians," and then more ominously "every German soldier sees himself as a condemned man." In July Stalin issued a fierce new order: "Not One Step Backwards. Anyone who surrenders is a traitor to the Motherland. Panic-mongers and cowards must be destroyed on the spot."

In the Soviet Order of Battle, behind the first wave of infantry there was to be second line of tanks and Battle Field Police to shoot down anyone who wavered. Being taken prisoner was a death sentence. The families of those known to have become POWs were sent to the work camps. Commanders permitting retreats were summarily dispatched to penal companies, which were used to perform suicide tasks. Surrounded by death, the Russian soldier had no alternative but to fight to the last. Collaborators, of course, were shot on the spot.

At the same time, Hitler was becoming increasingly uneasy with the tactical situation. Always discontented with his generals, he became more and more intolerant and rude. One of the field commanders, General Whilhelm Groener, made an entry in his diary for August 30, 1942, that reads:

> Today's conferences with the Führer were again the occasion of abusive reproaches against the military leadership of the highest commands. He charges them again with intellectual conceit, mental inadaptability, and utter failure to grasp essentials.

The Battle for Stalingrad

In late August of 1942, the Germans reached the outskirts of Stalingrad and the ultimate battle was joined. On August 23, German Henkel aircraft carpet bombed the center of the city, setting on fire the huge petroleum storage tanks and causing an immense conflagration. Burning oil spread across the Volga even as the Germans tried to cross in rubber boats creating the nightmare scenes seen in newsreels and later recreated in movies. In the days that followed, the German artillery reduced the city to rubble. By mid-October they almost had gained control of the city, and the Russian positions had been reduced to a few concrete strong houses on the right bank of the Volga.

But the Germans were exhausted and could not press their advantage. Their supply lines were stretched across 500 miles, their tanks were breaking down, and there were no spare parts. The two sides settled into what came to be called *Rattenkreig,* "the war of the rats," sniper to sniper, squad sized street-fighting, often hand-to-hand warfare amidst the rubble of the ruined city. It was a type of fighting where the Germans' superior mobility and firepower counted for far less. A German officer wrote in his diary: "Stalingrad is no longer a town. By day it is an enormous cloud of burning blinding smoke, and when night arrives . . . the dogs plunge into the Volga and swim desperately to gain the other bank. . . . Animals flee this hell . . . only men endure."

In the grim stalemate of the ruins where combat never stopped, snipers inflicted heavy casualties on both sides and disrupted movement. It was an art at which the Soviets excelled, and eventually the Germans sent the head of their sniper school, SS Heinz Thorwald, to the city. The Russians dispatched their two-man crack sniper team to kill him. They stalked each other for days, until finally they faced off from two impregnable positions. One of the Russians, Nikolai Kulikov, fired a wild shot and then raised his helmet on a stick for a moment. The German fired, Kulikov screamed as if he had been hit, and the German raised his head and the other Russian sniper killed him.

Stalin demanded that Stalingrad be fought literally to the last child. He ordered there was to be no evacuation of women and children from the city, believing this would compel the local militia to fight more viciously. The city curved around the Volga River for 20 miles, and the authorities organized a ruthless defense. Every able-bodied man and woman in this large area and the surrounding countryside was conscripted and forced to leave their families. Failure to do so meant you were branded "a traitor to the state" and subject to death or assignment to a penal battalion. Old scores were settled in the tribunals. A woman who fled from her village when it was bombed was denounced and sent by a tribunal to a penal battalion for "deserting her place of work." Another who refused to leave her home and young children as the Germans approached was condemned as a traitor. A teacher who balked at deploying his 13-year-old boy and girl students in a frontline position was sent to a gulag in Siberia.

The Closing of the Russian Ring

As the battle for Stalingrad raged on throughout the fall, the Russians slowly strengthened their forces of men, planes, and tanks, and then in mid-November began closing a ring around Stalingrad with the objective of trapping the Germans in the city. Gradually, the *Luftwaffe* lost air superiority. The encirclement of Stalingrad could not have been completed if it had not been for a daring Russian raid. The Russian columns could not link unless they could pass over the wide Don River at the massive Kalach Bridge. The bridge had been prepared for demolition by the Germans with a platoon of combat engineers stationed on it to insure that it was blown if Russian tanks threatened this crucial crossing.

At half past four on the afternoon of November 23 the officer in charge of the detail heard the sound of tanks approaching and his initial reaction was that they might be Russian. However, through his glasses he identified them as Horch personnel carriers with 21st Panzer Division markings followed by a column of tanks. Assuming they were carrying German reinforcements for Stalingrad, he waved them on. The personnel carriers halted on the bridge and disgorged a hundred Russian commandoes armed with automatic weapons who killed most of the engineers and secured the bridge before it could be blown. The column of tanks then passed over the bridge and late that night linked up with the tanks of the 51st Russian division. Alan Clark wrote: "The first tenuous link in a choke chain that would throttle a quarter of a million German soldiers had been forged, and the turning point in World War II had arrived." After Stalingrad the Red Army held the strategic initiative, and although the Germans from time to time won battles, they were only of tactical significance.

In December, Hitler mounted a major effort under General Erich von Manstein to break through the Russian cordon of steel to relieve the desperately beleaguered 5th Army trapped in Stalingrad. After initial gains, the offensive stalled, still 50 miles from the city. Shortly thereafter the relief force itself had to retreat in disorder as it was outflanked. By now the 5th Army was so enfeebled by malnutrition and typhus that it was incapable of fighting its own way out. Efforts to resupply it from the air were inadequate. On January 8, 1943, the Germans rejected an ultimatum to surrender, and a major Russian offensive began. As always the Germans fought resolutely and bravely but they were gradually pushed back a mile a day. On January 22 with the Russians only 10 miles from the center of the city, a final push began. In violent and intense house-to-house fighting the Germans were forced into an oblong four miles deep and eight miles long where they were relentlessly bombed and pounded by artillery.

In these last days of the siege, the once proud members of the *Wehrmacht* were afflicted by hunger, disease, terror, and panic at the thought of capture by the Russians. The Hungarian, Italian, and Rumanian conscript divisions were mutinous despite floggings, and anarchy reigned. The Soviet ring closed tighter and tighter on the German enclave. Hitler raged at his field commanders to fight to the end, and elevated the senior general to field marshal while dispensing battlefield promotions to many of the senior officers still alive. It was all to no avail. At 19:45 on the evening of January 30 the radio operator at 6th Army headquarters sent a last message on his own: "The Russians are at the door of our bunker. We are destroying our equipment." He added the letters "CX"—the international wireless code signifying: "This station will no longer transmit." The battle was over.

Although to the end, Hitler refused to countenance surrender and exhorted fighting to the last man, the remnants of the 5th Army in the Stalingrad pocket surrendered on January 30, 1943, and by February 2 all resistance had ceased. By that time 91,000 Germans including 23 generals were being herded off in the deadly cold of the Russian winter to open-air prison camps with nothing but their tattered greatcoats for shelter. Rations were bread and a thin, watery soup, and the latrines were holes in the frozen ground. By the spring of 1943, typhus, frostbite, and starvation had killed 45,000, and most of the survivors perished at hard labor in the years to come. Only 5,000 of the original 91,000 ever saw Germany again. This was all that was left of the once proud, all-conquering 5th Army, which only two months before consisted of 22 divisions and 285,000 men.

The surrender at Stalingrad shocked the German nation, and, as noted, had repercussions in the occupied countries. The press was rigidly controlled in Germany and across Europe, but it was impossible to hide the dimensions of the defeat. The Soviets released photographs of the captured German generals that showed them to be healthy and well fed, which were in bleak contrast to long lines of gaunt and ragged soldiers stumbling into captivity. For the first time it dawned on the German people that their armies might not only be repulsed from Russia, but that the Fatherland might actually lose the war. Fear of the revenge that the Russians would extract and of the future grew. Graffiti began to appear with the ironic slogan "Enjoy the War; the Peace Will Be Much Worse." Subversive jokes circulated in the officer corps with some no longer giving the traditional "Heil Hitler!" greeting. Plotting again began to assassinate Hitler, and then to negotiate a separate peace. Berlin had always been a city where delicious, malicious gossip was a currency unto itself. John Toland in *Adolf Hitler* cites the wives of Reich ministers Walther Funk and Wilhelm Frick whispering openly at a Berlin party in early 1943 that Hitler was insane.

Hitler Deteriorates—Physically and Mentally—and Germany Retreats

Hitler himself seemed shattered by the disaster. He retreated to his dreary command bunker at Raustenburg and became increasingly brooding, bitter, and reclusive. His health deteriorated and he suffered from gas, headaches, and insomnia. He aged noticeably and his hair went gray. His doctors gave him glandular injections and antidepressants. He spent hours studying maps and issuing orders for the taking of minor objectives by small units. Hitler had never followed a settled, orderly schedule, and he had always been a night owl. In this regard he was similar to Churchill. In the glory days he had moved constantly around Germany, visiting plants and schools, like a medieval monarch. Now his behavior became erratic and irascible.

Hitler's temper tantrums were monstrous. His generals were all "cowardly *schweinhunds.*" He no longer held forth at the evening mess with the senior officers and almost never left his personal quarters until after dark. Most meetings were held at night and often extended until almost dawn leaving the participants exhausted. Some historians now believe one of his doctors inadvertently poisoned him with doses of mercury, which caused his left hand to become numb.

His hold over the army, which was based on his previous infallibility, was gone. He became even more suspicious and began to worry (with good reason) about his personal security. The Stauffenberg assassination plot and the subsequent revelation that so many high-ranking officers whom he respected were involved had deeply wounded his pride and self-esteem. General Guderian, who was still his favorite, described the transformation as follows: "His left hand trembled, his back was bent, his gaze fixed, his eyes protruded but lacked their former luster, his cheeks were flecked with red."

Air Marshal Goring, winner of the Iron Cross as a fighter pilot in World War I and once Hitler's deputy and confidante, fell into disgrace. He had promised that the *Luftwaffe* could save the army at Stalingrad and that no allied bomber would ever reach the Ruhr. In August 1943 as the bombing of German cities increased, at a speech in Berlin he was heckled by angry shouts of: "You told us that you would protect us from the RAF," and "When will the air raids stop?" Goring, in late 1943, retired to his villa at Karinhall where he found solace in hunting, morphine, and his world-class art collection plundered mostly from the French museums and wealthy Jews.

After Stalingrad, all across the Eastern Front the German armies began to gradually pull back as shown in the map in Figure 12.1. Moscow was no longer menaced. The siege of Leningrad was broken. As for the plight of the army still in Russia, as one general put it, "We are in the position of a man who has seized a wolf by the ears and dares not let him go." Churchill in *The Hinge of Fate* wrote of Stalingrad: "This crushing disaster ended Hitler's prodigious efforts to conquer Russia by force of arms and destroy Communism by an equally odious form of totalitarian tyranny." The tide of Nazi conquest, which at its crest covered most of Europe to the frontier of Asia and the Volga and almost to the Nile in Africa, had begun to recede never to flow back again.

In the United States, which was preoccupied with its own bloody war in the Pacific, the importance of the surrender at Stalingrad was not recognized until much later. The stock market, which had returned to the doldrums after the Battle of Midway rally, pretty much ignored the news from Russia. However, as Antony Beevor points out in his epic history *Stalingrad,* the effect on the rest of the world was very significant. In occupied Europe, resistance movements were emboldened by the sense the tide had turned. The heroism of the Red armies and the flickering newsreels of long columns of ragged German prisoners stumbling across the steppes punctured the myth of the invincibility of German arms. Even more important the surrender at Stalingrad convinced many fellow travelers and skeptics around the world that Communism was the dynamic world force with the consequent effect on postwar politics. And as Churchill noted, Stalin became even more imperious and intractable. The concessions made to him at Yalta derived in part from Stalingrad.

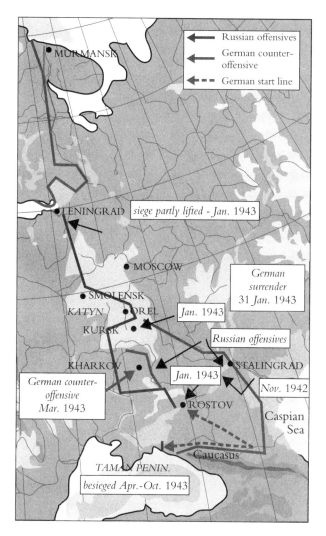

Figure 12.1   The Eastern Front, November 1942–March 1943
SOURCE: naval-history.net

The Effect of the Stalingrad Defeat on the German Economy

Immediately after the defeat at Stalingrad, concerned about the ebbing of confidence, the Nazi government imposed controls on stock prices for the remainder of World War II which concealed the damage. No

German legally could sell shares without first offering them to the Reichsbank, which had the option of buying them at December 1941 prices in exchange for government bonds, which remained in the bank's possession. Not exactly an attractive proposition, particularly since bond prices collapsed. German wealth was being destroyed not only by the allied bombing campaigns but also by edict. Anecdotal reports suggest that after Stalingrad and the imposition of controls, unreported sales of equities were infrequent and at deeply distressed prices. There is also evidence that at about this time the Nazi leadership gang and some of the generals began to hedge their wealth bets. Country estates in the Ukraine and Poland suddenly seemed chancy, and money and gold were being smuggled to Zurich, Madrid, and to bolt holes in Argentina and Chile.

By the spring of 1943, the German economy itself was becoming increasingly a barter economy. The German people now were hearing horror stories from soldiers on leave of the disasters on the Western Front, and there were rumors about atrocities and of slave labor and concentration camps. Soldiers warned that the Russians would extract terrible vengeance if they reached Germany. There was swelling unease and sullen discontent with Hitler, but everyone knew of and feared the sadistic thugs of the evil Gestapo. Germany was a police state ruled by fear.

The most interesting aspect of the actual chart of the German CDAX Index is not the huge advance prices had between late 1939 and the autumn of 1941, but that the index peaked so early (see Figure 12.2). Did German investors in the fall of 1941 actually perceive even then with the German army at the gates of Moscow and Lenningrad that Hitler had overreached in the attack on Russia? The Barbarossa advance (described in Chapter 6) didn't actually peter out until December of 1941, but by that October the specter of winter was looming for an army that was unprepared for it. It was then that the generals were becoming restless about the campaign, and were arguing with Hitler about strategy. It was then that Von Runstedt confided to his wife that "the vastness of Russia devours us."

Apparently investors must have learned of these misgivings (or sensed them) and taken them very seriously because, after all, there were great victories in the summer and fall of 1942. This book and most real historians argue that the surrender at Stalingrad more than a year later was the

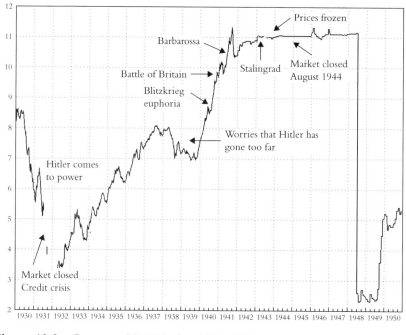

Figure 12.2   Germany CDAX Index: 1930–1950
DATA SOURCE: Global Financial Data, Inc.

true inflexion point. It was also such an obvious turning point. Everyone then could discern the dimensions of the defeat. The expending of the vital force of Barbarossa in the fall of 1941 was a much more subtle high-water mark. The timing of the peak also shows that even in a police state, stock markets can make dispassionate judgments. As shown in Figure 12.3 (which is indexed to 1918 equals 100) outlines the history of the German gold-denominated stock market as best Dan Ruprecht has been able to link indexes together over the 75 years that ended in 1945. This index does not include dividends (because there is no data), so it overstates the carnage. There certainly was stunning volatility in equity prices from 1914 to 1943, but there were some great buying opportunities, yet German stocks were not wealth preservers. Remember that from 1943 to 1946, prices were effectively frozen. As noted previously, what is striking is how prescient the German stock market was that World War I was going to be lost, that the reparations imposed by the victors would be a disaster, and that hyperinflation was coming and that it would crush equities. Talk about the wisdom of crowds!

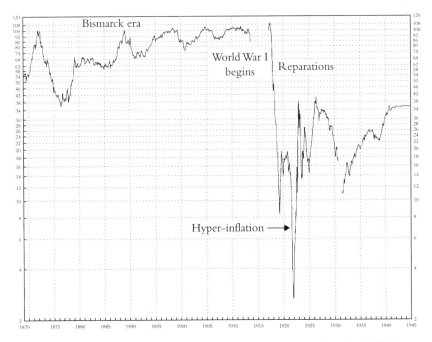

Figure 12.3   Germany Gold-Denominated Stock Price Index: 1870–1945
DATA SOURCE: Global Financial Data, Inc.

Joseph Goebbels in the spring of 1943 made a major effort to combat the gloom and defeatism of the German people. He argued that Germany was still a peacetime economy with six million people producing consumer goods, one and a half million women employed as domestics, and over one hundred thousand luxury restaurants still open. The German people must commit to "total war." With Hitler in seclusion, he made a series of speeches in which the message was: *Of course we can lose the war. The war can be lost by people who will not exert themselves; it will be won by those who try the hardest. Total war will be the shortest war.*

It was too late for heroics. Too many young soldiers had been killed; too many civilians had died in the bombings; the German people could not be fooled again. Nevertheless it has to be said that even as late as 1944 many Germans still believed in Hitler and the *Lebensraum* dream. The great author Gunter Grass in his autobiography relates how when the Stauffenberg plot to kill Hitler in July of that year failed, he joined his neighbors in decrying the conspirators as "that brood of treacherous aristocrats."

Nevertheless, by 1944 Hitler knew he was beaten. His physical deterioration was extraordinary. He shuffled when he walked, and his features were those of a weary and broken old man. In the last year of his life he became increasingly reclusive and seldom showed himself to crowds or his troops, and as he retreated back into Germany he spent more time on his special train. Albert Speer describes an incident one evening as he sat with Hitler "in his rosewood-paneled dining car."

> The table was elegantly set with silver, glass, china and flowers. As we began our meal, none of us at first saw that a freight train had stopped on the adjacent track. From the cattle car bedraggled, starved, and in some cases wounded German soldiers, just returning from the East, stared at the diners. With a start Hitler noticed the somber scene just two yards from his window. Without as much as a gesture of greeting in their direction, he peremptorily ordered the servant to draw the shades. This, in the second half of the war, was how Hitler handled a meeting with ordinary frontline soldiers such as he himself once had been.

I would argue that the December afternoon in 1941 when the patrol through the mist and snow dimly saw the spires of Moscow and the German army had never suffered a defeat was the high-water mark. If so then the Battle for Stalingrad, arguably the battle of the century, which ended in early 1943 with the German surrender, was the tipping point where the tide turned in the Russian-German war. Two years later the Russians inflicted the same devastation that reduced Stalingrad to rubble on Berlin. Before the war was over, the Russian colossus had lost nine million men with another 18 million wounded, and 4.5 million captured of which only 1.8 million ever returned. It is believed about 18 million Soviet civilians died.

As discussed previously, Hitler had long been obsessed with creating a German *volk* of 200 million people stretching from Germany to Moscow. He told his generals in the final meeting before the launching of Barbarossa that destroying Russia was the "real" war, the war he had always intended to wage. In retrospect, his decision to invade Russia was the most fateful of his career. He made three miscalculations.

First, he overestimated the dissatisfaction of the Russian people with the Soviet regime and underestimated their fighting spirit and loyalty to

Mother Russia. He was guilty of "ignorant condescension, mainly racially motivated" of what he thought was "a primitive Slavic society."

Second, by deciding to rescue Mussolini in Greece, the start of Barbarossa was postponed from the middle of May, as originally planned, until the third week of June. That six-week delay resulted in the failure of the *Wehrmacht* to reach winter quarters, take Moscow and Leningrad, and complete the campaign as originally planned well before the brutal Russian winter descended. Assuming the same rate of advance, the Germans would have been in Moscow and Leningrad by October comfortably warming their feet by the fire and in command of the capital and nerve center of the Soviet Union. In retrospect, the whole course of the campaign was fatally altered by this decision.

Third, by turning over the administration of the captured Russian territories to the bloodthirsty, depraved, criminals of the Waffen SS, Hitler lost the opportunity to capture the minds and souls of many Russians in the Western provinces. Instead he created a ferocious resistance that drained the German army's resources and imperiled its supply chain. It was a stupid and fatal error.

God only knows what the outcome of the entire war would have been and how long it would have lasted if the Soviet Union, having lost its capital and communications center, had capitulated and made a separate peace.

Russian Invasion of Germany: The Crushing of Lives, Property, Possessions, and the Economy

The financial history of Germany in the twentieth century is so fascinating and terrifying because the country endured the ultimate *plague,* the most extreme *cholera.* Germany's condition, the environment at the end of the World War II was even worse than Japan's. Hitler believed that in the end the Western Allies would intervene to save Germany from the Soviets, and as a result he demanded that the *Wehrmacht,* or what was left of it, keep fighting on the Eastern Front. By January 1945, the Russian offensive consisted of three million men against perhaps 450,000 Germans who ranged in age from 14 to 60. They had no chance, but they fought with the braveness and tenacity of desperation and they made the Red Army pay. The city of Berlin was fought street by street. All this served to further enrage the Soviet soldiers.

In the winter of 1945 when the Red Army entered East Prussia and then Germany, they were obsessed with blood and revenge. German soldiers trying to surrender were shot on sight. That January five million German civilians, to escape the terrible wrath of the Russians, fled west toward the British and American armies. Long caravans of people with their basic essentials jammed into wagons, carts, and old cars struggled down snow-choked roads. Many carried their valuable possessions with art folded in pipes and their life savings in gold and jewelry stuffed into knapsacks. The documented stories about what happened to them are grim reading.

When the Russian tank columns caught up with these pathetic caravans, they indiscriminately used their heavy tanks as bulldozers, smashing through the columns, and crushing people and carts like huge steam rollers. Those that fled into the fields in knee-deep snow were machine gunned. Children were herded into ditches, and then grenades were thrown at them. The living and the dead were stripped of watches, rings, boots, and fur gloves. The Russians' vengeance cry was *"Khleb za khleb, krov za krov!"*—"bread for bread, blood for blood."

When the Russians reached a town, they always jovially asked for the *burgermeister.* He was usually an older, respected man, and when he appeared in the town square, he was immediately shot. Any men under 60 were also killed, and younger women were brutally gang raped and sometimes nailed naked to the doors of their houses afterwards. Then the soldiers, who by now were often drunk, searched for loot, shouting *"uri, uri"* their version of the German word for watches. In the houses they went from room to room deliberately smashing treasured dishes and glassware. Sometimes homes and barns were set on fire. Large houses and manors were invariably burned to the ground. For example in the town of Nemmersdorf, 72 civilians were left dead after the Red Army passed through. Twelve French slave laborers also were rounded up and their rings were taken away—by slicing off their fingers. Then they were executed. It was senseless, murderous, vandalism. Such is life when the Four Horsemen ride again!

There was no way wealth could be preserved in the face of this indiscriminate carnage and cholera. However, after the surrender most of the atrocities stopped although food was in desperately short supply. The refugee German civilians began to return to their looted, ravaged homes, but at least the farmland was still there. In the early months of the occupation, stock prices were released from the Nazi controls, and even the informal quotations collapsed. For the next five bleak years, Hershey bars, Lucky Strikes, and lumps of coal were the mediums of exchange in Germany.

There is no linked stock market data for Germany prior to the creation of the Commerzbank index in 1956. Prior to that, less precise indexes calculated by Gielen, the Bundesamt, and the Reichsamt provide a general sense of direction and magnitude:

- In the first decade of the twentieth century, German stocks were strong, reaching a high in 1912.
- However the political unrest in Europe and the onset of World War I caused a steep decline as the war dragged on.
- In 1913 the German Mark was worth 2.38 U.S. dollars.
- After Germany surrendered in 1918 it had collapsed to 7 cents.
- By 1922 one U.S. cent was worth 100 Marks.

Later, some experts blamed this steep decline and the hyperinflation that went with it on the harsh reparations imposed on Germany by the Allies. In reality the collapse of the currency and the hyperinflation had very little to do with reparations.

In the third decade, German stocks were at first staggered by the hyperinflation, but then did better in the worldwide bull market of the late 1920s. After Hitler came to power and the economy began to recover, equity prices rose and for the full decade had a real return of 6.5% a year—the best real return performance in a still-sick world. However, after the initial euphoric gains of 1940 and 1941 ended in the snow outside of Moscow, German stocks suffered for the rest of the decade. For the decade of the 1940s they fell 6.4% per annum in nominal terms and minus 10.3% per year inflation adjusted. By 1949 they had lost two-thirds of their 1940 purchasing power. These are the numbers that were produced by Dimson, Marsh, and Staunton from the London Business School, but I suspect they would be the first to say that the precision of the decimal points is highly questionable.

German government bonds were even worse, with their purchasing power eroding at a rate of 20.8% per annum or a loss of 90% of their

1940 purchasing power in the course of the decade. Government bills were better, falling *only* 2.4% a year, although German bill owners had lost everything in the hyperinflation of 1923.

As a German investor in 1950 looking back at a half-century of war, debasement of the currency, hyperinflation, total defeat, and occupation, your equity portfolio adjusted for inflation had fallen from its purchasing power value in 1900 by 1.8% per annum, which means that 100 Marks had become 40 Marks. Government bonds in an inflation and war-ravaged economy declined 7.8% per annum, which amounted to a 90% loss of value since 1900. To compound the damage, the Mark had fallen 96% versus the dollar and 86% against the pound. Owners of financial assets paid a high price indeed for the sins of their leaders.

At mid-century, wealth had not been preserved during this wartime devastation and destruction. Both equities and bonds obviously had totally failed to preserve, much less enhance, the wealth of their holders. The semi-log chart shown in Figure 12.3 makes all percentage changes similar and to some extent masks the extent of the damage. When the stock market reopened in the late summer of 1948, the first trades were at a level 90% below the high in the fall of 1941. Although the index more than doubled by the end of 1949, the losses were still staggering.

However, after this grim first half of the century and from these profoundly depressed levels, beginning in 1950 German stocks increased more than tenfold in real terms in the next 10 years, compounding at an astounding 24.6% a year in real terms. As a result, by 1960 the German investor had a positive return since the turn of the century of 2.4% a year. Not bad for a country that lost two wars, endured a brutal dictatorship, and was partially occupied by the still vengeful Soviets. A surprisingly large number of the great, old German companies such as Siemens and Bayer had survived the war, and they prospered in the 1960s. In the late 1940s and 1950s, many new businesses were started that were to become the *mittelstand,* the medium-sized, family controlled, wealth machines of the future that restored Germany's economic power—and made a lot of Germans rich again.

From 1950 to 2000 German equities had a real annual return of 9.1%. Bonds earned 3.7% per annum, and the mark rose 50% versus the dollar. What an incredible turnaround! Obviously staying power, faith, and a strong stomach were required.

Chapter 13

Defeats and Then Victories in Asia and North Africa

As 1942 dawned, Churchill was confident that with the United States and Russia now engaged, final victory was insured unless what he called "the Grand Alliance" broke under the strain or unless some entirely new instrument of war appeared in German hands. Nevertheless the early months of the year were not promising as the full force of the Japanese onslaught fell on Britain and the United States. Carping about the conduct of the war was growing, particularly in London, but also from Australia, where (as mentioned in Chapters 2 and 5), the Australian Prime Minister John Curtin was a perpetual thorn in Churchill's side. Singapore had long been thought to be the impregnable fortress that anchored the English empire in Asia, and the prospect of its loss was frightening to Australia.

The British retreat down the Malaya peninsula was a dispiriting and bloody disaster. The old Royal Air Force planes flying out of Singapore were no match for the speedy Japanese Zero aircraft, and the new planes shipped from Britain in boxes had to be assembled. Their first flights were in combat against some of the most experienced combat pilots in the world flying superior aircraft. As a result, the Japanese quickly established air-superiority over Malaya, but the British, Indian, and Australian forces under General A.E. Percival still numbered 86,895 men versus only some 26,000 Japanese soldiers. General Percival, a tall, thin man with two protruding, rabbit-like teeth, by all accounts was not a forceful or effective leader.

By contrast the Japanese general, Tomoyuki Yamashita, later known as the Tiger of Malaya, was a towering, strong warrior who led from the front and inspired his troops with his personal valor. The British had not one single tank because years earlier some genius in London had decided armor would be ineffective in jungle warfare. The Japanese had lots of tanks to go with their bicycles, a combination that gave them firepower and mobility. The Indian troops who had never seen a tank before were terrified by what they called "metal monsters." The senior Australian, Major General Gordon Bennett, was appalled by the "total lack of the offensive spirit" of the British troops and warned Melbourne of a disaster unless reinforcements were sent. Australia's Prime Minister Curtin harassed Churchill to do something before it was too late. Churchill responded by sending an Indian brigade and a British division, but unfortunately the reinforcements were of little help. The Indians were young, inexperienced, and had not been trained in jungle warfare. The new British division that came had been on board ship for almost three months, and was unprepared for the jungle or the superbly conditioned Japanese. By contrast the Japanese had done extensive prewar reconnaissance of the terrain. Secret agents and equipment had been slyly infiltrated and preparations for the offensive had been made. For example before the war a large number of bicycles had been smuggled in and stored in various locations on the peninsula to provide mobility for the Japanese infantry. The Imperial army employed a unique combination of tanks and bicycles in their lightning advance. The jungle, the climate, and the night were allies of the Japanese. Relentless heat, stifling humidity, insects, snakes, and dysentery were the same for both sides, but the Japanese soldier had been through extensive jungle and night warfare training. He had been taught how to stay healthy and make do in the jungle on meager rice and water rations for weeks on end. Thus these jungle conditioned troops were able to effectively utilize small unit raids and infiltration to undermine the British front. Eventually the British were compelled to make a major withdrawal just to stabilize their lines, and by then it was too late. As they fell back toward the Singapore causeway they were continually infiltrated and outflanked with small amphibious landings and raids.

In early February the Allied forces withdrew to Singapore itself, the foundation and keystone of the empire in Asia. The Japanese, led by the Imperial Guards, were in relentless pursuit. The defenders in Singapore outnumbered the attackers by two to one, they were ensconced in fixed defensive positions, and by all military theory they should have been able to hold out. Churchill, sounding a little bit like Hitler haranguing his generals, exhorted Archibald Wavell, now the commanding general, as follows:

> I must admit to being staggered by your telegram. . . . It never occurred to me for a moment . . . that the gorge of the fortress of Singapore, with its splendid moat half a mile to a mile wide, was not entirely fortified against an attack from the northward. What is the use of having an island for a fortress if it is not to be made into a citadel? . . . How is it that not one of you pointed this out to me at any time when these matters have been under discussion?
>
> In these present circumstances the defenders must greatly outnumber the Japanese forces who have crossed the straits, and in a well-contested battle they should destroy them. There must at this stage be no thought of saving the troops or sparing the population. The battle must be fought to the bitter end at all costs. . . . Commanders and senior officers should die with their troops. The honor of the British Empire and of the British Army is at stake. I rely on you to show no mercy to weakness in any form. With the Russians fighting as they are and the Americans so stubborn at Luzon, the whole reputation of our country and our race is involved. It is expected that every unit will be brought into close contact with the enemy and fight it out.

However, the troops holding Singapore by now were demoralized by the retreat and exhausted from the heat, combat, malaria, and dysentery. Of the 100,000 soldiers deployed, 33,000 were British and 17,000 Australian. The rest were Indians and Malayans whose commitment understandably must have been a little soft. Wavell messaged Churchill on February 11, 1942, that his troops had "an inferiority complex." Furthermore he, Wavell, had slipped and broken some bones in his back, and he would be in hospital for a few days and crippled for a few weeks. His commander on the ground, General Percival, reported his forces were "too exhausted to withstand an attack" much less counter-attack. Ammunition, supplies, and water were running low, and the large civilian population of the city, much of it Chinese with memories of the rape of Nanking, was disorderly and panicked at the prospect of being occupied by the Japanese army. Churchill, disgusted with his generals, again ordered the timid Percival to "stand-fast in the citadel."

The Fall of Singapore

The Japanese continued to press their assault, and skillfully breached the first line of defenses. The heavy guns that faced the sea were fixed in place and useless. On February 13, 1942, 3,000 specialists vital to the Allied war effort were evacuated from Singapore in small boats. Tragically, Japanese navy patrols discovered them, and they were all killed or captured. Once again, the Allies lost key technical people. The following day, the defenders fell back further, and conditions within the city continued to worsen with some disorder and shortages of food and water. Japanese commandoes were beginning to infiltrate the city, but it was not a chaotic situation by the standard of sieges.

However, within a few days it was all over. On February 15, 1942, the Allied forces in Singapore surrendered to a Japanese army it **outnumbered two to one.** Churchill said it was "the worst disaster in British military history." Stock markets shuddered. In London, stock prices, which had been falling anyway, took a nasty fall although they were still well above the 1940 low. The Australian market sold off sharply.

Several days later over a 100,000 prisoners, some accounts say 130,000, led by General Percival, were paraded through the streets on the way to the Changi prison camp from which most of them would never emerge. The Japanese took control of the huge naval base with most of its prime dockyard facilities intact. After the war, General Yamashita admitted his army was as short of water and ammunition as the defenders and that his offensive was a bluff. His supply lies were so extended that if the garrison had resisted for another week, he said he would have had to withdraw. This formidable and impressive warrior later bravely held out in the Philippine mountains but finally surrendered to avoid further bloodshed. A bitter McArthur insisted he be tried as a sacrificial war criminal to appease popular sentiment, and he was executed in 1946.

The sudden and inexplicable surrender of Singapore shocked and frightened the Allied world. Japan's military prowess appeared comparable to the invincibility of the Nazi war machine, and its advance across Asia by land and sea seemed unstoppable. In the course of the campaign, the British and their allies had suffered 138,703 killed or wounded compared with 9,824 for the Japanese. The Australians were most immediately threatened. Prime Minister Curtin spoke of a "shameful betrayal." The loss of Singapore not only deepened Australia's peril, but one of her elite four infantry divisions had been sacrificed. Why for over 20 years had the defenses of Singapore been constructed to face the sea rather than the land? Who was responsible for such stupidity? The answer was that the British General Staff had believed an aggressor could not approach by land because of the thick jungle. Churchill was not to blame since he had not been in power, but nevertheless in London and Melbourne he was being castigated for his conduct of the war.

Later some historians such as the Paul Johnson in his epic *Modern Times* argued that Churchill, encouraged by FDR, unwittingly caused the fall of Singapore. As noted previously in the summer and fall of 1941, Stalin vociferously complained that Russia was fighting for its survival and diverting the Germans from attacking Britain yet was receiving no military supplies. This, of course, was a ridiculous charge since the British were at great cost supplying arms to Russia while in a life or death struggle as well. In any case, Churchill, at FDR's insistence succumbed and rushed tanks and modern fighter aircraft intended for Singapore by convoys to Archangel and Murmansk. The losses of ships, men, and arms as U-boats and raiders prayed on these convoys were huge, but the tanks and aircraft that got through definitely played a part in the Soviet Christmas counterattack of 1941 and the battle for Stalingrad. Johnson wrote: "Thus, by one of the great ironies of history, Churchill, the last major British imperialist, may have sacrificed a liberal empire in order to preserve a totalitarian one."

Threats to Burma and India by the Japanese Army

From Burma there was more bad news. In late February 1942, British and Indian brigades were caught by the Japanese in front of the wide Sittang River. Forced to retreat, the British blew up the lone bridge across the river leaving one of the Indian brigades trapped on the far side. The abandonment didn't do much for the morale of the rest of the Indians. The dreaded prospect of the Japanese army invading India and linking with the Germans now appeared possible. Extremely concerned, Churchill tried to divert to Burma two Australian divisions that were on their way home to defend Australia, wiring Prime Minister Curtin that "there is nothing else in the world that can fill the gap." Curtin, who basically had lost confidence in Britain's handling of the war, refused to permit the diversion. The bonds of kith and kin within the British Empire were fraying.

At home Churchill was beleaguered by the press and his critics. General Sir Alan Brooke wrote in his diary: "most unpleasant remarks by various ministers in connection with defeats by our forces ... I found it hard to keep my temper with some of the criticisms that were raised. Politicians prefer to be fed on victories than gorged on reverses ... there was a most unpleasant cabinet meeting."

As shown in Figure 13.1, the London stock market sold off in reaction to the fall of Singapore and then fell further in response to the continuing flow of defeats and losses:

- The Dutch East Indies on March 8, 1942.
- The Philippines on April 9.
- Mandalay on April 29.
- Corregidor, at the entrance to Manila Bay and the last strongpoint in the Philippines on May 6.

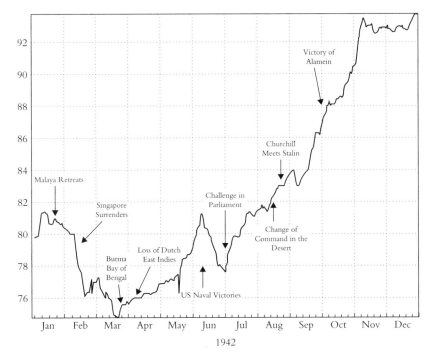

Figure 13.1   UK Financial Times 30 Industrials: 1942
DATA SOURCE: *Financial Times;* Global Financial Data, Inc.

- Losses in Ceylon.
- And the Bay of Bengal.

Now there was grumbling in Australia, and rumors of a rebellion brewing in India. It was truly a dark time. In late March, Roosevelt wrote an intimate, commiserating letter to Churchill in which he described the harangues and criticism he was receiving from prominent columnists "who have little background and less knowledge." Nevertheless, this carping created a negative, almost defeatist mood in the United States and was a definite factor in the stock market losses of that spring. FDR concluded with some personal advice that every similarly beleaguered portfolio manager should take to heart:

I know you will keep up your optimism and your grand driving force, but I know you will not mind if I tell you that you ought to take a leaf out of my notebook. Once a month I go to Hyde Park for four days, crawl into a hole, and pull the hole in after me. I am called on the telephone only if it is something of really great importance. I wish you would try it, and I wish you would lay a few bricks or paint another picture.

More Defeats for the Allies in North Africa and the North Atlantic

At the same time in the spring of 1942, the earlier, hard-won gains in North Africa were reversed: General Auchinleck had been defeated in the desert; Tobruk, Libya (in the northeast, near the border with Egypt), with its garrison of 25,000 men, fell in a single day, which meant that Libya was gone. The British armies had fallen back 400 miles across the desert towards the Egyptian frontier. A total of 50,000 men had been killed or captured, and massive amounts of equipment lost. Rommel seemed a military genius. The Germans were advancing in captured English vehicles running on captured oil and firing captured weapons and ammunition. The Allied forces were back to where they had been two years before with a triumphant Rommel pressing forward. It was not inconceivable that Cairo could be his next victim. In fact, Mussolini, wanting in on the glory, was preparing to join Rommel in the conquerors' victory parade through the streets of Cairo.

Furthermore, a "U-Boat Paradise," as Churchill described it, existed in the North Atlantic, and the Arctic convoys to get arms to Russia came under continuous attacks from U-boats, German destroyers and cruisers, and from the air. Convoys often lost half of their merchant ships and their escorts, and conditions were brutal with 10 or 20 degrees of Arctic frost and brutal ice storms. Tuberculosis was rampant on these ships because of the extreme cold and wet living conditions, and men became zombies from the fatigue of endless watches and battle stations. The superstructure of the warships was often sheeted with ice, a man's hand without gloves froze on contact with steel, and if his ship was torpedoed he could only expect to survive a minute or two in the freezing water. (Two great novels on these epic convoys are *The Cruel Sea* by Nicholas Monseratt and *H.M.S. Ulysses* by Alistair MacLean.) Even after all England had done and the losses it had suffered in doing it, Stalin continued complaining to FDR that the British were not sending enough convoys, and in late April of 1942 FDR chided Churchill. He replied:

> Moreover, difficulty of Russian convoys cannot be solved merely by antisubmarine craft. Enemy heavy ships and destroyers may at any time strike. Even on this present convoy we have been attacked by hostile destroyers, which were beaten off with damage to one of ours. *Edinburgh,* one of our best six-inch cruisers, has been badly damaged by U-boats and is being towed to Murmansk where *Trinidad,* damaged in the last convoy, is still penned. Just now I have received news that *King George V* has collided with our destroyer *Punjabi, Punjabi* being sunk and her depth charge exploding have damaged *King George V.*

Loss of Confidence in the British Military and in Churchill

In those times Churchill, although he was loath to admit it, felt under constant siege as every day new bad news arrived from somewhere. He was losing faith in his generals and the ability of British arms to combat on anywhere near equal terms their two enemies, Germany and Japan. A portfolio manager enduring a run of poor performance and facing cascading losses from some new unexpected source day after day can empathize with the prime minister's ennui.

But this was war not investing, and the injuries were not financial flesh wounds; they were mortal. All these setbacks resulted in heavy losses of life, equipment, aircraft, and ships. Nothing seemed to go right. The winter and spring of 1942 was a grim time for the Allies everywhere, and press criticism of the conduct of the war was fierce. Living conditions in London and the other major cities that were being bombed were abysmal. Lord Beaverbrook ("Max" to Churchill and a close friend and confidant) wrote to the prime minister on February 17, 1942: "The people have lost confidence in themselves, and they turn to the Government, looking for a restoration of that confidence."

However investors and the London market never totally lost confidence nor probed toward the depths of despair touched in the mortally dangerous summer of 1940. The smart, intuitive stock market, similar to wise old Churchill, was now sure that with the United States involved, the Allies would eventually win. It was just a question of how painful and long the struggle would be, and how impoverished England would be when it was all over. But it was a dark, grim time.

It is fascinating to see the rally in the London market after the battles of the Coral Sea and Midway, and then the weakness throughout most of June as the war news from the desert worsened and Churchill's leadership was challenged. Reading the press at the time, it sounds as though investors were also disconcerted by the growing criticism of the way the war was being managed and the developing movement in Parliament to replace the prime minister. In early June 1942, Churchill had gone to Washington for a consul of war with FDR, which went well, but a mutiny was brewing at home. He returned home to find himself facing a vote of "no confidence" in the House of Commons. Writing five years later in the *Hinge of Fate,* Churchill wrote:

> The chatter and criticisms of the press, where the sharpest pens were busy and many shrill voices raised, found its counterpart in the activities of a few score of Members in the House of Commons, and a fairly glum attitude on the part of our immense majority.

In a by-election for a seat in the House of Commons, the government candidate got only 6,226 votes out of almost 20,000 cast, which was widely interpreted as dissatisfaction with the administration of the war. There was talk in the lobbies of the House and in the London newspapers of a "decisive political crisis." Remember that Churchill was not only prime minister but minister of defense as well and some of the criticism focused on this dual role. On June 25, 1942, the motion for censure was placed before Parliament in the following terms:

> That this House, while paying tribute to the heroism and endurance of the Armed Forces of the Crown in circumstances of exceptional difficulty, has no confidence in the central direction of the war.

The sponsors of the motion were distinguished men who had known Churchill for years, in some cases since childhood. One, Sir Roger Keyes, was disgruntled because even though he was a longtime friend, Churchill had removed him from power, and he felt Churchill had not listened to his advice. Another, Sir John Wardlaw-Milne, was a highly regarded statesman. They all knew that if the motion was passed by the House, the prime minister would have to go. None of the ministers in Churchill's National Coalition Government backed the motion, and there was no political intrigue within the Cabinet but the debate was hot and sometimes personal.

Bevan, always a thorn in Churchill's side, said: "The Prime Minister always refers to a defeat as a disaster as though it came from God, but to a victory as though it came from Himself." A friend asked Bevan why he was attacking the prime minister.

"What do you think will happen if he goes?"

"Well," snapped Bevan, "suppose he does. What should we do? Send a postcard to Hitler giving in?" Bevan was no fan. On another occasion he described Churchill "as a man suffering from petrified adolescence ..."

Past defeats in Churchill's long career such as Gallipoli and Norway when he was First Sea Lord were brought up, and the charge was made that the government had been consistently too optimistic about the course of war. Some said he interfered too much with the military leadership on the ground. Wardlaw-Milne argued Churchill was stretched too thin. Churchill didn't help himself by saying: "I do not suffer from any desire to be relieved of my responsibilities. All I wanted was compliance with my wishes after a reasonable discussion."

While all this was going on, Churchill was suffering through a nasty, enervating crisis at home. His son Randolph was in William Manchester's words "a cad," and he and his father frequently quarreled. Randolph was even harder on his mother, maintaining that she "hated" him. A handsome man, he drank too excess and was loud, outspoken, overbearing and generally obnoxious. He was widely disliked, and had made many enemies. The constitution of one London club had actually been amended to read: "Randolph Churchill shall not be eligible for membership." When he had a tumor removed from his alimentary canal, Lord Stanley of Alderly, again according to Manchester, when he learned that the tumor was not cancerous remarked while standing at the bar of his club: "what a pity to remove the one part of Randolph that is not malignant."

According to John Mecham, as recounted in *Franklin and Winston* during the war while Randolph was stationed in Egypt, his young wife Pamela had an extended affair with the much older Averill Harriman, at that time the American Ambassador in London. In the spring of 1942, when Randolph learned of it, he came to believe that his mother and father had known of the relationship and neither warned him nor intervened. In fact, both Pamela and Harriman had been with the Prime Minister at Chartwell, late in the evening of Pearl Harbor. A tremendous family quarrel ensued which must have been deeply upsetting to the already beleaguered Churchill. Great men, like investment managers, sometimes face emotionally enervating private life distractions even as they are facing life or death professional crises.

While all this was going on, the war news continued to be bad. Rommel and his Afrika Korps were dazzling the British generals and the Eighth Army with lightning strikes and the tenacity of the troops. By mid-June 1942, he had laid siege to the key fortress city of Tobruk, which had changed hands several times. Heavy fighting took place over the next week and the Germans breached the perimeter against the 11th Indian Brigade and took possession of a great part of the fortress. On June 21, 1942, 33,000 British, Indian, and South African troops capitulated at Tobruk, Libya. As at Singapore, a large body of men and equipment had been prematurely surrendered. Many of the troops who had hardly been engaged could not believe they were giving up without further resistance. However, their position probably was hopeless. Rommel now seemed poised to enter Egypt and seize Cairo. After surveying the spoils, Rommel's chief of staff reported to Berlin with the second sentence emphasized:

> The booty is gigantic. It consisted of supplies for 30,000 men for three months and more than 10,000 cubic meters of petrol. **Without this booty adequate rations and clothing for the armoured divisions would not have been possible in the coming months.**

With this new defeat on everyone's minds, Lord Winterton led the attack on Churchill. His argument was that the prime minister must be held accountable for the series of disasters since he was in command and now he should be replaced. All this text is excerpted from *The Hinge of Fate.*

> We all agree that the Prime Minister was the Captain-General of our courage and constancy in 1940. But a lot has happened since 1940. There is more than one suitable man for Prime Minister on the Treasury bench . . . and the Right Honorable Gentleman (Churchill) should take office under him as Foreign Secretary because his management of our relations with Russia and the United States has been perfect."

The former Secretary of State for War, Mr. Leslie Hore-Belisha, concluded the case saying:

> How can one place reliance in judgments that have so repeatedly turned out to be misguided. That is what the House of Commons has to decide. Think what is at stake. In a hundred days we lost our Empire in the Far East. What will happen in the next one hundred days?

Churchill spoke last. He began with this powerful closing statement:

> This long debate has now reached its final stage. What a remarkable example it has been of the unbridled freedom of our Parliamentary institutions in time of war! Everything that could be thought of or raked up and has been used to weaken confidence in the Government, has been used to prove that ministers are incompetent and to weaken their confidence in themselves, to make the Army distrust the backing it is getting from the civil power, to make the workers lose confidence in the weapons they are striving so hard to make, to represent the government as a set of non-entities over whom the Prime Minister towers, and then to undermine him in his own heart, and if possible before the eyes of the nation. All this poured out by cable and radio to all parts of the world, to the distress of our friends and to the delight of all our foes.

He then went on to make a vigorous and eloquent defense of his stewardship. He accepted responsibility, but pointed out that many of the problems of inferior equipment and inadequate force were long-standing and therefore predated his administration. In the end, he stood by his "original programme, blood, toil, tears, and sweat" to which he added "many shortcomings, mistakes, and disappointments." He ended with this passionate cry for overwhelming support:

> Every vote counts. If those who have assailed us are reduced to contemptible proportions and their Vote of Censure is converted to a vote of censure upon its authors, make no mistake, a cheer will go up from every friend of Britain and every faithful servant of our cause, and the knell of disappointment will ring in the ears of the tyrants we are striving to overthrow.

On July 1, 1942, the motion was defeated 475 to 25. It was an overwhelming and impressive win for the prime minister. After all the setbacks Britain and its allies had sustained, that only 25 votes could be mustered against Churchill was an invigorating signal of the unity of the British people. Comfort was not given to the enemy. FDR wired Churchill: "Good for you."

The London stock market's June 1942 swoon ended that very day, and a strong rally that lifted prices 20 percent by early November 1942 followed. The stock market wanted Churchill. The market did better as the year progressed, and as slowly the tide turned in the desert. Mussolini, greedy for glory, now committed more Italian troops to the desert war and again babbled about joining Rommel in a great victory parade through the streets of Cairo. However in late July 1942, a German offensive failed to break the British defense perimeter thanks to the heroic conduct of a New Zealand Division. In hand-to-hand fighting under the moon, Rommel's own battle headquarters was almost over-run. The German's supply lines were extended and the panzers were in need of maintenance. The German advance stalled. Cairo was saved.

In August 1942, a raid in force by 5,000 Canadians and British commandoes was made on the port of Dieppe on the northwestern French coast. It was the first large-scale amphibious Allied operation against the Germans, but unfortunately it did not go well. Surprise was achieved, but almost everything else went wrong. The German defenders were stronger and the cliffs were steeper than anticipated. Landing boats came in on the wrong beaches and the naval gunfire was misdirected. The Canadians lost 900 men killed and almost 2,000 taken prisoner. It was not an encouraging rehearsal for a full-scale invasion of France.

That summer in Parliament, Churchill faced another irritating crisis. The Lord Privy Seal was now Sir Stafford Cripps who, as ambassador to Moscow had, for his own reasons, sidetracked and delayed Churchill's warning to Stalin of a German attack. Cripps was a Labor party leader, a liberal, a vegetarian, a teetotaler, and abhorred cigars. As one wag in the House of Commons said: "Cripps was descended from a long line of maiden aunts." "He has all the virtues I dislike and none of the vices I admire," Churchill had famously remarked.

Cripps was self-assured, righteous, and pompous: "there but for the grace of God goes God," but he was a very able administrator. As Lord Privy Seal and Leader of the House of Commons it was his role to explain the government's actions to the House. It was essential that he and the prime minister be in close communication.

In September Cripps began feeling neglected, and he wrote to the prime minister complaining. Furthermore, he said, he was not satisfied with the central direction of the war. The morale of the English people was deteriorating and they were becoming frustrated and discontented by the "inadequate leadership." He proposed a dualism of command, which presumably meant him. Churchill replied: "My Dear Cripps, I am surprised and somewhat pained to receive your letter." He then went on to dissect Cripps' arguments. It is fascinating to read the letter exchanges between the two of them because amidst all the elegant salutations of "My Dear Prime Minister" there is the vitriol of two men who grudgingly respect one another, but who not so *cordially* dislike each other. In the end Cripps resigned and was transferred to the Ministry of Aircraft Production.

An amusing story is told about Churchill and Cripps. As Lord Privy Seal, the fastidious and self-important Cripps often pestered Churchill with petty matters. One afternoon Cripps ordered his aide to reach Churchill immediately to have him sign some papers. The aide found Churchill in the Members Only bathroom where his presence in a stall was signaled by clouds of cigar smoke. The aide rapped on the door. Churchill told him he was busy and to go away. The aide politely informed the prime minister that the Lord Privy Seal wanted an immediate response. Churchill replied in a loud voice. "Pray tell the Lord Privy Seal that I am locked in a privy and can only deal with one shit at a time."

Stalin's Meeting with Churchill to Demand British Assistance

In early 1941, Stalin had flirted with Hitler, but now he needed weapons to fight him. His manner toward both FDR and Churchill was invariably hectoring and often rude. He continually demanded that "a second front" be established by the western allies to take some of the pressure off his armies. In 1942 and 1943 the American and British convoys up and around Norway's North Cape and Bear Island bearing arms for the Russians paid a brutally heavy price in both ships and men. When the surviving ships reached Murmansk, in the Russian Arctic, their crews often were inhospitably treated by the Russians.

Later in the summer of 1942, Churchill made the long and dangerous journey to Moscow to meet with Stalin. In *The Hinge of Fate* he tells how when they shook hands, he noted how strong and hard Stalin's handshake was and what a powerful, stocky body he had. Their first formal meeting was "most unpleasant." Stalin berated the allies for not launching a second front in Europe and for not sending more supplies. He said they were "too much afraid of fighting the Germans" and "that if the British army had been fighting the Germans as much as the Russian army had it would not be so frightened of them." Then he asked "Has the Royal Navy no sense of glory?" In subsequent meetings, Stalin continued with this insulting and hectoring tone, even mocking the losses in the Arctic convoys. After the final meeting, which ended at seven in the evening, Stalin said: "Why don't you come over to my apartment for some drinks."

Churchill agreed. Various staff members joined them. Stalin's daughter was introduced. Churchill later gossiping with FDR wrote that "she kissed him shyly but was not allowed to dine." After much vodka drinking, a huge suckling pig was served at one-thirty in the morning, which was Stalin's preferred hour for dining. There was some animated, frank conversation but no *bon homme.* The evening finally ended at three in the morning with the usually alcohol-impervious Churchill nursing a splitting headache.

Churchill never warmed up to Stalin the way FDR did and always basically distrusted him. At a dinner during the Yalta Conference in February 1945, FDR, in the spell of the evening, made a glowing toast to Stalin as a man of peace and progress. Churchill sat in stony silence. The Soviet delegation stared at the prime minister expecting him to respond. His foreign secretary nudged him. "But they do not want peace," Churchill whispered back. Finally he said: "To Premier Stalin, whose conduct of foreign policy manifests a desire for peace." As everyone drank in a stage whisper away from the translator he said: "A piece of Poland, a piece of Czechoslovakia, a piece of Romania. . . ."

British Victory in North Africa Marks a Major Turning Point

In August 1942, Churchill shuffled his generals in the desert, and General Montgomery took command of the British Eighth Army. Montgomery was always difficult with an immense ego, but he was a daring general and an inspirational leader. The Eighth Army was rebuilt and reinforced with new U.S. Grant and Sherman tanks.

At the end of September 1942, Rommel had gone to the hospital in Germany suffering from fatigue, and was replaced by General Georg Stumme. In October, an immense battle was joined in Egypt with the Afrika Korps 15 miles from El Alamein (on the northern, Mediterranean coast of Egypt, about 65 miles west of Alexandria). As the great battle began, Stumme died of a heart attack, and at Hitler's request, Rommel left his sickbed and resumed his command. Rommel immediately took the offensive with his panzers, but this time he suffered crippling losses.

The British forces counterattacked with highly effective close-air support from the RAF, and on the second day the German front was penetrated. By the third day, the bloodied German divisions were beginning to withdraw with a rearguard covering. By now the Italian army was already in full retreat, and nine Italian generals had been captured.

Hitler ordered that there be no further retreat, but the Führer's commands had lost their magic and it was too late for last stands. Montgomery pressed forward hoping to cut off the Afrika Korps and destroy it once and for all, but suddenly the rains came and it was impossible to continue the pursuit. Nevertheless the Battle of El Alamein was a magnificent British victory: four German and eight Italian divisions had been destroyed, 30,000 prisoners had been taken, and great masses of supplies seized. The British losses came to 13,000 men.

For the first time the supposedly unbeatable Rommel had been defeated. Suddenly England had a hero general. Churchill believed El Alamein was an epic event and a major turning point in the war. After El Alamein the British and American forces in Europe, on the so-called Western Front, were on the offensive, not the defensive. In November, Operation Torch, a joint British and American force, successfully invaded North Africa. Combined with the Russian victory at Stalingrad and the American triumphs in the Pacific, the momentum of the war had clearly turned. Churchill wrote in his memoirs: "It may almost be said, before Alamein we never had a victory. After Alamein we never had a defeat."

By May of 1943, all the German and Italian forces in the desert, and for that matter on the African continent, had been killed or captured.

The Allies Go on the Offensive

During 1943, Sicily was invaded and subdued after another fierce struggle with a still powerful German army led by Rommel. The next step was Italy, but these victories were not major stock market events.

In 1943, Britain and the United States also established domination of the seas. By the spring of 1943 the long battle with the U-boats reached the decisive phase, and by 1944 the Channel, the North Sea, and the Mediterranean were reasonably safe. The elite German submarine force, the *Kriegsmarine,* over the course of the war had 35,000 men who went to sea in U-boats. Ninety-two percent of them perished. In the Pacific, the U.S. Navy had gained clear dominance over the Japanese fleets. Without control of the seas the amphibious invasions in Europe and America's Pacific island hopping could never have been undertaken.

The improved performance of Allied arms shows the importance of the United States' direct entry into the war with vast resources, fresh manpower, and improved weapons. Suddenly the criticisms in Parliament ended, and Churchill was lauded as a master strategist. The analogy to a portfolio manager fully invested before the bottom of a bear market and under attack for it, and then prospering and being restored to grace as a bull market unfolds is inescapable.

As you would expect with diverse allies and such temperamental egos in play as Montgomery, de Gaulle, and General George Patton, there was intense competition for conquest and glory among the supposed allies. Patton and Montgomery were both difficult egomaniacs who despised each other. In the invasion of Sicily, their race to be the first to take the city of Messina allowed two German divisions to escape to Italy. Churchill described Montgomery as "in battle invincible, in defeat unvanquishable, in victory insufferable."

Patton was flamboyant, fearless, and truly believed he was the direct descendant of a long line of warriors going back to Roman times. He was a poet and a military genius. However, he also disobeyed orders he deemed too cautious and slapped and abused soldiers whom he thought cowards. He died in 1945 in a car accident in Germany. However by then the turning point in the Second World War had been passed. The survival of the cause of freedom was no longer in doubt, but as Churchill warned at the time, between survival and victory there are many stages. The danger was not destruction but fatigue and stalemate. Patience and persistence were essential just as they are in the relationship between an investment manager and clients.

The bombing of Germany by the RAF and the American Air Force was now intense. Cities were destroyed and tens of thousands of civilians and children were killed. An American pilot, Randell Jarrell, captured some of the mood of the pilots in his poem *Eighth Air Force.*

The other murderers troop in yawning:
Three of them play Pitch, one sleeps, and one
Lies counting missions, lies there sweating
Till even his heart beats: One, One, One.
O Murderers! . . . Still, this is how it's done:
. . .
Men wash their hands, in blood, as best they can.

How the Allies' Successes in 1942 and 1943
Affected the New York and London Markets

Both the London and New York stock markets had strong gains in 1942 and 1943 and to a large extent they were still linked together by war news at this point. Later that would change as the postwar economic outlook became the more overriding factor for both equity markets.

London dipped in early 1942 with the fall of Singapore but then had a steep climb right through year-end and throughout most of 1943 although there was a correction in December. As noted (in Chapter 8, see Figure 8.1), the New York market in 1942 declined into the battles of the Coral Sea and Midway and then celebrated throughout the rest of the year. As measured by Ibbotson and shown in Figure 13.2, large company stocks rose 20% and small company shares soared 44%. However, volume in 1942 fell even further to an average daily level of only 455,000 shares and stocks ended the year at 8.2 times earnings.

The year 1943 was an even better year for markets although it started out slowly. However, when it was over, large-company stocks were up 26% and small-company share prices had climbed an astounding 88%. The enthusiasm for smaller stocks was triggered by speculation that many of these companies that had either been kept alive or put into business by the War Department would have plants, machine tools, and patents that would be very valuable when peace came. Volume on the New York Stock Exchange reached a million shares a day again in 1943, and at year-end the market was trading at 12.8 times earnings. In late June 1944 stocks rallied strongly after D-Day and then fell in December with the Battle of the Bulge, the last-gasp, German counterattack.

To fully understand what happened to the U.S. market from 1943 to 1945, it's helpful to step back a bit and review what happened to American financial assets between 1929 and 1945. This 16-year period spanned two eras of extreme stress and anxiety for the nation: the Depression and deflation of the early 1930s and the war years of the 1940s. They included first the most crushing secular bear market in U.S. history, a powerful cyclical bull market, then another steep decline, and finally the beginnings of the huge secular postwar bull market.

Asset Class Perfomance, 1929–1945

Year	Large Stocks	Small Stocks	Long-Term Government Bonds	Treasury Bills	Inflation
1929	−8.4%	−51.4%	3.4%	4.7%	0.2%
1930	−24.9	−38.1	4.7	2.4	−6.0
1931	−43.3	−49.8	−5.3	1.1	−9.5
1932	−8.2	−5.4	16.8	1.0	−10.3
1933	54.0	142.9	−0.1	0.3	0.5
1934	−1.4	24.2	10.0	0.2	2.0
1935	47.7	40.2	5.0	0.2	3.0
1936	33.9	64.8	7.5	0.2	1.2
1937	−35.0	−58.0	0.2	0.3	3.1
1938	31.1	32.8	5.5	0.0	−2.8
1939	−0.4	0.3	5.9	0.0	−0.5
1940	−9.8	−5.2	6.1	0.0	1.0
1941	−11.6	−9.0	0.9	0.1	9.7
1942	20.3	44.5	3.2	0.3	9.3
1943	25.9	88.4	2.1	0.3	3.2
1944	19.8	53.7	2.8	0.3	2.1
1945	36.4	73.6	10.7	0.3	2.3
Average (No Compounding)	7.4	20.5	4.7	0.7	0.5
Compounded Average	3.5	7.6	4.6	0.7	0.4
Growth of $1	1.8	3.5	2.14	1.12	1.06

Figure 13.2   The Ebb and Flow of American Financial Assets 1929–1945
SOURCE: Ibbotson; Traxis Partners.

The volatility of the swings in the returns from stocks is startling, but once again if the holder of equities stuck with them through thick and thin they worked out reasonably well, particularly considering that the 1929 entry date was close to the top of one of the biggest, speculative equity bubbles of all time. For the 10 years from 1930 to 1940, in the heart of darkness of the Great Bear Market, equities actually had a negative nominal return but a positive real return of 1.9% per annum because of the effect of deflation, and real returns are what it's all about. Government bonds were the best place to be with a lovely real return of 7.1% a year for the 1930s. A lot of investors' psyches never recovered.

From 1929 to 1945, government bonds did better than large capitalization stocks, which is not surprising considering it was a time of deflation, recession, and low inflation. Furthermore, government bonds were far less volatile than stocks and had negative returns in only 2 out of the 16 years. The rich returns from small stocks, as always, vindicate this volatile but dynamic asset class. They, too, surged after the Battle of Midway, and then embarked on a spectacular run from 1942 to the end of 1945!

For the half century that ended on December 31, 1949, the nominal return on U.S. equities was 7.4% per annum and 3.8% per annum on bonds. The real return was 4.9% and 1.4%, respectively. For the same period in the U.K., equities and government bonds had annual nominal returns of 5.1% and 2.9%. Real returns were 3% and 0.9%.

From 1946 to 1948 inflation soared, both large and small company stocks faltered, and bonds posted small, positive total returns. Investors generally believed the inflation was transitory, that deflation would return, and they were still traumatized by the volatility of equities. The conventional wisdom was that a prolonged recession would follow the end of hostilities because the draft had only temporarily solved the unemployment problem, and that industrial production would collapse without armaments-related demand. The crowd didn't understand that the huge pool of savings and deferred demand would transform the economy. As a result they continued to gravitate away from equities and toward bonds. Few investors were in the mood for speculation.

The story of the Allied invasions of Europe and the Japanese islands has been told many times. It was a monstrous task to invade the aggressor nations in their homelands, and the problems of coordination between Britain, the United States, and the Soviet Union were formidable but that's another story. By late 1944 and 1945 the equity markets were looking ahead to the postwar world, mostly with trepidation rather than anticipation.

After the termination of hostilities in 1945, as noted most fiduciaries resolutely staring backwards worried that the postwar global economy without the stimulus of defense spending would slip back into the stagnation and deflation of the 1930s. The average institutional portfolio was 60% to 70% in bonds and 30% to 40% in equities. It was a monumental miscalculation. By the end of the decade of the 1940s, U.S.

equities were poised for a great bull run that would last for almost two decades. Bonds, by contrast, were on the brink of an epic secular bear market. It was *the* asset allocation decision of the third quarter of the century and almost all of the big institutional investors of the time got it backwards.

Chapter 14

The Test in Korea:
The Last Battle of WWII

In the immediate aftermath of World War II, the Soviet Union and China plotted expansion and probed the resolve of the West and particularly of the United States. By far the most dramatic event occurred in 1950 on the Korean Peninsula. In many respects, the Korean War may be thought of as the last battle of World War II because in 1945 the nation of Korea had been artificially divided by the United States and Britain into two zones at the 38th parallel, one capitalist, one Communist, as a bribe to induce the Soviets to attack Japan: Figure 14.1 shows how the country was divided.

The unintended consequences of this cynical action turned out to be profound to say the least. The Korean War was fought by the men of World War II and with essentially the same weapons. It was also an interesting test of the wisdom of markets, particularly in Japan.

Figure 14.1   North and South Korea

These consequences included the dreaded land war in Asia against the Chinese. The Korean War resulted in the death in action of 54,000 Americans, almost as many as died in Viet Nam. In addition, tragically, at least a million Koreans and a quarter of million Chinese also were killed. During the course of the war there was a devastating North Korean surprise attack; a horrendous retreat down the peninsula (which was perhaps the most humiliating in U.S. military history); an incredibly daring amphibious landing at Inchon, South Korea, by the First Marine Division that outflanked and cut off the North Koreans; a push by the American forces almost to the borders of China; and then a violent counterattack by the Chinese. The capital city of South Korea, Seoul, changed hands four times in the first year of the war as the tide of battle swung violently back and forth. Before the war was over, the president of the United States had summarily relieved of command the iconic hero, General Douglas MacArthur, and the war virtually insured the election of Dwight D. Eisenhower as president. Finally, that year, 1950, there was also another interesting test of the wisdom of markets, when a very bizarre event occurred in the U.S. that had nothing to do with the war in Korea, but which caused an abrupt loss of confidence in President Truman and greatly upset U.S. investors.

The U.S. vs. Communist Aggression

The attack on South Korea was the first major test of the post-World War II military will of the United States to stand up to Communist aggression in remote parts of the world. The North Korean invasion was no local grudge match. North Korea was a client state of the Soviet Union, and clearly the Kremlin had selected the Korean peninsula where the aggressors had a huge advantage as their location of choice. Dean Acheson, the U.S. secretary of state, was later to say that he couldn't imagine a worse place from the West's point of view to fight. So the first test was to take place in Asia rather than Europe as the West had expected, but no one in the chancelleries of the free world questioned its significance.

If the North Koreans took South Korea and established it as a Communist state, the future of Asia in general and Japan in particular as free bastions of capitalism and democracy were in doubt. Defense strategists in London and Washington also worried that the invasion of South Korea was the prelude to an attack on Japan or even the beginning of World War III. In the early days of the war, it appeared that the Republic of Korea (ROK) and the hastily assembled American forces were going to be swept ignominiously down the peninsula and into the sea. When the North Koreans launched their surprise attack on South Korea on June 25, 1950, stock markets around the world panicked.

As shown in Figure 14.2, in New York, the Dow Jones Industrial Average plummeted. There was a brief rally a few days later after the fall of Seoul when American troops were committed, but as the war news worsened and it appeared that the U.S. forces would be pushed all the way back to Pusan and into the sea, the market continued to fall steeply. However by late July 1950, even as the battle continued to go very badly, the market bottomed at the time command to the desperately beleaguered

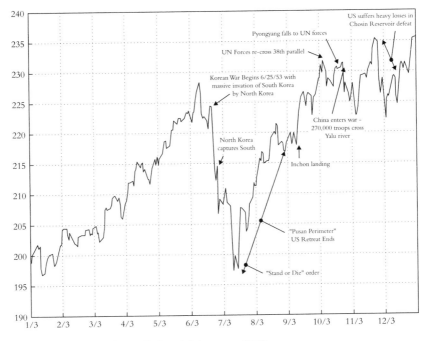

Figure 14.2   Dow Jones Industrial Average: 1950
DATA SOURCE: Dow Jones & Co.; Global Insight.

American Army and Marine forces was a dramatic order. "Stand or die! There will be no Asian Dunkirk. No Batan."

By August 1, 1950, there were 50,000 U.S. troops at Pusan with more reinforcements and heavy equipment including motorized 155mm howitzers arriving every day. As it became clear the Pusan beachhead was going to hold, stocks began to rally. When the market learned of the daring Inchon landing, prices surged higher. It is interesting that the fall of the North Korean capital, Pyongyang, failed to stimulate further gains perhaps because the market sensed that within days the Chinese would enter the war with calamitous consequences.

In London the pattern was similar but more muted. The Financial Times Industrials early in the fourth quarter of 1949 had begun a strong rally that had pushed the Index up 25% by June 1950. In view of Britain's large interests in Asia and in particular, Hong Kong, the news from Korea knocked the market for a loop. Prime Minister Atlee was so concerned he flew to Washington to consult directly with Truman.

The Japanese stock market had by far the most violent reaction. For one thing, it was still immature and tender. By the spring of 1949, the clandestine over-the-counter-stock market in Tokyo was on fire. According to Albert Alletzhauser in *The House of Nomura* there were 360 dealers, 40 floor clerks, and 24 newspaper reporters fighting for position in a small room in the Securities Association next to the closed Tokyo Stock Exchange. Trading volume exceeded a million shares a day—far above the total volume of 68 million shares for all of 1944. Thus, the occupation authorities were virtually compelled to allow the reopening of the Tokyo Stock Exchange, which resumed formal operations on May 16, 1949, in a wild burst of celebratory, drunken euphoria about the emergence of the New Japan.

Prices soared over the next 12 months. However, when on June 25 the North Koreans attacked, the bullish mood was abruptly and utterly shattered. The news of North Korean victories and advances down the peninsula was terrifying. The Japanese press questioned whether the United States would fight, and what would be the fate of Japan if North Korean, a client state of Japan's two historic enemies—China and Russia, prevailed. Wouldn't Japan be next? Japan's nascent Self Defense Forces were totally incapable of defending the home islands.

Furthermore, the Koreans had scores to settle with the Japanese. Japan had brutally occupied Korea for almost half a century, and anyone who was troublesome or resisted had his or her nose lopped off, often with fatal results. The noses were then piled in a huge mound as a warning, and the Japanese had no illusions about how they were regarded by the Koreans. Japanese investors panicked. In the first 11 days after the attack, the Nikkei halved from 176 to 85 on July 6, 1951. That day, July 6, was the low of the second half of the century for the Japanese stock market. There were no victories; no turn of the tide on the Korean peninsula on July 6, 1950 for the battered ROK and U.S. forces, just a dogged, fighting retreat south. Nevertheless, with early prescience the Japanese market bottomed that day. The good guys did not get pushed into the sea, and although the Korean War was a long bloody stalemate, the U.S. and the West proved they would and could stand up to Communist aggression in a land war in Asia. The next test of this resolve did not come for 15 years.

Equally important, the Japanese market sensed something else. The Korean War was about to give Japan's still depressed economy a tremendous boost from special war-related procurements as the U.S. poured troops and resources into the war zone. At the end of 1950, stock prices briefly sold off in reaction to the Chinese offensive, but then surged steeply for the next 18 months because of the war-related prosperity. Japanese companies were also reaping rich profits from government contracts for rebuilding Japan. The stock market was perceptive and smart.

But it was more than just war profits and rebuilding the domestic economy that propelled the incredibly steep ascent of the Japanese market from the 1951 bottom throughout the 1950s. Investors began to sense Japan was poised for an era of secular growth of historic proportions. Forty years later in mid December of 1989 the Nikkei Index was up from 85 to over 39,000. The big chart shown in Figure 14.3 is semilog. As shown in the insert in Figure 14.3, when we ran it traditionally, the ascent was so vertical it made the descent in 1950 virtually invisible. As you can see (but barely), stock prices reacted to the Chinese offensive at the end of 1950 but then in 1951the raw power of the recovery in the Japanese economy dwarfed all other considerations.

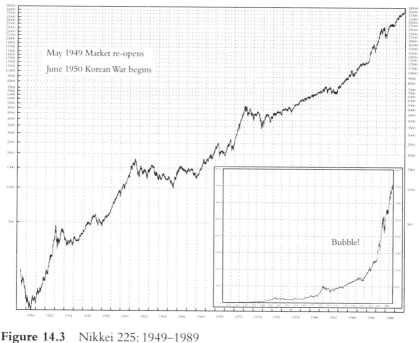

Figure 14.3   Nikkei 225: 1949–1989
DATA SOURCE: Nikkei; Bloomberg; Datastream.

Background on the War in Korea

Well before June 1950, U.S. defense planners knew that North Korea had powerful military capabilities compared to the Republic of Korea (ROK); however they never imagined that Korea would be the site of a major confrontation. In 1949, following the withdrawal of Russian forces from the North, they approved the withdrawal of American troops from the ROK. In a major address, Secretary of State Dean Acheson didn't even include South Korea in the U.S.'s strategic defense perimeter. The assumption that the United States operated under was that a war in Korea would only be an adjunct to a general war with the Soviet Union and possibly China. In this scenario, the Korean peninsula had little strategic value, and it was judged not worth committing scarce U.S. resources to defend. General Mathew Ridgeway, the army's deputy chief of staff, later said: "The concept of limited warfare never entered our councils.

The atomic bomb for us created a psychological Maginot Line." On the other hand, there were many signs that trouble was brewing. In 1949 alone, 874 border violations by the North Koreans were recorded. Some of these were pitched battles with over a thousand men involved and significant casualties on both sides. Short, fierce firefights between ROK border guards and North Korean infiltrators were virtually a daily occurrence throughout 1949 and the spring of 1950. North Korea with substantial Soviet training and equipment had built a formidable, tough, and fanatical military machine with one of the largest armies in the world. Their army and air force were far bigger and better than those of South Korea. The United States had given the ROK army minimal equipment and aid.

The reason for the niggardly assistance was that the president of South Korea, Syngman Rhee, a feisty, little, bellicose man, in 1949 had boasted that if turned loose his army could quickly defeat and occupy North Korea in spite of the Soviet presence. The American defense establishment was appalled. The last thing they wanted was for Rhee to start World War III by attacking the North and involving the Chinese. As a result, worried that he would launch an attack, the United States had severely restricted the ROK's offensive capability. The four divisions of ROK infantry deployed on the border along the 38th parallel were really just a constabulary force armed with carbines and without artillery or tanks.

Basically the North Koreans had skillfully set up the United States and South Korea. As MacArthur wrote in his *Memoirs,* "the North Koreans showed great shrewdness in masking their preparations for the attack." Beginning in April 1950 they had abruptly changed their tactics. The raids across the border virtually stopped, and Pyongyang issued "peace" proposals for unification and elections. Because the population of the south substantially outnumbered that of the north, this proposal raised hopes about the reunification of the two Koreas, and, at the very least, of a more reasonable attitude about the future of Korea. Along the border, the North Koreans had deployed a screening force of light infantry similar to the ROK forces. However at the same time, they were secretly moving regular infantry armed with heavy weapons and tank divisions, including the latest model Russian T-34 tanks, closer to the border, telling the troops they were on maneuvers. Neither U.S. nor

Korean intelligence was alarmed, and on June 25 one-third of the ROK's army was on leave.

The Attack by North Korea

On June 25, 1950, at dawn in the midst of a heavy rainstorm, the North Koreans struck across the border with a force of 100,000 men consisting of six infantry divisions, three full-strength brigades, 200 tanks, and considerable close air support. Amphibious landings from junks and sampans also were made behind the ROK lines. The invaders achieved complete surprise. Initially, the attack was made by the light infantry, but once they penetrated the unprepared ROK defense line, they swung right and left to get out of the way, and the heavy main force led by Soviet T-34 tanks charged through the gap, decimating the underequipped four ROK divisions.

The ROK forces fought bravely but briefly as they were desperately overmatched. They were armed with World War II bazookas whose shells bounced off the Russian tanks like stones. Again this was a conscious U.S. policy to discourage them from an invasion of the North.

The ROK divisions on the border were virtually destroyed in the first 24 hours, and on June 26 the T-34s were in the suburbs of Seoul, the capital of South Korea. On June 27 the North Koreans took Seoul, and Rhee and his government fled. The roads to the port city of Pusan were already choked with refugees.

From the capital of North Korea, Pyongyang, the formidable Communist premier, Kim Il Sung, vowed to "crush" South Korea in a month. Kim Il Sung was a large, powerful man who was an authentic hero of the resistance against the Japanese occupation. He still had his nose, and he modestly described himself in his own newspaper as a "great thinker and theoretician . . . a matchless iron-willed brilliant commander who has worked countless legendary miracles . . . who is ever victorious as well as the tender-hearted father of the people, embracing them in his broad bosom." Kim Il Sung was a horse of a totally different color from his pudgy son, "The Dear Leader," who now is the premier.

U.S. Reaction to the North Korean Offensive

By mid-June the educated opinion in London, Washington, and Tokyo was that the ROK forces would be pushed south into the sea and Korea would be overrun. *The Washington Post* wrote that it was all frighteningly reminiscent of the Nazi *Blitzkreig* across France in 1940. In Washington and London there were worries that this offensive was a prelude to a Soviet land grab and attack on Japan. On June 27 stock markets around the world sold off again and then steadied. The *New York Times* ran a front-page story with the headline, "Stocks Rally After Big New Losses In War Scare; Sales near 5 Million." The article reported that at one point the Dow was down 5% but on huge volume recovered to end off a mere 0.73%. "London was the worst sufferer among the major exchanges," said the text, "while Canadian markets followed the lead of New York."

However, President Truman acted forcefully and quickly, and on June 28 ordered MacArthur to deploy U.S. troops from Japan. The instantaneous reaction around the free world was overwhelmingly positive. When the decision was announced, cheers broke out in the U.S. House and Senate. Editorials and columnists such as the Alsop Brothers and Scotty Reston in the *New York Times* and *Washington Post* praised the president for his courage and boldness. Stock markets rallied. America was going to stand up! The White House mail was strongly in favor. David McCullough in his epic biography, *Truman*, relates one message to the president: "You may be a whiskey guzzling poker playing old buzzard as some say," wrote a Republican from Illinois "but by damn for the first time since old Teddy left there in March of 1909, America has a grassroots *American* in the White House."

President Harry Truman did guzzle some whisky, but at age 67 he was a healthy, vigorous, earthy and appealing, man. He worked hard and loved his job and people. Every morning he rose at 5 A.M. and had a breakfast of one piece of dry toast, fruit, one egg, a strip of bacon, and a glass of skimmed milk. Then he briskly walked two miles at the old army quick march tempo of 120 pace to the minute, did some "setting-up" exercises, and drank an ounce of *Old Grand Dad* or *White Turkey* bourbon "to get the engine going." He was at his desk shortly after 7 A.M. his head bolt upright. He was always impeccably dressed in double-breasted suits, which he proudly announced were 15 years old and still fit perfectly, and he exuded vitality and cheerful confidence. Everyone that worked for Harry Truman or came in contact with him liked him.

A Weak, Unprepared U.S. Army

From his headquarters in Japan, MacArthur quickly inserted the regular army 24th infantry division under the command of General William Dean that had been on garrison duty and a Marine regiment. The 24th was a mixture of salty career soldiers who had elected to stay in after the end of World War II and young draftees with no combat experience. Garrison duty in Japan at the time was considered to be a choice and luxurious assignment because the yen was so cheap. Officers and non-commissioned officers lived off base with their Japanese girlfriends, and Japanese *momma-sans* made the soldiers' beds, washed their clothes, and shined their boots. Beer at the Officer's Club and the Non-Commissioned Officer's Club was a dime a draft. The most strenuous maneuver the division had made in the previous year was a climb of Mount Fuji. The 24th was understrength, out of shape, and mostly equipped with World War II weapons. The North Koreans chewed them up.

MacArthur in his memoirs vividly describes a visit he made to the battlefield on June 29. For all his foibles, the general was a brave man. Despite advice to the contrary, he had his plane, the *Bataan,* land at a forward airstrip and he went forward under fire so he could observe the battlefield.

> Only a mile away I could see the towers of smoke rising from the ruins of this fourteenth-century city … in its agony of destruction. There was the constant crump of Red mortar fire as the enemy swooped down toward the bridges. Below me, and streaming by both sides of the hill, were the retreating, panting columns of disorganized troops, the drab color of their weaving lines interspersed here and there with bright red crosses of ambulances filled with broken, groaning men. The sky was resonant with shrieking missiles of death, and everywhere were the stench and utter desolation of a stricken battlefield. Clogging all the roads in

a writhing dust-shrouded mass of humanity were the refugees. But among them there was no hysteria or whimpering.

The general had just missed a ghastly incident. Screaming masses of South Korean civilians in carts, old cars, and on bicycles fleeing south from the city choked the four bridges across the Han River. It was a panic, mob scene. The ROK Command ordered three of the bridges to be blown despite the crowds on them, and they went up in huge blasts blowing hundreds high into the air. There was one bridge left for the ROK troops still in Seoul to escape over but the North Koreans were approaching fast. According to William Manchester, MacArthur studied the situation briefly through his field glasses and then ordered: "Take it out." Then his motorcade headed back to his plane.

The U.S. and South Korean Armies' Fighting Retreat

When he returned to Tokyo, the general decided to stage an "orderly withdrawal" toward Pusan 275 miles to the south. He recognized that he didn't have sufficient strength to halt the North Korean offensive and that he needed time. His sensible strategy was to trade space for time as he gathered reinforcements and brought them into Pusan by sea and air. The front across Korea was 150 miles wide. The terrain was a brutal mixture of valleys with rice paddies laced with irrigation ditches and unpaved roads interspersed with steep hills and even small mountains. The mud roads were chaos, clogged with hundreds of thousands of refugees with their possessions in ox carts fleeing south. Marine Corps lore became that Korea up hill and down dale was the biggest country in the world. By mid–July, MacArthur had deployed the 1st Calvary and the 25th Division, but neither was in any better shape to fight a physical land war in the extreme heat than the 24th.

By then the ROK army was in total disarray, and the American and ROK forces were often outnumbered three to one or ten to one. The retreat down the peninsula was fought in the drenching rains of the monsoon season with 100 degree temperatures and choking humidity. Clothes rotted, the M-1 rifles rusted, and the troops suffering from dehydration, drank water from paddies fertilized with human manure resulting in violent, crippling dysentery. The American soldiers knew nothing of the terrain, of the Korean people, or the language. McCullough relates how an infantry soldier later remembered those days. "Guys, sweat-soaked, shitting in their pants, not even dropping them, moved like zombies. I just sensed we were going to find another hill and be attacked, and then find another hill and so forth, endless forever. What a place to die!" Within a week of being committed, a third of most units were dead or wounded, and some young soldiers just "bugged out" and ran. One young Marine officer scrawled a note to his wife paraphrasing Rupert Brooke's sonnet *The Soldier.*

> If I should die, think only this of me:
> That there's some corner of a foreign field
> That is forever America.

The withdrawal quickly degenerated into a retreat through steep mountain passes, immensely complicated by ten of thousands of fleeing refugees clogging the road. The North Koreans were brutal, vicious, and fanatical fighters who routinely tortured prisoners in the field for battle-field information. Their special forces discarded their green uniforms, dressed like peasants in dirty white trousers and blouses, and mingled with the refugees. They then used the refugees as cover to attack the beleaguered American and ROK units. The American troops didn't know who was friend and who was foe, and sometimes indiscriminately fired into groups of refugees or mistakenly shelled villages believed to be sheltering the North Korean commandoes. Atrocities by both sides were common.

The 24th bravely tried to make a stand on the high ground before the Kum River, and then at the ancient city of Taejon, where intense house-to-house fighting took place. On July 19, with the city in flames and many units cut off and surrounded, General William Dean, the commander of the 24th, disappeared and was last seen trying to stop a tank with his .45 pistol. His body was never recovered. On July 22, 1950, the *New York Times* ran a front-page story of seven slaughtered American soldiers found by a roadside with their hands tied behind their backs and shot in the face. The front was so fluid that units often would find themselves behind enemy lines in a strange country in which they did not know whom to trust. A reporter from *The Baltimore Sun* told of a group that had fought their way out on foot over 50 miles of mountain trails.

There originally had been 80 but only 25 made it. The others had either been killed or became so exhausted they opted to fight where they collapsed. The retreat south, Truman said, was one of the most heroic rearguard actions in American military history. It was also one of the darkest and most humiliating.

North Korea Continues Its Offensive

By July 20th MacArthur had deployed most of the units located in Japan including the First Calvary and the Eighth Army under General Walton Walker. Still the North Koreans advanced, chewing up 20 miles a day. It was a desperate decision to keep deploying these fresh troops into a chaotic battlefield on a piecemeal basis, but there was no alternative. An attempt was made to integrate American and ROK troops, but by then the South Koreans were demoralized and were deserting in droves. By early August the battlefield situation was disorganized and desperate. From Tokyo MacArthur made it clear to his field commander, General Walker, that there be no evacuation "no vast Asian Dunkirk, no Bataan" from the Korean peninsula. The American units were told to "stand or die." MacArthur's imperial lifestyle in Tokyo was well-known to troops, and this exhortation was not taken well, in particular by the marines. The sardonic joke was: MacArthur says: "You dumbheads stand or die. I'm going out for dinner and a cigar."

The North Koreans poured in fresh troops, artillery, and tanks and now had 13 divisions involved in the offensive. The North Korean forces were deployed in a series of columns of battalion and regimental size, probing roads and mountain trails in an effort to penetrate and outflank the American positions. However, the North Korean supply lines were becoming extended. Reconnaissance flights showed heavy tonnage of supplies was coming by truck from Chinese Manchuria and Russian Siberia. Moreover, U.S. airpower was beginning to assert itself. Daytime movement across the 38th parallel was strafed, and bridges and roads were bombed. Thus all North Korean resupply had to occur at night.

In addition, the best North Korean frontline divisions had been badly depleted by their reckless and fanatical assaults. In late July the momentum of their advance began to slow. Meanwhile, both the U.S.

Army and Marine divisions involved were being reinforced, and equipment was pouring into Pusan by sea. By August 7th a defensive perimeter behind the Naktong River in the form of an arc of 130 miles around Pusan had been established by the battered American units and what was left of the ROK forces. The U.S. Air Force was now providing close air support over the battlefield, and the navy was assisting with naval gunfire employing "spotter" units. A regiment of 50-ton Pershing, self-propelled tanks with 90-mm cannons arrived along with a battalion of 155-mm howitzers. The North Korean advance ground to a halt. Their momentum was broken. The U.S. forces had made a valiant stand.

As both sides dug in and reinforcements arrived in Pusan, a stalemate developed throughout August 1950. The British sent 2,000 soldiers from Hong Kong and there were other allies as well. The Turkish regiment proved itself to be particularly fierce fighters. The rainy season had ended, but the midsummer heat was stifling, and McCullough writes that the dust was so thick trucks kept their headlights on at midday. Fierce fighting continued as the North Koreans tried but failed to penetrate the beachhead, and both sides suffered heavy casualties. On the other hand a breakout assault by the American and ROK forces across the river and into entrenched fortifications would have been very costly.

Support for the Korean War Wanes in the U.S.

Back in the United States, the mood had completely changed. Truman was under intense attack from the public, the media, and the Republicans. The general refrain was, "Why are American boys being sacrificed in this faraway God-forsaken country?" Truman's mail and the polls were running 20 to 1 against the war, and the media was highly critical of the way the war was being conducted and questioning why the United States was so unprepared for it. The Republican leader, Senator Robert Taft, called for the resignation of Dean Acheson, and the influential Alsop brothers wrote that Secretary of Defense Louis Johnson's policies had been "catastrophic."

On the other hand, some hawks were demanding the use of the atomic bomb before more American boys were sacrificed. One banner headline read: "YOU DID IT BEFORE, HARRY! DROP ONE ON

THEM AND GET IT OVER WITH." To add to the president's problems, the Nationalist Chinese were offering to send troops, and on his own MacArthur flew to Formosa and expressed support for his old comrade, the slippery and egotistical Generalissimo Chiang Kai-shek. Furthermore, Mac had been photographed bestowing a long and lingering kiss on the beguiling Madame Chiang Kai-shek's hand, which enraged the anti-Chiang faction in the State Department and Congress.

As for the Dow Jones Industrial Average, by mid-July it had fallen 15% from 229 to 197 in just over a month, but then as the front stabilized and the Pusan perimeter held, rallied back to 222 by late August. Nevertheless commentary was pessimistic as market letter writers worried about an excess profits tax and what was going to happen next in Asia. There was much talk of falling dominoes.

MacArthur's Strategy to Beat North Korea

In fact, MacArthur was increasingly becoming a problem for the president as he manipulated the media and his friends in the Congress for more freedom of action in Korea. Reading MacArthur's speeches now it is hard to see what so exercised Truman and Acheson, but basically it came down to MacArthur wanting to go for a knockout punch against the North Koreans and the Chinese regardless of the global consequences. Truman and Acheson were afraid he would blunder into igniting World War III. Incredibly, neither one had ever met MacArthur, who, in fact, had not been back to the United States since the late 1930s.

This was the situation: a bloody stalemate on the battleground and vociferous discontent at home when MacArthur came up with what he modestly describes in his memoirs as a masterstroke—a turning movement deep into the flank and rear of the enemy that would sever his supply lines and encircle all his forces south of Seoul. The only other alternative was a frontal breakout from the Pusan perimeter which, if successful, would have resulted in a protracted and bloody campaign up the length of the peninsula.

MacArthur had selected as his entry point for an amphibious landing the port of Inchon, 20 miles west of Seoul, and over 200 miles north of Pusan. Inchon, about as large as Jersey City, had always been considered by military experts as absolutely invulnerable to an amphibious landing. The port could only be approached by a narrow, winding channel that could easily be mined and would be blocked if one ship was sunk in it. There were no beaches at Inchon, the tides were huge (30 feet or more), and only high tide would carry landing craft up the high sea wall protecting Wolmi-do, the elevated, heavily fortified island that commanded the harbor. Two hours after high tide, landing craft would be stuck in the mud. When the tide was at full crest, the sea wall loomed 60 feet above the high-water mark and was believed to be suicidal to scale. In addition, it had guardhouses manned with elite troops spaced along it. Even if the fortress were taken, the landing force would have to cross under fire a long stone causeway to Inchon and fight house-to-house through the very heart of the city.

When Averell Harriman, the president's special envoy, visited Tokyo in August 1950, MacArthur laid out the plan to him in a brilliant two-and-a-half hour presentation. He stated that he would astonish and defeat the North Koreans by also doing the impossible (comparing himself to the eighteenth century British General Wolfe who had been victorious over the French General Montcalm in the Battle of Quebec in 1759. MacArthur believed in reincarnation, and he had a habit of comparing himself to long-dead generals when making his battle plans). A decision had to be made promptly. The tides would be right on September 15 and the attack had to be made before the Korean winter came. The plan was completely MacArthur's idea. Harriman, a wise old fox, was impressed.

However, when he got back to Washington and laid out the plan to the president, the Joint Chiefs, and the National Security Council they were appalled. General Omar Bradley, the chairman of the Joint Chiefs and a widely respected strategist, said it was, "the riskiest plan I have ever heard of." Admiral Forrest Sherman, the Chief of Naval Operations, announced: "If every possible, geographical and military handicap were listed—Inchon has 'em all." The other Joint Chiefs agreed, and even some of MacArthur's own staff admitted it was a 1-in-50 shot. Bradley wrote that "a failure could be a national or even international catastrophe, not only military but psychologically." There were just so many things that could go wrong."

But Truman bought the idea. He knew it was a tremendous gamble and he understood the consequences if it failed. The weight of military opinion was against it, and basically he didn't like, trust, or respect MacArthur whom he thought was "a stuffed-shirt egomaniac." He also had a low opinion of generals, of their West Point education, and the military caste system. But he liked the plan and ordered three members of the Joint Chiefs, Harriman, and Secretary of the Army, Frank Pace, to go to Tokyo for one final council of war with MacArthur.

At the meeting the military experts resisted the Inchon plan as too dangerous. The Joint Chiefs argued Inchon was too far in the rear, that the Pusan beachhead would be weakened and endangered by the removal of the First Marine Division, and that an operation of this size could not be kept secret. But above all it was too risky. The Marines were to be the first wave, and the experts questioned their ability to scale the looming seawall in the very face of the garrison and under fire. The amphibious experts said landing craft would be sitting ducks on the mudflats; the navy maintained the channel was too narrow. Harriman pointed out that because of the extreme tides, all the troops had to be got in that first day and that there could be no resupply. It was an all or nothing shot.

When everyone had spoken, Mac wrote in his memoirs that he waited a moment to collect his thoughts. "The tension rose in the room. If ever a silence was pregnant, this one was." He began by saying, "My father warned me: 'Doug, councils of war breed timidity and defeatism.'" Frank Pace, Secretary of the Army, who was present, years later told me that with those words the hair literally rose on the back of his head. Mac went on:

> The very arguments you have made as to the impracticabilities involved will tend to ensure me the element of surprise. For the enemy commander will reason that no one would be so brash as to make such an attempt. Surprise is the most vital element for success in war. . . . The Navy's objections as to tides, hydrography, terrain, and physical handicaps are indeed substantial and pertinent. But they are not insuperable. My confidence in the Navy is complete, and in fact I seem to have more confidence in the Navy than the Navy has in itself.

He then went on to say that the only alternatives were to stay in Pusan and continue to suffer heavy casualties in a defensive position, or to attempt a breakout and then fight up the peninsula. His estimate was that this latter course would cost the lives of 100,000 Americans and Koreans. Speaking completely extemporaneously he dramatically concluded:

> If we lose the war to Communism in Asia, the fate of Europe will be gravely jeopardized. Win it and Europe will probably be saved from war and stay free. Make the wrong decision here— the fatal decision of inertia—and we will be done. I can almost hear the ticking of the second hand of destiny. We must act now or we will die.
>
> If my estimate is inaccurate and should I run into a defense with which I cannot cope, I will be there personally and will immediately withdraw our forces before they are committed to a bloody setback. The only loss then will be to my professional reputation. But Inchon will not fail. Inchon will succeed.

There was complete silence. Nobody said anything. The force of Mac's enormous personality and conviction was so overpowering. Finally, Admiral Sherman, the Chief of Naval Operations, spoke: "Thank you. A great voice in a great cause!" The attack was on. MacArthur had taken full responsibility, and for all his hubris, he was a compelling and charismatic leader!

The Surprise Attack at Inchon

In the next two weeks the invasion force of 62 ships and 70,000 men was assembled in complete secrecy and by September 8 was preparing to proceed to the target. The Marines were in the final stages of embarkation when MacArthur received a message, which he said, "chilled me to the marrow of my bones," from the Joint Chiefs who had returned to Washington and met with the president and the National Security Council. It read:

> We have noted with considerable concern the recent trend of events in Korea. In the light of the commitment of all the reserves available to the Eighth Army, we desire your estimate as

to the feasibility and chance of success of projected operation if initiated on planned schedule.

MacArthur was convinced this was Washington covering its posterior in case of failure, and he immediately replied with a summary of his reasoning.

A day later he got a cryptic reply from the Joint Chiefs saying that in view of his reply they had "approved the operation and so informed the president."

In the early morning of September 13, 1950, the assault began. Complete surprise was achieved. The North Koreans had assumed that Womi-do was impregnable. In a synchronized operation, just prior to the naval gunfire beginning, elite, superbly trained Marine recon units in canoes reached the seawall on Wolmi-do and then using rope ladders and grappling hooks scaled the seawall and garroted the sentries, still undetected. It wasn't as easy as it sounds, and there was fierce hand-to-hand fighting on the seawall and in the guard houses. Thirty-seven of the raiders were wounded, but miraculously none were killed. For their heroic actions, two Marine members of the raiding party were awarded the United States' second highest medal, the Navy Cross.

Immediately, carrier-based aircraft and the escorting cruisers pounded Wolmi-do and targets in Inchon as the first wave of the Marines in landing craft reached the seawall and scaled it. By 9 A.M. the tide had gone out, and some of the landing craft were left on the massive mud banks but it didn't matter as Womi-do had been secured. The Marines crossed the causeway and hard fighting began house to-house in Inchon itself. The 7th Army Division landed and followed the Marines in. MacArthur himself went to Womi-do on the afternoon of the first day and was gratified to discover that the North Koreans had started intense fortification of the island. If the attack had been delayed a month it might not have succeeded.

Once having secured Inchon, the Marines and the army moved quickly inland with one column headed for Seoul and the huge Kimpo Airfield from which the North Koreans were flying MiGs. Kimpo was secured by the third day. The other column, the Northern Force, moved towards Suwon and another major airfield. Then the northern column was to press across the peninsula thus closing the pincer movement.

When the two prongs of the pincers were forged, the combined army would turn south to take Seoul and surround the main North Korean army. It all worked perfectly. The North Koreans were completely unprepared and had few firstline troops this far behind the front. In two days the ring had been closed.

At the same time combat patrols detected weakness on the North Korean side of the Pusan beachhead. MacArthur immediately ordered the Eighth Army and ROK divisions to go on the offensive and break out of the beachhead. Initially the resistance was fierce, and there was considerable difficulty in crossing the Naktong River. However, once the U.S. and ROK units were on the other side, the North Koreans panicked. They were being strafed and bombed continuously, and the prime targets were tanks and self-propelled artillery. The North Koreans now knew they were cut off to the rear, 250 miles from the border, and that their supply lines had been severed.

Meanwhile, powerful American armor and infantry divisions were driving north. Some North Korean regiments completely disintegrated, and the troops abandoned everything and either surrendered or tried to melt into the countryside and then work their way north to escape. The roads and trails were littered with abandoned tanks, self-propelled artillery, mortars, and weapons of all types. The retreat became a rout. In the next two weeks 130,000 North Koreans surrendered or were captured. Twelve days after the Inchon landing it was all over. The huge North Korean army that was holding siege to Pusan had been virtually destroyed and Seoul had been retaken.

On September 29, 1950, Seoul was formally restored as the capital of the South Korean government. Here is the way MacArthur described the moment in *Reminiscences*. The general either wrote very well or had a great editor.

> In the war-shattered assembly room sat row on row of heavily armed officers and men of both the U.N. and ROK armies. On both sides of the room, the windows gaped brokenly, and the smell of death drifted through them. My thoughts went back to that day in Malacana Palace in Manila when I handed the seat of government over to the authorities of the Philippines. I asked that all present rise and join me in reciting the Lord's Prayer.

The steel helmets and mud-caked fatigue caps came off as everyone rose to his feet. Together we recited the Lord's Prayer, and
I remember particles of glass tinkling down from the shattered
roof of the assembly room as I concluded, ". . . Thine is the
Kingdom, the Power and the Glory, for ever and ever, Amen.

MacArthur recounts how afterward President Rhee clasped his
hand. "We admire you," he said with tears flowing down his cheeks. "We
love you as the savior of our race!" MacArthur loved it, and as the conquering proconsul, basking in his glory, then rode through the streets of
Seoul, which were lined with people who clapped and waved paper
American flags. Once again MacArthur had returned.

Meanwhile Washington and, in fact the whole country, was jubilant
and euphoric. It was one of the most dramatic turns of fortune in the
history of war. The resident and the Joint Chiefs could hardly believe
the news. In his memoirs, Mac chronicles the messages of congratula-
tion and adoration that poured into him from all over the world. (Of
course, the Inchon naysayers had selective memory, recalling that they
had been for the Inchon operation all along and just wanted to make
"constructive suggestions"). As always, victory has a thousand fathers but
defeat is an orphan.

The U.S. Push to Destroy
the North Korean Army

In the weeks that followed there was much discussion of whether to
advance into North Korea and end once and for all its capability to make
war. There was always the worry that China with its massive manpower
would feel threatened and would enter the war. The Joint Chiefs and
MacArthur argued the North Korean military machine must be
destroyed, or South Korea would be living forever under the Sword of
Damocles. The U.N. equivocated. In the end, the Joint Chiefs ordered
MacArthur to cross the 38th parallel with the mission of destroying the
North Korean army. MacArthur choose to divide his forces and sent
the Eighth Army up the west coast toward Pyongyang while the X Corps
drove up the east side of North Korea. Then, said MacArthur, they would

link in one "massive comprehensive envelopment ... that would end the war." MacArthur in his hubris like Humpty Dumpty climbed to the top of a very high wall, and Humpty Dumpty took a great fall.

The two coasts of North Korea are separated by a spinal range of steep mountains that made communication and transportation between them extremely uncertain and difficult. McCullough says that the Joint Chiefs viewed this separation of forces as "an immensely risky maneuver," but that after his last masterstroke, no one wanted to argue with the military genius. MacArthur makes no reference to any such objections in his memoirs. In any case, after initial success and the capture of Pyongyang, the war took another totally unexpected turn and suddenly the U.S., ROK, and U.N. forces found themselves in a desperate retreat.

Abruptly with no warning, the Chinese entered the war and counterattacked with a massive army of 260,000 men. This great Chinese horde tore a gaping hole in the Eighth Army's flank and drove it back toward Pyongyang, and, at the same time, exploited the divided American front to force the X Corp back to the 38th parallel. These developments left the First Marine Division isolated and surrounded in the dead of winter at the Chosin Reservoir. The fighting withdrawal of the Marines in temperatures of 30 below zero carrying their dead with them 40 miles to the port of Hungnam and evacuation would be compared to Xenophon's retreat of the Immortal Ten Thousand. "Retreat hell," said the division commander, "we're just advancing in another direction."

The Market's Response to Korea— and to Unusual Events on the Home Front

The Dow Jones Industrial Average celebrated the capture of Pyongyang but then sold off when China entered the war. However, in late November it rallied again as the fighting in Korea settled into a bloody stalemate. The front had stabilized from exhaustion and the cold into fixed-position trenches and sandbagged bunkers in the hills along the 38th parallel. The best description of that stage of the war comes in James Brady's fine journal *A Memoir of Korea: The Coldest War*. On one side were a million Chinese and what was left of the North Koreans, and on the other six American divisions, ROK, and U.N. contingents.

Then in the first week in December 1950, a bizarre but very human altercation in Washington involving the president of the United States, his daughter Margaret, and a music critic gave the Dow Jones Average the jitters. The story of what happened is a fascinating case study of how a totally unforeseeable, random, apparently insignificant event can unravel financial markets. In fact, it is an example of the foolishness of markets rather than their wisdom.

Margaret Truman was the only child of Harry and Bess and she was literally the apple of her father's eye. In 1950, she was 26 years old and an attractive if somewhat plain young woman with a pleasant smile and personality. She had long cherished aspirations to be a concert singer, and she trained hard, took voice lessons, and was very determined.

However, the fact of the matter was that her soprano voice was not strong, and she could not project it. At the time she was working with Helen Traubel, a Wagnerian opera diva, who had warned her that she was still inexperienced and needed five more years of study. When Traubel told the president this, he reportedly banged his fist on his desk and said that was exactly what he wanted.

However, Margaret had other ideas. She had performed at numerous small recitals, and when the opportunity came to perform at a major concert she insisted on going ahead. The president himself was a music lover, played the piano, and frequently attended many concerts to which he often brought the score of the pieces that would be played.

On December 5, Margaret Truman gave her first serious concert at Constitution Hall. She sang a light program according to the historian David McCullough, drew enthusiastic applause, and was called for four encores. Nevertheless some people in the large audience were not particularly impressed. One comment heard after the concert was that if she had not been the president's daughter she would not have been on stage at Constitution Hall.

Paul Hume, the 33-year old music critic of the influential *Washington Post,* wrote a devastating review that ran the next morning.

> Miss Truman is a unique American phenomenon with a pleasant voice of little size and fair quality. She is extremely attractive on stage. . . . Yet Miss Truman cannot sing very well. She is flat a good deal of the time—more last night than at any time we

have heard her in past years. There are few moments during her recital when one can relax and feel confident that she will make her goal, which is the end of the song.

Miss Truman has not improved in the years we have heard her . . . she still cannot sing with anything approaching professional finish. She communicates almost nothing of the music she presents . . .

The next morning at 5:30 A.M. when the president opened his *Post* the first thing he turned to was the reviews. When Truman read Hume's comments he exploded, and immediately wrote in his own hand a short letter to Hume, which he had a messenger mail. Truman had a quick temper, and he was aware as he told Dean Acheson later, that he was prone to emotional "longhand spasms," which invariably got him into trouble. McCullough cites some of them. For example he had fired off angry rockets to Bernard Baruch ("that old goat") to congressmen ("the Marine Corps is nothing more than the navy's police force with a publicity machine comparable to Stalin's") and had once called the columnist Drew Pearson "a son of a bitch." He also particularly disliked the rabble-rousing columnist Westbrook Pegler. Truman was not repentant concerning his venting. As he once said: "I never give them hell. I just tell the truth and they think it's hell." The letter to Hume written on a scratch pad bearing the White House imprint read as follows.

Mr. Hume:

I've just read your lousy review of Margaret's concert. I've come to the conclusion that you are an eight ulcer man on four ulcer pay. It seems to me that you are a frustrated old man who wishes he could have been successful. When you write such poppycock as was in the back section of the paper it shows conclusively that you're off the beam and at least four of your ulcers are at work.

Someday I hope to meet you. When that happens you'll need a new nose, a lot of beef streak for black eyes, and perhaps a support below. Pegler, a guttersnipe, is a gentleman alongside you. I hope you'll accept that statement as a worse insult than a reflection on your ancestry. H.S.T.

By contrast, the *Times Herald,* a lesser Washington newspaper, said in its review that the Mozart aria Margaret sang was fresh and unforced and that her voice was "charming." However the President didn't read that review until later in the morning.

Hume and the editorial management of the *Washington Post* to their credit decided to do nothing about the letter. However, copies of it were made and circulated around the newsroom. Someone gave it to the tabloid *Washington News,* which ran it in full on the front page. The rest of the national media and all of the president's enemies had a field day with it. Hume himself was graciousness itself. "I can only say that a man suffering the loss of a close friend [Truman's press secretary had died suddenly on the day of the recital] and carrying the terrible burden of the present world crisis ought to be indulged in an occasional outburst of temper."

Others were less charitable. The *Chicago Tribune* said the letter was evidence that the president lacked the "mental competence and emotional stability" for his position. Editorials in various papers criticized him for being focused on his daughter's reviews rather than the soldiers and marines who were dying every day in Korea. The *New York Times* on December 9 discussed the letter and quoted it as shown in the preceding excerpt. However the story said, "The language was reported to be even earthier than the expurgated version." Another publication wrote: "Among President Truman's many weaknesses was his utter inability to discriminate between history and histrionics." MacArthur, whom Truman was in the process of relieving of his command, later used the letter incident with his congressional supporters to disparage the president's judgment and his mental stability. He wrote disdainfully of it in his *Reminiscences.*

The letters and telegrams that poured into the White House chastised Truman for his "uncouth language" and "petty, infantile mind" at a time of national crisis. "You showed the whole world that you are nothing but a little, selfish pipsqueak," one screamed. A few were sympathetic saying that he was only reacting as any loyal father would. However, the incident caused the intellectual elite and the media in New York, Chicago, and Washington to lose even more confidence in a president they disdained as a mental lightweight. They mocked him mercilessly. It was one of the low points of his presidency. Remember that Truman was not appreciated while he was president, and it was only afterward that he became a kind of folk hero—"the captain with the mighty heart" as Dean Acheson described him. As for Margaret Truman, she was initially mortified by her father's letter but later touched by his loyalty.

In any case, the New York Stock Exchange sold off steeply for about a week after the Hume letter. The decline turned out to be a great buying opportunity as shown in Figure 14.4. The U.S. equity market was about to take off on a fantastic bull run. The market crowd can be irrational in its immediate reaction to an unexpected event. Sometimes it becomes misled by the conventional wisdom or is too emotional, and the market can be wrong in its initial, instinctive reaction. In this case it changed its mind very quickly and shrugged off the recital letter as an insignificant event. There are no eternal verities in the stock market.

On this occasion, the stock market mistook a relatively minor incident and a very human reaction as a major event that cast doubt on the

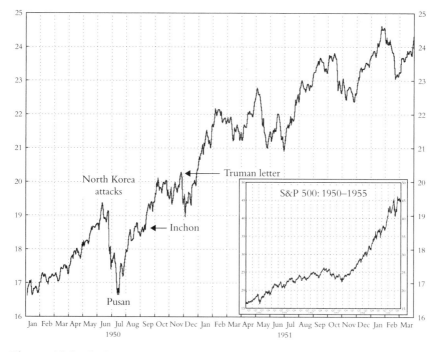

Figure 14.4   S&P 500: January 1950–March 1952
DATA SOURCE: Standard & Poor's; Global Insight, Inc.

president's ability to govern and make decisions. Part of this knee-jerk response was the volatile nature of the times with victory apparently being transformed into defeat by the entry of the Chinese into the war, and U.S. forces caught in an unpopular war from which there seemed no righteous exit.

In any case, the Pusan stock market lows and then the Truman letter bottom were levels that were never seen again. As for wealth in Korea, there was virtually none after years of Japanese occupation, and if there had been it would have been totally destroyed by the rampaging armies. Perhaps it was "creative destruction." Owning land was the only thing that mattered. In the next 50 years, Korea would rise from the ashes to become one of the most dynamic economies and stock markets in the world.

Chapter 15

Preserving Wealth
in a Time of Cholera

Those who cannot remember the past are condemned to repeat it.
—GEORGE SANTAYANA

The years of World War II were a time of horrors and agonies not just for the fighting men but most of the people of the world. Asia suffered endless deprivation and pain under a cruel and harsh Japanese occupation, and both the Communist and Nationalist Chinese armies ruthlessly lived off the land. There is less documentation of what happened in Asia, and there had been far less wealth created there prior to the war although the fortunes of the colonial families were shattered forever.

Across the vast expanse of the continent of Europe in the 1940s people were just trying to survive. Water supplies were polluted, food was in terribly short supply, disease was rampant, and cruelty and perverted brutality by invading armies were omnipresent.

Some, but not many, lucky families found rural Shangri-Las. There are a number of anecdotes about affluent French families that shuttered their houses in Paris in 1940 and retreated with their most precious possessions to family farms in the deep countryside far from the beaten track where they survived the war in deprived but reasonably comfortable circumstances. Not attracting attention from the Germans or the collaborators by any kind of a display of wealth or overt resistance to the occupation was crucial. You did not want your house or farm to be too grand or to appear to be unusually fertile. The same was true in Belgium, Holland, and Denmark and to a lesser extent in Eastern Europe.

During World War II in much of occupied Europe *physical* real estate (houses and buildings as compared to agricultural land) was usually not a good asset to hold. As Norman Davies' superb book, *Europe at War,* points out, physical property is a dangerous thing to possess in wartime. It gets stolen, bombed, destroyed, and expropriated. And the more attractive it is, the more likely it is to get taken away from you.

Unless the owners were Jewish, the Fascist Nazi dictatorship generally respected property rights in Germany. In fact, during the 1930s in both England and the United States there were conservative people who believed that a Fascist government was less threatening to wealth than a democratic one. As is well known, Joseph Kennedy was bitterly opposed to the United States entering the war on Britain's side, and was a real thorn in Roosevelt's side and even a threat to his reelection for a third term in 1940. In his fine new book, *Presidential Courage,* Michael Beschloss explicitly recounts the president's maneuvers to muzzle Kennedy. By way of explanation of Kennedy's opposition, FDR later remarked that Kennedy distrusted democracy and was "thoroughly obsessed with the idea that he must leave each of his nine children a million dollars apiece. . . . To him, the future of a small capitalist class is safer under a Hitler than under a Churchill . . ."

In the occupied countries of Eastern Europe, it was another story. Prime land and real estate were almost always expropriated by the occupying forces, regardless of whether they were German or Russian. When the fog of war and the terrible chaos of occupation, and Communism cleared years later, it was very difficult to establish the original ownership. The occupying British and U.S. armies commandeered property and held it for long periods, but even in Japan houses and buildings were eventually returned to their original owners.

The Plunder of Land in Poland

Hitler knew the mentality of his soldiers, and he was well aware that since the beginning of conquest, armies wanted spoils. As was related, it was made clear to the *Wehrmacht* that with victory in the West and the implementation of *Lebensraum,* the reward would be farms on the rich, black soiled agricultural lands in Poland in 1940 and the Ukraine in 1941. The higher the rank of the German recipient, the bigger the farm. Iron Cross winners were to get special consideration. The grand estates of the Polish nobility were allocated as the vast private preserves of victorious generals or high Nazi officials.

The Prussian generals were particularly enamored with estates because most of them came from aristocratic but relatively impoverished families. Some of them (such as Guderian) when on leave from the front in the halcyon days of 1940 and 1941 spent considerable time searching for the perfect property. Others requisitioned slave labor to refurbish their ancestral properties in Prussia. It was the last grasp for glory for the old, Prussian nobility. By the end of the war, they had been virtually wiped out. One historian claims that of 8,800 nobles, 6,400 were killed in the war, 500 committed suicide after the war, and 500 died in Soviet prison camps. Another 200 were murdered by slave workers on their estates.

As World War II raged back and forth across Eastern Europe, towns and cities were serially occupied. The city of Vilnius in Poland was first occupied by the Russians in September 1939, by the Lithuanians from 1939 to 1940, by the Red Army again in 1941, and then by the Germans until the middle of 1944 when the Russians came back on their way to Germany. Not much private property rights except on remote farms or timberland survived that onslaught.

Individual situations were extremely complex to unravel. For example, take the actual case of a large estate in Poland. In 1941 it was commandeered by the German army from the aristocratic Polish family that had owned it for generations, and the manor house became a German army hospital. The occupation authorities divided up and deeded the farmland to collaborating Polish families as part of the resettlement program. In 1945, as the Red Army approached, the doctors and nurses fled but there was no transport to move the wounded patients.

The estate was on a road near a village that was approached from the east by a stone bridge across a river. One day in the fall of 1944 a battalion of Germany soldiers retreated across the bridge with the Red Army in hot pursuit. The German convoy stopped in the village, four soldiers and a corporal got out of a truck, and unloaded a 50-caliber machine gun. The major commanding the battalion ordered the corporal: "Hold this bridge!" The corporal saluted. When the Russians arrived the next morning, the Germans held their fire until the advance guard was half-way across the bridge. Then the camouflaged heavy machine gun blasted the trucks filled with Russian troops. When later in the day, more infantry tried to cross, they were driven back. It was the following after-noon before the Russians could get two tanks up to take out the machine gun. The other three Germans fought to the death. The villagers fled into the countryside.

When the Red Army soldiers finally took the village, they shot in their beds the wounded Germans left behind in the hospital and killed the three Polish nurses who had loyally stayed with their patients. They took any food they could find and did some minor looting, but they had been ordered by their political officer to behave because "Poles are Socialists like us. Save your revenge for the Germans." Later the Communist regime converted the hospital into an orphanage, and the farmland was given to peasant Polish families.

For the next 35 years the estate's original owners lived in genteel poverty in France since there was no point in appealing to the Communist regime for compensation. In 1993, after the Communists were over-thrown, the descendants of the original family filed a claim. How was the issue to be resolved? Ownership rights couldn't be unraveled. They received no compensation from the state.

The Seizure of Estates in Hungary

Hungary was different. The Hungarians historically had been allied with Germany and had fought and hated the Russians. About 10% of the population was Jewish, and they owned the manufacturing companies, the banks, and the brokers. The non-Jewish Hungarian wealth was concentrated in land and houses. In 1941 the Hungarians, after some arm twisting, joined the Germans, and three Hungarian divisions fought the Soviets on the Eastern Front. In 1944, the Germans occupied Hungary, rounded up all the Jews they could find, seized their assets and packed them off to death camps. Later when the Russians invaded, and Hungary became a Communist state, the land and property of the wealthy were confiscated and distributed to the commissars and the people.

The saga of Andras, an aristocratic Hungarian born in 1912, is illustrative. His family had for generations owned a magnificent manor and 2,000 acres of farmland in the countryside plus rental apartments and a grand home in Budapest. An accomplished horseman, Andras graduated from the military academy in 1930 and joined an elite cavalry battalion. When war came, he had no choice but to fight with the Germans on the Eastern Front, and besides he had never been too fond of the Russians. In 1942 cavalry still worked as a fast striking attack force, and horses could move on muddy terrain or through woods where tanks got bogged down. In 1944 the tide turned and the German army was in retreat. As his regiment was pushed back across Hungary and into Austria, he found a way to surrender to the Americans rather than the Red Army where as an officer he would undoubtedly have been shot. Andras spent seven months in an American POW camp and then, after Germany surrendered, was released.

Returning to Hungary he found that the family estate had been seized by the Communist regime. The rental apartments and the home in Budapest had been destroyed by bombing, and he was virtually penniless. In the postwar chaos he escaped to the West and finally made his way to the United States where he married, raised a family, and for 35 years taught riding on Long Island to the horse-besotted daughters of stockbrokers. When the Communists were finally ousted, his son (Andras was now dead) filed for restitution. After much wrangling and searching through musty papers, the new Hungarian government gave him back the old manor house (which was a dilapidated wreck) and 200 acres. That was it! The son estimates that the family's recompense was equivalent to about 5% of the 1940 value of his father's net worth. As for the Hungarian Jews, if they were still alive, they got nothing.

The price for Andras of not having diversified his wealth was high as he was reduced to fairly menial labor in the United States. As he described it, in the early postwar years no matter what your education and qualifications were, when you filled out an application form that disclosed you had fought in the Hungarian army and spent time in a U.S. prisoner of war camp, even in America doors got slammed in your face. The story has a happy ending, though. Andras' two sons, who grew up in America, either because of good genes or the immigrant mentality, worked hard, got scholarships to Harvard, and have been financial successes. Their daughters now take their riding lessons on Long Island from Argentines. Perhaps brains or a skill are the most portable and best wealth preserver.

The Theft of Land and Valuables in Czechoslovakia

With wealth in the form of land and possessions, bizarre, unpredictable outcomes occur. In 1939, the aristocratic Lobcowitz (not the real name) family in what is now the Czech Republic had great, inherited wealth in the form of estates with farmland, art, fine furniture, antique silver, priceless collections of china and porcelain, and a fabulous palace on a hill just outside of Prague. The Germans invaded, seized the palace for *Wehrmacht* headquarters, and with food in short supply, the agricultural land was worked by slave laborers. Four years later when the Russians came they distributed the farmland to Communist partisans.

Meanwhile, in 1940 the Lobcowitz family had fled to the United States and settled in Boston. They had long owned some U.S. Treasury bonds, and they survived but were far from affluent. The patriarch had brought with him the family records, deeds, and accounts, but when he tried to use them as collateral for loans, the bankers rolled their eyes. Possessions in a Soviet satellite were not bankable collateral. His offspring went to high school and college in the Boston area, and in the early 1990s when the Czech Republic emerged from behind the Iron Curtain, the oldest son was working as a real estate broker. He returned to Prague and assisted by a lawyer, presented the family's documentation and petitioned the government for restoration of the family's possessions.

After much wrangling, the Czech government ruled that the family should be allowed to recover all the physical possessions it could find, including silverware and furniture, provided that it could prove it had owned them in 1939. It was also entitled to the estates, the palace, and their immediate grounds but not the adjoining farmland to which "it had ceded title to by willfully abandoning." Over the next six months, armed with family records and the fact that many of the household possessions bore the family crest, the oldest son and his brothers were able to find and recover much of the silver, art, and furniture that had been in the palace. Armed with the government's ruling, they literally expropriated items whenever and wherever they came across them in restaurants, homes, hotels, or museums.

However their euphoria quickly faded as they discovered that the manor houses and even the palace itself were in abysmal condition. The palace had great historic value, but it would take massive amounts of money to restore it and the manor houses. The brothers had no money. In fact, they owed substantial fees to their lawyer and property taxes were beginning to accumulate. So now they are house and possessions rich but still money poor and are paying their bills and taxes by selling off the antiques and acting as tour guides. As the oldest brother puts it: "Presumably eventually there will be a happy ending, but in the meantime I missed the bull market in Boston real estate."

Rape and Robbery by the Red Army

There were many different threats to life and wealth preservation in an occupied country. People who were there point out that the soldiers of the occupying power were usually only part of the problem. In most cases they were second rate, garrison troops that tended to hang out in their barracks and were mostly interested in petty looting, drinking, and women. The more serious menaces to life and wealth were those who had gambled that Germany would win or that the Soviet Union would rule Eastern Europe forever. They were the brutal policemen, the venal administrators, and the scummy local politicians of the occupying regimes. In the case of the German occupations either they were lower class Germans, often from the SS, or they were collaborators. Plagued by guilty consciences but with local knowledge and grudges to settle, the collaborators were deadly threats. The indigenous populations despised and hated them, and at the end of the war they were sometimes executed and always subjected to humiliating public punishments.

The secondary consequences were wrenching family dislocations. A father torn by seeing his wife and children starving to death or in desperate need of medicine, might be inclined to do something to aid the occupiers or their administrators in return for the necessities of life for his loved ones. Ostracism and often terrible vengeance would subsequently be inflicted on him and his family. Young women who became mistresses of German soldiers paid a high price after the war, and their children were forever taunted and scarred for life as "the child of a whore for the Germans." It was a cruel, hard time.

During the war years, being a landowner or a businessman had some major risks attached to it if you lived in countries that were overrun and then occupied by the Soviets. The Red Army as it surged back across Eastern Europe and into Germany in 1944 and 1945 was an undisciplined, brutal, marauding horde out of the Dark Ages. It had been in the field and in combat conditions for years on end. The soldiers had seen men sheared in half by grenades, decapitated by machine guns, and comrades bleed to death on frozen tundra and hot roads. Its uniforms were torn, dirty rags, and like General Sherman's army when it marched through Georgia during the Civil War, you could smell the stink hundreds of yards away.

The men of the Red Army had been dehumanized mentally and morally. Almost everyone they loved or had cared for had been killed or murdered either by the Germans or by their own regime. Death and horrendous wounds were a daily occurrence. They had no mercy; they wanted revenge, loot, liquor, and women.

Landowners were classified as "oppressors of the people," businessmen were "blood suckers" and both deserved to be shot. Red Army soldiers were actually encouraged to violate people and property.

Krasnaya Zvyezda, the official army newspaper, blatantly exhorted revenge and warned that political officers would view leniency and pity to civilians and "collaborators" in Hungary, Rumania, and particularly Germany as a crime against the Soviet state. With the barbarians coming, civilians in these countries abandoned their homes, disguised their girls as boys, and fled into the woods and deep countryside.

Norman Davies vividly describes the Red Army. The Soviet soldiers fancied watches and bicycles and had no qualms about murdering to get them. They had been hungry for so long that the sight of plump German civilians enraged them, and their joke was that after the men were killed, "the fatty Nazis' wives" were to be raped first. When they reached the work camps where Russian prisoners and civilians had been held by the Germans in appalling conditions, with the political officers egging them on, they often shot the men as traitors and raped their own women.

One book, Austin J. App's *Ravishing the Women of Conquered Europe,* estimates that in 1945 two million German women were raped, not just by Russians but by American and British troops as well. Gang rape was often accompanied by murder, and thousands of German women, particularly in the Eastern provinces, committed suicide either to avoid being raped or in post-traumatic self revulsion. In the first four months of 1945, the U.S. Army's Judge Advocate division had to deal with 500 rape cases per week. In the Soviet zone, a third alternative for German women was to seek protection by becoming a concubine for an officer or a sergeant. The Russian army had long condoned this practice of "frontline wives."

Civilians who had experienced invasion by both Germans and Russians write that by contrast the conquering German soldiers of the early 1940s were disciplined, clean, generally polite, and paid with Reich Marks for what they took. According to *Europe at War,* it is a surprising fact of history that the German army was not an extreme abuser of women. The frontline troops were far from perfect as they overran Europe in the early 1940s, but rape was never widespread. For reasons of sexual hygiene, the *Wehrmacht* provided brothels for its troops, and they were lectured on the crime of race defilement—*Rassenschande*—which the Nazis took seriously. The SS, when they came later, of course, were another matter entirely.

In the grim winters of 1945 and 1946 when Europe was gripped by famine, women sold themselves to soldiers for food and cigarettes. Just as in Japan in 1945, American cigarettes became virtually legal tender as they could be swapped for food or warm clothes. In the American and British zones, allegedly the price of an all-nighter was five Marlboros. The Red Army was also used by high Soviet officials to plunder for them. Freight trains loaded with clothes, cars, fine china, jewelry, art, and even grand pianos were shipped back to Russia. The amount of art expropriated this way is not supposition: After the fall of the Soviet Union, the loading documents and inventory records became available.

The Red Army was not the only looter. American soldiers, although generally interested in Lugers and helmets, stole numerous treasures from Germany. In 1995, a priceless Carolingian Bible was discovered among the possessions auctioned in the estate of a former sergeant from Texas. The original German owners have sued for restitution, but so far to no avail. Possession is 99% of the law. Wealth is ephemeral in a country that is conquered and occupied.

Stocks versus Bonds: Which Preserves Wealth Better during War?

So were public equities and government bonds less conspicuous and better wealth preservers and enhancers in the perilous first half of the twentieth century? The answer is that it depends on your time frame. As shown in Figure 9.1 (refer back to Chapter 9), for the full century, equities in the Lucky Stable countries that won the wars had an annual real return of 6.5% and the government bonds of these fortunate countries returned 1.8% real. Even bills had a positive real return. These are impressive numbers! Although the world economy had spectacular growth and there was great technological progress, the century was marred by two great bloody wars, hyperinflation episodes, and two deep secular bear markets in equities that afflicted both the Luckies and the Losers.

As for the countries that were Losers, (refer back to Figure 9.2 in Chapter 9), all things considered, the 4.2% annual real return *for the full century* posted by equities was eminently respectable. After all, over the course of a hundred years, stocks enhanced the purchasing power of capital even in countries like Japan, Germany, and Italy that lived through extended national nightmares. But that was for the full century. In many countries in the first half of the century, particularly in those unhappy nations that lost wars and were occupied, equities provided minimal or **negative** real returns and for the disastrous decade of the 1940s, had double-digit negative annual real returns, as is evident in Figure 15.1.

It is also a fact that only four of the fifteen countries studied (the United States, Australia, Canada, and Sweden) had positive real returns in every twenty year period in the first half of the century. In the other eleven, the loss of purchasing power over their twenty year downers was generally minimal but that's not much consolation if that twenty years came at a time in your life when you wanted to spend. However, considering their liquidity, you have to conclude equities are the best place to be with the bulk of your wealth.

As shown in Figure 15.2, when these returns are *compounded,* the results for equities in France, Germany, Italy, and Japan were abysmal both for the half century and catastrophic for the decade of the 1940s. The declines of that sad 10 years were so severe, they completely wiped out 40 years of moderate gains. The returns for government bonds are a calamity. And 10 years was a long time in the 1940s if you lived in France or the Axis countries and had your fortune in pieces of paper that were in the process of losing most of their purchasing power value

	1900–1949		1940–1949	
	Equities (%)	Bonds (%)	Equities (%)	Bonds (%)
Belgium	−1.5	−1.7	−1.7	−6.5
Denmark	+3.9	+1.9	+1.0	+0.3
France	−0.5	−6.3	−7.6	−21.7
Germany	−1.9	−7.8	−10.3	−20.8
Italy	+0.2	−6.2	−11.5	−27.6
Japan	+0.3	−6.0	−25.7	−35.2
Netherlands	+2.5	+1.2	+2.2	−1.5
Spain	+3.4	+1.6	−2.0	−1.8

Figure 15.1   Annual Real Returns
DATA SOURCE: *Millennium Book II; ABN Amro.*

	1900–1949		1940–1949	
	Equities (%)	Bonds (%)	Equities (%)	Bonds (%)
France	−22	−96	−55	−91
Germany	−60	−98	−66	−90
Italy	+11	−96	−71	−96
Japan	+16	−96	−95	−98
Netherlands	+243	+81	+24	−14

Figure 15.2   Total Real Returns
DATA SOURCE: *Millennium Book II; ABN Amro.*

and in addition were quite illiquid. Moreover, it was no consolation that other forms of wealth were also declining in value. By 1944, virtually no one was paying rent on land and buildings. At least you could try to grow food on your farm and barter your gold and jewelry.

These numbers, although academically correct are almost certainly not precise because the equity markets in both Germany and Japan were administered or closed for much of the 1940s and there were long periods when all of them were barely functioning. In the aftermath of the war, inflation soared as high as 30% in France, over 40% in Italy, and 50% in Japan. Although officially lower it was probably impossible to measure in Germany. In two of the occupied countries, Denmark and Holland, equities actually rose marginally in real terms in the 1940s, in part because neither experienced serious inflation. In any case, public equities in the principal Loser Countries lost huge amounts of real wealth during the war years and immediately after. By contrast, during World War I from 1914 to 1918 world equities peak to trough lost only 12% of their purchasing power although German stocks lost 66%.

Beware of Investing in "Keeper" Stocks: Nothing Lasts Forever!

Another message from history is that even in the Lucky Countries wealth invested in equities should be diversified. There are no magnificent long-term, "keeper" stocks to put away forever, and there never have been because no company has ever had a sustainable, *forever* competitive advantage. Excellence that lasts over multiple decades is virtually nonexistent. Some advantages last longer than others, but all are temporary. Furthermore, there is overwhelming evidence that the duration of corporate competitive advantages has shortened, which is not surprising in a world where the rate of change is accelerating. It's the nature of business evolution. Also bear in mind that wars, as Joseph Schumpeter might have said, are "gales of creative destruction" and in the aftermath lead to accelerated technological progress.

Corporate evolution seems to consist of a company developing a competitive advantage, exploiting its edge, and becoming successful. Then its share price soars, and soon it is discovered and thereafter becomes a *keeper* growth stock. As the company grows and gets bigger, it attracts competition and inevitably becomes less nimble and creative. Then as it ages, its growth slows and eventually it either becomes stodgy or obsolete. Studies of organizational ecology show that while there is immense innovation in the world economy as new companies create new businesses, there is far less innovation in large, mature companies. To express the same concept differently, companies don't innovate; entrepreneurs do. IBM and Intel were once great innovating companies, but now they are corporate research laboratories. Bill Gates was the innovator, not Microsoft.

For example, back when the pace of change was much slower, there were stocks that retained a competitive advantage for a long time. Eric Beinhocker in *The Origin of Wealth* writes how the British East India Company in the seventeenth and eighteenth centuries had a total monopoly in four countries, possessed worldwide dominance in everything from coffee and woolens to opium, had its own army and navy, and was actually empowered by the Crown to wage war if necessary. However the world changed, it didn't, and its "massive wall of core competencies" collapsed in the face of technological innovation. It went out of business in 1873.

In 1917, *Forbes* published a list of the 100 largest U.S. companies. Over the next 71years there was the Great Depression, World War II, the inflation of the 1970s, and the spectacular postwar boom. When *Forbes* reviewed the original list in 1987, 61 of the companies no longer existed for one reason or another. Of the rest, 21 still were in business but no longer were in the top 100. Only 18 were, and with the exception of General Electric and Kodak, they all had underperformed the market indexes. Since then, Kodak has had serious difficulties so GE is the sole, truly successful survivor. In 1997, Foster and Kaplan checked the endurance record of the Standard & Poor's 500 Stock Index since it was created 40 years earlier. Only 74 of the original companies were still in the select 500, and that group had underperformed the overall index by 20%.

Warren Buffett is a certified immortal, but even investment clairvoyants can misjudge individual companies. Eleven years ago, I listened to him extol Coca Cola as an impregnable franchise growth stock you could safely lock away and own forever. The shares then sold at a substantial premium valuation. He misjudged the various social, industry, and company-specific ailments that have afflicted the company and crushed its stock price. The same applies to another of his favorites: the *Washington Post*.

In another study cited by Beinhocker, two academics, Robert Wiggins and Tim Ruefli, created a database of the operating performance of 6,772 companies across 40 industries in the postwar era. They sorted for **persistent,** superior business, not stock market, performance lasting 10 years or more relative to the industry the company was in. They discovered that *there was no safe industry.* The pace of change was faster in the high-tech groups than in the more mundane ones, but the velocity was increasing in all industry groups over time. They also found that only five percent of the companies achieved a period of superior performance that lasted 10 years or more, and a mere half of one percent sustained competitive advantages of 20 years. Only three companies, American Home Products, Eli Lilly, and 3M reached the 50-year mark.

Diversification of wealth in equities over decades or generations means either buying index funds or somehow finding the unusual investment management firm that with wisdom and vision can construct a diversified portfolio that will at least keep up with and hopefully beat the averages—*after taxes and fees.* Two important advantages of an index fund are that it minimizes taxes and transaction costs because of its low turnover and charges a miniscule investment management fee. You can now buy an index fund to replicate almost any equity sector. A number of recent studies show that over time the average American investor whether he or she buys individual stocks or active mutual funds, earns a return considerably less than that of the S&P 500. It pains me to write it, but professional investors don't do much better on a statistically significant, risk-adjusted basis.

The record indicates that public equities over the long run are (to use the infamous phrase) *highly likely* to earn a return well in excess of the inflation rate. If you live in a stable country and you know with a high degree of certainty you can achieve a long-term *real* return of 400 to 700 basis points in an index fund why fuss with anything else? Maybe if you still believe in fairies and are a skilled professional investor you can do better but don't count on it. Above all, don't hold your eggs in a few big baskets. The old saying: "put all your eggs in one basket and then watch the basket" is broker baloney. The risks in holding an undiversified portfolio are astronomical.

Common sense and the message of the past is that reversion to the mean is an over-powering, gravitational force in all aspects of the investment world, but particularly in equities. There are no super-return asset classes! It is written in stone that exceptional returns attract excessive capital, and size is the enemy of performance. No one should have any illusions that private equity or hedge funds will be any different.

The Gold, Art, and Bonds Are Problematical

Third, the history of Europe during World War II indicates gold and jewelry work fairly well to protect a small amount of a wealth. Think of them as your "mad money." However, as noted previously, the history of World War II warns not to keep them in a safe deposit box *in-country*. Conquerors demand the key, and your bank will give it to them. Have your own safe deposit box at home or secrete your valuables in a safe haven. Above all don't tell anybody. When your neighbor's children are starving (as so many were in the lawless winters of 1945 and 1946), they will do anything. If the barbarians come next time as a terrorist attack or a plague, you are going to want to have your mad money close at hand.

Fourth, art is not particularly good either. It is vulnerable to destruction by fire, can easily be damaged, quickly plundered, and it's difficult to hide. At the end of the war, Warsaw alone reported 13,512 missing works of art of one kind or another. That said, some Europeans successfully removed valuable pictures from their frames and smuggled the canvases out of their home countries and transported them to safe havens. The caveat was that when they tried to sell them, they were only able to get a fraction of their true value.

Fifth, at least based on the last century, fixed-income investments are nowhere near as good as equities. Even in the Lucky countries, they provided returns far below stocks, although they did offer much lower volatility. Across the various countries, bonds had a standard deviation about half of that of equities, and bills had volatility about a quarter that of equities. In terms of liquidity, they were fine. Fixed income markets remained relatively liquid in London and New York throughout the war years.

In the Losers, fixed income had severely negative returns, and although government paper is normally considered to be relatively risk free, German bill investors lost everything in 1923, and German bonds investors lost over 92% in real terms after World War I. Admittedly inflation was virulent in a war-torn world, and fixed income is not the place to be in such an environment. In the chaotic, disorderly environment of the war years in the Loser nations, you can't sell bonds or cash in bills any more that you can trade stocks. However there was a period in the 1930s when because of deflation, bonds were the best performing asset everywhere.

Complacency Is a Deadly Enemy!

One message from both the past and the present is that if you are part of a prosperous minority in a country, particularly a religious minority, you always should be looking over your shoulder. Don't become complacent. Your abundance, your affluence inevitably is attracting envy and envy leads to hatred. Get some serious capital out of the country. Having money outside of your country was a life-saving act if you were a European or Asian citizen of a Loser country during World War II. The case of Georges Levin, the wealthy Jew mentioned in Chapter 10, who had the foresight to have money outside of France, is a perfect example of the benefits of anticipation. The hard thing is to extricate your fortune without suffering a brutal diminishment of it. Having money somewhere was certainly helpful in rebuilding after the war was over.

On the other hand, your overseas fortune didn't do you much good if you were caught *in-country* trying to survive during the war years. Have a bolt hole, an escape hatch, a sanctuary for yourself as well. It's not a happy situation if you have plenty of money outside the country but are stuck in the homeland starving, imprisoned, or in a concentration camp. Many wealthy Frenchmen, both Jews and Gentiles, had money in Switzerland but had to endure the unendurable hardships of the occupation in France.

The record and the interviews cited suggest that the rich almost always become smug, assured, too confident—prosperous fools. Many of the German Jews, brilliant, cultured, and cosmopolitan as they were, were too complacent. They had been in Germany so long and were so well established, they simply couldn't believe there was going to be a pogrom that would endanger them. They were too comfortable. They thought they knew all the right people and were too crucial to the business life of Germany. They believed the Nazi's anti-Semitism was an episodic event and that Hitler's bark was worse than his bite. Their businesses, the banks, the department stores, the shops, were so profitable they couldn't bear to sell them at distress prices, pay outrageous transfer taxes, and then put the dreadfully diminished proceeds into sterile bank accounts in Zurich.

As a result the German Jews had relatively little wealth outside of Germany, and reacted sluggishly to the rise of Hitler for completely understandable but tragically erroneous reasons. Events moved much faster than they could imagine. Before they knew it, their government and their neighbors had become barbarians and their wealth, art collections, estates, and often their very lives were gone. Their art and antiquities are even now emerging from private hands. Recently there has been considerable publicity about the provenance of a priceless 2,350 year old, five-foot-tall, bronze statue, Apollo Sauroktonos, that disappeared from a French collection in 1941. In 1994, it was surreptitiously sold by an East German family, changed hands four times in the next 10 years, and was most recently bought by a museum in Cleveland. The original owners are suing, but off course no one admits to being the looter.

The patterns of financial persecution of Jews, Armenians, overseas Chinese, and other successful minorities has been repeated endless times. In Iraq the wealthy Iraqi Jews who had lived there for centuries misjudged how fast and ruthlessly Saddam Hussein, when he came to absolute power, would move to expropriate their wealth. At the first hint of expropriation and Jewish flight, the price at which they could sell their property, art, or businesses collapsed as the potential buyers immediately sensed their desperation. The same calamity befell the Indonesian Chinese who failed to anticipate the rapidity of the fall of Sukarno.

Achieving diversification by transferring money out of lucrative, *in-country* investments to sterile assets in a safe haven is wrenching and very expensive but it has to be viewed as catastrophe insurance. No matter how safe and secure your home country appears, even if it's the United States, every truly wealthy person should have some assets elsewhere. History suggests that nothing is forever. Extreme political change, a terrorist attack, a meltdown of the financial system can happen anywhere. Currency diversification is also essential. Consider carefully what currency or currencies you want your wealth to have purchasing power in.

Some of the wealthy now choose to own property in a relatively secure place outside of their home country. New Zealand recently has become the Shangri-la of choice for paranoid American hedge-fund grand masters. Currently wealthy Russians are paying up for residential properties in London, New York, and the south of France. They know they are buying at inflated prices, but their primary motivation is not value but to get money out of Russia and to obtain some diversification. As one Russian oligarch commented: "I hope I'm making a bad buy," meaning he hopes the insurance turns out to be unnecessary.

At the same time the rich in the developing countries are opening bank and investment accounts in the financial centers of the world. It's not just the Russian oligarchs. The same rationale applies to entrepreneurs and investors who have made a lot of money in countries such as Brazil, Argentina, Indonesia, the Philippines, and China. The destinations of choice are in no particular order New York, London, Singapore, Zurich, and Geneva. Dubai has aspirations to join the club, but to make it very painful for an impoverished, populous neighbor to fuss with it, Dubai, like Singapore needs an air force, not just an airline.

If you're wealthy, just remember "nothing is forever." and pay attention to markets. They know more than they can tell.

Chapter 16

Barbarians at the Gate

For those who have wealth, it is well to always bear in mind that inevitably there will be another plague, "a time of cholera," that the Four Horsemen will ride again, and that someday, suddenly *the barbarians* will be at your gate. Wealth arms the eyes of the envious, and breeds complacency in the rich. It was Aristotle who more than 2,300 years ago said: "The character which results from wealth is that of a prosperous fool."

The last half century has been a time of immense wealth creation. Of course, wealth will cause envy, and will be whittled away by spoiled second and third generations and redistributionist politicians. But the issue of this book is will there be apocalyptic events that will destroy fortunes (both great and modest) as has continually happened over the centuries? "History," said Cicero, "illuminates reality, vitalizes memory, and provides guidance in daily life." The history of the chaos of World War II, the destruction of wealth that ensued, and the flashes of clairvoyance shown by stock markets is provocative. They suggest that wealth is ephemeral, diversification is essential, and that stock markets have surprisingly good intuitions at the epic tipping points. As the old saying goes, when coming events cast their shadows, they often fall on the New York Stock Exchange.

Since time immemorial people of affluence, owners of property, businesses, and financial assets, have faced threats to their wealth from envy, revolutions, invading armies, natural disasters, plagues, famines, and depressions and hyperinflation. Technological change and new innovations, of course, are a danger and a destroyer, but they are a different class of threat entirely. Technology ravages commercial enterprises that fail to adapt and the fortunes attached to them, but this is the evolutionary, creative destruction of the way the world works and vigilance and diversification can mitigate their impact.

History suggests that by far the most deadly menace and the most destructive threat to wealth has been war and especially defeat and occupation by an invading army. The history of Europe is stuffed with episodes of violent wealth destruction, and if you lived in the South during the American Civil War, you certainly encountered the Four Horsemen. Sherman's march through Georgia for sheer property devastation rivaled the rampages of the *Wehrmacht* and the Red Army.

War seems to be endemic to mankind, and the record of the second half of the twentieth century is not encouraging. After the agonies of two great wars, you would have thought mankind, urged on by the mothers of the world, would have turned from war, but new sources of conflict always seem to emerge. Now the so-called civilized world faces a new kind of war—this time with militant Islamic terrorism. A German warlord, Count Moltke a hundred years ago summarized the inevitability and glorification of war: "Perpetual peace is a dream, and it is not even a beautiful dream. War is an element in the order of the world ordained by God. Without war the world would stagnate and lose itself in materialism."

This sentiment was echoed by Nietzsche in an even more chilling paragraph:

It is mere illusion and pretty sentiment to expect much (even anything at all) from mankind if it forgets how to make war. As yet no means are known which call so much into action as a great war, that rough energy born of the camp, the deep impersonality born of hatred, that conscience born of murder and cold-bloodedness, that fervor born of effort in annihilation of the enemy, that proud indifference to loss, to one's own existence, to that of one's fellows, that earthquake-like soul-shaking which a people needs when it is losing its vitality.

If wars and apocalypses are recurring and inevitable, what should the person with wealth do? Experience suggests, that for *in-country* wealth, land and properties in your own country are the safest havens in a chaos prone, vulnerable world. An unostentatious farm or farmland, not a great estate, is probably best. Bricks-and-mortar real estate can be expropriated or bombed, but the land is always there. It can't be plundered or shipped off to somewhere else. During World War II in most of the occupied countries, if you had a self-sufficient farm, you could hunker down on it and with luck wait out the disaster. At the very least you were sure of food in a starving country, and in France and Italy owning and operating a vineyard was a wonderful wealth protector.

The twentieth century marked the end of an era, and a particularly turbulent one at that. However, the history of the world demonstrates that wealth destruction, whether through wars or plagues or technology, has been endemic to mankind, and there is no sign as yet that sophistication and progress will change this eternal verity. What will be the threats to wealth of this new century? Terrorism, religious warfare, or a collapse of the financial system caused by an implosion of derivatives? Who knows? But be alert. The barbarians will come again.

Terrorism, of course, is a form of war, and terrorism is just as capable of destroying wealth. A natural or technological disaster would cause similar carnage. Supposing the tsunami comes not from the ocean but from either an ecological plague that made an area of the world uninhabitable or from a technological terrorism attack in which all the data documenting financial wealth was destroyed. Or it could be in the form of a derivatives-leverage driven, financial tsunami that bankrupts major record-keeping institutions. Was the sub-prime mortgage debacle of the summer of 2007 a warning? What would happen to the all the connected dominoes if a major financial institution failed? Perhaps the barbarians next time come dressed as investment bankers, traders, and leveraged hedge fund managers.

There are no easy solutions or conclusions as to the best way to preserve and enhance wealth. If you have your wealth in a country that is conquered, occupied, or that suffers an ecological or technological disaster, you are going to suffer immense losses unless you have escaped to a safe haven well in advance of the hostilities. Disasters and their side effects ranging from bombings to power failures and epidemics are bound to cause a breakdown of law and order, which is by definition inimical to wealth. Waiting until the barbarians are at the gates is no good. You have to act in anticipation that *some day in the future barbarians in one disguise or another will be at the gates.* The difficulty is that the barbarians next time will not look or act the same as the barbarians last time—but they will be just as confiscatory and rapacious.

Watch for "Black Swans": They Prove to Be Turning Points

In his new book, *The Black Swan,* Nassim Taleb, an original and creative philosopher, introduces the concept of the *Black Swan.* The black swan is a freak of nature, and until Australia was discovered, civilized people could not believe a black swan could happen.

> It illustrates a severe limitation to our learning from observations or experience and the fragility of our knowledge. One single observation can invalidate a general statement derived from millennia of confirmatory sightings of millions of white swans.

For Taleb, a Black Swan is an outlier event far beyond the realm of regular expectations because nothing in the past can convincingly point to the possibility of it occurring. A Black Swan is a very low probability, extremely high impact event. It does, however, have retrospective probability. In other words, after it has occurred, we can and do manufacture plausible explanations for it.

Black Swans are totally unpredictable happenings, 20 standard deviation events that come out of the great nowhere of the inconceivable to change the world. The assassination of Arch Duke Ferdinand, the rise of Hitler, Pearl Harbor, the fall of the Soviet Union, September 11, 2001, and the Crash of 1987 were all Black Swans. What were the odds that the two biggest buildings in New York would be leveled in a morning? Based on a normal distribution of stock market returns, there was no chance that the U.S. market could decline 22% in a single day as it did in 1987 even if the market were to be open for the estimated lifespan of the universe.

The Battle of Midway was a *good* Black Swan for the United States and a *bad* Black Swan for Japan in that the outcome was a multi-standard deviation event. It also was *the turning point* for both the war and the U.S. stock market. Nobody anticipated the stock market bottom except an obscure market letter writer for *Barron's*—and the investor crowd. Only the poor, benighted German stock market understood that Barbarossa and Hitler's dreams of empire had crested in the late fall of 1942 in the birch and scrub pine forests outside of Moscow.

Taleb does not provide much of a solution for an investor for dealing with Black Swans. He correctly points out that when investors assess risk they do not include the possibility of the Black Swan. He also says, "We don't learn that we don't learn." He considers most investors as "traders picking up pennies in front of a steamroller;" in other words, exposing themselves to a life-ending event for pittances. These are all true statements, but unfortunately he doesn't tell us what to do about them. How do you prepare yourself for Black Swans? His point seems to be that you can't! In the conclusion of his book he says, "My antidote to Black Swans is precisely to be noncommoditized in my thinking. Half the time I am hyperconservative in the conduct of my own affairs; the other half I am hyperaggressive." I don't know what he means, but that is what he says.

Kiril Sokoloff of 13D Research writing about Taleb and Black Swans maintains: "If you are perceptive and intuitive enough, there is no reason why you can't see most of them coming." He says that many of the most recent Black Swans were anticipated by others and by him. Maybe so but I am skeptical. It's easy to conjure up Black Swans but it's no good unless you get the timing reasonably right—say within a year or two. Being too early is the same as being wrong.

However, you can try to conjure up the unthinkable and consider the cost of insurance.

In the spring of 1987 a young, very smart and analytical proprietary derivatives trader at an investment bank (not Morgan Stanley) became convinced (based on a quantitative model that he had developed) that the soaring U.S. stock market could have an immense decline. Not a 10% or 15% decline, but a 25-standard-deviation, Black Swan fall of 20% to 25%. Furthermore, he presumed that the collapse would be in the form of an extreme break over a few weeks, not a long drawn-out bear market. For the firm and himself (he committed 70% of his meager net worth) to buying insanely deep out-of-the-money puts on the S&P 500 with an expiration date at the end of 1987. Obviously when the Crash came, he made tremendous money for the firm and himself and the firm rewarded him with a huge bonus.

What happened thereafter? Today the young trader is 20 years older and has had a strong bearish bias on equities ever since. His quantitative model became very popular, and from 1988 to 1998 three times falsely signaled another Black Swan. The model was closed down in despair in 1999. From 1988 to perhaps the mid-1990s, another 10 to 12 smart young traders who had seen firsthand the life- and career-transforming effect of forecasting a Black Swan squandered an immense amount of money putting on similar trades. I can't say for sure, but I suspect a lot of them by the late 1990s had their Black Swan obsession beaten out of them, and went over the cliff with technology in 2000.

What is the point? The happening and timing of Black Swans are utterly unforecastable. Beware you do not become obsessed with them. Nietzsche said it succinctly: "Stare too long into the abyss and you become the abyss." As a wealthy person, you should have 5% of your money in a safe haven. You should have another 5% in a farm. You should own some Treasury Inflation Protected (TIPS) bonds. But, in my view, the right percentages are 5% to 10%; not 50%. Again Nietzsche said it best. "Ignore the past and you will lose an eye. Live in the past and you will lose both of them."

Speaking of financial safe havens, in the course of writing this book, I reviewed a large number of stories of wealthy families that had money in Swiss banks over the war years. In many cases a father had secreted money in a bank before the war for his heirs. After the war Swiss banks rigorously followed (for understandable reasons) the policy that absolute legal documentation of account ownership had to be presented, and if it wasn't no matter what the circumstances, the money would not be paid out.

For example, Estelle Sapir was the daughter of a wealthy Warsaw investment banker, Joseph Sapir. The family's apartment was filled with fine furnishings, silver, and art, and was staffed by live-in servants. When the Germans invaded Poland, the Sapirs fled to France. When the Germans came, they were arrested. Estelle had a final conversation with her father through a prison fence. "Don't worry for money," he said, "You have plenty of money in Switzerland." He named the bank where he had the account. Then reaching through the barbed wire with a single finger to touch his daughter, he made her repeat the information to be sure she would not forget. A day later he was transported to the Majdanek death camp and was never heard of again.

Estelle survived the war in France, and in 1946 went to the Credit Suisse bank in Geneva to get her money. The attendant returned with a folder labeled "J. Sapir." She identified herself with her passport and showed him handwritten notes from her father about the account, but he insisted that the money could not be disbursed until she provided her father's death certificate. In frustration she asked: "Who do you want me to get the death certificate from, Adolf Hitler?" But he was adamant. She visited the bank twice in 1946, once in 1957, and then in 1996 to no avail. Thanks to American intervention, the bank finally made a token payment of $500,000 in 1998 but she died a few months later at the age of 73. In retrospect it was her father's fault that he signed a document with such a provision.

Many banks at the time followed the practice that if after a number of years no legal contact was made with an account holder, the money would be transferred into the bank's reserve fund. This enraged many applicants and a number of articles and books were written. For example, Tom Brower wrote a book that was published in 1997 whose title tells its message: *Nazi Gold: The Full Story of the Fifty-Year Swiss-Nazi Conspiracy to Steal Billions from Europe's Jews and Holocaust Survivors.* I don't believe there was a conspiracy, and banks have to have rules, but the moral of the story is that safe haven accounts must be crafted with the bank to provide flexibility of future identification. Read the fine print.

How do you preserve wealth in anticipation of a time of chaos in the future? No one knows. Uncertainty means that uncertainty compels diversification. Diversification is and always has been the first tenet of the Prudent Man Rule of investing. Diversify your assets in terms of allocation between stocks, bonds, private equity, income producing property, and real businesses. In sub-Saharan Africa, for centuries, people believed cattle were the safest repository of wealth. That was until the great drought came along.

Diversify as to where you have your financial assets for safekeeping. Don't keep all your securities in the computerized databases of giant banks and brokers in New York, London, and Zurich. Make sure they are registered in your name and not in Street Name. Derivatives are like chain-smoking cigarettes. The odds are very high that eventually they are going to give you cancer.

Charles Darwin in *The Origin of the Species* wrote:

> It is not the strongest of the species that survives, not the most intelligent, but the one most responsive to change.

The same applies to the endurance of fortunes over time.

Always pay close attention to what the collective wisdom of the investor crowd is as reflected in what the markets themselves are whispering. They are not infallible, but they are far wiser than the experts and the media. However, recognize that they are better at bottoms than tops, and you cannot expect them to forecast terrorist attacks, plagues, or crashes.

As for the wisdom of stock markets at the big turning points, the record speaks for itself.

The London Market

In the early summer of 1940, after Dunkirk and while the Battle of Britain still raged overhead, the London stock market somehow sensed that the high-water mark of German conquest in its war with Britain had been reached. There is no record that at the time anyone of influence believed this. The war news couldn't have been worse and England stood alone. As noted in Chapter 4, Churchill himself was cautious in his public statements at the time, emphasizing that "the Battle of Britain is about to begin." In fact, he was very depressed as the British army and navy suffered defeat after defeat.

The London market bottomed in the last week of June 1940, at almost the same level that it had touched in the post-crash Depression lows of the 1930s. It was one of the great buying opportunities of all time but only the collective of investors sensed it. The date was June 27, 1940 to be precise. That day Churchill warned FDR and the prime minister of Canada "that if this country were invaded and largely occupied ... some Quisling government would be formed to make peace. ... in this case the British Fleet would be the solid contribution with which this peace government would buy terms." On June 27, the strategic Joint Planners in the United States War Department led by the great and good General George Marshall submitted to FDR their conclusion, "according to which no further American war material should be sold or sent to Britain since the survival of the British was very much open to question. At about the same time, John F. Kennedy made a contribution to the isolationist organization America First, and a German spy in London was counting the discarded bottles in the trash bin at 10 Downing Street to assess whether Churchill was an alcoholic as Hitler suspected.

As noted previously, American stock prices made a bottom for 1940 at about the same time only to drift lower in 1941 and 1942. The only market that didn't get it was Paris, although after Stalingrad it began to understand that the Third Reich wasn't going to last a thousand years. British investors were also prescient in 1941 when stocks rallied in the fourth quarter in the face of awful war news and carping about British military incompetence. London investors must have been anticipating the United States' entry into the war, and it is tempting, but probably farfetched, to suggest they foresaw an event such as Pearl Harbor.

The Berlin Market

As the winds of war turned, stock prices in Japan and Germany became administered, which meant it became "unpatriotic" to sell. Thus the evidence of their wisdom of markets is murkier. Nevertheless German investors were prescient. Stock prices in Berlin peaked in November of 1941 just *before* Barbarossa stalled at the gates of Moscow. It was an amazing perception in a totalitarian state where the news was strictly controlled. At the time, a few of Hitler's generals were beginning to express privately doubts about being consumed by "the vastness of Russia," but they had never been believers anyway so why would anyone have listened to them?

The Japanese Market

It was much the same story in Japan. The war news was even more tightly controlled, and losses were either not reported or minimized. Defeat was utterly inconceivable to the Japanese public. Throughout 1942 the public was told only of conquests, and the battles of the Coral Sea, Midway, and Guadalcanal were heralded as glorious victories. As mentioned, the crews of the warships sunk at the Coral Sea and Midway were not allowed shore leave in Japan. There was much talk of Japan's new and rich empire in Southeast Asia.

Somehow investors saw through the propaganda, and stock prices in real terms peaked in the fall of 1942. Food was beginning to be in short supply, and the iron railings in city parks were being melted down for steel. Could be that investors voted their money with their stomachs rather than the Samurai tradition.

In 1950, immediately after the North Korean attack, the Japanese market fell 50% in the first 11 days after the attack. Then in early July even as the South Korean and American troops were in headlong retreat and it appeared they would be forced into the sea, the market began to rally putting in a bottom for the ages, months ahead of any good news and the Inchon break out.

The U.S. Market

The U.S. story is equally dramatic. American equities made a secular, all-time bottom in the late spring of 1942 as Coral Sea and Midway were occurring. In the first months after Pearl Harbor, the official dispatches and the media grossly misreported the news from the Pacific. Small successes were wildly exaggerated. This was not propaganda; the warriors in the flush of battle were mistaking near misses for hits. Washington wanted to believe Japanese ships were sinking like stones. A torpedo striking a Japanese destroyer appeared like the torpedoing of a battleship to a fevered imagination looking through a periscope. In one egregious example, a navy pilot reported sinking a Japanese cruiser. In actuality, flying in a broken overcast, he had dive bombed an American submarine. The sub crash-dived, and in the pilot's excitement, he *misreported* the incident. As the war went on, the evaluators on both sides learned to divide their pilots' unconfirmed estimates of casualties always by two and sometimes by three.

What is interesting is that by the middle of 1942, skepticism was widespread in the United States. Battle reports had been inflated so often that they were no longer believed. The American media was full of criticism of the conduct of the war and the inefficiencies of the mobilization. The incompetence of the military, particularly the navy, was a recurring theme after the disaster at Pearl Harbor and in the Java Sea. Some people maintained (and still do) MacArthur should have been court-martialed for being inaccessible and allowing his air force to be destroyed on the ground after Pearl Harbor. The Coral Sea encounter was reported as another set-back, and in press reports, the losses at Midway of the torpedo bombers and of the *Yorktown* were emphasized. As noted, the Japanese officially proclaimed Midway as a victory, and as Rommel's panzers had just taken Tobruk, Libya, and were a mere 65 miles from Alexandria, Egypt, despondency bordering on despair reigned. The war news was abysmal.

Conclusion

Equity markets are wise. The investor crowd has great intuitive wisdom. Stock markets, in their long run judgements, are the perfect, dispassionate, seperately but directly motivated crowd. Disregard the ranting and raving of the self-proclaimed elite thinkers and alleged experts on wars, economies, politics, and, above all, the stock market. They are empty suits with vacant heads, and their opinions cluster around the probable. They lack the imagination and the courage to predict the unexpected, the 10 standard deviation events that transform the environment. History usually doesn't evolve in a slow and orderly way; often it leaps forward in disorderly, chaotic jumps.

People with wealth should assume that somewhere in the near or far future there will be another time of cholera when the Four Horsemen will ride again and the barbarians unexpectedly will be at *their* gate. By definition, the next Black Swan will be some form of a total breakdown of civilized society and the social and financial infrastructure as we know it.

The issue is what form will it take, what costume will it wear? It is likely it will have the general effect of the anarchy of an occupying army in World War II. The trigger event could be a massive terrorist or nuclear attack that disrupts the economy for months and maybe for years. A power failure that lasted not a day but a month would paralyze a modern economy. Or it could be a plague, a massive SARS epidemic, in which hundreds of millions die, or an electronic explosion that cascades into a complete breakdown of the world's financial accounting systems. Whatever happens, it most likely will be an event that is both unexpected and we will not be prepared for. The world is very good at locking the barn door after the horses have been stolen.

What can you do? In simplest terms, the conclusions are to diversify your fortune both as to asset class and location, anticipate *the anticipation of trouble,* and pay attention to the message of the markets. Equities are the place to be in the long run because of their proven and virtually unique ability to increase the purchasing power of capital.

In my considered but not necessarily correct opinion, a family or individual should have 75% of its wealth in equity investments. A century of history validates equities as the principal, but not the only, place to be. As David Swensen likes to say, you as an investor in an inflation prone world want to be an owner—not a lender. Most of that commitment should be in publicly traded *global* equities. Don't try to time short term market swings. What you want to capture is that wealth purchasing power compounding from the real return of stock. Tilted, refreshed index funds, or even just plain vanilla index funds, are fine. Don't fuss with high fee investment alternatives, and in general, don't get fancy and try to pick the best global managers or hedge funds. Last year's superstar may be next year's bum.

Another, much smaller part of your diversification strategy should be to have a farm or a ranch somewhere far off the beaten track but which you can get to reasonably quickly and easily. Think of it as an insurance policy, and for rich people in the developed economies a farm is a fine diversifier and probably an excellent long-term investment. Perhaps its purchase price should amount to five percent of your net worth. The control of food-producing land is a basic instinct of mankind, and landowners seem to find considerable psychic satisfaction just from the knowledge of possession. There are few things as fulfilling as having drink in the sunset and looking at your fields and cows.

There is no way of knowing how much time we will have to reach our Shangri-La next time. It will not be of much use having a wonderful estate in New Zealand if you can't get there. Long-range air travel is likely to be one of the first things to go. On the other hand, you want your sanctuary to be remote enough to be inaccessible to the dispossessed hordes.

You should assume the possibility of a breakdown of the civilized infrastructure. Your safe haven must be self-sufficient and capable of growing some kind of food. It should be well-stocked with seed, fertilizer, canned food, wine, medicine, clothes, etc. Think Swiss Family Robinson. Even in America and Europe there could be moments of riot and rebellion when law and order temporarily completely breaks down. A few rounds over the approaching brigands heads would probably be a compelling persuader that there are easier farms to pillage. Brigands tend to be cowards.

I repeat that history suggests that the rich almost always are too complacent, because they cherish the illusion that when things start to go bad, they will have time to extricate themselves and their wealth. It never works that way. Events move much faster than anyone expects, and the barbarians are on top of you before you can escape. Black Swans by definition have to be unexpected. The temptation always is to try to salvage wealth, but by the time it is apparent that you need to, it is usually too late. It is expensive to move early, but it is far better to be early than to be late.

Confucius said: "Study the past if you would divine the future."

Notes

Chapter 1

Page 13   "How does the weighted averaging get done?" Henry G. Manne, "The Welfare of American Investors," the *Wall Street Journal,* June 13, 2006.

Page 13   "The efficient market hypothesis was based almost entirely on empirical observations . . ." Henry G. Manne, "The Welfare of American Investors," the *Wall Street Journal,* June 13, 2006.

Chapter 2

Page 23   "They reminded me of paintings I had seen of the Medusa . . ." William L. Shirer, *The Nightmare Years,* p. 127.

Chapter 4

Page 55   "1940 was the most splendid, most deadly year . . . " Winston Churchill, *Their Finest Hour,* p. 628.

Page 55   "If the British Empire lasts for a thousand years . . ." Winston Churchill, *Their Finest Hour,* p. 628.

Page 58   Victorian England's anthem cited by William Manchester, *The Last Lion Alone.*

Page 59   "Churchill, if I was your wife . . ." James Humes, *The Wit and Wisdom of Winston Churchill,* p. 64.

Page 59   "Winston, you are drunk again . . ." op. cit., p. 190.

Page 59   "Feeling a little standoffish are we today, Winston?" op. cit., p. 44.

Page 59   "He is an adolescent . . ." op. cit., p. 39.

Page 59   "Fifty percent of Winston is genius . . ." Clement Atlee, quoted in Lord Moran's, *Churchill: Taken from the Diaries of Lord Moran,* Houghton Mifflin, 1966.

Page 60   "Fortune attended me lately in finances." William Manchester, *The Last Lion Alone,* pp. 300–304; also Paul Johnson, *Modern Times,* pp. 230–231.

Page 61   "Occasionally he stumbles over the truth . . ." Winston Churchill remark; 1936: Miriam Ringo, *Nobody Said it Better,* p. 183.

Page 61   "Must the right honorable gentlemen fall asleep . . ." op. cit., p. 56.

Page 61   "a half breed American . . ." op. cit., p. 60.

Page 62   "unsteady and drinking too much." op. cit., p. 73.

Page 62   "Winston Churchill is 80 years of age today . . ." Lorn Moran, Lord, *Taken from the Diaries of Lord Moran,* Houghton Mifflin, 1966.

Page 62   "many beautiful women admired him . . ." John Lukacs, *The Duel,* p. 44.

Page 63   "Winston has always seen things in blinkers." Clementine Churchill remark in 1945 to Lord Moran, op. cit.

Page 68   "I have nothing to offer but blood, toil, tears, and sweat." Winston S. Churchill, *Never Give In! The Best of Winston Churchill's Speeches,* p. 206.

Page 68   "You ask, what is our policy?" Winston S. Churchill *Never Give In! The Best of Winston Churchill's Speeches,* p. 206.

Page 74   "We must be very careful not to assign to this deliverance . . ." Speech to the House of Commons, on June 4, 1940, Winston S. Churchill, *Never Give In! The Best of Winston Churchill's Speeches,* p. 214.

Page 75   "surrounded by generals and high officials" Countess Helene de Portie, H. Freeman Mathews comment; William L. Shirer, *The Collapse of the Third Republic,* p. 817; also Robert Wernick, *Blitzkreig,* p. 187.

Page 76   "we have found it necessary to take measures . . ." Winston S. Churchill, *Never Give In! The Best of Winston Churchill's Speeches;* p. 217.

Page 77 "the news from France . . ." Winston S. Churchill, , *Never Give In! The Best of Winston Churchill's Speeches,* p. 218.

Page 77 "disastrous military events . . ." Winston S. Churchill, *Never Give In! The Best of Winston Churchill's Speeches,* p. 221.

Page 77 "the colossal military disaster" Winston S. Churchill, *Never Give In! The Best of Winston Churchill's Speeches,* p. 219.

Page 77 "who are found to be consciously exercising . . ." Winston S. Churchill, *Never Give In! The Best of Winston Churchill's Speeches,* p. 234.

Page 79 "rejects terror bombing and Goering's comment, but the Führer does not want to destroy the Empire." From the diary of Josef Goebbels.

Page 84 "Horrified by ghastly sight in the Tubes." Comment by Rosemary Black as recounted by Leonard Mosely, *The Battle of Britain,* p. 145.

Page 87 "The soul of the British people and race proved invincible." Winston Churchill, *Their Finest Hour,* p. 610.

Page 89 "The able-bodied male population . . ." William L. Shirer, *The Rise and Fall of the Third Reich,* pp. 782–783.

Page 89 "Anyhow, sir, we're in the Final . . . " Winston Churchill, *Their Finest Hour,* p. 615.

Chapter 5

Page 92 "wanted to make history, not endure it." Paul Johnson, *Modern Times,* p. 96, sourced Opera Ominia, p. 32.

Page 92 "Well that's fair. Last time they were on our side." James Humes, *The Wit & Wisdom of Winston Churchill,* p. 211.

Page 92 "This whipped jackal, Mussolini . . ." Winston Churchill, speech, April 27, 1941, Guildhall, London.

Page 92 "Dear Churchill: Wendell Wilkie will give you this." Winston Churchill, *The Grand Alliance,* pp. 26–27.

Page 94 "At one of the rest centers . . ." Winston Churchill, *The Grand Alliance,* pp. 359–361.

Page 95 "deluded and evil warmongers" Winston Churchill, *The Grand Alliance,* p. 50.

Page 95 Corporal Hitler and this bloodthirsty guttersnipe and the repository of evil; June 22, 1941 speech.

Page 96 "[Hitler] was the greatest son; William L. Shirer, *The Rise and Fall of the Third Reich,* p. 1141.

Page 96   "When I make a statement of facts . . ." Winston Churchill, *The Hinge of Fate,* pp. 497–499.

Page 97   "We have a very daring and skillful opponent . . ." Winston Churchill, *The Grand Alliance,* p. 97.

Page 98   "If Hitler invaded the realms of hell . . ." John Colville, *The Fringes of Power,* p. 183.

Page 101   "You are the pride of the navy." Hitler visiting Bismarck. William L. Shirer, *The Deadly Hunt,* p. 65.

Page 103   "Ship unmaneuverable," Op. cit., p. 135.

Page 107   "In a few weeks we lost . . ." Winston Churchill speech to the House of Commons, Winston Churchill, *The Grand Alliance,* p. 78.

Chapter 6

Page 109   "the battle of annihilation" (Hitler quoted); William L. Shirer, *The Rise and Fall of the Third Reich,* pp. 798–806.

Page 110   "smash in the door . . ." Morin Bishop, *An Illustrated History of World War II,* p. 113.

Page 113   "A German master sergeant . . ." John Toland, *Adolph Hitler,* p. 82. Also other sources.

Page 121   "We Germans make the mistake of thinking . . ." Nicholas Bethel, *Russia Besieged,* p. 90.

Page 124   "One final heave . . ." Hitler to General Jodl. William L. Shirer, *The Rise and Fall of the Third Reich,* p. 863.

Page 124   "The Russian recovery and their winter offensive . . ." op. cit., p. 183.

Page 125   "Is it any less cold fifty miles back?" Quote from General Blumentritt. Alan Clark, *Barbarrossa,* p. 26.

Page 125   "Hitler's fanatical order that the troops must hold fast . . ." Quote from General Blumentritt. Alan Clark, *Barbarrossa,* pp. 26–28.

Page 126   "so disgraced the uniform," alleged comment by Hitler. Alan Clark, *Barbarrossa,* p. 246.

Chapter 7

Page 131   "a wise statesman" Winston Churchill, *The Grand Alliance,* pp. 190–191.

Page 132   ". . . Eta Jima had been modeled on the British Royal Navy." Evan Thomas, *Sea of Thunder,* pp. 28, 85.

Page 133 "spirit bars" op. cit., p. 205.

Page 134 "a ferocious bushido ideologue . . ." Paul Johnson, *Modern Times*, p. 311.

Page 138 " . . . the finest naval weapon in the world." Ronald Spector, *Eagle Against the Sun*, pp. 33–50.

Page 140 " . . . mortifying personal defeat." Ronald Spector, *Eagle Against the Sun*, pp. 33–50.

Page 147 The dive bombers came out of the sun . . . Ronald Spector, *Eagle Against the Sun*, p. 177.

Page 147 "Looking around I was horrified . . ." Walter Lord, *Incredible Victory*, pp. 172, 173.

Page 147 "scratch one carrier." U.S. Navy records, pilot source unknown.

Page 148 "Captain, I have come on behalf . . ." John Toland, *But Not in Shame*, p. 422.

Page 149 "There is a beautiful moon tonight." John Toland, *But Not in Shame*, p. 428. Also, Walter Lord, *Incredible Victory*, pp. 249–250.

Page 151 "a great victory had been won." John Toland, *Adolf Hitler*, p. 716.

Page 151 "There are still eight carriers . . ." various sources, including Evan Thomas, *Sea of Thunder*, pp. 85–86.

Chapter 8

For general background information for this chapter, the author talked in great detail with John Alkire, whose family lived in Japan before, during, and after the war years. Alkire also introduced the author to numerous Japanese who provided much information.

Page 154 By mid-1942 Japan was virtually a planned economy . . . Jon Halliday and Gavan McCormack, *A Political History of Japanese Capitalism* (Monthly Review Press: 1978), pp. 156–157.

Page 157 "Revenge by the Bull" *New York Herald Tribune*, February 5, 1942. Also, Evan Thomas, *Sea of Thunder*, p. 49.

Page 158 "should give more attention to the ill-housed . . ." James Grant, *The Trouble with Prosperity*, pp. 77–87.

Page 168 "Courageous the pine . . ." James Webb, "The Emperor's General," pp. 135–137.

Page 170 There was one other asset class in Japan . . . Data on Japanese housing and land prices, Stefan Rheinwald, *Polarisation and Extremes*, CLSA Research, June 25, 2007, pp. 8–11.

Chapter 9

Page 179 Hitler convened a meeting . . . Robert Herzstein, *The Nazis*, p. 43.

Page 180 . . . dressed in a plain brown uniform . . . William L. Shirer, *The Rise and Fall of the Third Reich*, p. 325.

Page 182 "It used to be called plundering . . ." Robert Herzstein, *The Nazis,* p. 116.

Chapter 10

Page 188 flaccid parliamentarism and regime of palaver; William L. Shirer, *The Collapse of the Third Republic*, pp. 922–927.

Page 188 So France, like its stock market, sulked listlessly . . . Robert Paxton, *Vichy France;* William L. Shirer, *The Collapse of the Third Republic;* Richard Vinen, *The Unfree French;* Gerhard Weinberg, *Life Under the Occupation;* and Norman Davies, *Europe at War: 1939–1945 No Simple Victory.*

Page 192 "Vichy has done more reform in one year . . ." William L. Shirer, *The Collapse of the Third Republic,* p. 487.

Page 194 The three Rothschild brothers . . . *The Lost Museum,* Chapter 4.

Page 199 His old age was a shipwreck." Charles De Gaulle on Marshal Petain, Robert Paxton, *Vichy France,* p. 350. Also, Norman Davies, *Europe at War: 1939–1945 No Simple Victory.*

Chapter 11

For general background information for the first half of this chapter the author referred to *The Fall of Mussolini* (Oxford University Press, 2007) by Philip Morgan and *A World at Arms* by Gerhard Weinberg.

Page 204 "If I advance follow me . . . " Mussolini on himself, quoted in "Time Capsule," 1943. Miriam Ringo, *Nobody Said it Better,* p. 250.

Page 204 . . . he had 169 mistresses . . . Paul Johnson, *Modern Times,* p. 410.

Page 204 "One would have thought . . ." Malcolm Muggeridge, introduction to Galeasso Ciano's *Hidden Diaries.*

Page 205 "Even Michelangelo needed marble . . ." op. cit., p. 236.

Page 207 . . . in the North, there was virtually a civil war . . . Philip Morgan, *The Fall of Mussolini* p. 321.

Page 208   Once after the war at a dinner . . . James C. Humes, *The Wit & Wisdom of Winston Churchill,* p. 210.

Page 211   To understand the trauma of German wealth . . . George Bittlingmayer, "Output, Stock Volatility, and Political Uncertainty in a Natural Experiment: Germany 1880–1940, " *Journal of Finance,* December 1998.

Page 219   When the Nazis invaded Poland . . . Lynn H. Nicholas, *The Rape of Europe,* Chapter 3.

Page 219   In desperation, Countess Matgozata Radziwill . . . Lynn H. Nicholas, *The Rape of Europe,* Chapter 3.

Page 223   "To Members of the Community . . ." Mirham Pressler, *Anne Frank: A Hidden Life,* pp. 39–40.

Page 226   "He [Hitler] understood nothing whatever about economics." Schacht on Hitler in *The Warburgs,* p. 435, by Rob Chernow.

Page 226   "fighting the war of our system . . ." Schacht to Morgan, in *The House of Morgan,* pp. 393–394, 398, by Ron Chernow.

Page 228   A similar fate befell the Bleichroder family . . . Fritz Stern, *Gold and Iron: Bismarck, Bleichroder, and the Building of the German Empire,* pp. 546–549.

Page 229   "Friction produces warmth . . ." Paul Johnson, *Modern Times,* p. 277.

Chapter 12

Page 232   "Once when a quite objective report . . ." Antony Beevor, *Stalingrad,* page 123. Also, Alan Clark, *Barbarossa,* pp. 109–112.

Page 233   "If he has an arm left . . ." Descriptions of partisan war behind German lines. Nicholas Bethel, *Russia Besieged,* pp. 88–95.

Page 233   "The progress of the columns . . ." Alan Clark, *Barbarossa,* p. 205.

Page 234   German communiqués, "wild beasts" "barbarians"; Description of "Wehrmacht at high tide." Alan Clark, *Barbarossa,* p. 222.

Page 235   "Today's conferences with the Führer . . ." William L. Shirer, *The Rise and Fall of the Third Reich,* pp. 53–55. Also, John Keegan, *The Mask of Command,* p. 272.

Page 236   "Animals flee this hell . . ." Alan Clark, *Barbarossa,* p. 238.

Page 237   "The first tenuous link on the choke chain . . ." Alan Clark, *Barbarossa,* p. 248.

Page 238   "The Russians are at the door of our bunker." On the circumstances of the German surrender, Antony Beevor, *Stalingrad,* pp. 381–385.

Page 239   Hitler is insane. John Toland, *Adolf Hitler.*

Page 239   "His left hand trembled . . ." Alan Clark, *Barbarossa,* p. 297.

Page 240   . . . he was heckled by angry shouts . . . John Toland, *Adolf Hitler.*

Page 240   "We are in the position of a man who has seized a wolf . . ." Alan Clark, *Barbarossa,* p. 275.

Page 243   "the vastness of Russia devours us." Guderian, letter to his wife. Alan Clark, *Barbarossa.*

Page 245   "The table was elegantly set." John Keegan, *The Mask of Command,* p. 308.

Chapter 13

In addition to the sources that follow, the author drew on these references for background information for this chapter: Richard Collier, *The War in the Desert*; Arthur Bryant, *The Turn of the Tide*; and John Colville, *The Fringes of Power.*

Page 253   The training of a Japanese soldier. Arthur Zich, *The Rising Sun,* p. 89.

Page 253   "I must admit to being staggered by your telegram." Winston Churchill, *The Hinge of Fate,* p. 100.

Page 254   Wavell messaged Churchill . . . Winston Churchill, *The Hinge of Fate,* pp. 99–105.

Page 254   Percival reported his forces. . . . Winston Churchill, *The Hinge of Fate,* pp. 99–105.

Page 254   "stand fast in the citadel." Winston Churchill, *The Hinge of Fate,* pp. 105–107.

Page 256   "Thus, by one of the great ironies of history . . ." Paul Johnson, *Modern Times,* pp. 468–469.

Page 256   "there is nothing else that can fill the gap." Winston Churchill, *The Hinge of Fate,* pp. 160–161.

Page 257   "I know you will keep up your optimism . . ." op. cit., p. 201.

Page 259   "Moreover, difficulty of Russian convoys . . ." op. cit., p. 259.

Page 261   "The Prime Minister always refers to a defeat . . ." speech, November 12, 1942. and disparaging comments. Miriam Ringo, *Nobody Said it Better,* p. 190.

Page 261   "I do not suffer from any desire to be relieved . . . " op. cit., p. 190.

Page 261 Randolph "a cad" William Manchester, Winston Spencer, *Churchill Alone* p. 254.

Page 262 "what a pity to remove the one part . . ." op. cit., p. 254.

Page 262 Pamela affair with Harriman and family quarrel, John Mecham, *Winston and Franklin.*

Page 262 "The booty was gigantic . . ." Winston Churchill, *The Hinge of Fate,* p. 419.

Page 265 Disparaging remarks about Cripps from Marion Ringo, *Nobody Said it Better,* pp. 194–195.

Page 265 Letter exchanged between Churchill and Cripps. Winston Churchill, *Hinge of Fate,* pp. 558–560.

Page 266 ". . . tell the Lord Privy Seal I am locked in a privy . . ."; op. cit., p. 208.

Page 267 "A piece of Poland, a piece of . . ." James Humes, *The Wit & Wisdom of Winston Churchill,* p. 297.

Page 268 "It may almost be said . . ." Churchill after Alamein: op. cit., p. 603.

Page 269 "in battle invincible, in defeat . . ." Winston Churchill's description of General Montgomery Hume, p. 157. Also, Miriam Ringo, *Nobody Said It Better,* p. 323.

Chapter 14

Page 277 Descriptions of the Korean order of battle, Richard K. Betts, *Surprise Attack,* p. 55.

Page 279 "Stand or die!" Order issued by General Walton Walker on July 29, 1950. David McCullough, *Truman,* p. 788.

Page 281 "The concept of limited warfare never entered our councils . . ." (General Ridgeway). Richard K. Betts, *Surprise Attacks,* p. 52.

Page 283 The invaders achieved complete surprise. Also, citing Dean Acheson speech to National Press Club, Dean Rusk, etc. Also, David McCullough, *Truman,* p. 777.

Page 283 The Attack by North Korea. William Manchester, *American Caesar,* pp. 545–546.

Page 283 "a great thinker and theoretician . . ." David McCullough, *Truman,* p. 780.

Page 284 Every morning he rose at 5 A.M . . . . op. cit., pp. 857–858.

Page 285 "Only a mile away I could see the towers . . ." Douglas MacArthur, *Reminscences.*

Page 286 . . . they went up in huge blasts . . . William Manchester, *American Caesar,* p. 555.

Page 286 Description of the retreat. op. cit., p. 787. Also, author's conversations with Marines involved.

Page 287 "If I should die, think only this of me . . ." Young marine officer's note to his wife, quoting from Rupert Brooke's poem (told to the author).

Page 288 "stand or die" and "You dumbheads stand or die." Author's conversations with Marines. Also alluded to by David McCullough, *Truman,* pp. 788–789.

Page 291 Pusan beachhead description. William Manchester, *American Caesar,* p. 561. Also, as described in Marine training manuals.

Page 291 "the riskiest plan I have ever heard of." David McCullough, *Truman,* p. 797.

Page 292 At the meeting the military experts resisted the Inchon plan . . . Douglas MacArthur, *Reminiscences,* pp. 349–350. Also, direct transcript of what happened at council, confirmed and expanded on to author by Frank Pace.

Page 293 "chilled me to the marrow of my bones" Douglas MacArthur, *Reminscences,* p. 352; reply, p. 353.

Page 299 "Mr. Hume: I've just read your lousy review . . ." op. cit., p. 829.

Chapter 15

Page 304 "thoroughly obsessed with the idea . . ." Michael Beschloss, *Presidential Courage,* p. 182 (quoting John Boettiger, March 3, 1941, Franklin Roosevelt Papers; Harold Ickes diary, July 3 and September 5. 1938).

Page 305 The city of Vilnius in Poland . . . Norman Davies, *Europe At War,* p. 407.

Page 306 As recounted to author by Polish American which corroborated above about Vilnius.

Page 307 The saga of Andras, an aristocratic Hungarian. Recounted in detail to author by the son of Andras.

Page 308 In 1939, the aristocratic . . . Lobcowitz friend of the family as told to author.

Page 310 "Landowners were classified as oppressors of the people . . . blood suckers." Norman Davies, *Europe at War,* p. 445.

Page 311 "fatty Nazi wives" op. cit., p. 358.

Chapter 16

Page 327 For example, Estelle Sapir was the daughter . . . Stuart E. Eizenstat, *Imperfect Justice: Looted Assets, Slave Labor, and Unfinished Business of World War II,* p. 78.

Page 329 Comments on what happened on June 27, 1940. John Lukacs, pp. 141–143, 150.

Bibliography

World War II Sources—Histories, Biographies, and Novels

Bailey, Ronald H. *Partisans and Guerillas.* New York: Time-Life Books, 1977.

———. *Prisoners of War.* New York: Time-Life Books, 1981.

Beevor, Antony. *Stalingrad: The Fateful Siege 1942–1943.* Harmondsworth, England: Penguin Books, 1998.

Beschloss, Michael. *Presidential Courage: Brave Leaders and How They Changed America 1789–1989.* New York: Simon & Schuster, 2007.

Bethell, Nicholas. *Russia Besieged.* New York: Time-Life Books, 1980.

Betts, Richard K. *Surprise Attack.* Washington, DC: Brookings Institution, 1982.

Bishop, Morin. *An Illustrated History of World War II Crisis and Courage.* New York: Barnes & Noble Publishing, 2006.

Black, Conrad. *Franklin Delano Roosevelt, Champion of Freedom.* New York: Public Affairs, 2003.

Botting, Richard. *The Second Front.* Alexandria VA: Time-Life Books, 1978.

———. *The U-Boats.* Alexandria, VA: Time-Life Books, 1979.

Bryant, Arthur. *The Turn of the Tide 1939–1943.* London: Collins, 1957.

Churchill, Winston. *Blood, Sweat, and Tears.* New York: G.P. Putnam's Sons, 1941.

————. *Closing the Ring.* Boston: Houghton Mifflin, 1951.

————. *The Gathering Storm.* Boston: Houghton Mifflin, 1948.

————. *The Grand Alliance.* Boston: Houghton Mifflin, 1950.

————. *The Hinge of Fate.* Boston: Houghton Mifflin, 1950.

————. *Never Give In! The Best of Winston Churchill's Speeches.* Selected by his grandson Winston S. Churchill. New York: Hyperion, 2003.

————. *Their Finest Hour.* Boston: Houghton Mifflin, 1949.

————. *The Wit & Wisdom of Winston Churchill.* Compiled by James C. Humes. New York: HarperCollins, 1994.

Clark, Alan. *Barbarossa—The Russian-German Conflict 1941–1945.* New York: Morrow, 1965.

Collier, Richard. *The War in the Desert.* New York: Time-Life Books, 1977.

Colville, John. *The Fringes of Power: 10 Downing Street Diaries 1939–1955.* London: Hodder and Staughton Ltd., 1985.

Davies, Norman. *Europe at War 1939–1945: No Simple Victory.* London: Macmillan, 2006.

Ellson, Robert T. *Prelude to War.* Alexandria, VA: Time-Life Books, 1976.

Gilbert, Martin. *Churchill: A Life.* New York: Henry Holt, 1991.

Halberstam, David. *The Coldest Winter: America and the Korean War.* New York: Hyperion, 2007.

Herzstein, Robert Edwin. *The Nazis.* New York: Time-Life Books, 1980.

Hoopes, Townsend, and Douglas Brinkley. *Driven Patriot: The Life and Times of James Forrestal.* New York: Vintage Books, 1993.

Johnson, Paul. *Modern Times.* New York: Harper & Row, 1983.

Jones, James. *From Here to Eternity.* New York: Charles Scribner's Sons, 1951.

Keegan, John. *The Mask of Command.* Middlesex, England: Penguin Books, 1987.

————. *The Price of Admiralty.* New York: Penguin Group, 1988.

Kerr, Walter. *The Secret of Stalingrad.* Chicago: Playboy Press, 1979.

Koestler, Arthur. *Darkness at Noon.* New York: Bantam Books, reissue edition 1993.

Lord, Walter. *Incredible Victory.* New York: Harper & Row, 1967.

Lukacs, John. *The Duel: The Eighty Day Struggle between Churchill & Hitler.* New Haven, CT: Yale University Press, 1990.

MacArthur, Douglas. *Reminiscences.* New York: McGraw-Hill, 1964.

MacLean, Alistair. *H.M.S. Ulysses.* New York: Doubleday, 1955.

Manchester, William. *American Caesar: Douglas MacArthur 1880–1964.* Boston: Little, Brown, 1978.

———. *The Last Lion: Winston Spencer Churchill: Visions of Glory.* Boston: Little, Brown, 1983.

———. *Winston Spencer Churchill Alone.* Boston: Little, Brown, 1988.

Marnham, Patrick. *The Death of Jean Moulin: Biography of a Ghost.* London: John Murray, 2000.

McCullough, David. *Truman.* New York: Simon & Schuster, 1992.

Mecham, John. *Franklin and Winston: An Intimate Portrait of an Epic Friendship.* New York: Random House Audio, 2003.

Miller, Russell. *The Commandoes.* New York: Time-Life Books, 1981.

———. *The Resistance.* New York: Time-Life Books, 1979.

Monsarratt, Nicholas. *The Cruel Sea.* Springfield, NJ: Burford Books, 2000.

Mosley, Leonard. *The Battle of Britain.* New York: Time-Life Books, 1977.

Nagorski, Andrew. *The Greatest Battle.* New York: Simon & Schuster, 2007.

Paxton, Robert O. *Vichy France: Old Guard and New Order 1940–1944.* New York: Columbia University Press, 1972.

Presler, Mirjam. *Anne Frank: A Hidden Life.* New York: Puffin Books/Penguin Books, 2001.

Ringo, Miriam. *Nobody Said It Better.* Chicago: Rand McNally, 1980.

Russell, Francis. *The Secret War.* New York: Time-Life Books, 1981.

Salisbury, Harrison F. *The 900 Days: The Siege of Leningrad.* New York: Harper & Row, 1969.

Service, Robert. *A History of Modern Russia.* London: Penguin Books, 1997.

Shirer, William L. *The Collapse of the Third Republic.* New York: Simon & Schuster, 1969.

———. *The Deadly Hunt: The Sinking of the Bismarck.* New York: Random House, 1962.

———. *The Nightmare Years.* Boston: Little, Brown, 1984.

———. *The Rise and Fall of the Third Reich.* New York: Simon & Schuster, 1960.

Snyder, Louis L., and Richard B. Morris. *A Treasury of Great Reporting.* New York: Simon & Schuster, 1949.

Spector, Ronald H. *Eagle Against the Sun: The American War with Japan.* New York: Free Press, 1984; Vintage Books, 1985.

Speer, Albert. *Inside the Third Reich: Memoirs.* New York: Macmillan, 1970.

Spooner, Rick. *The Spirit of Semper Fidelis.* Williamstown, NJ: Phillips Publications, 2004.

Stern, Fritz. *Gold and Iron: Bismarck, Bleichroder, and the Building of the German Empire.* New York: Vintage Books, Random House, 1977.

Stevenson, William. *A Man Called Intrepid.* New York: Harcourt Brace Jovanovich, 1976.

Thomas, Evan. *Sea of Thunder.* New York: Simon & Schuster, 2006.

Toland, John. *Adolf Hitler.* Garden City, N Y: Doubleday, 1976.

———. *But Not in Shame: The Six Months after Pearl Harbor.* New York: Random House, 1961.

Tooze, Adam. *The Wages of Destruction: The Making and Breaking of the Nazi Economy.* London: Allen Lane, 2006.

Tuchman, Barbara W. *Stilwell and the American Experience in China.* New York: Macmillan, 1970.

Vinen, Richard. *The Unfree French: Life under the Occupation.* London: Penguin/Allen Lane, 2006.

Webb, James. *The Emperor's General.* New York: Broadway Books, 1999.

Weinberg, Gerhard L. *A World at Arms: A Global History of World War II.* Cambridge: Cambridge University Press, 1994.

Wenick, Robert. *Blitzkreig.* New York: Time-Life Books, 1976.

Wouk, Herman. *The Winds of War.* Boston: Little, Brown, 1969.

Young, Desmond. *Rommel: The Desert Fox.* New York: Harper & Brothers, 1950.

Zich, Arthur. *The Rising Sun.* Alexandria, VA: Time-Life Books, 1977.

Books about Financial Markets, Wealth, and the Times

Alletzhauser, Albert J. *The House of Nomura: The Inside Story of the Legendary Japanese Financial Dynasty.* New York: Arcade Publishing, 1990.

Auchincloss, Louis. *The Embezzler.* Boston: Houghton Mifflin, 1966.

Beinhocker, Eric D. *The Origin of Wealth.* Boston: Harvard Business School Press, 2006.

Bittlingmayer, George. "Output, Stock Volatility, and Political Uncertainty in a Natural Experiment: Germany 1880–1940." *Journal of Finance* (December 1981).

Bower, Tom. *Nazi Gold: The Full Story of the Fifty Year Swiss-Nazi Conspiracy to Steal Billions from Europe's Jews and Holocaust Survivors.* New York: HarperCollins, 1997.

Chernow, Ron. *The House of Morgan: An American Banking Dynasty*. New York: Atlantic Monthly Press, 1990.

———. *The Warburgs: The Twentieth Century Odyssey of a Remarkable Jewish Family*. New York: Vintage Books, 1993.

Dimson, Elroy, Paul Marsh, and Mike Staunton. *The Millennium Book II: A Century of Investment Returns*. London: ABN-Amro and London Business School, 2001.

Eizenstat, Stuart. *Imperfect Justice: Looted Assets, Slave Labor, and the Unfinished Business of World War II*. New York: Public Affairs, 2003.

Felicano, Hector. *The Lost Museum*. New York: Basic Books, 1997.

Grant, James. *Bernard Baruch: The Adventures of a Wall Street Legend*. New York: Simon & Schuster, 1983.

———. *The Trouble with Prosperity: The Loss of Fear, the Rise of Speculation and the Risk to American Savings*. New York: Times Books, Random House, 1996.

Ibbotson, Associates. *Stocks, Bonds, Bills, and Inflation Yearbook*. Chicago: Ibbotson Associates, 2006.

Mauboussin, Michael J. *More Than You Know: Finding Financial Wisdom in Unconventional Places*. New York: Columbia University Press, 2006.

Mayer, Martin. *Wall Street: Men and Money*. New York: Harper & Brothers, 1955.

Menschel, Robert. *Markets, Mobs, and Mayhem*. New York: John Wiley & Sons, 2002.

Morgan, Ted. *FDR: A Biography*. New York: Simon & Schuster, 1985.

Morton, Frederic. *The Rothschilds: A Family History*. Philadelphia: Curtis Publishing Company, 1962.

Nicholas, Lynn H. *The Rape of Europa*. New York: Alfred A. Knopf, 1994.

Rheinwald, Stefan. "Polarization and Extremes CLSA Japan Market Research." June 25, 2007.

Sobel, Robert. *The Big Board: A History of the New York Stock Market*. New York: Free Press, 1965.

Surowiecki, James. *The Wisdom of Crowds*. New York: Anchor Books, 2005.

Taleb, Nassim Nicholas. *The Black Swan*. New York: Random House, 2007.

Tetlock, Philip. *Expert Political Judgment: How Good Is It? How Can We Know?* Princeton, NJ: Princeton University Press, 2006.

Index